This book is dedicated to my parents
Helen and Harold;
to my grandmother Elsie King
(a promise kept at last);
and to Dolores Brown,
my sophomore high school English teacher,
who first introduced me to theatre.

Thank you all for helping to give me
the life I love today.

Acknowledgments

Many people helped make this book possible. I'd like to thank my contributing writers, both official and unofficial: Mark Barrett, Hal Barwood, Bob Bates, Jim Buchanan, Noah Falstein, Nate Fox, Chris L'Etoile, Bill Link, Steve Meretzky, Matt Mihaly, Ken Rolston, John Szeder, and Mark Terrano.

Those who performed above and beyond the call of duty by reading the manuscript and offering insight and critiques were Bob Bates, Mark Barrett, Hal Barwood, Noah Falstein, Steve Meretzky and Mark Terrano.

Thanks are also due James Ohlen at Bioware; Jennifer Hicks and Scott Jennings at Mythic; Alex Bradley; Chris Foster at Turbine; Jurie Horneman at Rockstar; Chris Klug; Dorian Newcomb; Graham Sheldon; and the Game Design Workshop. My appreciation goes out to all of the members of the workshop list for putting up with my book questions for the past seven months.

More general acknowledgments are owed Chris Abbott, Ron Austin, Sandy Bianco, Eddie Bowen, Glen Dahlgren, Steve de Souza, Mike Dornbrook, Elonka Dunin, Phil Fehrle, Eric Goldberg, Brian Green, Hope Hickli, Geoff Howland, Amy Jo Kim, Raph Koster, Peter Lefcourt, Niki Marvin, Di Meredith, Andrew Nelson, Nick Nicholson, Otto Penzler, Jeff Perkinson, François Robillard, Liz Robinson, Jeri Taylor, Jeff Tyeryar, John Valente, Doug Walker, Steve Wartofsky, Johnny Wilson, and Gary Winnick. Some of you will know why. The others will just have to take my word for it that you belong here.

And last, but not least, from Course Technology I'd like to thank Mitzi Koontz and my superb editor Sandy Doell.

I'm sure I've missed a few. My sincere apologies! To all named and unnamed go my deepest thanks.

About the Author

LEE SHELDON was a writer/producer for 20 years on TV shows such as *Star Trek: The Next Generation*, *Charlie's Angels*, *Quincy*, and many more. Over 200 of his original scripts were filmed, and he has produced and edited hundreds more. Lee was twice nominated for awards by the Mystery Writers of America. He was also nominated by the Writers Guild of America for the daytime serial *Edge of Night*. Since 1994, he has been writing and designing games. His titles include solo games such as the award-winning *The Riddle of Master Lu*, *Dark Side of the Moon*, and *Wild Wild West: The Steel Assassin*. He has worked on massively multiplayer worlds for companies including Cyan (*URU: Ages Beyond Myst*) and Disney (*Disney's Virtual Kingdom*).

Lee is known as one of the leading experts on storytelling and character development in games. For seven years, he ran a full-day tutorial on these and related issues at the Game Developer's Conference and has appeared on panels and given talks elsewhere. He is a charter member of the Game Design Workshop, which includes most of the major game designers in the industry. He is the author of the mystery novel *Impossible Bliss* (Mystery & Suspense Press, Mystery Writers of America Imprint for iUniverse, ISBN: 0595194818).

CONTENTS

INTRODUCTION

Character Development and Storytelling for Games is meant to be a resource for writers and designers and those who must work with us and who may want to talk intelligently with us at some point.

This is not a book of rules that, if slavishly followed, will guarantee success. You'll see that just about every time I try to lay down some canonical law to follow, I immediately think of exceptions. Don't be afraid to break any rules as you write, as long as you know exactly what they mean, and why they're rules to begin with. Pablo Picasso knew this, as you'll soon see. It is one of the continuing themes running through this book.

Think of it as a book of ideas and of choices. With any luck, it will help you to generate ideas of your own. And you will feel more comfortable when choices present themselves as you write. Knowing which choices to make is not teachable. It's part of that creative instinct we call talent whose secret voice guides us in our decisions every time we sit down at the keyboard. And anyway, they will be different for different people. Despite what writing gurus say, all stories are not identical. They are shaped by all those unique facets of the human beings who write them.

I have some strong opinions, and you will find them in here. Hopefully, if you disagree with them, you will still discover much that is helpful to you as a writer of games. Even better, your disagreement can lead to enlightenment for all of us. Debate is a necessary part of learning. Sometimes, as I wrote, I wished I could just stop and ask my own questions of you.

For those interested in such things, I'll confess up front that in the way I've chosen to write this book can be found all of the major concepts I'm writing about. The book itself has been designed as a quest. Considering how much I'll promote non-linear storytelling in the following pages, you may be surprised to find it is a linear quest. I originally laid the book out in modules that could be read in any order, something like Geoff Ryman's novel *253*, but in the end I went for a straight read instead of distracting page flipping. Write the story in the way that fits your medium. I practice what I preach as much as I preach what I practice. This book is an illustration of both.

I warn you in advance that I'm going to drag in anecdotes and examples from all sorts of strange places. This is how ideas blossom. I encourage you in your life as well as in your writing to be open to all of the arts, and the world they seek to depict. Limiting oneself to a favorite genre or type of entertainment may be okay for our audience (although I wouldn't encourage it), but we owe it to our audience to draw from a much broader world of knowledge and experience.

This book is as much about game design as it is about writing for games. The two are virtually inseparable. I'll seem to stray off course occasionally into topics that appear to be only about design, but hopefully, the discussions are of value to our chief concerns, character and story, if only for context. Ideas without context may be great for bumper stickers, but they are useless to us as creators. Don't worry; I won't stray far.

When we look to other media to understand how to write for games, literature is surprisingly a common first choice. We can learn much from literature, but games are visual, a medium of action, as are drama and film. Game stories, like stories in film and television, need not—should not—be convoluted, but as the mystery writer knows, it's all in the telling, and an apparently complex plot can actually be quite simple underneath.

We cannot talk about plot or character development or emotion in a vacuum. To do so is about as helpful as trying to study medicine by examining only the left foot. All of the weapons of drama must be aimed at what we write. Story and gameplay should evolve simultaneously. Attempting to tack one form of entertainment on to the other is to lessen the benefits of both. Even though they are very different, both can be woven together to create a single entertainment experience.

I am not a programmer. I am a professional writer. Through several careers, no matter what else I have been—story editor, producer, director, or game designer—I have always been a writer first.

You don't have to be a programmer to be a game designer, but you do need to know enough about programming to carry on meaningful conversations with programmers on your development team. You need to know enough to be able to at least suspect the difference between a firm commitment and wishful thinking. Contrary to popular belief, programmers aren't all liars, but they are the most optimistic bunch you'll ever meet.

You don't have to be an artist, but you should know quite a bit about art. It saves time to be able to dismiss Jackson Pollock as a potential conceptual artist for your Disney treasure hunt game. His Mickey Mouse would make you unhappy.

You don't have to be a writer. But it helps to be able to recognize that fact. Just as you do have to be a programmer to program, you really should be a writer to write. Everybody seems to think that because writing doesn't require manual dexterity the way art often does, or an ability to do math, that anyone can do it.

One problem we come across when attempting to discuss games is our lack of a common vocabulary. We've borrowed terms from other media and then changed their definitions. We've made up our own words. A few gray areas of terminology should be mentioned here.

For the most part I use *video game* and *computer game* interchangeably, particularly if the platform is irrelevant to the topic under discussion. At times, I will just be sloppy and not modify the word *game* at all. Unless I specifically say so, assume I mean the same thing as video game or computer game. The distinction becomes important only when discussing hardware. Then computer games are played on personal computers and video games are played on consoles.

In game development, the word *genre* is often mistakenly used when talking about action, role-playing, adventure games, and so forth. In this book, I reserve the word genre for its more traditional definition of an artistic category. In painting, this could be expressionism or minimalism. In arts that tell stories, genres are mystery, romance, science fiction, and so on. Since we have these kinds of genres in games as well, I differentiate action, adventure, role-playing, simulation, and strategy as "types" of games.

Another tricky word is *script*. A script in my former life as a Hollywood writer was a teleplay or screenplay, the dialogue and descriptions of the action. In games, we also use script to mean a simple sort of pseudo-programming language that can be translated into program code. I have often been called upon to write scripts in script, compounding the confusion when I meet with other developers to discuss a project. You'll find both types of script are discussed in the following pages, but the context should make which one I mean clear.

Finally, there is the bewildering alphabet soup surrounding our most recent type of game: massively multiplayer. Virtual worlds, persistent worlds, massive persistent worlds, and tongue-torturing acronyms such as MMORPG (Massively Multi-Player Online Role-Playing Game), MMO (Massively-Multiplayer Online) and MMP (Massively-Multi-Player) are only *sort of* synonymous. I prefer the term *virtual worlds* used by Richard A Bartle in his book *Designing Virtual Worlds*. It covers all of them: persistent or non-persistent, massively multiplayer or the MUDs and MUSHes upon which they're based. But you'll be subjected to most of them at one time or another when we explore their differences.

I try and provide the birth and, if appropriate, death dates for many of the real people you'll meet in these pages who have contributed to my understanding of, and love for, writing. I don't do this because of some textbook convention, but because I believe it is important to realize that we're not creating new paradigms here from scratch. We're building on concepts that, in some cases, date back to primitive men like Urk (790,067 BC–790,025 BC), that great mastodon hunter who became the "father of the campfire story." The dates will hopefully put into perspective how long people have been thinking about characters and story and, yes, writing about their creation too.

In a book with the scope of this one, there are thousands of details. Every human effort has been made to confirm historical references, quotes, and facts. Sometimes primary sources were available. Sometimes they weren't, but reliable secondary sources were. Often, I have had only anecdotal references to draw upon. In other cases, attempts to verify specific examples failed, and I've had to rely on my own powers of observation (good) or memory (fanciful). I'm going to make mistakes. This isn't a newspaper. I'm not a journalist.

If I get an example wrong, forgive me. Look at the substance of the argument instead. I guarantee, even if the example is inaccurate, it at least supports my thesis! Please send me corrections or additions. If there is a second edition of the book, I'll be happy to incorporate them.

I've used the word *hopefully* quite a lot in this short introduction. This is a hopeful book. You hold in your hands most of what I know about writing for games and much of what I believe and practice, no matter what kind of writing I'm doing. It is meant to inform, to instruct, and maybe even inspire. Use the ideas you can, discard the rest. Make your own choices. We are all of us on a journey toward a destination for which there is no single road.

PART I

BACKGROUND

Prelude in a Fire-Lit Cave

The body of one hunter was already cooling in the patch of low fern where it had been thrown. A second hunter, gored twice in chest and shoulder, lay nearby, blinking at the sun filtered through the broad leaves of a towering tree. He would be abandoned; his bones picked clean by scavengers, bleaching memorials and sacrifices to the hunt.

Men wielding stone knives were chopping meat into manageable slabs and scraping gristle from great swatches of hide. The work was done with little grace, speed the only importance. The meat must reach the tribe's current camp as soon as possible to be seared and consumed within a few short hours. Each lost minute tainted it and increased the chance of illness, possibly death, instead of nourishment.

Death was every bit as much a member of the tribe as the hunters, the gatherers of roots and berries, the cooks, and the artisans who fashioned the stone heads of spears and blades of knives. Death was a constant companion, sometimes cruel, at others merciful; inevitable as nightfall, a companion to be depended upon.

Once all that could be carried had been harvested from the shaggy, long-tusked beast, the hunters began their weary trek back to the cave where they had taken refuge when autumn's first frost had touched the land only a few sunsets before. Their burden meant the traveling was slow. And they must always be on guard against some other predator that caught the scent of the easy meal they carried. At last the mouth of the cave was spotted; other members of the tribe gathered about it, awaiting their return.

Once inside, amongst the women, children, and infirm—there were no old ones in this life—the meat was skewered on long stakes and placed in the central fire pit. Hide was distributed to the women to be fashioned into protection against the fast approaching winter.

Lamentations were sung for the two hunters lost to the beast, the meal consumed, and the fire stoked against the encroaching darkness. All gathered round that fire now: hunters, women, children. Finally the work-a-day chatter died, and all eyes turned to the chief of the hunters.

He was possessed of only one good eye, and his left hand had withered to a frozen claw after it had been savaged by the teeth of a great cat three winters gone. Yet he was the bravest of them all, the most cunning, and ablest of the hunters.

The chief hunter waited in the silence, biding his time, allowing the stillness to linger. He gazed into the fire as it sparked and spit from animal grease. At last, when the quiet was stretched taut as a tendon, he looked round at them and began to speak . . .

And with every word he knew, he told the story of the hunt . . .

CHAPTER 1

MYTHS AND EQUATIONS

Ever since tales of great hunts and hunters were told to awestruck listeners huddled around the protecting fire, consumers, from cave folk to moviegoers, have been drawn to the power of storytelling. The story is the single thread that is woven through the entire fabric of what entertains us. The appreciation of a good story is a gift not granted to any other species on this planet. It is reserved for Homo sapiens alone.

Like other species, Homo sapiens play games. From professional sports to the puns and word juxtapositions that pepper our conversations, games appeal to us on many levels. We enjoy games because they have been a major source of our entertainment and a stimulus for our consciousness since we first focused our newly born eyes on a world of possibilities. Play was a way of dealing with the unknown. If our toes could be successfully played with, maybe they weren't something we needed to fear!

Games and stories have much in common. Both deal with how we handle fear. Both can teach us about the world and ourselves. Both can challenge us, move us to laughter or tears. Both spring from the child inside, and both can keep us young. Each can exist separately from the other, and be consummately entertaining, yet there are also times when the two meet, feed off of one another, and grow into something greater than they were separately. One of the most interesting opportunities for games and stories to coincide is in the still relatively new form of entertainment called computer games. And that is the focus of this book.

Before we get down to the nuts and bolts of manufacturing stories and constructing characters, there are two fundamental questions we should think about, a few myths that need to be dispelled, and an acknowledgement made that since games are an interactive medium after all, we do want to hear from our audience. First, the questions.

Why Make Games?

Is it a need to create? A need to express ourselves? A need to entertain? A need to illuminate the human condition? A need to make great wads of cash? Ask yourself why you want to make games as you read this book. We will never arrive at an answer that pleases everyone, but it's important to arrive at an answer that satisfies you.

Interactive entertainment will never replace passive entertainment any more than movies replaced the theatre, or TV replaced movies. It will, however, grow to be an equal source of pleasure and satisfaction for millions of people throughout the world. Opportunities are boundless for those who have the time and the patience to learn the skills necessary to build games, and the talent to take advantage of them.

There are two goals many say we need to reach as an industry. The first is mass market entertainment. The game industry may appear to be there by virtue of its sheer bulk, but until a single title reaches true mass market numbers, we're just flirting with the concept. One night in 1977 an episode I wrote of the television series *Charlie's Angels* was seen by close to 60 million people. Now, we're not necessarily talking about quality of product here, but the quantity of people who experienced it. Even in today's highly fragmented television industry the audience for a *single* episode of a hit TV show is measured in tens of millions. That is mass market penetration. And our most successful titles do not come close.

The second goal is achieving some sort of legitimacy in the eyes of critics, other media, and the population at large. I don't believe art (or even quality entertainment!) is achieved by someone who sets out to make Art. I'm talking now about Art with a capital "A," a painting or symphony or book or film that is considered classic because it "stands the test of time." What does this well worn phrase mean? That the creator of that piece of Art has succeeded in touching the hearts and minds of generations unborn when the Art was created.

Antonio Salieri was the star composer of socially conscious Holy Roman Emperor Joseph II's court, but it is Mozart we treasure. Salieri would have remained a footnote in music history were it not for Peter Shaffer's brilliant play, *Amadeus*, and the film adapted from it. But even with his new found fame, Salieri's work does not get performed much today. Art endures. Popular opinion fades.

Gemalde-Galerie

Figure 1.1 Antonio Salieri, famous footnote.

So while it would be pompous to suggest that any game creators should be attempting to make Art, we should also be aware of those qualities that may be conducive to its generation.

The game industry has failed to reach true mass market penetration; and few of our products even flirt with Art. And while they aren't as out of reach as many might think, nor are they waiting around placidly for us to catch up with them. What is needed is a solid body of work we can learn from, and a critical perspective with which we can study it. You can begin to *suspect* how a watch runs by watching the hands move, or hearing the ticking sound it makes. But you learn how it works by taking it apart, and putting it back together. We can see examples of how this happens in other youngish industries with aspirations to the capital "A."

My mentor at California Institute of the Arts was a screenwriter and director named Alexander MacKendrick. Sandy was a product of the "golden age" of British film comedy, a period from the late 40s to early 60s when motion picture studios (most famous of them was Ealing Studios, where Sandy worked for nearly all of his early career) released what are considered by many to be classics of film comedy. The Ealing Studios' films such as *The Man in the White Suit, Kind Hearts and Coronets, The Lavender Hill Mob,* and *The Ladykillers* were notable for (amongst other things) their impeccable story structure, non-stereotypical characters, and their illumination of the humanity and truth in the goofiest of characters and situations.

Figure 1.2 Alec Guinness sports the funny teeth in the first version of *The Ladykillers.*

In one course Sandy taught, we watched a handful of films over and over again: *North by Northwest*, *On the Waterfront*, Sandy's own *The Ladykillers*. The purpose was to see beyond the entertainment value each film possessed, to see the seams, to see how all the elements came together to create a unified entertainment experience. If you can get to the point where your favorite game no longer entertains you, you will have taken a crucial step toward understanding how it worked its magic. It can be a sad moment and an exhilarating one all at the same time.

Why Tell Stories in Games?

Should games try to tell stories? Not all of them. But they can, if we want. If we would like to involve emotions higher than an adrenaline rush, we need to reach the human spirit, not just endocrine glands. If we would like some day to be legitimized, stories and characters are time-honored ways to begin.

Can we do it? The answer is obvious: yes. Stories have gone from being the afterthought of early games to at least being considered of some value. Story and gameplay need to stop fighting with each other though, like naughty siblings competing for parental attention. We come to this struggle again when we explore Myth #2 below.

Can we do it *well*? Of course. Given some imagination, talent, and craft. Imagination and talent cannot be taught, but they can be encouraged. Give a craftsman the tools he needs to create, and both imagination and talent can blossom.

Stories are present in all other forms of crafted entertainment. In some, like live theatre or soap operas, the story is often pre-eminent. Production limitations place a necessary premium on good writing. If we want to eventually achieve some sort of critical recognition at least the equal of television and film, or simply reach the true mass market, it's time we accorded the writing of computer games respect and professionalism at least equal to that we currently reserve for graphics and sound and programming.

Myth #1: Interactive storytelling first appeared in computer games.

Some of us who make games have a tendency to believe that our civilization came to interactive storytelling late in our dramatic development. In fact, interactivity was a part of storytelling from the very beginning. There is a scene in the film *The Wind and the Lion*, written and directed by John Milius, where the "last of the Barbary pirates," a desert chieftain portrayed by Sean Connery, is relating the story of his life at yet another campfire. As he spins his tale to his captive, played by Candace Bergen, his men, having heard it many times and knowing it almost as well as he does, prompt him to retell the most significant and impressive parts. They attempt to shape the story, and the storyteller, wise leader that he is, molds his yarn to suit their requests.

Figure 1.3 Stories and games in *The Wind and the Lion*.

We can trust that as the chief hunter tells the story that opens this chapter the men who were on the hunt with him will interject their recollections, and those members of the tribe who were not part of the experience will ask questions and respond with exclamations of amazement, satisfaction, or sorrow. Both the additional material added by the chief hunter's men and the response from the rest of the tribe will help shape the narrative.

Live dramatic performances have always taken into account that extra character, the audience, and adjusted accordingly. If the audience is responding with enthusiastic laughter to a comedy, the actors will draw on that energy to enliven their performances. If the audience is bored and restless, the actors may try harder to infuse their words with intensity, or they may just speed up their dialogue to minimize the experience for both them and the audience. William Shakespeare acknowledged the role his audience at the Globe Theatre, most notably those standing in the pit armed with vegetables, played in his productions. Andrew Lloyd Webber's *Cats* creep and crawl through the audience as the play is about to begin.

Figure 1.4 *Cats* on the prowl begin each performance.

Many years ago I was at a performance of Paul Giovanni's Sherlock Holmes pastiche *The Crucifer of Blood* at a theatre in London's West End. In the midst of the play there was a sudden disturbance in the balcony. It quickly became impossible for either the audience or the actors to ignore. A man actually shouted from the balcony, "Is there a doctor in the house?" Keith Michel, the actor portraying the famous detective in the play, repeated the question. There was indeed a doctor in the orchestra section of the audience, and a man who had suffered a heart attack was removed by ambulance to a hospital.

When the play resumed the actors replayed the beginning of the scene that had been interrupted. Mr. Michel, to draw the audience back into the fun of the experience, sped through his lines, giving them deliberately comic overtones the text did not possess. Even though it broke "the fourth wall," a term we'll discuss in Chapter 8, the audience loved it, and was able to relax back into the play-going experience. His leading lady, Susan Hampshire, was not as taken with his efforts, and kept glaring at him, until he finally lapsed back into the rhythm of the play as directed, and the reality of the performance.

Interactivity, that two way street of storytelling, has always been with us, even if later media, such as film, radio, and television, have been largely insensate of the audience, at least during the actual performance. Happily we still have live theatre! If we were to express this relationship as an equation, it might look something like this:

Scripted/Rehearsed Story + Audience = Entertainment Experience

So we have in computer games a far more natural approach to storytelling than one might at first suppose, one that includes the participation of the audience, those individuals we call players.

Myth #2: Games and stories don't mix.

This is often the first observation out of the mouth of someone who believes we shouldn't attempt to tell more than cursory stories in games, or that we need to throw out all the old "outdated" rules of storytelling, and find some completely new paradigm like Artificial Intelligence to drive non-player characters in games, or force the players to do all the work and create any necessary story. Both actually have a place in games, but not as replacements to imaginatively drawn characters or carefully crafted stories.

Jerome Lawrence and Robert E. Lee's play *Inherit the Wind* was inspired by the Scopes Monkey Trial in 1925 where a teacher was prosecuted for teaching evolution. At the end of the film version, Henry Drummond (a fictionalized Clarence Darrow), played by Spencer Tracy, picks up a copy of the *Bible* and a copy of Charles' Darwin's *Origin of the Species*, weighs each for a moment, then packs them away together in his briefcase. The symbolism is obvious. Biblical teaching and evolution can coexist. The same is true for stories and games.

MGM/UA

Figure 1.5 The *Bible* and *Origin of the Species* side by side.

Games are a very different animal from stories. We all know that. While the word *game* is often taken to mean a competitive activity, the most general definition is simply "a way of amusing oneself."

In fact, games that encourage active participation in storytelling are as old as games themselves. Children learn through playing games. They act out stories, play characters, and mold their stories and characters in reaction to their friends' actions. Adults role-playing at their kitchen tables enjoy the structure of a game that allows a fluid storytelling that adjusts to their play. Here our equation might resemble the following:

Game Rules + Scripted/Rehearsed Story + Players = Entertainment Experience

The key to a satisfying entertainment experience is in the balance of its parts. Balance is a key concern in many areas of game design as well as writing. You'll discover it is one of the main themes we come back to again and again in this book.

If, in our first equation above, the storyteller is unable to adjust to his audience, audience participation will diminish (or degenerate into heckling!), and the entertainment experience will be adversely affected. (In the case of theatrical productions in Shakespeare's day, of course, the heckling was an acknowledged part of mass entertainment. Polite society was forced to endure it, or sponsor private productions.)

In the second equation, if the game rules or the scripted story are too rigid to adjust to the improvisations of the players, the entertainment experience will suffer.

What games played on computers have altered in this mix is the replacement of human beings with algorithms on one side of the equation or the other. Instead of human story-tellers responding to their audiences or actors adjusting their performances, we require the game's programming to adjust, a far trickier proposition, and one we will address often in the following pages.

Since we're messing around with equations, let's look at one more common myth.

Myth #3: Life equals drama.

Webster's Dictionary gives the following definitions of drama:

1. A play in prose or verse
2. Dramatic art of a particular kind or period
3. The art or practice of writing or producing plays
4. A real-life situation or succession of events having the dramatic progression or emotional content typical of a play

It is that last definition that is of most interest to us here. I remember a debate during a roundtable at the Game Developer's Conference several years ago where a number of game designers insisted that if we witness a child struck by a car on the street we are see-ing drama. But this position reflects a misunderstanding of the colloquial or common usage of the word, as in "Wasn't that a dramatic basketball game?"

What we really mean is "Wasn't that basketball game as exciting as the Disney movie about a basketball game we saw?" There is more to drama than real life. Drama only exists in real life when real life events mirror dramatic structure and remind us of created drama we have witnessed. This is not to say that intense emotions cannot be aroused by an injured child or a close score in a sports contest. We may even call these examples "drama." But it is dangerous for creators of drama to assume that all we must do is follow Hamlet's famous advice to *his* players: "To hold, as 'twere, the mirror up to nature."

According to definition, we must start with drama as a structure in which to wrap real life. Drama begets Real Life Drama. Therefore the progression looks like this:

Drama -> Real Life Drama

But wait! Which really came first? Wasn't it life? Shouldn't the cause and effect look like more like this?

Real Life -> Drama

No, because even in the very beginning of storytelling and drama, back around that campfire after the woolly mammoth fell, there was an added step in the equation:

Real Life + Interpreter = Drama

Drama is built on the reflection human beings bring to the incidents and conflict of real life that is then communicated to other human beings. And drama is built from the human context that we wrap the realities of life within.

Just adding an interpreter to the equation doesn't guarantee drama of course.

Life + Interpreter (Shakespeare) = Drama

Life + Interpreter (My Next Door Neighbor Bob) = Trivialization

When you add insight and perspective to life it can become drama. It speaks to us as human beings and can enrich our lives. However, when you add imagery without meaning, life is not dramatized, it is cheapened. We will explore some of the building blocks of drama shortly, and see how they relate to the craft of writing for games.

One Last Equation

Okay, let's put all of the highfalutin' concepts we've just talked about aside. Forget Art. Forget drama. There is one primary equation that drives all entertainment industries:

Entertainment = Fun

Sounds obvious, doesn't it? Yet we are an industry awash in pet theories that disregard fun, new paradigms that ignore past, and earth-shaking "discoveries" that only seem new to their discoverers because they are unaware of even the short history of our industry. A lot of these pet theories, new paradigms, and earth-shaking discoveries have been tried time and time again, and have failed miserably. To paraphrase George Santayana: "Those who are ignorant of the past are condemned to overlook it."

We'll take some requests from our audience.

We storytellers have a pretty good idea of what we want from our audiences. We want them to be entertained. But what do they want from us? If we listen closely, they will tell us:

- Take me to a place I have never been.
- Make me into someone I could never be.
- Let me do things I could never do.

Obviously, all entertainment media has the opportunity to take the audience to a place it's never been. But only a few mediums add the other two: theme park rides, masquerade balls, simulators, live-action role playing, and of course, computer games.

If we can fulfill those three far from trivial requests, we will have succeeded. As authors, we may add more at our pleasure. We can share our philosophies of life; air our political views; teach; titillate; shock; comfort; challenge; empower; suborn. The choices are limitless. But it is those three requests from our audience that open the door for all else to follow. They are at the heart of certain mystical guarantors of entertainment like *willing suspension of disbelief* and *immersion.*

It will do us a lot of good if we keep these concepts and questions in mind as we work.

CHAPTER 2

THE STORY
REMAINS THE SAME

W hy bother with all this old stuff? Games demand a new paradigm, don't they? You can't apply the techniques of linear, non-interactive media to games, can you?

Well . . . yes, you can.

An examination of art styles is far beyond the scope of this book, but I want you to take a look at these two paintings by Pablo Picasso. Each is a portrait. The first is of Picasso's mother, painted in 1896 when the artist was *fifteen* years old.

The second is Picasso's daughter, painted in 1938 when the artist was fifty-seven.

Figure 2.1 Portrait of Pablo Picasso's Mother, 1896.

Figure 2.2 Portrait of Pablo Picasso's Daughter, 1938.

13

The point is not which person Picasso was more fond of, or which portrait you may like better. The point is that Picasso did not wake up one morning and, through sheer creativity and imagination, start painting in the cubist style that he and Georges Braque pioneered in the years before World War I, and that is today most associated with him. He began by applying his considerable talents to far more traditional work. In short, he learned the rules he was later to break. He first learned composition, perspective, light, anatomy, all the principles he needed to feed his vision. As he matured, his vision evolved, and his training enabled him to pursue it.

Now an argument can be made that these were at least both paintings. Games are very different from books or movies. One of the central themes of this book is (apologies to Marshall McLuhan) the medium is *not* the message. The principles of *storytelling*, as much as they may appear to change, in fact remain the same. To tell stories, even in the relatively new medium of computer games, we may extend those principles, even find new ones. To ignore the fundamentals of storytelling found in other media is to create work that fails to touch our audience, the players, yet we hear some people in our industry advocating to do exactly that. They argue that computer games are an entirely new form of entertainment that must develop its own new paradigms.

Yet other aspects of our medium that we embrace as ours alone are actually built upon principles borrowed from other media. Our interfaces imitate real world control systems. Our graphics are grounded in art history and traditional animation. Pioneering work in artificial intelligence was done long before the first computer game. If programmers can embrace research from nongame sources; if artists can apply rules of composition and use *chiaroscuro* lighting in our games; then it should be obvious that writers of games can also learn from those writers who came before us.

note

CHIAROSCURO: a painting technique that starkly contrasts light and shade.

George Santayana is oft quoted and just as often misquoted or paraphrased. Here, from *Reason in Common Sense*, is what the poor man actually wrote: "Progress, far from consisting in change, depends on retentiveness. Those who cannot remember the past are condemned to repeat it."

Richard A. Bartle in *Designing Virtual Worlds* writes, "You have to *understand* a system before you can challenge it."

Here then is an introduction at least to that linear, non-interactive stuff some are so eager to change.

Aristotle and Those Other Greeks

Aristotle

Aristotle (384-322 BCE) was a philosopher, writer, and teacher; student of Plato; and possibly a tutor to Alexander the Great. Although there is some question about whether this popular belief is actually true or not, it makes for a great story. His treatises, covering a variety of scientific and philosophical matters, from physics and natural history to politics, logic, ethics, and even dreams, are still published today. In fact Aristotelian thought shaped Western culture for centuries, and remains one of the pillars of our intellectual history.

Figure 2.3 Aristotle.

It is through him that we are introduced to the concept of the Deus ex Machina, the "God Machine," that is today trotted out to describe a fortuitous (to the author) plot twist that wraps up the final action in a story. We may frown on it, but in Aristotle's day of course, it was simply a perfectly respectable plot device given that most stories were set in motion by those hands-on gods atop Mt. Olympus.

It was Aristotle who proposed the bedrock logical argument consisting of two premises and a conclusion:

- Every Greek is a person.
- Every person is mortal.
- Every Greek is mortal.

The work that most concerns us as writers is, of course, his *Poetics* written in 350 BCE. Like most of Aristotle's writing, there are not a lot of words in the *Poetics*, but it is packed with ideas. Even though Aristotle chiefly concerned himself with tragedy and epic poetry (and, briefly, comedy), several ideas resonate even today in our drama, literature, film, and games. He was the first writer to talk about the dramatic reversal that in the past few years enjoyed revived attention in books on screenwriting. This concept is important enough to have its own topic in Chapter 9, "Bringing the Story to Life," and we'll examine it then.

Expanding on Plato's observation that "art imitates life," Aristotle begins the *Poetics* with three elements of that imitation, or representation: the medium, or type, of art, such as music, poetry, and drama; the objects of imitation who are defined as "men in action," the protagonists of today; and the manner in which the imitation is presented, either as narration or drama.

Aristotle notes that the ability to imitate is with human beings from birth. It is how we learn. And he points out we enjoy seeing others imitating. This pleasure gave rise to everything from earliest man mimicking the animals he hunted in ritual dances to one of the main reasons people today watch plays, films, and television drama. Acting is pretending, make-believe, imitation.

The second element is of interest to us because this "man of action" is the player-character in games. He categorizes this man of action in three ways. First are characters who are better than people in real life. These can be tragic heroes such Oedipus, Hamlet, Citizen Kane, Anakin Skywalker, or even Dave Boyle, the character played by Tim Robbins in the film *Mystic River*.

In 1983 Michael Berlyn's text adventure *Infidel* gave gamers a tragically flawed character to play. The *PC* is obsessed with his work, arrogant, and driven, and this *Achilles' heel* ultimately kills him. Some reviewers considered this a "twist" ending. It's not, of course, but rather the only logical conclusion for a classical tragic hero. It was a controversial ending, and players were understandably split on whether they liked it or not.

note

PC: stands for player-character, the character controlled by and representing the player in the game.

note

ACHILLES' HEEL: refers to the one weak spot on the Greek hero's body that literally brings about his fall. It is popularly used synonymously with tragic flaw.

We don't find many tragic heroes in games for two main reasons. First, they are uncomfortable figures, haunted and often alone. Games are meant to be fun. These guys are not fun. Second, the hero role is most often taken by the player-character as in any First Person Shooter like *Judge Dredd: Dredd Versus Death* or most Third Person Action games like *Prince of Persia: The Sands of Time*. The very fact that a game's interactivity puts the player into a story means players really don't want to be a tragic hero who comes to a bad end.

On rare occasions we see this type of character as an *NPC*.

note

NPC: an acronym that stands for non-player character. In a game all of the characters not controlled by the player are NPCs.

Because it's rare, it can add surprise as well as depth to the story of a game. Aribeth in *Neverwinter Nights* is an example of a woman who starts out as a typical heroic babe, but as the story develops, bitterness over the death of her sweetheart and a desire for revenge twist her thinking to the point where near the climax of the game story she has become one of the chief villain's most prized generals. We'll discuss the various roles NPCs can play in games in Chapter 4, "Character Roles."

A way to have your heroic cake and eat it too is to have the player-character come to a bloody end, but by sacrificing himself for a good purpose. The character can be a noble figure from the beginning, or redeem himself for past wrongs. We have plenty of examples of the former, but games shy away from the latter, again because the game element, the reason players buy the game, is to feel heroic in the more common definition we discuss next.

Heroes in games are more commonly archetypal heroes (see the section on Joseph Campbell below). In the first *FPS* games like *Doom*, no attention was paid to the player-character at all. He was just a rough-looking face in the corner of the interface who got more battered and bruised as he took hits. Later games have added more character: *Lara Croft: Tomb Raider* or Sam Fisher in *Tom Clancy's Splinter Cell*.

note

FPS: stands for first person shooter, a standard type of action game.

These characters rarely change through the course of the game story, and they have little depth. This is one of the reasons attempts at creating emotion in the second Lara Croft film, *Lara Croft Tomb Raider: The Cradle of Life* fail to resonate with audiences. When they are faced with characters about whom they know nothing except a checklist of facts—characters with no capacity for growth—audiences should be forgiven if they don't care what happens to them.

More recent games have attempted to portray, or at least suggest, more complex characters even given the restrictions on player-characters already mentioned above. JC Denton in *Deus Ex*, or his clone Alex D in the recent sequel *Deus Ex: Invisible War*, or the enigmatic Master Chief from *Halo*, are all more interesting to watch, and to play. In Chapter 3, "Respecting Characters," we'll explore the voyage of discovery players can take to learn about the character they are guiding through the story.

There are also heroes in strategy games like *Heroes of Might and Magic* who function more as celebrity walk-ons, just special characters with unique powers at the disposal of the player. In *Age of Empires* and similar strategy games, the player becomes the hero, with god-like powers to manipulate warriors, farmers, and entire civilizations.

The second type of character Aristotle discusses is one who is worse than most people. This is not the villain/antagonist for a protagonist to contend with, but the actual protagonist or central figure of a story. This type of character was, in Aristotle's day, confined to comedy. Comic figures like Moliere's hypocritical *Tartuffe* and, to some extent, Phil Connors, Bill Murray's insensitive boor of a weatherman in *Groundhog Day*, are deliberately written to seem worse than the rest of us. Such characters often end as badly as *Oedipus* or *Hamlet*, if not outright dead, at least with all their high blown pretensions and convoluted schemes in tatters. Of course, the audience takes delight in this: the difference between tragic and comedic characters. Phil Connors is redeemed in the end, a more common fate these days for these characters. In each case, however, Aristotle's term "poetic justice" accurately describes their fates.

The third and last type of character Aristotle addresses is the one who is representative of the way people really are. By this, he is rounding out a dramatic class system and simply means those that are not worthier than ourselves or lower, but somewhere in between. He is discussing drama, after all, and does not mean to suggest a character that may have its direct counterpart in real life.

Today we often break down these three classifications, twist them and turn them, combine them, or subtract essential elements that define the classic models. It's important to remember that the drama and poetry he analyzed were very restricted and had been for centuries. While there is much to learn from him and his friends, we must also be aware of the ways in which our modern literature and drama have evolved.

For example, today we have the anti-hero, a popular character particularly in the late 1960s and early 1970s, when writers in all media created characters who struggled against the establishment: McMurphy, the rebellious patient at an Oregon state mental institution in *One Flew Over the Cuckoo's Nest*; and Luke, from ex-convict Donn Pearce's novel, *Cool Hand Luke*. The film version gave us the famous phrase, "What we have here is . . . failure to communicate." Paul Newman, the actor who played Luke in the film, had already carved out an anti-hero niche all his own a few years earlier in such films as *The Hustler* and *Hud*.

But what happens to anti-heroes? They can often come to messy ends just like their tragic forebears. McMurphy is lobotomized. Luke is killed. Again, not necessarily characters players might want to play. And since these types of characters are invariably extremely colorful, outrageous, and shocking, players wouldn't be too fond of the very real possibility of their characters being over-shadowed if anti-heroes were NPCs.

Probably the most famous concept we take from Aristotle is that of the unities of time, place, and action. We first need to understand that Aristotle based this concept on the prevailing forms of drama and epic poetry that existed in his day. And there are many stories that do not observe them. *Gone with the Wind*, *Cold Mountain*, and the James Bond films cover large amounts of geography and incident, and are no worse for it. Even so, the unities apply directly to all dramatic media today, and especially to computer games.

Unity of Time

The story we are telling takes place in a limited, and sequential, time frame. This can be as little as an hour or two as in films such as *Die Hard* or *Nick of Time*; or as long as a day or two or maybe even a week. The key points are that the time of the story is purposely limited to the time it takes to play out the action. There is no extraneous passage of time covered by a title reading "Later that Day," cuts to revved up clocks, or the pages fluttering off a calendar. And the tighter the time, the more tension can be created.

This is perfect for computer games. From the intimate, squad-level firefights of the *Tom Clancy's Rainbow Six* series to the real-time battles of *Command and Conquer* and *Age of Mythology*, the action plays sequentially. While the levels of these games, as well as First-Person Shooters and action games can be connected in a looser timeline, each level is an episodic story complete within itself. And because that story is confined to a limited and sequential "real-time" it is all the more suspenseful.

Unity of Place

One of the jobs computer games can do well is simulate an environment. We can't capture the realistic look of live action films, but we can create geography with consistent physical laws, recognizable terrain, and objects that can be manipulated. In single-player games the environment must be extremely interactive. Players enjoy seeing the destruction their bullets and bombs make in the world of the game. They want to be able to open the drawers of a desk or run water from a tap.

In order to accomplish this level of physical interaction, these games limit the place where the action plays out. Each level or area is bounded either by logical physical barriers, barriers that fit within the fiction of the world such as NPC guards, or by less logical blockages in the landscape: impassable forests, unswimmable rivers, and so on. If we didn't limit the geography *and* the number of interactions possible within the environment, the number of interactions would overwhelm an engine that must stay lean and mean to accommodate the game's action, and the number of locations would tax even the largest art staff.

This level of physical interaction becomes more problematic in massively multiplayer worlds. Here the trade-off is allowing a much more expansive geography for players to explore at the expense of fewer interactions with the world.

In both cases, the storyteller should gladly accept the limitations imposed in the same way we were limited in television to a limited number of locations and constructed sets. By confining the story in this way, less attention is paid to the environment. Each new setting ore that a player or audience must absorb. Maintaining unity of place forces us as writers to pay attention to what is important: character and story. And like unity of time, it helps us to create the necessary tension and suspense. *Die Hard* (and all its clones), *Nick of Time*, and of course, James Cameron's *Titanic* all benefit from observing the unities of time and place and the third one as well: action.

Unity of Action

This unity is interesting because it encompasses both stories limited in time and place and epics such as *Gone with the Wind, War and Peace*, and *The Odyssey* by Homer. It eliminates all extraneous action that is not of central importance to the plot and theme. In each of the above cases the scope of the story is immense, yet each scene is chosen with care.

Again, game authors limited by budget and time constraints can use this unity to help us decide what scenes and levels are necessary to the game story and which ones are a waste of resources. Any level may be a standout due to geography, effects, puzzles, uniqueness of enemies, and many other factors. But if that level does not advance the story, it is better saved for another game. As we explore the ways writers and designers can meld story with gameplay in Chapters 7, "Once Upon a Time," 8, "Respecting Story," and 9, "Bringing the Story to Life," we'll see we must take advantage of every opportunity presented to us, even more so than in other media. Superfluous material, however brilliantly conceived and executed, makes our job all the more difficult.

Keeping unity of action in mind while we write is also important because it focuses our attention where it belongs: on the story and the characters who drive it. It can rein in creative flights of fancy that may seem fun and exciting when they first grab us, but become dead ends once they're fully explored. Experienced writers— particularly those used to tight deadlines and budget constraints—develop instincts as to what to include and what to discard as they write. This process of selection can pass almost unnoticed as the writer works, but it is as vital to a successful story as the impulse that gave it birth.

Homer

"It is Homer who has chiefly taught other poets the art of telling lies skillfully."

—*Aristotle*

Figure 2.4 Homer.

Homer (born circa 750 BCE) did not, as we may think, make up the stories of *The Odyssey* and *The Illiad*. Nor did he simply set down popular myths or historic events. The epic poetry of Greece was handed down from generation to generation, mostly in oral form. There is even evidence to suggest many hands were involved in the creation of these epic tales. Homer is certainly the best known of these, and the romantic notion of this blind man dictating stories to a faithful scribe is certainly in keeping with the bardic tradition he exemplifies. This shouldn't take away from our admiration of him. Shakespeare freely adapted others' stories, history, and mythology for his own purposes. That Homer was a skilled interpreter, natural storyteller, and inspired poet can be deduced from the fact that it is his name that is most revered by later Greek writers and philosophers when they discuss epic poetry.

Homer is important to us, the creators of games, because of the style in which his epic stories were told. Alfred Lord, in his book, *The Singer of Tales*, explicitly relates this type of storytelling to bardic tradition. The prelude of this section of my book is meant to illustrate the origins of it, forever lost in the swampy miasma of pre-literate history. Every story told by a loving parent to a child just before the child drifts off to sleep follows in the same grand tradition.

Two points are of most interest: the fluidity of this type of storytelling, and its fundamentally episodic nature. The ever-changing story of bardic tradition that is influenced by teller, by audience, by region and culture closely reflects the interactive story. Interactive stories must react to the player just as bards and cavemen reacted to their audience; just as parents must adjust their bedtime stories to a child's question, "But Mommy, the prince wasn't really evil, was he?"

The episodic nature of the Homeric epics have even more potential for us as writers of computer games, particularly massively multiplayer games. Here we see the first building blocks of a modular system that we will explore further in Chapter 13, "The Roots of a New Storytelling," and we'll revisit Homer, copying and refining oral tradition, then.

Sophocles

In Sophocles (circa 496–404 BCE) we have one of the great playwrights of Greece's golden age, an era that included such heavy hitters as Aeschylus and Euripides. The plotting of his *Oedipus Rex* feels as up-to-date today as it did centuries ago. In *Antigone* and *Electra*, his women characters are brilliantly etched, strong, and complex.

Figure 2.5 Sophocles.

Like Shakespeare, Sophocles often acted in his plays, and was apparently something of an amazing juggler. One of his major accomplishments was adding a third character to plays. That's right, Greek drama up until that time was all duets. Something to keep in mind the next time you're faced with cutting your cast of NPCs! He was also responsible for abandoning the practice of presenting a single story as a trilogy, preferring instead to tell a complete story in a single play.

These single plays were of the same basic length as the single part of a trilogy, yet they were based on the same stories and myths as their predecessors. And this is why he is of interest to the computer game writer. What was the result of taking the action of a story spread out over three plays and reducing it to a single play? Pace was quickened. Drama was heightened.

Just as earlier I talked about the paradoxical benefits of the Aristotelian unities as they seem to limit time, place, and action, yet in fact serve to focus our writing, this condensing of Sophocles' stories made them that much more involving. Writers of computer games start at the apparent disadvantage of having to find ways and means to tell our stories without interrupting the natural flow of the gameplay. Other media do not have this additional challenge.

As a result, we are also continually condensing our stories to fit within our own specialized restraints. What this process demands is clarity of vision. When Sophocles sped up the action to fit within the shorter performance time, he had to make sure that action remained comprehensible to his audience, so he needed to simplify the stories. Also, many of his audience knew the stories by heart before they entered the amphitheatre. They would not have been receptive if their favorite parts were removed.

What a challenge! Yet he was able to pull it off with enough virtuosity that he won 18 first prizes, and never finished worse than second in over 120 plays. In fact, in his first competition he beat Aeschylus, the "Father of Tragedy" himself. Maybe it was because people were relieved by the shorter running times.

The point is that simply because we work under many restrictions not piled upon other forms of storytelling, this doesn't mean we need to settle for anything less. There is nothing more intrinsically difficult in writing a computer game than in writing a play all those centuries ago. For every new challenge we face, there is a solution. There is no need for a badly written game, and no excuse.

Aristophanes

There are other Greeks worth checking out, including Plato, Aeschylus, and Euripides, but the only other golden Greek I'm going to talk about here is Aristophanes (circa 448–380 BCE). Like Homer, his versions of popular stories are the only ones that survived, the only extant examples of Greek comedy.

Figure 2.6
Aristophanes.

There is much more comedy than tragedy in computer games. Why? We've talked about players' reluctance to play heroes who end up face down in a pool of congealing dreams. The other major reason is that it is much easier to make people laugh than it is to make them cry. To write comedy, you only need to be able to take a certain impish outlook on life, combine it with a knack for timing and surprise, and you'll have them rolling in their cubicles. To write tragedy, you need to explore some darker sides of your character. While this doesn't seem to deter all those writers of the books that end up on Oprah's list, it's a voyage many writers of computer games seem unwilling to take.

Mark Barrett, one of my sidebar contributors, suggests, "The main reason that games have emphasized humor is that people who are laughing will forgive almost anything in exchange for those laughs. String enough laughs together and you can even convince people that a game is a comedy—which is a specific narrative form—when, in fact, it is more closely related to a collection of jokes or gags. Humor in the form of jokes is also inherently self-contained, meaning you can slip it into the 'holes' in gameplay, where other narrative forms require significant preparation and continuity over the course of the game."

Moreover, the humor in computer games is generally confined within certain limits. It is, for the most part, doggedly mainstream, relying heavily on verbal wit that is, after all, easier to animate than pratfalls. Writers of computer games are also fond of winking at the players, reminding them that the author is aware of them, however much that might harm their involvement in the story.

Computer game humor isn't confined to subject matter as much as it is style, full of puns and put-downs, and it can be as deliberately gross as a Farrelly Brothers' film. What's missing is an edge. There is nothing edgy about fart jokes any longer. They have successfully made the leap from the playground to Disney films.

Aristophanes, who wasn't above the occasional scatological moment himself, wrote his comedies in an uncertain era of war and political upheaval. Greece was a nation in transition. All Greeks felt it, even if they didn't know where that transition was taking them. The comedy of Aristophanes was therefore a comedy shaded by melancholy and uncertainty and suffering.

The Peloponnesian War was over two decades old when one of his most famous plays, *Lysistrata*, told the story of wives who refused to have sex with their husbands until they brought the war to an end. It should not surprise anyone that it enjoyed a popular revival during the late 1960s for its sexual themes as well as its explicit anti-war statement. In *The Wasps*, he explored the decline of Athenian culture, particularly its legal system. In *The Knights*, he satirized the powerful, unloved and unlovely politician, Cleon. Today we may be shocked that a comedian might lose his TV show over political comments. Aristophanes could have lost his life. He even went after respectable figures like Euripides and Socrates in other plays.

Aristophanes' comedy was comedy with a purpose, and that purpose was not only to make his audiences laugh. He used comedy to challenge them and to make them think. Other than a handful of titles such as *Grand Theft Auto: Vice City* with its utterly despicable, yet funny characters, *Grim Fandango's* meditations on life and death, and the skewering of corporate greed in *The Space Bar*, computer games haven't attempted much meaningful comedy. We'll return to comedy in Chapter 11, "Story Anatomy."

Jung's Collective Unconscious

If Sigmund Freud is the father of modern psychology, Carl Jung (1875–1961) is his free-spirited nephew. Whereas Freud's view of the unconscious mind was that of a dark and roiling mass of hidden secrets and dangerous passions, Jung saw it as a connection, a doorway between the individual mind and all of humanity.

Jung defined three parts of our psyche: the ego, or conscious mind; the personal unconscious, repository for memory both accessible and suppressed; and the collective unconscious, containing a memory shared in common with all humanity. Phenomena such as déjà vu and love at first sight, the similarities across different cultures of various symbols and myths, as well as parallels in everything from dreams to fairy tales, Jung wrote, are all examples of this collective unconscious, which can be studied only through its effects, and never directly.

Figure 2.7 Carl Jung.

Jung's last book, *Man and His Symbols*, is a perfect synthesis of his ideas on the symbolism of dreams. It covers everything from the influences of ancient myths on modern man to symbolism in the visual arts. To understand Jung's theories, begin here at the end. Even though the material is all theory, it is great fuel to fire our creative thinking.

Jung is of primary interest to us for three reasons. First is his theory of the collective unconscious, this shared history of humankind we all carry within us. It can help us understand why others react in the ways that they do to what we create. If we can learn from it, we will be better able to touch the hearts and minds of our audience, the computer game player.

The second reason is the importance of symbols, those atavistic signposts that show up unexpectedly in a phrase, a shape, a composition of light and color, and immediately imbue the moment with a greater significance that it might ordinarily have. We see symbols everywhere around us: in an expressionist painting, a church sermon, or a national flag. How those symbols can be used to invoke a particular reaction in the player will be explored in Chapter 8.

The third reason for taking a look at Jung is his cross-cultural studies of symbols and myths, spadework that directly influenced our last subject in this chapter: Joseph Campbell.

Campbell's The Hero's Journey

"The latest incarnation of Oedipus, the continued romance of Beauty and the Beast, stand this afternoon on the corner of Forty-second Street and Fifth Avenue, waiting for the traffic light to change."

—Joseph Campbell, *The Hero with a Thousand Faces*

I first stumbled across Joseph Campbell's *The Hero with a Thousand Faces* when I was a college student many years ago. First published in 1949, the book was enjoying a minor revival of interest in the turbulent late 1960s and early 1970s. It was a revelation to me. Here was the best book I'd ever read about my burgeoning vocation, writing, and it wasn't even about writing.

Figure 2.8 Joseph Campbell.

Campbell gives us the story of the hero's journey, a story that is remarkably and significantly the same in myths from around the world. He uses this story to mirror nothing less than how we develop as human beings. We act out this journey in our lives, and to recognize it is to recognize ourselves.

The hero's journey is broken down into three major parts, almost like acts in a play. First there is a Departure. Here the hero is called to adventure. Someone is in need of aid, and the hero, an unimportant local character like Jack in *Jack, the Giant Killer*; someone with standing, but not perceived as a hero like Sir Thomas Moore in *A Man for All Seasons*; or a wanderer with no particularly notable deeds to his credit such as the gunslinger called *Shane*, is pressed to help. He may be confronted by a mentor figure, or seek one out to assist him in his quest.

The next step Campbell calls Initiation, and this is the trek to reach the goal that will secure the needed aid. This journey may be physical or spiritual or both. As Campbell says, "Popular tales represent the heroic action as physical; the higher religions show the deed to be moral . . ." This second part is what we generally refer to as the quest or mission, and plays a great part in the structure of computer games today, even though games often pay far greater attention to it at the expense of the Departure, which becomes little more than a briefing or assignment. One of the most important facets of this step is the necessity for the hero to change, and this directly ties in to character progression that we will look at in the next chapter.

The third step is Return wherein the hero accomplishes his task, aid is rendered, and lives or reputations or souls are saved. In this part, the hero is rewarded with acclamation, riches, the hand of a fair maiden, or most importantly, peace of mind. For the journey has been more than a voyage of discovery. It has effected a significant change in the hero's perceptions and beliefs that will continue to the end of his days.

George Lucas has acknowledged that Luke Skywalker's journey is heavily influenced by *The Hero with a Thousand Faces*, although he didn't need to, the evidence is there in front of our eyes. More recently the computer games industry has rightfully rediscovered Campbell's work. And while it may be taken way too literally, this journey's importance cannot be overstressed. We'll return to it throughout the course of this book.

Primary Sources

One final note before we move on, and that concerns primary sources. Aristotle's *The Poetics* and *The Art of Dramatic Writing* by Lajos Egri both have much to teach us as writers of computer games. I'll be referring to both throughout this book. Yet if I'd only read Egri, I might not have bothered with Aristotle, since Egri has little use for him (not to mention such accomplished playwrights as Eugene O'Neil and Noel Coward, and most of the other people with books on playwrighting in his day!). There is much we can learn from Egri, but we must take anyone's opinions with a grain of our own insight.

There are many books that will gladly interpret the original plays and books we've been discussing here, as well as all the plays, films, books, and games I'll give as examples. I'm doing the same after all. But none should be considered a substitute for experiencing the originals. I fervently recommend that you seek out as many as you can, study them, and form your own conclusions. It is far more likely that you'll be able to absorb and synthesize the ideas in their original forms, and even come to disagree with others' interpretations, including mine!

From *The Great Train Robbery* to *Birth of a Nation*

People say our technology is changing so fast these days it's impossible to keep up with it. Janet Murray in *Hamlet on the Holodeck: The Future of Narrative in Cyberspace* suggests that we are in our industry still at the incunabula stage, using a technology still in its infancy. She points out that it took 150 years from Gutenberg's printing press to *Don Quixote*, a book we both find significant, but for different reasons. We will be examining *Don Quixote* in Chapter 13. For now, it is enough that it is regarded as the first true novel in western culture. Maybe it's no coincidence that this novel gives us hints of how to handle interactive storytelling today in the infancy of OUR technology.

But I would argue that things move much faster these days. Information and ideas spread like wildfire, or e-mail viruses, threatening to overwhelm us. Innovation runs at a much faster pace.

What can we say about *The Great Train Robbery*? Produced at Thomas Edison's studio in 1903, it was written, directed, and edited by the head of production, Edwin S. Porter. The film ran about 12 minutes, chronicling the title robbery, the outlaws' escape, and their eventual comeuppance. It is credited as being the first narrative to use *parallel cutting* to create suspense and move the story forward. Reportedly, women fainted (I expect a few men did too.) when a villain pointed his gun directly at the camera and fired it. (Something network censors refused to let us do in the opening credits of the television show *Blacke's Magic* in 1985!)

Figure 2.9 Yes, *The Great Train Robbery* is about robbing a train.

note

PARALLEL CUTTING: (aka parallel action) an editing technique where two related stories are intercut as they move forward.

D.W. Griffith's controversial epic *Birth of a Nation* appeared in 1915. And to this day it is an excruciating embarrassment to critics and scholars who rightfully honor its breakthrough filmmaking achievements while at the same time having to deal with the undeniable fact that it is virulently racist, historically inaccurate, and politically naïve. It's as if Aristotle's *Poetics* extolled child molestation at the same time as they laid the foundations of drama. Film critic James Agee said of Griffith, "To watch his work is like being witness to the beginning of melody, or the first conscious use of the lever or the wheel; the emergence, coordination, and first eloquence of language; the birth of an art; and to realize that this is all the work of one man."

Figure 2.10 *Birth of a Nation*: Seminal and reprehensible all at the same time.

Twelve years separated the very first one-reel narrative film, *The Great Train Robbery* (1903), and D.W. Griffith's epic *Birth of a Nation* (1915).

Will Crowther's and Don Wood's *Colossal Cave*, the first adventure game, showed up on mainframe computers in its present form in 1976, a greatly expanded version of the original work Crowther began four years earlier. This game introduced interactive fiction to the world.

In 12 years nearly a century ago, the narrative film went from gurgling infancy to mass entertainment produced by a host of competitors. As we charge into the new century, 30 years after the debut of that game, let's look around. Games are little changed in content despite the addition of the latest audio/video trimmings, and for the most part, the core audience for them remains a small portion of the entertainment market. Why?

The Language of Drama and Film

The word language in this heading refers to terms that describe and techniques that utilize some basic concepts to dramatic writing and screenwriting. Much of the vocabulary of drama and film must be juggled before it can apply to computer games, as we shall see. But there are several concepts that can be translated directly. We'll be returning to them again and again, but for now, here are some brief discussions to lay the groundwork.

Universal Themes

What is the story about? Good vs. Evil? Is that enough? You want an audience to willingly suspend their disbelief? Give them a theme they understand, and are interested in. Whether it's the universal heroic quest tracked from culture to culture by Joseph Campbell, or the Greek-tragedy of families torn apart, give the story for your game, as any story, a reason for being told beyond the fact that it would be fun.

Don't give in to the mechanical repetition of cliché. Find new stories, or at least new meaning in old stories. Do RPGs really need another "There was a great conflict in the past between good and evil, now evil is coming back!" story that offers nothing more than a change of scenery, and different names for weapons and spells?

In contrast, look at *Sly Cooper and the Thievius Raccoonus*, a console action game that takes players on a basic treasure hunt that is also a quest to retrieve family honor. The theme is "There is no risk too great that is not worth taking for the sake of one's family."

In *The Art of Dramatic Writing* Lajos Egri speaks of the word *premise*. However, his definition of this word is closer to what we call today *theme*. Premise is reserved for the idea or situation upon which a story is based. If we take premise to more closely resemble theme though, his thoughts give us several important points to consider.

Every game story, as every play, should begin with a theme. This theme gives you your ending, and all the steps leading up to it.

Egri: "And it must be a premise worded so that anyone can understand it as the author intended it to be understood. An unclear premise is as bad as no premise at all."

The theme of Gary Ross's film version of *Seabiscuit* is there is worth to be found in every person. It is personified in this story of the little horse who could, and a generation of human beings squashed by the Great Depression, yet still managing to survive and to find hope in the future. Almost every scene is infused with this theme. It is the reason the film was made. It is easily understood, and adds incredible depth to what could have been just another movie about a come-from-behind team winning the big game.

Egri again: "You... should not write anything you do not believe. The premise should be a conviction of your own, so that you may prove it wholeheartedly."

If Gary Ross didn't believe that there is worth to be found in even apparently broken human beings, he could not have made his film with the passion he did. It's that simple. Your theme does not have to be unique, but you must believe in it. That belief will not only convince your audience, but will give you better insight into the theme, suggest more ways to present it that rise naturally from your characters and story, and make it all the more powerful.

Egri even gives us hope when during the writing it seems we are losing touch with the theme that ignited us to begin with. He says, "If in the process you find your premise untenable *because you have changed your mind as to what you wished to say*, formulate a new premise and discard the old."

Everybody makes mistakes. The story you are telling may take a new direction away from the theme you started with. If it does, you have two choices: rein it back in until it is again on theme, or search it for the theme you are illuminating at the expense of the original. Don't be afraid to throw anything away! As hard as it might feel at the time, you cannot fit square plot moves in round stories. It will be an exercise in frustration that, carried to its logical conclusion, will result in a bad story. And you can take heart in the fact that all that work is there waiting to be used again in support of another story or theme.

Egri: "You can arrive at your premise in any one of a great many ways. You may start with an idea which you at once convert to a premise, or you may develop a situation first and see that it has potentialities which need only the right premise to give them meaning and suggest an end."

You can start with politics or war or jealousy, and build many different themes from each depending upon how you want to treat them. In 1964 two films with remarkably similar situations were released. One was *Fail Safe*. The second was *Dr. Strangelove, or How I*

Learned to Stop Worrying and Love the Bomb. Both carried themes about the horrors of nuclear war. Both followed similar scenarios. Both are entirely different in treatment and how they chose to explicate their common theme. Take a look at *Platoon* and *The Green Berets*, two films about the Vietnam War that couldn't be farther apart in theme.

One last point from Egri: "No one premise is necessarily a universal truth. Poverty doesn't always lead to crime, but if you've chosen this premise, it does in your case. The same principle governs all premises."

This can save us a lot of grief. Writers who try to search for truths that are too universal often end up with the clichés I mentioned in the opening paragraph of this topic. Themes like "Doing bad stuff is bad" and "Evil must be fought" are obviously pretty universal, but instead of inspiring us to new interesting characters, settings, and stories, they often lock us into the same old themes of every other game out there. Want to make your game stand out from the crowd? Find a theme that is less lofty, but more personal. It will focus your writing and your game.

Drama

As we discussed before, life is not drama. A senseless death in real life is not drama until we human beings react to it, place it in a context that touches us and others. What then is drama? William Archer in *Playmaking* says "the essence of drama" is crisis. He quotes another writer, "No obstacle, no drama." Obstacles exist to be overcome by strength, intelligence, force of will. How do we apply this to the creation of games? We create a game structure that is built on conflict, that provides obstacles (including traditional puzzles, but not limited to them) to the player.

Obstacles can arise during action, conversation with other characters, and are present everywhere in gameplay. Traps, bosses, locked doors, all are obstacles. But think of them as obstacles, not just puzzles or targets. These obstacles can be the natural next step beyond those that have dominated games up until now, replacing them with dramatic confrontations and suspense-filled predicaments that are the meat and potatoes of drama.

Conflict

Drama is not simply about conflict, but conflict certainly gives it momentum. Conflict gives the player a need to continue. Too often, games fall into the trap of emulating Golden Age mysteries from the 1920s and 30s. Too many detective stories of that era confined all the action to the unraveling of the crime instead of a mystery that unfolds and deepens as we read.

In *Myst*, the story is static, set in the past, and simply revealed bit by bit. In *Jak & Daxter*, on the other hand, we have the ongoing attempt by the Lurkers to release dark eco into the world, and the ongoing quest to help Daxter revert back to his more natural form.

The conflict, of course, doesn't have to include danger except in the broadest sense: the danger of the breakup of a relationship can be just as compelling as the breakup of an alliance between two planets.

Egri has some things to say about conflict, too: "Conflict is the heartbeat of all writing. No conflict ever existed without first foreshadowing itself. Conflict is that titanic atomic energy whereby one explosion creates a chain of explosions."

Figure 2.11 *Myst:* a story as static as its beautiful images.

His thesis is that drama is built in a series of ever-rising conflicts leading directly to the climax pre-ordained by the theme. Why are we so drawn to conflict in entertainment, even as we may try to avoid it in our own lives?

Egri: "Since most of us . . . hide our true selves from the world, we are interested in witnessing the things happening to those who are forced to reveal their true characters under the stress of conflict. . . . In conflict we are *forced* to reveal ourselves. It seems that self-revelation of others or ourselves holds a fatal fascination for everyone."

Character

We'll have a lot to say about character in the following chapters. The important point here is that theme alone is not enough to get your story rolling; neither is conflict. It is characters who will drive the story, whether they are the player-character (solo games), many player-characters at once (multiplayer), or non-player characters. All are important, and each presents its own special challenges as we shall see.

Cut Scenes

For years, cut scenes have been the standard means to tell story in all sorts of computer games. Real-time strategy games put the next campaign or level in context with a cut scene, as do squad-level games and single-character action games. Even in *Final Fantasy*

XI and *Asheron's Call 2*, two massively multiplayer games, cut scenes are used to further the story, provide eye candy rewards at the end of quests, or illuminate back story. This is understandable. It's very simple to segregate gameplay from story. It means that all the tricks of film are available to you the writer. The player realizes that we're in story mode, and takes her hand off the mouse or game pad to passively watch.

However there are several problems inherent in stopping gameplay dead in its tracks to run a passive cut scene.

- You destroy any momentum built up in the previous gameplay section. The cut scene must re-establish momentum on its own.

- The shift in method of delivering the entertainment is jarring and serves to accentuate the differences between gameplay and storytelling, harming immersion in the entire experience.

- Players play games to . . . well play! They don't *want* to take their fingers off the buttons. They will impatiently stab at those buttons until the cut scene is done. It's become habit with many players. What is the normal solution to this? Allow players to escape out of the cut scene and advance directly to the next level of gameplay. This may not be much loss in a game that has given only perfunctory attention to the storytelling, but it enforces the habit, and makes it harder to use the cut scene effectively. And we should be trying to create story that is as entertaining as the game. We don't *want* players to click out of it.

We'll return to cut scenes in the chapters on storytelling that follow. They will always have a place in games. But used exclusively and indiscriminately they are the lazy writer's shot at shoehorning story into games. We will attempt to find better, less obtrusive, more organic ways of accomplishing the same thing.

PART II

CREATING CHARACTERS

Interlude with a Man on a Stair

As I was going up the stair
I met a man who wasn't there
He wasn't there again today
I wish, I wish he'd stay away.

—William Hughes Mearns, *The Psycho-ed*

The light on the landing above me was out and the stairs climbed into deep shadow. It occurred to me, as it does to many people, I think, that the light bulb might have been shattered or removed; that someone might wait for me there under cover of darkness with harm in mind. But I continued up the stairs thinking, as many do, that my imagination was playing tricks on me, and I was being silly or, worse, paranoid.

He was standing there on the next flight of steps, silhouetted against the light from the top landing: a tall athletic-looking man, features indistinct. My eyes grew more accustomed to the dim light, and I saw the automatic clutched in his hand. I stopped in mid-stride, glancing back over my shoulder down the stairs.

"Don't run," he said. His voice was low and very calm, almost a monotone. "Bullets travel faster than anyone can run."

"If this is robbery," I replied, trying to keep my voice from shaking, "I don't have much money. I'm a writer."

"I know what you are," he said. "Better than you know me." He must have seen something in my eyes, because he went on. "You think I'm crazy, don't you? If it isn't robbery, and you don't recognize me, then I must be a stray loose cannon rolled to a stop in your path."

"I wasn't thinking that. What do you want?"

"I want to kill you. Not because I'm crazy, but because I should be."

I shook my head. "I don't understand."

"Then let me explain. I know nothing about myself. Nothing up until the moment I woke up a fully grown man with a gun in my hand. My family was dead at my feet, and even though I never knew them, I was filled with the lust for revenge! Every moment now I must protect myself from madmen determined to kill me. So I kill. Over and over again!"

"I'm not one of those madmen!" I protested.

"No, you're not. But let me go on. I have no family now. I never had any friends. I'm never hungry. I never sleep. I pop pills to keep myself going, different pills that I have to scrounge for in dirty corners and in garbage cans. I kill those hunting me in order not to be killed myself. That is my life. My *entire* life. Who would wish a never-ending nightmare like that on anyone?"

"I wouldn't."

His hand tightened on the automatic. "But you did!" he screamed. "You don't recognize my face, because you didn't give me one! I don't know my enemies any more than I knew my family! You think I must be crazy because I fight without real purpose, but you gave me none! What little reason I have to go on is nothing more than the clichéd revenge story you trapped me in!"

I stared at him, realization dawning. "You're Brutus Forss! The hero of the shooter I'm writing!"

He slowly brought his emotions under control, and his voice returned to the flat monotone with which he'd begun. "Yes, and you didn't respect me enough to give me a life. You killed my family for no reason, saddled me with a bad pun for a name, filled my mouth with hackneyed dialogue, and forced me into a violent, purposeless existence. Staying true to the unthinking, vengeful nature of my character, I've decided to take my revenge on *you*. And if you say 'Et tu, Brute!' I'll shoot you in the kneecaps first."

His finger tightened on the trigger.

CHAPTER 3

RESPECTING CHARACTERS

There's a double meaning in the title of this chapter. The word *respecting* can mean "about." It can also mean "bestowing respect." It's not enough to populate a story with characters because you're supposed to. It's not enough to heedlessly scatter characters throughout a game like chicken feed in the barnyard mud because we need an adversary at this moment, a merchant here, or a puzzle-giver there. Characters in games must be more than clones of Vanna White, magically revealing those letters on *Wheel of Fortune*. Characters have a right to their own lives in the game. And giving them that right—granting them purpose beyond the designer's convenience—in fact makes it easier for us to tell our stories. There's no reason not to respect characters as much as we respect *collision detection*.

note

COLLISION DETECTION: algorithms monitoring the intersection of solid objects as in a computer game.

Not all characters need be well rounded because not all can be major characters. Minor characters can be brought to life with less detail, much the way an artist's sketch can still capture certain telling details, yet is not as explicit a likeness as a portrait in oil. We'll cover minor characters and even the lowly extra later in this chapter.

Three Dimensions

William Archer in *Play-Making* notes that "the power to observe, to penetrate, and to reproduce character can neither be acquired nor regulated by theoretical recommendations." And despite what the current vogue in how-to-write books might want us to believe, Archer also reminds us that ". . . specific directions for character-drawing would be like rules for becoming six-feet-high." What we can do, however, is present some ideas to consider as we bring to life the inhabitants of our games.

We call well-rounded characters *three-dimensional*. The same term is applied to the physical world around us and computer art that is represented by height, width, and depth. That description of characters is often used as is, but it actually does have a definition. The three dimensions of a character are physical, sociological, and psychological. And they apply to all major characters in a game, whether they are the player-character or significant non-player characters.

The Physical Character

The easiest dimension of character to reveal is the physical, particularly in visual media. What does Chuck Noland look like in *Castaway*? A chubby Tom Hanks. What does Carl Hanratty look like in *Catch Me if You Can*? Tom Hanks in glasses and a bad suit. In games, we draw our heroes to fit their parts the same way Mr. Hanks binges to fit his. Do we run the risk of stereotyping our characters? Unfortunately, yes. A stereotyped character is not a respected character. It is a tool of the author, the artist, the marketing department, or all three. We'll return to stereotypes later in this chapter.

So we draw (both in word and picture) our characters to fit their roles in our games. And most often, they're drawn to reflect the character's personality or function in the game. But often we stop there, simply layering on a toolbox of skills, mannerisms, and catch phrases as we need them in the game. To create the well-rounded character, we need a bit more.

In the game *Ico*, a boy is born with horns, a physical deformity that recurs in his small village and is viewed by the villagers as a bad omen. Their attempt to kill him leads directly to the adventures that make up the story. Here, the physical character is notable both for the unique entry point it provides into the story, and the fact that at the beginning of the game it is more important than either of the boy's other two dimensions.

Figure 3.1 That's not a Viking hat. Ico's horns are real.

The Sociological Character

This includes the character's past, her upbringing and her environment, both local and cultural. By giving a character a past, we put her actions in perspective. They are no longer simply authorial conveniences, but they add weight and interest to the character. Sly Cooper's character is drawn and animated as a wily raccoon. But add family tradition, and the recovery of the Thievius Raccoonus becomes more than just the final goal of the game. It becomes an essential character-driven goal, and underlines the game's theme.

Environment in this context is not only where the character grew up, but where the character is *now*. This can be by choice as in a treasure hunt game like *Jak & Daxter* where there are many environments, and the player doesn't necessarily have to finish one before exploring another. Or it can be by circumstance in the more structured levels of an action game like *James Bond 007: Everything or Nothing*. The characters may need to draw on different skills or knowledge dependent on this environment, but they cannot be dragged out the first time they are needed. Even the James Bond franchise (not heavily into three-dimensional character) attempts to set up Bond's later actions as early as possible, if only to get him out of a new jam with a new gadget.

A word of caution: it is far too easy to go overboard on a character's background. It is easy to confuse lists of details of a character's past with pertinent information that helps mold the character. Just as drama is selective of incident where life gives us every moment, so too a character's past should be filtered by necessity. If you know where you want your character to go, it is only necessary to provide a route, not a map of the world.

The Psychological Character

We build a relationship with the characters we write—just as we do with people we meet in our lives. If we want that relationship to grow stronger, we need to know the person as well as we can. The difference is that we theoretically know *everything* about a character we write, every treasure buried on the lost islands of their minds. But as we can spend too much time on their past, we can also spend too much time on what that past has made them, if we're not careful.

Instead, we take a look at the actions of the character, his attitudes, his opinions, his view of the world. And we do it without letting the character in on the fact that we know as much as we do. Characters who explain themselves are not only boring, they are not true-to-life. We writers know a secret. Even the most self-centered of human beings knows less about himself than he may think. If the characters are too self-aware— "I know I'm a self-made man, Pamela, and am rough around the edges. But gosh darn it, honey, underneath it all I have a warm heart and a pretty decent brain to boot."—it's a sure way to spot a hack writer.

Sometimes the most unaware of characters can be the most interesting. There is a sweet delight in the audience that is ahead of a character whose own actions or words condemn her. "But how did you know the killer had carved a star into the lieutenant's left palm?" "Well, I read about it in the newspaper account of his death." "That fact was never published! Take him away!"

Figure 3.2 *Blood Simple*: Only the audience knows what's going on.

The Coen brother's first film, *Blood Simple*, takes this delicious moment of the audience knowing more than the character to a relentless, hilarious, and ghastly extreme: none of the characters knows who is doing what to whom. They all think they have a grasp on the situation, but they're all totally wrong.

We reveal the character, particularly the psychological dimension, through action. We don't stop the story dead to do it, anymore than we should stop the action for exposition, a topic we'll get to in Chapter 9, "Bringing the Story to Life." "By His works ye shall know Him." A well-written character doesn't have to explain himself. He may not even know how. He is revealed by what he chooses to do.

When is the best time to reveal the psychological dimension of character? In a moment of crisis. It's easy to wear a mask when everything is going smoothly in drama as well as in life. But watch the mask get stripped away when the character is faced with a crisis.

Character Progression

As Lajos Egri reminds us, "There is only one realm in which characters defy natural laws and remain the same—the realm of bad writing. And it is the fixed nature of the characters which makes the writing bad. If a character in a short story, novel, or play [or game!—ed.] occupies the same position at the end as the one he did at the beginning, that story, novel, or play is bad."

Minor characters may not need to change. They may only be present for a single moment of time, and not every one of the moments can or should be a satori for every single character. But major characters, whether PC or NPC, must, like sharks, keep swimming or they will die. This change takes two forms: growth and development. They are often thought to mean the same thing. They don't.

Growth

Character growth describes the changes that occur to the character as she progresses through the story.

In *Dark Side of the Moon*, written by Mark Barrett and me, the player-character Jake Wright moves from a shy, lackadaisical young man to a relentless seeker of the truth, then on to the determined protector of an entire alien race. The growth would have been artificial and unbelievable if we had not planted the seeds for this transition early in the story. The first clue that there is more to Jake than meets the eye is the fact that he has embarked on this trip to a distant moon in the first place, instead of shrugging it off, as he has most other things in his life. It is the love of his uncle that gives him the initial impetus that simple curiosity alone could not have. And in his search he finds the strength to stand up against corporate slavers and the soulless creature who murdered his uncle. Jake is the player-character, and as such, his growth brings us other issues to deal with that we will explore later in this chapter.

Beyond helping to portray a fully developed character, growth assists us in our storytelling. Growth implies forward momentum. Character growth helps to propel us through the story of the game. Matching moments of character growth to moments of conflict in the story is surprisingly easy once you know the character and have mapped out the conflicts she must face.

We need character growth. For that reason, we must know where, psychologically, the character is when the story begins. If the character begins triumphant we'll have to tear him down. If he starts in the gutter, it will be a lot easier to enjoy the road he takes to the throne.

Development

Character development is, as William Archer says, "... not change, but rather unveiling, disclosure." He compares it to the developing of film. A drama ought to bring out character as the "photographer's chemicals 'bring out' the forms latent in the negative." He uses Ibsen's Nora in *A Doll's House* as a prime example: "... we cannot but feel that the poet has compressed into a week an evolution which, in fact, would have demanded many months." At the end of a play Archer insists, "We should ... know more of the protagonist's character than he himself, or his most intimate friend, could know at the beginning ..."

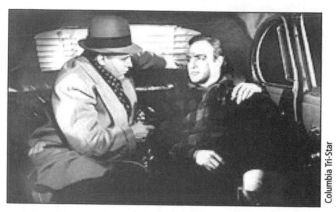

Columbia Tri-Star

Figure 3.3 Marlon Brando and Rod Steiger in the famous cab scene from *On the Waterfront.*

Terry Mallory, Marlon Brando's character in *On the Waterfront* both grows and develops. As he moves through the film toward his ultimate bloody confrontation and triumph on the docks, his character grows from a man who has always played by the rules of the corrupt union to a man driven by the developing realization of where his life has brought him. "I coulda been a contenda, Charlie!" he cries in the famous taxi cab scene.

So if Jake Wright grows, how does he develop in the game? He learns along with the player a truth about his past, and the player at last sees what Jake himself may never know: the source of his strength and courage. It was in the genes all along.

The Pivotal Character

The pivotal character is the character who sets the story in motion. It can be the protagonist Hamlet who sets out on his course of revenge after the visitation by his father's ghost, or "honest, honest" Iago, apparently dedicated to the interests of his lord, Othello, until his promotion is turned down.

Egri tells us, "Without a pivotal character, there is no play. The pivotal character is the one who creates conflict and makes the play move forward. The pivotal character knows what he wants. Without him the story flounders . . . in fact there is no story."

The protagonist can be the pivotal character. Sly Cooper is an example of a player-character protagonist who is also a pivotal character. In many games, the pivotal character is the antagonist, who, with *Pinky and the Brain* determination, is bent on world domination in one form or another. Most RPGs begin with an evil force already at work. The player-character reacts to the resulting crisis.

If neither the hero nor the villain is the pivotal character you still need one. In *Jak & Daxter: The Precursor Legacy*, it is the sidekick character, Daxter, who sets the story in motion.

His transformation into a rodent by falling in a vat of dark eco sends Jak, the player-character, on the search that is the spine of the game's action to help him regain his original physical form. We'll have more to say about sidekicks in the next chapter.

"A good pivotal character *must have something very vital at stake.*" Egri emphasizes. He "is necessarily aggressive, uncompromising, even ruthless." Here we can see why both villains and anti-heroes make particularly strong pivotal characters.

Sony Computer Entertainment

Figure 3.4 Daxter is the pivotal character in *Jak & Daxter*, not Jak.

Is it necessary to have a pivotal character in every game that tells a story? It's hard to avoid it. And why should we? It works as well in games as it does in other storytelling media. It personalizes what's at stake, by giving it a recognizable face. It creates the initial crisis that drives the action. And it's a good reason why at least one of our characters is in the game to begin with beyond a simple gameplay function.

The Player-Character

First, a moment of silence for heroes everywhere. Villains are fun to write. Sidekicks can be wild and crazy. Even mentors with their air of mystery can seem deep and interesting. But what have heroes got going for them? Writers (and audiences) are forever complaining how hard it is to keep them as entertaining as all of the other characters in a story, yet they are arguably the most important character in a game story.

Take heart, heroes. You are only bland and uninteresting if you're written that way. You are actually the most complex character in the story. The player will learn more about you than any other character, and through you may even learn something about herself. It's a heavy responsibility. Don't get pompous or bombastic. Keep your goals simple, and your dreams infinite. The player must embrace you, and want to share your life in a bond that may seem like marriage however fleeting. And remember this: the game can't exist without you.

Identified by several names such as Player-Character, Player-Controlled Character, PC, or Avatar, this is the most important character in the game. Except in the example in the above paragraph, which as noted we'll cover separately, the PC is the direct link between player and game. How he interacts with the game world reveals much about his nature and the nature of the game. These are design choices as much as writing choices, but the two must go hand-in-hand. For just as the player-character has a function in the game, he is also the *protagonist* in the game's story.

note

PROTAGONIST: the principal character in a work of fiction.

Whether human being, furry animal, alien creature, faceless general, or smiley yellow bag that eats dots and has reason to fear ghosts, the character controlled by the player is the most complicated and challenging character there is to write.

And we must answer several questions writers of other media don't face before the PC can be written.

Is the PC meant only to be controlled by the player, or is it meant to *be* the player?

In most games, no matter of what type, the PC is distinct from the player, a puppet to be manipulated to carry out actions in the game world that the player desires. This is true whether the PC is original or borrowed from another medium. However, you will occasionally see one where the player becomes the lead character in the game. Most often the *point of view* (POV) for these games is first person, where you do not see your character, but are looking through your character's eyes. In a First-Person Shooter as we'll see later on, the POV may be first person, but you are still playing a character, however sketchy, in the game fiction.

One good example where the player-character and you are one and the same is the original adventure game, *Colossal Cave*. This tradition continued with text adventures from Infocom, such as *Zork*, and more recently *Myst* and its sequels. Further, the cancelled multiplayer version of the game *URU: Ages of Myst* allowed players to play themselves, or create distinct characters. It is the player's choice.

The theory behind allowing players to play themselves in a game is said to be a greater level of immersion. Certainly in the earlier text adventures, it helped the reality of the worlds to preface player actions with "you" as in "You find yourself in a maze of twisty passages, all alike." This is actually second-person, a POV rarely found outside of computer games. And it continues in use in many games today, even when, in the bulk of these, you control a player-character with its own personality. We'll go into POV in greater detail later on. Despite the use of second-person text, most games today feature player-characters distinct from players. There are three reasons for this:

1. Computer games are happiest as a visual medium, and text is usually suffered only as a necessity.

2. We have a tradition of *empathizing* with characters in other visual media such as film, television, and live drama.

note

EMPATHY: the ability of human beings to understand the feelings of others, even fictional characters, to such a degree that they enter into those feelings, and experience them almost as if they were their own.

3. Games today are attempting more sophisticated storytelling. We see this even in the development of the *Myst* games where the first is nothing more than the unraveling of a backstory, and the later sequels feature ongoing story in which the player-character becomes actively involved.

Because we are able to empathize with well-drawn fictional characters; because players recognize, if only unconsciously, the significance these made-up protagonists play in a story; and because with them it is far easier to involve a player in the fictional narrative, it is now accepted that a greater immersion is actually possible if the player-character is *not* a representation of the player. All of the rest of the questions here assume the player-character is only controlled by the player, and is not meant to actually be the player.

Is the PC original, or based on a character from another medium?

On the face of it when we are adapting a character from another medium (See Chapter 7, "Once Upon a Time," for related differences between original material and adaptations.) it would appear that a lot of our work has already been done for us. And while it's true some of it has been, new work is created.

Obviously, we don't have to create the character from scratch, either in its behavior or its physical appearance. In fact, to vary from these is to court disaster by ignoring audience expectations. But we must translate actions in response to game challenges that are true to the adapted characters in terms of both personality and abilities. If the player is faced with a challenge that requires the player-character to act in a way inconsistent with the way he was portrayed in a film or book, or to possess a skill the character didn't have, it immediately feels false to the player.

So the gameplay must be constructed with that character in mind. This may seem obvious, but consider this conundrum: many designers want as open-ended a world as possible. Games like *Duke Nukem* and *Grand Theft Auto* allow players to shoot or run over just about anything that moves. Imagine though Neo or James Bond wantonly gunning down innocent citizens.

Another challenge is imitating how the adapted character expressed herself in the original material. Being able to emulate the style of another author is an essential skill for writers adapting that author's work. We'll explore this ability in Appendix B.

Good screenplays are written lean and mean without a lot of extraneous detail. That's fine for a medium that can fill in additional detail thanks to directors, costumers, set designers, and so forth. It's not so good for adapters. Not only must you stay true to what you know from the previous work, you must often provide additional detail to flesh out the game.

For example if you want to provide an exciting action-sequence on motorcycles, but there is no moment in the original material showing the PC riding a motorcycle, include a single line of dialogue or a shot of the motorcycle in the PC's garage sometime *before* the sequence (and not right before!) to add that skill to those previously known. If you reveal that the PC can pilot a helicopter *right before* he is forced to escape from a high rise rooftop by piloting a helicopter, it looks like the *deus ex machina* it is. It will annoy the player. Whereas, if you plant your mention of the skill a few levels before, the player will accept it. This brings up another general point about skills and immersion that we'll take a look at in a moment.

Is there one solution? No. In *The Riddle of Master Lu*, I was faced with writing, not a known fictional character from another medium, but a character based on a real person, Robert Ripley of Ripley's Believe It or Not! fame. My choice was not to exactly recreate the man. This could have proved difficult. His unconventional private life, particularly his relationships with numerous women, was some cause for scandal, and not something the grantors of the license to his character would have appreciated in a family video game. I concentrated instead on his spirit, his boyish enthusiasm, his fascination for the bizarre, and his real-life love for adventure that reportedly made him one of the models for Indiana Jones. All qualities that served the character well in the game.

Figure 3.5 Robert Ripley, man of the world.

www.conceptattractions.com

Once the decision has been made to make the PC a character distinct from the player, the writer must next decide:

How much does the player know about the character?

Early on, the writer/designer must make choices about what we call the player-character's ego. This refers to the PC's innermost thoughts. Does the character share them with the player? This question and the next cover this two-way street.

Even after deciding the player-character is not the player, the writer/designer must decide how fleshed out the character should be. As I said, protagonists are usually not nearly as much fun to write as villains. Compare Leonardo di Caprio's character Amsterdam Vallon to Daniel Day Lewis's character Bill "Butcher" Cutting in *Gangs of New York*. Putting aside for the moment any opinion you might have of the actors' relative talents, the characters have many similarities: colorful names, distinct wardrobes, important missions, and more. Yet Cutting is written with such an obvious joy in his horrendous villainy, and Amsterdam, even with a revenge plot of Shakespearean dimensions, is written as more wishy-washy (at least in the central part of the film) than Hamlet.

Why? Because the filmmakers want us to identify with Amsterdam, not with Bill. And just like them, the game writer is faced with the possibility that providing a player-character who is too fully drawn, and who may have so many differences in speech, attitude, ethics, favorite sports, whatever, from players, they may have difficulty seeing themselves as the character.

Next the writer/designer must grapple with keeping knowledge between player and player-character balanced. The audience knowing more about what is really happening than the protagonists in the film *Blood Simple* may be wildly entertaining. But a player knowing more that the character she controls can harm the illusion of the player-character's life within the fiction of the world, just as the PC knowing more than the player can cause problems as well. This dilemma would seem to be unique to games, but luckily there are parallels in other media to help guide us.

First, here's a plea from the heart: never, ever, ever consider amnesia as a means to keep the knowledge shared by the player-character and the player consistent. It's such a cliché that to call it a cliché is a cliché. You may quote me. There are plenty of other ways to tackle the sharing of knowledge between player and PC.

One way to keep player and player-character knowledge balanced is to make sure the surprises in the story you share are surprises to both of you. This is the technique of first-person mystery novels and the films that mimic them with voice-over narration, detective in every scene, and so on. These rely heavily on Aristotle's unity of action. If you *must* cut away to a scene the PC is not observing, don't reveal a slew of information that puts the player ahead of the PC in the knowledge race. The only reason for doing this is if you are creating suspense, as we discussed in Chapter 2, "The Story Remains the Same."

Better still, avoid it even in that case. Instead of seeing mysterious hands wiring a door with explosives, force a zoom in when the PC approaches the door to focus on the tripwire barely seen through the crack between door and jamb. Yes, you've taken control (very briefly) from the player, but it is a technique we are all familiar with from TV and film. If you intend to use this device, just set it up early on, maybe a couple of times, in situations where it isn't so critical, to prepare the player for its use later on.

In *Dark Side of the Moon*, there is a secret about the player-character Jake's parentage that we needed to withhold from the player until late in the game, even though we learn quite a bit about his past through flashbacks and other clues. To preserve the surprise, we made sure Jake himself did not know the secret by establishing his bickering relationship with the woman he thought was his sister. It's psychologically valid. Players take it to be sibling rivalry, or even just two people who don't get along. Yet not only does it set up the surprise, it prepares the player for the revelation that they aren't so closely related after all.

Another approach is to put the PC in locations with which the character would be unfamiliar. If the player-character is assigned to investigate the disappearance of all the inhabitants of a space station, create a character who may be the 23rd century's equivalent of Sherlock Holmes, but confine his actual experience to earthbound mysteries. Now you can simultaneously reveal new information to both player and PC in the mission briefings. Puzzles can be concocted from simple operations. Give the player the challenge of adapting the PC's earthly skills to the new environment.

If you want to maintain the fictional reality of the character, try to avoid the mistake of setting up a PC who by his knowledge and training *should* know how to do something, then try to make it a puzzle how to do it. I'm reminded of the LucasArts game *The Dig*, with Steven Spielberg's name on the box, and written by Orson Scott Card, author of the wonderful science-fiction novel *Ender's Game*.

Here is the opening situation in *The Dig*: you are part of a crack team of experts headed for an asteroid on a collision course with earth. Your mission is to plant charges beneath the surface, and knock it off its course. Upon arriving near the asteroid the player discovers that he must learn how to guide the explosives to the asteroid's surface in an abbreviated version of the earlier game *Lunar Lander*. This crack expert, meticulously trained, has no idea how his controls work.

This first challenge completely trashes the fiction of the game world because you, the well briefed, thoroughly prepped, expert, must learn by trial and error how to place the charges just so the game can have a puzzle at that point. We'll revisit this when we take a look at simulations that feature story in Chapter 15, "Game Types."

How much does the character know about the player?

This is not as odd a question as it might first sound. Basically it is a reference to the fourth wall, defined in Chapter 8, "Respecting Story." The PC can be written with various stages of awareness of the player.

Click once on one of your player-controlled minions in the real-time strategy game *Warcraft* and you'll get an attentive response. Do it too many times in a row without issuing a command, and the character will complain, "Quit poking me!" Here the fourth wall is only broken if the player repeatedly tries an essentially useless action. Its function, in addition to eliciting a smile, is to help the player get back on track.

Save your game and Floyd, the irrepressible sidekick in *Planetfall*, will respond, "Oh boy! Are we gonna try something dangerous now?" Here we have a more overt wink at the player. Floyd is not only aware he's being manipulated by the player, he is even aware of the player's actions outside of the game world.

Breaking the fourth wall is nothing new. Even before there were actual characters in Greek drama, the chorus would address the audience directly. Shakespeare and his own interactive audience standing in the pit both loved the soliloquy. Actors were lucky if all the pit population did was yell back at them and not lob the dregs of their dinners as well. Characters in Eugene O'Neill's *Strange Interlude* voiced their inner thoughts to the audience. The play was hilariously parodied by Groucho Marx's Captain Spaulding in *Animal Crackers*:

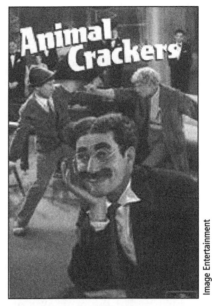

Figure 3.6 Groucho Marx takes on Eugene O'Neil in *Animal Crackers*.

"Pardon me while I have a strange interlude. . . . Here I am talking of parties. I came down here for a party. What happens? Nothing. Not even ice cream. The gods looked down and laughed. This would be a better world for children if the parents had to eat the spinach."

It's no accident the richest cracks in the fourth wall are usually found in comic games, often in response to a player attempting to do something the game engine can't handle such as in *Full Throttle*: "I ain't puttin' my lips on that!" It's far easier in comedy games to accept these asides aimed at the player than in more serious games where they can undermine immersion. Yet it was often a staple form of humor in early computer games, and still crops up today.

Our struggle creating immersion in a game and empathy in its characters is already difficult enough without additional pitfalls. Outside of a humorous world fiction it is unnecessarily jarring. It's a gamer's choice, not a storyteller's choice, to remind the player she is playing a game and not inhabiting a realistic world, in a world where the willing suspension of disbelief is crucial to believing in it. If a writer feels the need to do it in a normally inappropriate setting, he should have damn good reason to break the rules, and enough skill as a writer to pull it off. Otherwise, it can come across as sophomoric and amateurish.

If the player-character needs certain skills, must the player have them too?

Many types of gameplay can coexist inside a single game. Shooters feature adventure-game–like puzzles. Role-playing games can require the hand-eye coordination of an FPS. Yet one type doesn't travel so well: simulations. Much of the fun and challenge of a simulation is in learning to operate the intricate controls of a jet plane, a tank, a train, a spaceship, any number of exotic vehicles we may never get our hands on in real life. Simulations pride themselves on getting the controls, physics, and feel as accurate as possible. Nothing breaks a player's willing suspension of disbelief more than when she is required to be a master marksman, but must work like crazy to hit the broad side of a barn.

A similar dilemma occurs when an RPG aimed at a large audience requires a certain level of FPS skill to be successful in combat. Lots of people who love RPGs don't have the reflexes to be skilled swordsmen, or to "chain" a number of keystrokes triggering special combat moves.

If the player can control more than one character, how does this affect the NPCs and storytelling?

Non-Player Characters

Non-player characters, or as they are commonly known, NPCs, populate the world of a game. They shoulder a large portion of the burden of moving the story of the game forward, and come in many shapes and sizes. They also provide a focus for the player's emotion. The only emotion a player may feel on the death of a player-character who can be resurrected at the beginning of a level or back at a bind point might be frustration. The deaths of thousands of soldiers in a strategy game might mean defeat, but the player will not be attending their funerals as Commander-in-Chief. However, the death of a companion the player-character has adventured with, come to know, even rely upon, can be a potent source for much deeper emotion. We'll explore this next as we look at major non-player characters.

Major Characters

Presenting and developing the story of your game through static game-world elements like books, journals, scrolls, historic markers, or any other kind of voluminous text is all very well and good, but there are a number of drawbacks. For one, no matter what E-Book publishers want you to believe nobody, *NOBODY* wants to read text on screen, or chapters of books, or even long paragraphs. The resolution of a computer's screen, or even worse, the resolution of the TV screen a console game is played on, is nowhere near as easy to read as the words on this page.

For another, the more a player is reading, the more he isn't playing, and players don't like this. Forcing players to wade through great swatches of text only makes them impatient and irritable. So designers are forced to allow them to skip through the text by continually pressing the ESC key or spacebar or a mouse button. Now the players with the itchiest trigger fingers miss essential exposition that might have drawn them into the story; brought them greater insight into characters; or given them clues to help them in the game. When that happens, designers have to find other ways to supplement the information.

If designers try to counter this by demanding that every text passage be as short as possible, we are stuck with ingame "books" that consist of a few lines, breaking the fiction of the game.

Recorded video (whether live or animated) and sound bites can remove the need for reading, but of course, they only work in certain settings. A video in a medieval world would look wildly out of place unless its form was stylized into a vision, say, which fit the fiction of the world. Recorded sound bites, even professionally voiced, can get tedious after a short while. And both of these methods of delivering story- or character-related material suffer from the same problem as text if they run on too long. Players want to play!

We'll explore some other solutions to this problem in Chapters 15, "Game Types," and 16, "Game Genres," when we look at techniques specific to different types and genres of games. But one solution common to all is providing NPC characters. I only played *Asheron's Call 2* for a couple of months early in its development cycle. It may have changed, but the world of Dereth was a cold land of empty cities and vast landscapes populated only by creatures to be slaughtered. It made me think of a brightly-colored amusement park where there were no barkers or ticket-takers or ride operators and all the attractions were closed.

Contrast this with *Star Wars Galaxies* and its bustling cities. The more NPCs you have, the more digestible pieces you can break your story into. We'll be talking a lot about all the ways in which NPCs populate game worlds and facilitate storytelling in the chapters that follow.

Finally, as stated above, not only can major non-player characters help move the plot along, they also help us to generate emotion. Floyd, the robot in *Planetfall*, who I mentioned in the opening paragraph of this chapter, is a prime example. Steve Meretzky, one of the original Infocom text adventure writer/designers is Floyd's proud papa, and tells us in our first sidebar how his baby was born.

Steve Meretzky, Writer/Designer

My first design decision when I started working on *Planetfall* was to have a strong main character (or, a strong secondary character, if you consider the player to be the main character). In games up to that point, there had been lots of very minor characters (the thief/troll/cyclops in *Zork I*, the wizard/demon/dragon/princess in *Zork II*, various suspects in *Deadline*), but because there were so many, none of them was very fleshed out. I wanted to "put all my eggs in one basket" and have one really good character instead of many half-baked ones. After that, deciding that Floyd would die was just about my second major decision. Certainly well before I decided to give the game a humorous streak, perhaps even before I decided on the game's setting. I just thought that if I put all that effort into creating a character

Figure 3.7 Steve Meretzky.

the player would care about, that character's death would be the best possible payoff; the most bang for the buck. Only much later did the death scene get integrated into a puzzle/solution.

While I assumed it would be an impactful scene, I certainly never imagined it would have the reception that it did, either right away, or two decades later! I was most moved while writing Floyd's death scene by writing the lyrics for "The Ballad of the Starcross'd Miner" that your character sings to Floyd as he dies. You'd be told now and then over the course of the game that Floyd was singing his favorite song, "The Ballad of the Starcross'd Miner," but you were never told the words; this was the first time you saw the lyrics. That, for me, personalized the death, and made the writing of the scene much more emotionally potent than it would have been without it. But it was merely a "lump in the throat" experience, not tears. And I cry fairly easily. I always weep like a baby at the end of *It's a Wonderful Life* or *Field of Dreams*.

The only time I've tried to go for the same effect since has been in the sequel, *Stationfall*, and in the never-produced *Planetfall 3*, which I scripted for Activision circa 1993 but which died in bureaucracy. I don't think *Stationfall* was as effective, because Floyd gets progressively more evil as the game progresses (as he gets "taken over" by an evil alien machine), and you actually have to kill him to save humanity . . . but he does get released from the power of the alien machine long enough before he dies to become unevil again, and tell you that he doesn't blame you for what you did, before he dies. *P3*, I guess we'll never know how effective it would have been there.

The Space Bar, in which you play a cop, did have a best-friend/partner character, who gets kidnapped and progressively more threatened by the bad guy. But he gets kidnapped so early on, you don't have much time to form a Floyd-like bond with him (although with every threat, we throw in another flashback in which he takes a bullet for you, donates a kidney to save your mother's life and so forth.) Also, we played the situation much more for laughs than for pathos.

Minor Characters and Extras

Populating the game world with only major characters essential to story and/or gameplay works fine if the scene is the commercial towing vehicle Nostromo in the film *Alien* or the islands of the best-selling adventure game *Myst*. And game designs cognizant of budget restraints often keep character animation to a minimum. Even major characters are often modeled upon identical skeletons. However, these days, no matter what the type of game, genre, or platform, if the setting is the city streets of *Grand Theft Auto* or the towns of *Neverwinter Nights*, minor characters and extras add to the verisimilitude of the setting.

We don't have to paint minor characters with the detail we lavish on major characters—we rarely have the time—but they often have crucial, if brief, roles to play in the game, if not in the story, such as merchants or quest givers. Here we can shorthand the character creation process. Charles Dickens was a master at capturing his characters great or small in a single paragraph. Here is his description of that old reprobate, protagonist, *and* pivotal character Ebeneezer Scrooge:

"Oh! But he was a tight-fisted hand at the grindstone, Scrooge! A squeezing, wrenching, grasping, scraping, clutching, covetous old sinner! Hard and sharp as flint, from which no steel had ever struck out generous fire; secret, and self-contained; and solitary as an oyster. The cold within him froze his old features, nipped his pointed nose, shriveled his cheek, stiffened his gait; made his eyes red, his thin lips blue; and spoke out shrewdly in his grating voice. A frosty rime was on his head, and on his eyebrows, and his wiry chin. He carried his own low temperature always about with him; he iced his office in the dog-days; and didn't thaw it one degree at Christmas."

It passes as a description of the physical dimension of Scrooge's character, but also ties the physical so tightly to the psychological we don't just see him, we *know* him, and we don't like him much either! Now meet a relatively minor character in Dickens' *Bleak House*: Inspector Bucket:

"Mr. Snagsby is dismayed to see, standing with an attentive face between himself and the lawyer at a little distance from the table, a person with a hat and a stick in his hand who was not there when he himself came in and has not since entered by the door or by either of the windows. There is a press in the room, but its hinges have not creaked, nor has a step been audible upon the floor. Yet this third person stands there with his attentive face, and his hat and his stick in his hands, and his hands behind him, a composed and quiet listener. He is a stoutly built, steady-looking, sharp-eyed man in black, of about middle-age. Except that he looks at Mr. Snagsby as if he were going to take his portrait, there is nothing remarkable about him at first sight but his ghostly manner of appearing."

Using his almost magical entrance, Dickens is able to describe his character through the eyes of another; not just his physical appearance, but his intelligence, his stealthiness, his own ability to study character, all traits that add up to a very special, and possibly dangerous man. Bucket is, by the way, the first detective in English literature.

We may not have the luxury of longish descriptive paragraphs in games where we want to move the action along, but we can certainly sketch our characters equally vividly. The tools at our disposable include:

- Recognizable character types or personalities: the garrulous salesman, the flirty serving wench, the hard-as-nails assassin, and so on. These serve as shorthand readable by the player. "Ah!" the player exclaims. "I know what's up with him!" These can easily become stereotypes if we're not careful though. The trick is to then give the character some attitude that will rescue her from the clutches of stereotype: the serving wench is actually very prim and proper. The assassin is dictating his memoirs into a cassette recorder as he focus the sights of his rifle on his next victim.

- Professions that can quickly tell our player, who has played many other games, what role to expect him to play: the librarian, the policeman, the ticket clerk.

- Physical mannerisms. Does the character twitch? Does she shy away when the PC approaches. Does he reach for a weapon?

- Turns of phrase or accents. Do you trust a character who insists you can trust him? Probably not. Is someone with a Scots accent a native of the fishing village in the Hebrides where you find yourself? Probably.

- Clothes. Will that beggar in rags be a good sort to hit up for a loan? Will you want to take the young lovely sitting at the bar in bustier and garters home to mom? Probably not.

- Distinct attitudes and opinions. A few short phrases sprinkled throughout the conversation. "Yup, the mayor has a mule for sale, but count yer change. He's a politician." "I'd like ta hep ya out stranger, but I been watchin' the sky. It just ain't a good day fer it, no sireee, not a good day at all." "Well, as my dear mother used to say . . ."

Extras don't even get to talk. But we notice them even when they're not around. The lack of extras in a haunted house at midnight is easy to justify. The lack of extras on a city street at noon is more difficult. It's one of the reasons we have so many games set in artificially closed environments or with justifications like a post-apocalyptic theme, or an alternate universe: "Where the race who had built the towering structures of steel and concrete had gone remained a mystery . . ."

Figure 3.8 Robert Culp is the "Demon with a Glass Hand."

Maybe they all ended up in Robert Culp's palm in the Outer Limits episode "Demon with a Glass Hand." (Set incidentally in one closed environment: The Bradbury Building in downtown Los Angeles.)

It is refreshing to see populations going about their business peripheral to the forward thrust of a game. It allows for *Matrix*-like irony: "Little did they know the truth about what was going on!" It also creates opportunities for suspense, as we shall see in a moment.

I confess I'm using the term "extras" a bit loosely here. In other dramatic media such as TV and film, the word refers to non-speaking parts, also known as background. If extras are given a single line of dialogue or a special bit of "business," they immediately are elevated into bit players who are paid more and might even get an onscreen credit. In computer games, extras are often given at least one line of dialogue along the lines of "I have no time to talk now," or "I'm late, I'm late! For a very important date!" to politely or impolitely brush off the player-controlled character within the fiction of the game, and to inform the player that they have nothing to offer that will further the story or enhance gameplay.

There can be exceptions. True non-speaking extras can be used to good account if they add something to a scene or level, especially in games where the player cannot talk to every NPC. For example, to their credit numerous first-person shooters, particularly those in contemporary real-world settings, now include "civilians" as well as hostile targets, and often penalize players for killing non-hostiles, much the way such targets are added to police academy firing ranges. It can instill a sense of caution in the player if it's clear that blasting everything in sight will result in losing the level, or crucial points necessary to achieving the highest score.

Another use for extras is as true background. This works in single-player games and squad-based multiplayer games where the world is explicitly narrowed to contain players and propel the action forward. It would be difficult in virtual worlds where players are supposed to be able to range anywhere. But even in these worlds, fiction enhancing choke points like locked gates or guards can prevent players from entering a certain location, at least part of the time, and at least from that entry point. Don't you love qualifications?

Here are a couple of ways non-speaking, or at least non-interactive, extras can add drama to the game. First we have a shooter level where the player is being pursued by enemies through sewers beneath the city streets. It's a nice, contained, easy-to-model setting for a level, but the designers also want to indicate the irony that just above our heads the regular world goes on oblivious to the dire happenings below, and also create some additional suspense in the bargain. So we devise a section of the sewer tunnel with rungs set in the concrete wall. The player climbs the rungs to a grate where simple passing shadows and the sound effects of shoes on pavement, car horns, and so forth tell us a city street lies just beyond. But the grate is immobile. As the shadows flick across our player-character's face or strobe the screen in first person, the player realizes that no escape lies that way. Perhaps the PC in this game has voice commands like "Yell." But the yell, when played by the game in this locale comes across as muffled. There's no way those above will hear it.

More adventurous designers with a little more time and art budget on their hands could enhance the scene by an omniscient cut of the street above. This could be a low angle, tilted down at the sewer grate. We see only passing feet: polished men's shoes, sneakers, high heels, and maybe unseen by pedestrians, the PC's fingers wiggling through the holes in the grate à la Harry Lime in *The Third Man*. This quick shot, lasting no more than two or three seconds, is the least obtrusive, and often most dramatic, use of cut scenes.

In a virtual world, players may be able to see into the courtyard of a high-level NPC's home, but are blocked from entry by the locked gate or guards mentioned above. They could then take note of another brief cut scene of security precautions; glimpse a kidnapped prince; overhear a brief exchange of NPC dialogue between nameless minions indicating a breach in trust between enemy commanders; or so much more. This same situation works equally well in single-player games. How players are allowed to react to what they see is, of course, up to the designers. Is this only information to be learned? Does it imply a possible quest? Will brute force provide entry, or is there another way into the apparently inaccessible area?

In a multiplayer game, the other consideration is how the moment is treated: it could be simply a pantomime repeated endlessly for anyone who pauses while passing by. Or with some thought, it could be constructed as a variable experience with many permutations.

Separating true extras in a game world from the NPC quest givers or merchants we will cover soon can sometimes be a chore. One design decision distinguishes the notable NPCs in some way. A very gamey solution is to float explicit markers like question marks above the heads of important NPCs. This solution certainly serves its purpose, but at the expense of immersion and the fiction of the world. Another solution is to establish that certain *types* of NPCs can be useful, such as town criers and bartenders.

Another decision is to just ignore the problem, letting players discover which NPCs may be of importance. This school of thought well maintains the fiction of the world. People in real life rarely have signboards floating above their heads. The problem is that it can become an artificial obstacle to a player's progression through the game. It is frustrating to players if they don't have any idea who they should speak to, and it's frustrating for designers if they build intricate sub-stories that players rarely stumble across. As this problem more directly relates to story delivery, we'll go into more detail in the later chapters on story.

Of course, most NPCs that are important to story or gameplay are usually easy to distinguish. They are our major characters, and as discussed earlier, we can provide players many pointers to locate them.

Avoiding Stereotypes

Square jawed heroes, hook-nosed villains, gravity-defying big-breasted women, wise-cracking cowardly sidekicks, wily thieves, scheming clerics, wise bearded magicians, old crone-like witches, stubborn dwarves, grass-chewing rustics . . . the list is a long one. Take a profession or race or physical trait and, thanks to centuries of character-creation, almost immediately a personality trait pops into your mind. These are *stereotypes*.

note

> STEREOTYPE: a generalized, non-contextual portrait of an individual that does not take into account unique qualities all individuals possess.

Relying on them in narrative fiction is not as bad as in real life where failing to see the real person behind a stereotype can harm a relationship, even with a stranger, prevent communication, or even be dangerous. There may be cases where deliberate stereotyping to make a point is even advantageous in fiction. But for the most part, stereotypes work

Konami

Figure 3.9 *Cy Girls:* Stereotypes
are alive and well in games.

against the veracity of the narrative. Since they are so common, we don't notice them, or take them for granted, particularly because they appear to be staples of most genre fiction, and stories in games are, without exception, genre fiction.

We might understand how many human beings can fall into the trap of stereotyping through parental indoctrination, peer influences, and a parochial view of the world they inhabit. But what excuses might a writer, someone hopefully a bit more worldly and open-minded, have? There are several.

- We don't realize they *are* stereotypes.

  As writers, we owe it to ourselves to observe and absorb as much of the world as is humanly possible: its art, its people, its geography. There is simply no telling when a random bit of information or a serendipitous insight might be useful. I'm still waiting for my childhood hobby of paleontology to become useful in the construction and history of a virtual world. However, there are many writers who have grown up not reading outside of their favorite genres, or taking the time to explore, however briefly, what other people are doing and thinking in the world.

- Stereotypes are easy to write. All the work has been done for us.

  They almost write themselves. We know how the dark-eyed vixen is going to act before she can get a word out. Other similar characters have worked in other games or other media. We want to repeat their successes. Why not borrow their characters?

- We may justify their inclusion by citing time constraints.

  We've all been faced with impossible deadlines, and seemingly unmeetable milestones. There is such a temptation to just pencil them in and tell ourselves that we can always go back and flesh them out later. But there never is a later. Characters are due some proper respect, and their fair share of our consideration. Take a break from the cool action scenes, and take the time to give the characters their due.

- Stereotypes are often confused with archetypes.

  Archetypes are universally recognized. Men want the chance to interact with goddesses in leather. Women want to team up with dashing, romantic men who will sweep them off their feet, or succumb to their charms. We want men and women to play our games, to live out their fantasies, sure, but unless we turn those fantasies into living, breathing individuals, the experience will be hollow.

- Some types of games, like RPGs, rely on them for player-character creation.

  Players want to play the stealthy rogue, the benevolent cleric, the elven archer. Since these characters are developed very mechanically *on purpose*, they should occupy a special exception to the rule. The largest problem with your game in this case may not lie with stereotyped characters at all, but the stereotypical setting you want them to live in. We'll look at setting in Chapter 8, "Respecting Story."

Falling back on stereotypes is certainly easier than finding new characters either in life or in our imaginations. Certainly some of the appeal in RPGs is allowing the players to assume roles more glamorous and enviable than we might play in life. But stereotypes diminish the overall gaming experience. They limit the sophistication of our stories. And as a result, limit our audience. Try to catch yourself doing it. Take the extra time and struggle to avoid stereotypes.

To recognize when you are writing stereotypes, ask yourself questions: Does the character look, talk, and act exactly as you'd expect her to? If there are no surprises, you've got a stereotype. Do the concept sketches the artists are making from your description look a lot like the concept sketches from other games? Stereotype.

To write characters the player will want to know and play with, we first must respect them. We must take the time to know them even better than they know themselves. We must give them a life within the game, not just a gameplay reason for being there. We need to choose how they will grow, and how much they will learn about themselves. If they are stereotypes, they are stillborn. There is no possibility for growth or development, and players will quickly tire of them. Characters drive the story. If they are boring or derivative, the story will be the same.

CHAPTER 4

CHARACTER ROLES

In Chapter 3, "Respecting Characters," I introduced some concepts from drama and film that can be useful to us as we write characters in games: the three dimensions of character; character progression through growth and development; and the pivotal characters. We then moved into the types of characters we find in games such as PCs, NPCs; a breakdown of NPCs into major and minor characters and extras; finishing with stereotypes and how to avoid them.

Using that as a foundation, let's look at the various roles characters play in our games. There's no better place to start than story.

The Character's Role in Story

Story structure can spring from many sources: a situation, a relationship, an ideal, a need to educate, whatever. But it is borne on the backs of the characters that inhabit it. We can be touched by the death of an "old yaller dog," but we are most often and easily touched by the plight of our fellow human beings. Our stories should be populated by characters who compel us to watch them, or interact with them. These are characters that we want to spend time with, maybe because we like them (Floyd, the Robot from *Planetfall*, is a classic example), maybe because we are mesmerized by their evil as we are mesmerized by the swaying cobra (Hannibal Lecter).

Figure 4.1 The cobra-like gaze of Anthony Hopkins as Hannibal Lecter in *Silence of the Lambs.*

If we want players to care what happens to characters in our games, it isn't enough for them to be three-dimensional. Static characters don't freeze gameplay, but they confine it to the purely mechanical act of making the correct moves. If reviews of a game says it's just more of the same, no matter what genre, you can bet the mechanics of its genre have been copied, maybe a few new cool moves have been added, but not much attention has been paid to character or story or both. Even a great story is not enough. It must be inhabited and driven by characters.

Much can be made of Lajos Egri and others decrying Aristotle's insistence that *action* (*muthos* in the original Greek) is the essential element in drama, and not character (*êthos*). As William Archer points out, it is a waste of ink. Of course, action is the most important element. Stories can exist without character (many Hollywood action films and most action games do), but none can exist without action. The word "drama" means doing, not simply saying or existing.

note

ACTION: It can often be thought to be synonymous with activity as in an "action" film. Its more correct definition for our purposes is "something done, as opposed to something said."

However, accepting action as the fundamental element in drama doesn't mean it is the noblest. When talking about action preordained by the gods, maybe it is. That is the model Aristotle was working from after all. As Egri says, "Fate was supposed to play the chief role in the drama. The gods spoke, and men lived or died in accordance with what they said." But William Archer puts the debate in perspective when he writes:

"The skeleton is, in a sense, the fundamental element in the human organism. It can exist, and, with a little assistance, retain its form, when stripped of muscle and blood and nerve: whereas a boneless man would be an amorphous heap, more helpless than a jelly-fish. But do we therefore account the skeleton man's noblest part? Scarcely. It is by his blood and nerves that he lives, not by his bones; and it is because his bones are, comparatively speaking, dead matter that they continue to exist when the flesh has fallen away from them."

Action equals bones. Character equals all that other messy stuff. As Archer concludes, "Action ought to exist for the sake of character: when the relation is reversed, the play may be an ingenious toy, but scarcely a vital work of art." We're going to discuss that tricky word "art" in Chapter 20, "The Responsible Writer."

Characters drive the story. They create the conflicts. The only emotion in a game experience without good characters is the emotion derived by the player from the game play: frustration, anger, exhilaration, triumph . . . the thrill of victory, the agony of defeat. . . . To create emotion through story we must start with character.

In computer games the *protagonist* is almost invariably either the primary character controlled by a player, or the player himself. I say "primary" character because players can alternate control of two characters in succession as in the adventure game *The Beast Within: A Gabriel Knight Mystery*. Players can also concurrently control an additional character such as a sidekick or parties of several characters in single-player RPGs like *Baldur's Gate*. Some games provide a single group of fellow adventurers either in the beginning, or acquired throughout a game. Others allow players to recruit and drop party members at will. We'll get to the benefits and drawbacks of each approach shortly.

In war games, or strategy games like *Civilization* and *Age of Empires*, the player may control armies or the populations of entire cities or kingdoms. In these games, discussed in more detail in Chapter 15, "Game Types," the player is very much the protagonist with little or no emotional attachment to his minions, treating each NPC or unit as nothing more than a piece on a game board. In the other examples, however, a very real emotional attachment is possible, and can be exploited by the author.

Populating the World

The original *Myst* is set in an empty world where the player is the only living, breathing character in it. *Asheron's Call 2* is its massively multiplayer equivalent. In, one supposes, an effort to simplify massively multiplayer games and make them more accessible to a wider range of players, *AC2* presented us with a world almost entirely empty of NPCs. There were sentient *mobs*, but they were cannon-fodder, nothing more.

note

MOB: short for mobiles, a term coined by Richard Bartle to describe creatures moving in a controlled, but unpredictable way.

Sequels to *Myst* have added characters, and as different designers try their hands at *AC2*, more NPCs have appeared. They are only thinly drawn functionaries, handing out quests, and when I stopped playing the game many months ago, did little to dispel the feeling of an empty, essentially lifeless world. Yet obviously the designers of these games came to realize that populating these worlds even with minor characters gave them a needed touch of life.

We spoke in Chapter 2, "The Story Remains the Same," about Aristotle actually helping us as writers of games by insisting on unities that, while heightening drama, allow us to create games with few characters and locations. Some games lend themselves to this far better than others. The designers of *Star Wars Galaxies* by necessity needed to populate their universe. Players would expect at least an approximation of the busy streets of Mos Eisley and other cities. So we have many NPCs added as window dressing, as well as droids beeping past and spaceships roaring overhead. All of these add tremendously to the atmosphere of the game.

NPCs can function as more than local color too, as we'll explore in this chapter. To confine NPCs to the background is to miss opportunities of character development as well as storytelling, not to mention the gameplay functionality they can provide.

Commentary and Gossip

We rely on characters in stories to help us understand how we feel about the events that are unfolding. We can share a character's *point of view*, or POV. In *Full Throttle* the player-character is Ben, a Harley-riding, hard-hitting biker with a rough-and-tumble sense of humor. We see the game story through his eyes, and are able to experience the world in character. One of the standard menu items is "kick." The exact same game without Ben would be an entirely different experience, and not nearly as much fun.

In a more general way, NPC characters can provide commentary on a game's action, filling in gaps in the exposition; putting the action in perspective; and clarifying the murky parts. Players need not identify with minor character commentators to benefit from their knowledge. And we as writers can use such characters in all sorts of interesting ways.

The song "Master of the House" from the musical *Les Miserables* describes in melody and *recitative* the character of the landlord, Monsieur Thenardier:

> "Mine host Thenardier
> He was there so they say,
> At the field of Waterloo
> Got there, it's true
> When the fight was all through
> But he knew just what to do
> Crawling through the mud
> So I've heard it said
> Picking through the pockets
> Of the English dead
> He made a tidy score
> From the spoils of war"

note

RECITATIVE: Lyrics that are spoken rhythmically with slight melodic variations rather than sung.

I mentioned in Chapter 3 how Dickens could sketch a character in a paragraph. Here's one in song. The point here is not to bemoan the lack of musical games with NPCs breaking into song, but to give them another purpose as commentators or gossips.

We find NPC town criers, bards, and bartenders in many massively multiplayer games handy sources of information. They are always passive, unfortunately, waiting without

Cameron Mackintosh International

Figure 4.2 Thenardier and customers from *Les Miserables.*

lives or thoughts of their own until a player clicks on them, and they can offer tidbits of general information on monthly events, locations of quest givers (see the last section in this chapter), hints of where good hunting may be found, and so on. Other minor characters and extras wander the streets as nothing more than local color, as we saw in the preceding section.

Yet, here is a perfect opportunity for illuminating characters. These NPCs shouldn't explain who they are, or what they're about, but who their neighbors are, particularly if their neighbors are major characters.

In any game, single-player or multiplayer, NPCs can gossip about other characters to avoid the amateur writer's characters who explain themselves. Even better, the character being gossiped about can have an entirely different story like Monsieur Thenardier, who also sings in "Master of the House."

> "Welcome, M'sieur
> Sit yourself down
> And meet the best
> Innkeeper in town
> As for the rest
> All of 'em crooks
> Rooking their guests
> And cooking the books
> Seldom do you see
> Honest men like me
> A gent of good intent
> Who's content to be
> Master of the house"

Let's go down this road even farther. There can be disagreement among the NPCs about another's character. In fact, depending upon whom players speak to, different players could have entirely different views of a character, something our games offer that other media do not. We can then mold player opinion by turning off negative comments about a certain character if the player speaks to three with positive gossip first. We then can replace the more accurate gossip with non-committal comments to lead the player down any garden path we choose. Player impressions may get them into trouble with NPCs if players act on one set of information. Non-committal comments might then switch to a third state: "That'll teach you to listen to the wrong kind of people! Too bad you didn't come to me first!"

One of the things all massively multiplayer games concentrate on is building the community of players. The more friends a player makes in the game, the more likely she is to hang around and pay her money every month. One way to do this is to seed conversation between players. Having NPCs give conflicting information is a good way to do this.

The first massively multiplayer game I worked on was *The Gryphon Tapestry*, a game that unfortunately didn't make it past a limited closed beta before financing dried up. I'll go into the relationship matrix we set up to track players' relationships with non-player characters in Chapter 6, "Character Encounters," but mention it here because it affected the gossip function that was built into all of our NPCs. If a player's relationship wasn't very good with a particular NPC, that NPC would be less forthcoming with gossip, and might even lie. In addition, different NPCs were inherently better sources of gossip than others, and not along stereotypical lines. The cook at the manor house in one village wanted to

Figure 4.3 Character sketches from *The Gryphon Tapestry* by artist Alex Bradley.

be thought of as someone in the know, yet her gossip was usually quite worthless. There was one exception to this. She had helped raise the daughter of the house, who was devoted to her and often let her in on secrets the daughter might be expected to know.

We are respecting the characters enough in this example to make them more than functional props in the game. By giving them character and lives of their own, we enrich the world they inhabit. By giving them their own opinions and prejudices, we can weave fairly sophisticated relationships between them. The result is not towns that are little more than theatrical sets with cigar store Indians standing in front of them, but communities of living, breathing characters who are far more interesting to interact with as they fulfill the functions the design requires.

Mark Terrano was lead designer on *Age of Empires II: The Age of Kings*, a developer on the other *Age of Empires* games, and is currently an Xbox technical evangelist at Microsoft. Mark has a longtime interest in storytelling. In his sidebar, he suggests a procedural approach to what he calls the propagation of conversation, a system giving NPCs the ability to react to the events around them in a massively multiplayer game.

Mark's conversation system is an excellent approach to commentary and gossip; and it works equally well in multiplayer and solo-player games, particularly if they are built modularly and not linearly. But I'm getting ahead of myself.

In *The Gryphon Tapestry*, commentary and gossip definitely added to the community feeling of the game. In beta we would watch as players met at the local pub to share their day's adventures, only to discover that the view of a particular NPC one might have been given was contrary to the impression another had. The debates about whom to believe and what the truth might be were extremely entertaining.

Living Useful Lives

Many games treat minor characters as functionaries only, assigning them a single role to play, and shoving a line or two of "character" dialogue—or simple dialect—in their mouths. This is not respecting the characters. This is ignoring all the many ways they can support the story and the overall game experience. We'll explore some typical roles characters play in games in a moment. But as we look at each, remember these need not be in isolation. Any NPC can be a gossip. Any NPC can be part of a faction that has attitudes towards other factions in the game. Any NPC can have needs, stated by soliciting players' aid in the form of errands or quests.

There is a definite benefit to both writers and their stories when we give NPCs multiple reasons for being in the game. It gives us multiple facets to their characters. Before we know it, even the lowliest minor character can blossom without much effort on our part. An NPC that functions as merchant/gossip/quest giver instead of just merchant *has* to have more going for him before we even start to apply those functions.

Mark Terrano, Programmer/Designer

A common complaint from MMO players is that they feel insubstantial—ghostlike—with their actions having no permanence and no real impact on the world around them. A living world reacts to what is happening—and intelligent NPCs would certainly notice and talk about any changes to 'their' world. They should express fears, recognize heroes, complain about injustices, and talk about the weather.

Developers are usually unable to let players make permanent changes to the objects or landscape, but simple recognition by those around you can be just as satisfying and even more personal. Games currently depend on players to build up their own social networks (guilds/friend lists) and let the recognition come from the other players.

Figure 4.4 Mark Terrano proposes a procedural approach to NPC conversations.

In the world where the NPC inhabitants notice and remark on changes, "Leveling up" isn't just a marker on your character page—but everyone in town seems to notice something is different about you, and mention it. Buying a new set of armor gets appreciative nods, cheers, and shouts of praise when you walk down the street. When your team returns from slaying the Evil Dragon, everyone in town seems to be already talking about it. In a big city they might not have all the details, but they'd all heard of one being killed nearby. Merchants seem to remember you and greet you by name. Rumors (developer foreshadowing) would be talked about in town, whispered in alleys, and of course, everyone still comments on the weather.

NPC 'scripts' are typically very limited, repetitive, and destroy the illusion that players are in a living world. In a real town (or office), information is retained and repeated by people that are most interested in it . . . the level of interest also governs how much detail is kept and passed forward. Conversational snippets, when tagged with just a little bit of information, can move through any game society and breathe life into the social landscape.

Each snippet of conversation, when created, is given a scope (how far it travels/age), and an impact (economic, social, health and safety), and how someone would normally react hearing it (good, bad, indifferent, trivial). NPCs can then have general behaviors that are triggered by information that is moving around in the world, conversationally connected in a great social web.

Player actions (killing a dragon, solving a mystery, leveling up, buying new clothes) will seed the database with new conversational items—these then spread out like ripples in a pond. Developers can add new content both manually and programmatically—so rumors of a war might persist and grow for weeks before the armies actually get within sight. Like the childhood 'whispering' game, where a phrase at one end of the room changes as it is whispered from child to child—exaggeration, substitution, and even mixing of rumors can take place on information stored this way.

Players will feel a sense of integration into a larger whole, a real community—and intimately part of your world as they see their own experiences woven into its history.

The downside is that multiple roles can mean additional user interface (UI) issues. The last thing we want to do is create more well-rounded characters only to have them buried beneath menus. This is one reason—and there are many—why all of the elements of the game experience—gameplay, story, character, graphic style, sound environment—should ideally be developed together. Too many times I've been stuck with the task of "adding" story to gameplay and an engine already in place, or adding gameplay to some linear story, sometimes original but most often derived from linear media.

My biggest challenge ever was a full-motion-video (FMV) game called *Temüjin* where I was handed completed video scenes with real actors on real sets and tasked with altering the story until it made sense, which required changing characters already committed to film, *and* adding gameplay. I wouldn't wish that on my worst enemy!

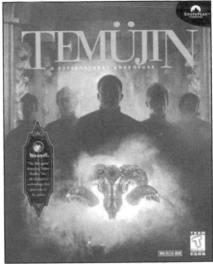

Figure 4.5 *Temüjin*, a big challenge for this writer.

If we start with the idea of our minor characters being multi-functional we have at least a fighting chance that the engine and its interfaces will not become bloated or complicated in the same way they might if we tried to add functionality to the characters after the work on engine and interfaces had already been done. Just as story grows out of characters and gameplay can emerge from story, story and character can emerge from gameplay. It is a two-way street, and we should be traveling both directions as we build our games.

Adding multiple functions to our characters does not, of course, guarantee that they will become three-dimensional all on their own, and if they're minor characters, there's no special reason they need to be. But to literally bring the world of a game to life, it must be inhabited by creatures who truly live in it. Giving them multiple functions can be as useful a tool to the writer as it is to gameplay, but we still need to think about *who* each one is, not just what functions that individual NPC can perform.

The Player-Character Revisited (Protagonist)

When talking about the character's role in story, I identified the protagonist as usually either the player-controlled character or the player herself. This is true of all games whether there is a single player-character, or multiple characters the player can control.

And here is one way in which games depart from other media. In drama the protagonist is, according to Egri, always the pivotal character. This definition, if it was shared even in 1946 when his book was written, is not that clear-cut today. Iago is not the protagonist of *Othello* even though he is the pivotal character. Daxter is not the protagonist or player-character in *Jak & Daxter: The Precursor Legacy*.

Confining the protagonist to the player-character is really not much of a limitation because look what we gain in the process. We give the audience, our player, active involvement in the progress of the story. Because of that, the player-character should be "the main character . . . the person at the center of the action."

But it does bring up an interesting dilemma, a variation of which writers face every week in series television: character death.

Death of a Player-Character

> "I'm gonna show you and everybody else that Willy Loman did not die in vain. He had a good dream. It's the only dream you can have—to come out number-one man. He fought it out here, and this is where I'm gonna win it for him."
>
> —*Arthur Miller, Death of a Salesman*

When I took over as head writer of the daytime soap opera *Edge of Night* (The "*The*" was dropped as the first word of the title during my tenure, I believe, to toughen it up. Edge is a stronger word than the article.) I was informed by the producers that the actress playing one of the show's longest running characters did not want to renew her contract, but wanted to try her luck in Hollywood. Television, including daytime, is often a good rung of the career ladder for actors to climb on their way to movies.

The character, Nicole, had already been recast several times throughout her life on the show. We discussed recasting yet again, but those who had been with the show longer than I pointed out that the usefulness of the character may have run its course. The once popular character of Miles had not had much to do since marrying her, and if she were out of the picture, it would liberate him. So we decided to kill her.

This was possible because soap operas have huge casts of characters, all of them protagonists to a point, though not always pivotal. Each character's life depended most on popularity with viewers, a fact an actor will quite rightly use to his advantage in contract negotiations when his popularity is high, and mention less if his character has fallen from grace with the audience. As it was, there was quite an uproar when we offed Nicole in a wonderfully nasty way. I received a letter from one stricken fan who had named her daughter after Nicole. Tear stains had smeared the ink.

Continuing characters on primetime series are a bit trickier. The recent trend toward serial stories has made it more possible to hire actors who appear to be characters that will live forever, or to take actors whose contract demands have gotten higher than their perceived value to the show, and dispose of them. But by and large, shows remain on the air because of their characters more than their stories.

In the fourth season of *Star Trek: Next Generation*, we were faced with the Wesley Crusher problem. Here was the only young character in the series, well acted by Will Wheaton, but who had been allowed to develop into a sort of Superboy. It was the writers' fault, no one else's, and the writers had to deal with it. We finally decided to send him off to Starfleet Academy (the place, not the game!) instead of killing him to give us the option of bringing him back at some point, particularly since his mom was still aboard the Enterprise.

Figure 4.6 What to do with Wesley . . . ?

We could have killed Wesley. It would have been much harder to kill one of *Charlie's Angels* or any member of the casts of so many shows. Yet in computer games we kill the player-character over and over again. Why? And why would anyone want to play a character so inept at survival?

It's no coincidence that so many games deal in death, just as it is no coincidence that many popular TV shows are set in arenas like crime and law and medicine where life and death struggles can be played out week after week. Game developers recognize, as do producers of television and motion pictures and publishers of books, that the stakes don't get much higher in a story than when there is a life in the balance.

But a challenge unique to our medium of expression is not just the potential of the player-character dying, but of that character dying more times than Christopher Lee got staked by Peter Cushing in all those Hammer Dracula movies combined. It is a primary game mechanic in many shooter and squad-based games to kill the player-character. There are two major reasons often cited for this: a) It provides a penalty when the player fails; and b) as in other media it hopefully raises the stakes.

(We can't, of course, kill off the player-character permanently except in arcade games where players must start from scratch each time they step up to the machine. To do so is to erase the investment the player has made in the PC, all that advancement in levels, skills, and loot. There is always a minority movement in virtual worlds for permanent death. They try to skirt the issue—as I'm about to with my chart of alternatives to player-character death—by coming up with reincarnation or passing items from father to children. Unless the context is very carefully established, these solutions can only become obvious placebos for the player to swallow as the character she's invested three years of her life in sails out to sea like the fiery funeral ship of the Vikings.

I've explored a generational game structure that I'll introduce later, but it is compelling to me for different reasons than softening the blow of player-character death.)

In other non-series media, there is a third important reason: the protagonist, the character we've invested the most empathy in can really die. We don't see this happen much in popular entertainment, but it happens enough in action films (*Armageddon*), and dramas (*The Human Stain*), and even comedies (*Four Weddings and a Funeral*), that it is always within the realm of possibility. However, as we saw in our discussion of tragedy, reason number three is all but removed from it. And remember, the "hero" we play in *Infidel* is not a particularly empathetic character.

We've seen how TV series in particular wrestle with this problem (as well as James Bond on the big screen). What do they do? They kill off with reckless regularity characters the immortal protagonist supposedly cares about. It is glamorous, but dangerous to be a Bond girl. You don't even have to marry him as Tracey Di Vicenzo, Diana Rigg's character did in *On Her Majesty's Secret Service*. TV has reduced this solution to an awkward cliché. Introduce the old friend or blood relation of the hero and nine out of ten times that old friend or troubled sibling is either a villain, or will die in his arms, or both.

Writers of games have fastened on "kill an NPC the player-character cares about" because we are apparently stuck between a rock and a hard place. Even in games that are *not* part of a series, we don't want to kill our player-character, as we discussed in Chapter 2. Yet we want the player to care about the character that is her avatar in the game. In a game where there is no death, it's not a problem. But if there are villainous opponents, and the opponents *can* die, it can upset the balance, and negate the "raised stakes" of a life and death struggle.

There is no universal solution to this dilemma, and I doubt we'll find one any more than the grail will turn up, or a chemical process will be found to alter the atomic structure of Pb into Au. The important point is whatever solution we come up with must be in context. A science fiction solution won't work in a real world setting. A comedic solution would jar the player in a realistic combat simulation.

Some possible ways to avoid player-character death are listed in the following table.

Alternatives to Player-Character Death

Genre	Method	Notes
Sci-Fi	Clone the PC	New clones will have a shared memory of the game up until now. (Thanks, Carl Jung!)
Sci-Fi	Artificial human/android	Brain circuits undamaged. The PC can be repaired.
Sci-Fi/Fantasy	Regenerating tissue	Whether through futuristic medicine, or the nature of the non-human the player manipulates. (Dwarves are supposed to be good at this.)
Sci-Fi	Auto-Teleportation	The PC automatically snapped back to command post when health reaches a critical level.
Sci-Fi	Time travel	The Time Travel device has a timer that resets automatically to moments before the fatal confrontation. This, of course, *is* a death, but without death's sting.
Modern combat	Unconsciousness	Evac'ed to field hospital.
Modern combat	Squad-based	NPC squad-member drags PC to safety.
Police action	Unconsciousness	GPS locates PC, and PC is rescued by paramedics.
Police action	Squad-based	Different arena, same method as modern combat example above.
Any	Capture	PC must escape. Different prison/detention method/guards each level.
Any	Simulator	As real as the others, but PC is actually in a simulator with an instructor overseeing.
Any	Plot-based	PC has something villains need. This is used over and over in film and TV to justify why bad guys don't kill heroes when they get the drop on them.
Any	Plot-based	Chief villain is related to/in love with PC. This can be happily combined with death of an NPC close to hero for a double-dose of emotion!
Horror	Undeath	Hero is an attractive zombie who can be incapacitated for a time, but eventually lurches back to his feet.
Any	*The Game*	Film with Michael Douglas and Sean Penn. PC appears to die and be resurrected, but it's all a hoax.
Fantasy	*Highlander*	Player *is* immortal except for one thing: (decapitation/stake through the heart). Just keep those swords and stakes away from the villains till the final level!

Do we really need an alternative? If we want to tone down the violence, it's better to start with theme, rather than player-character death, and create a game where other stakes are made as high as life and death. This is not to say you cannot have a story with relatively little onscreen violence, and still kill off your protagonist. Dickens' *A Tale of Two Cities* keeps violence and gore "offscreen," and even manages to achieve an upbeat ending while Sidney Carton is being trundled off to the guillotine:

> "It is a far, far better thing I do, than I have ever done; it is a far, far better rest that I go to, than I have ever known."

Here is a character at peace and triumphant. Not a tragic character even at the moment of his death.

But game writers actually have a couple of things going for us that other media don't have. Death of the player-character is a game mechanic. It is one of those elements of gameplay that is accepted by players, just as power pills and being able to carry an entire armory of weapons are accepted. If the context is preserved (the weapons are appropriate to the arena) it need not break immersion any more than the fact the player is holding a controller in his hands instead of an M-16.

And the other thing we have going for us is that *because* player-character death is a game mechanic, we can still find ways to empathize with the player-character even if he doesn't die. And herein lies a clue why we need not concentrate on creating all our emotion in the game only through an NPC. Players care about the player-character even before they boot the game simply because they *are* the player-characters.

We can give them any number of gut-wrenching and heart-tugging dramatic moments without killing the PC off. And we don't need to create a single NPC the player-character (or player!) cares about to do it. As human beings we can care about all sorts of issues, values, and ideas. Let's take just one: personal freedoms such as speech, liberty, equality, worship, privacy, and so many others. As in *Oddworld*, create forces depriving the player-character of any of these or any combination of these and you're going to rouse empathy in that character, even if life is not one of the freedoms you try and deny them. From totalitarian military states to mad wizards, any number of villains can be out to get the player-character through so many different means that strike to the heart of what makes us humans. That alone makes it worthwhile to find ways to avoid player-character death, so that we can break the monotony of story that it imposes.

Villains (Antagonists)

Villains can do all sorts of nasty things to player-characters. That's why we love them and hate them all at the same time. Villains also seem to have more fun than heroes, which is why we writers love to write them!

I try not to state out-and-out rules in this book, but here's one where I can't help myself: the _antagonist_ must be every bit as intelligent and powerful as the protagonist. A weak adversary creates a weak hero. Never ever _ever_ make the mistake of giving the villain an _obvious_ weakness in the same way we lame a tragic hero with an Achilles heel.

This rule is so important Egri repeats it twice on the same page:

> "The antagonist in any play is necessarily as strong and, in time, as ruthless as the pivotal character. A fight is interesting only if the fighters are evenly matched."

And:

> "Let me now repeat it again: the antagonist must be as strong as the protagonist. The wills of conflicting personalities must clash."

We will talk about reversals and surprise in Chapter 9, "Bringing the Story to Life." But it is the strong antagonist who forces such surprises and reversals to occur, those heart-stopping moments that can make us cry out loud at our monitors.

It would seem we have a dilemma here. How do we design the game so that the player can win, if the player's NPC opponent is his equal? Let's look at sports. No matter how evenly matched opponents may be, one always wins in the end. You may tie a game in hockey, but at the end of the season the tie will be broken, or rendered meaningless. The most exciting athletic competitions are those where the outcome is unknown up until the final seconds, and so should it be in our games.

How does the player manage at all to advance if the force he applies is met with an equal and opposite force? There are a number of ways. We:

- Saddle the antagonist with minions who _are_ minions because they are not as powerful as him. Take a look at a James Bond or Jackie Chan film to see how very strict the hierarchy of bad guys is, as they line up like homicidal ducks to be machine-gunned and flying-kicked out of their feathers. We've adopted this hierarchy literally in games.

- Provide the player-character with increasingly better weapons (not necessarily the kind that kill—information can be a powerful weapon in a non-combat game) to barely overcome the forces the villain throws at her.

- Create a McGuffin that both player and villain must constantly be striving and sacrificing for to obtain. The McGuffin can be powerful or as inconsequential as those in the films of the man who invented the term:

note

McGUFFIN: A plot-enabling device. A term coined by master director Alfred Hitchcock to describe the reason all the intrigue and running around is happening in his movies. It is ultimately unimportant. The chase is all. Examples include the microfilm in the sculpture in *North by Northwest* (who remembers that?); Mister Memory's memorized international treaty in *The Thirty-nine Steps* (The title is actually a reference to the parts of the treaty, but who remembers that?); the wine bottle stuffed with uranium salts in *Notorious* , and many others.

- Give him that tragic flaw, but don't make it obvious, or don't make how to take advantage of it obvious. Just make sure it's set up early enough so it won't feel like a deus ex machina dropped on the player like a Pb weight from our old friends the Greek gods.

- Subject both the player-character and the villain to the ironies of fate. This is tricky to do in the final confrontation, but to both help and hinder the player early on it can introduce an apparent random element that heightens suspense.

In the previous section on player-character death, I mentioned the very interesting dramatic situation where the protagonist and antagonist actually have an emotional bond. The ultimate version of this would be identical twins, or the many alternate Jet Li's in the film *The One*. An interesting variation on allowing one equal to defeat another in that film is that as Yulaw the antagonist (and pivotal character) kills his counterparts in other alternate universes, he gains their strength. He kills the first few easily because they're unaware they're being stalked. But by killing them off, he also increases the strength of the protagonist, Gabe.

It stands to reason that to create an antagonist worthy of our protagonist, we need to develop him as fully as our central character with his physical character, psychological character, and sociological character all in play. This can be difficult because while the player-character is always onscreen, the antagonist may not be very much until the end. This is especially true in boss mob story structures where we may see the villain being villainous only in cut scenes removed from the action. This is a device borrowed from genre fiction in other media.

* * *

```
CUT TO:

INT. BLOFELD'S LAIR—DAY

Ernst Stavro Blofeld, face in shadow, strokes his ice-
eyed white Persian cat.

                    BLOFELD
Find Bond, and kill him!
```

* * *

We'll discuss this point-of-view, called the *omniscient POV*, more in Chapter 6. A better way to reveal his character is through his moves and countermoves as play progresses. You don't need to know anything about a chess opponent you meet on the Internet. You'll learn all you need to know soon enough by his game.

And in video games, we can introduce the antagonist to the player by the nature of the McGuffin the antagonist relentlessly pursues; those she recruits to serve her; how she treats civilians; the wording of a ransom note; the architecture of her lair. As many dimensions as you need to fill out a character can be found by how he touches all aspects of the world around him. There is no need to rely on that dossier from Central Exposition. In fact, it's far more fun if a couple of those reversals we want to introduce are surprises because the mission briefing was flat-out wrong.

An even trickier situation arises in a mystery. How do we develop the character of the villain if we don't know who he is? We call upon all those gossipy NPCs. How does Christopher McQuarrie, the writer of *The Usual Suspects*, pull it off? Through witness accounts, rumors, and a list of crimes. We learn something of the psychological, sociological, and even physical dimensions of Keyser Soze's character. We know him by his works. And after all, realizing the rabbit McQuarrie has waiting in the hat, how else *could* he have built a complete portrait of his chilling, amoral, criminal mastermind?

We need to respect all of our NPCs, our villains more so than most. They must appear to be every bit as capable of winning the game as the player. Have I said that enough? Think the player-character might need even more help? Let's talk about another character who can help tip the scales in her favor.

Mentors

Joseph Campbell speaks of the mentor characters found in the mythology of many cultures in *The Hero with a Thousand Faces*:

"For those who have not refused the call [to adventure], the first encounter of the hero-journey is with a protective figure (often a little old crone or old man) who provides the adventurer with amulets against the dragon forces he is about to pass."

Where would Cinderella be without her fairy godmother? Still at home doing the floors. Where would Luke be without Obi-Wan Kenobi? Still on Tatooine raising crops.

Figure 4.7 Alec Guinness as Obi-Wan Kenobi in *Star Wars*.

"Protective and dangerous, motherly and fatherly at the same time," writes Campbell, "this supernatural principle of guardianship and direction unites in itself all the ambiguities of the unconscious—thus signifying the support of our conscious personality by that other, larger system, but also the inscrutability of the guide that we are following, to the peril of all our rational ends."

The mentor is a far more complex figure than popular entertainment usually dishes out. The mentor can be supernatural, or have unusual powers, but it is not a requirement. For our purposes in games it is a useful character for a number of reasons. Mentors can provide:

- Backstory: both generalized and personalized for the protagonist.
- Story hints like setting up a new level; pointing to where the next step in the story might be located; potentially help characters; and dangers to avoid.
- Gameplay hints on everything from special powers the player can draw upon to how to use the gamepad, an interesting breaking of the fourth wall to help ease the player behind it once again.
- Memory Jogger: Remind the player what she has completed, and what her immediate and long-term goals should be.
- Training.
- Quests in the form of jobs the player must accomplish.
- Support for the player's efforts. "Good work! Only four more wizards to defeat!"
- Rewards: interim rewards for players, as well as possibly bestowing the final crown.

Unlike other characters who may not know the protagonist, the mentor is often already a part of the player-character's life, if even in a minor role, and either expands his mentor role to face the new crisis, or moves into it from a seemingly innocuous former role, e.g. the wandering beggar who turns out to be a disgraced swordsman capable of training the player-character in new skills. In either case, the mentor knows the protagonist and has some idea of what the player-character is capable of, and what his background may be. Or the mentor can use supernatural means to bone up on the protagonist via devices such as a crystal ball or those fat dossiers that litter mentor's desks that can only have been provided by Central Exposition.

Story and puzzle hint systems have grown in sophistication over the years from printed documents apart from the game to in-game Help menus to props, such as books and computers player characters can access, to NPC characters. In my mind, it is the NPCs who can provide the most help and who damage the player's immersion the least. Story or puzzle hints can be built, depending upon how difficult the designer wants the game to be, in many layers of dialogue from the NPC. I would avoid treating the acquisition of these hints as a problem for players to solve the way we used gossip earlier. Hints are a sometimes necessary intrusion. It's best to get them over as quickly and as seamlessly as possible, and not frustrate players and remind them they're playing a game. That is the opposite of what we're trying to achieve.

Gameplay hints, as stated in the list, are problematic at best as far as immersion goes. But since it appears few gamers bother to read the documentation we provide them, an in-game solution must be found. One of the benefits console games have over games on a personal computer is that the controls are dedicated for the most part to gaming, and are very standardized across many games on a platform. If you play one game on an Xbox, you can get the hang of many more quite quickly. So in this case designers can at least keep world-breaking contact with the players to a minimum.

Mentors are excellent memory joggers. Obi-Wan Kenobi kept Luke (and the audience) from getting too sidetracked and forgetting what his ultimate goal was. In video games mentors work even better. We play games over a period of days, even weeks or longer, and not steadily. It may be fairly easy to remember exposition over the two-hour running time of a movie, but next to impossible to call it instantly to mind if we haven't picked up the game in a couple of weeks.

I know this is a painful reality for some designers to face. We may want our games to be so compelling players *can't* put them down for more than meals or a nap. But the reality is they will. Far better to worry about keeping them compelled when they *are* playing. If the game is fun, they'll come back like prodigal sons, forgetful perhaps, but ready to re-engage.

Mentors can be happily substituted for the ubiquitous journals in many RPGs. They save us an interface, and we can keep the text in the game to a minimum. Dialogue by necessity should be terser than the written word even when both are presented to the player as text. Mentors can respond in character, say, with irritation when a player-character returns to them before the completion of a mission or quest, and in character remind them of what they've accomplished or still have to do. Mentors have a stake in the story and in the player-character, and this can add drama where in a journal there may be only lists.

Mentors can cross dress as trainers. These are NPCs who teach new abilities to the player-character—or player-characters in a virtual world. Yoda, Luke's second mentor, was also his trainer. Obi-Wan sent Luke to him to learn the more practical aspects of the force like levitation and swinging that light saber. We can use the mentor as the sole trainer, or save only the special skills for him, if there are other trainers in the game. We'll take a deeper look at trainers in a moment.

Mentors can function as quest givers although they should probably be confined to the main quest of the story. It's a good thing to give an NPC multiple functions, but bad to burden a single NPC with too many. To keep the through line of the game clear, don't rely too heavily on the mentor for minor quests and side trips.

Players need constant pats on the back and reassurance just as they do in non-computer games and sports. Good coaches often become surrogate parents for players. The only equivalent we have in games is the game master in multiplayer worlds. In *Horizons*, for example, players are able to unlock new content as part of any ongoing story line. The "World Master" for the server I played on shows up now and then to offer encouragement or dire threats. But in most multiplayer games and all single-player games, we don't have coaches or game masters. Mentors are the perfect choice to fill that role, providing carrots of praise and the occasional stick of warning to help keep players engaged.

Finally, of course, the mentor can reward players with new skills, items, cash, any number of things to improve their chances in the game. Interim rewards are tremendously important to players. Of course, they can be handled by system messages like "Congratulations! You've just found a Horn of Creature Calling that will summon creatures to fight at your side!" But how much more immersive and dramatic it is to have our mentor reach up and pull that same horn from the shelf where we've seen it sitting from the beginning. "Here is a horn my father gave me. He was a simple shepherd who once saved a great magician's flock from wolves . . ."

And if the mentor should survive (no reason not to kill her off as a nice reversal near the end), and be present at the end of a story, then if they don't bestow the ultimate reward to the player, you can expect to find them winking nearby, or shuffling off into the distance with a slight wave of the hand, their mission accomplished.

We will talk about conflict in Chapter 5, "Character Traits." Here I want to mention that conflict between hero and mentor can be a good thing. The best part of the film *Remo Williams: The Adventure Begins* is the relationship between Remo and his mentor played by Joel Grey. They can barely tolerate each other, and each gives as good as he gets. He provides opportunities for great conflict and humor, particularly in the first act of the movie when Remo is learning his new trade.

We'll wave goodbye here to mentors, and move on to . . .

Sidekicks

Cortana in *Halo* is a shipboard AI harkening back to Arthur from *Journeyman Project II: Buried in Time*, a helpful but at times annoying AI personality on a chip you install in your time suit. Sidekicks don't have to be other physical beings, but most of the time they are. And whereas mentors are in many ways greater than their protégés (at least until the climatic action when all they can do is stand by and cheer, "Use the force, Luke!"), sidekicks are a step down the food chain.

Sidekicks provide comic relief, the occasional helping hand, sometimes useful exposition, or just a foil to bounce ideas off. Sometimes they're just there to make the hero look good. Robin isn't all that wonderful if all he does is ask questions so Batman can patiently explain what his Boy Wonder brain is unable to grasp.

But sidekicks can be much more. Daxter, as we've seen, is a pivotal character as well as a sidekick. Even Gabby Hayes could occasionally rescue Roy from calamity. The sidekick is the perfect NPC to generate emotion, if it is he who is in danger. Yorda in *Ico* is a good example of this. She is pretty much helpless without Ico's aid. He can't even communicate with her. Yet with charming animations, as when they run hand-in-hand; or through clever game mechanics such as making the safe places in the castle benches where when they rest she lays her head on Ico's shoulder, a tender relationship is built. And the final scene, much debated, provides, at least to me, a fitting conclusion.

Figure 4.8 Roy Rogers and his sidekick George "Gabby" Hayes.

We can go so far as to kill off sidekicks as in *Planetfall*. But in many games we run the risk of alienating the player. The death of a sidekick can make it look like the player has failed. Jak may fail to change Daxter back at the end of *Jak & Daxter: The Precursor Legacy*, but Jak has succeeded in a far greater purpose, and Daxter doesn't die, he is just still a rodent.

Figure 4.9 Jak and his sidekick Daxter go gritty in *Jak II*.

Another useful role for sidekicks is as surprise villain. Okay, not much of a surprise in *Othello* when Iago turns, and it happens right in the beginning. A much more famous example is one of Agatha Christie's first novels. Her audience was raised, as she was, on stories where detectives like Sherlock Holmes patiently pointed out clues to their befuddled Watsons while never really explaining anything at all until the very end. She cleverly played on her fellow mystery authors' habit of writing their detectives and sidekicks as these recognizable personalities (see the "Avoiding Stereotypes" section in Chapter 3), then dropped her brilliant bombshell. Her Watson character is the murderer. It's been done since, but never so well, or at the exact point in time where it worked the best. And, yes, I'm deliberately not giving you the title of the book.

As far as game mechanics go, sidekicks can be the hint system come alive or the pipeline to Central Exposition. The best use of a sidekick in storytelling terms though is somebody to whom the player-character can talk at any point in the game. Yes, occasionally the sidekick can get sidetracked: lost, kidnapped, or distracted by a mission of her own, but for the most part the player-character and sidekick go through the game as Siamese twins.

For this reason, because the sidekick can be a huge resource for the writer to reveal character exposition and backstory, the sidekick needs to be as vividly drawn as the hero with a distinct personality that complements the protagonist's character. Like mentors, sidekicks need not see eye-to-eye with their heroes. They are often sidekicks precisely because they don't worship the ground their heroes walk on. It helps the character of the protagonist, if he can tolerate an edgy relationship with his sidekick.

Do all player-characters need sidekicks? Not at all. Don't cram a sidekick into a game story like *Tom Clancy's Splinter Cell*. But if such a relationship fits the game story, it can be incredibly useful to the writer.

Servants and Pets

We are now segueing from the roles of major characters to the roles of minor characters, and while there can be some traffic back and forth—a servant can be a sidekick as a Sancho Panza to Don Quixote—we are now mostly dealing with characters who are almost defined by their roles. Servants and pets certainly fall into this category.

Servants are NPCs whose basic function in the game is to assist the player-character. Servant may not be a particularly politically correct word, but it adequately describes them. Sometimes they're friends, sometimes superior officers, but basically they're here to serve. Unlike sidekicks, they often do not follow the protagonist around. We'll find them back at headquarters researching leads or clues the player-character uncovers, or offering additional exposition or gameplay tips like Bentley and Murray in *Sly Cooper and the Thievius*

Raccoonus. Another is Lambert, the Third Echelon teammate of Sam Fisher in *Tom Clancy's Splinter Cell*. Bentley and Murray are delightful characters in their own right. There is no more to laconic Lambert than the world-weary attitudes he shares with Fisher. He's there as a servant, nothing more.

You can already see where I'm going with this. There is no reason not to flesh out a servant character. Bentley and Murray aren't three-dimensional, but they don't need to be. They are essentially minor characters, removed for the most part from the developing storyline of the game, although they show up in connective tissue cut scenes, and Murray does get into the act at one point. In Chapter 3 I suggested a number of ways to bring them to life without complete psychological and sociological workups. In comedy we can sometimes get by with less effort on characterizations, relying on distinct variations on established personality types, as long as we're careful not to leave them as simple stereotypes.

Pets are yet another link down the food chain. Don't worry; it's not a long chain. We're almost done. We run across them mostly in virtual worlds. Pets can be summoned by enchanters as in *Dark Age of Camelot*, or tamed by Creature Handlers in Star *Wars Galaxies*. Right now they're almost entirely functional, and that function is to kill other creatures. One idea that has been making the rounds is to increase their functionality by allowing them to carry a portion of the player-character's inventory. Another is to train them to loot mobs killed by the player-character. Both are sensible ideas, and as we know, every time you add to an NPC's functionality you are expanding her character.

But let's look at how Disney handles pets: Aladdin's monkey, Abu, or Jafar's parrot Iago (he turns up in the strangest places!) in *Aladdin*; or Flounder and Sebastian, Ariel's companions in *The Little Mermaid*. Children are delighted when pets talk back; seem to be smarter than their owners; get into trouble and must be rescued; or rescue their masters and mistresses in return. Most importantly they are characterized. How hard would it be to add some character to pets in games? Not very.

Again, they are minor characters. In massively multiplayer worlds like *Star Wars Galaxies*, players can already assign dialogue to them. And as we'll see in Chapter 19, "Enabling Story in Virtual Worlds," this is one way players can contribute to character and story. It shouldn't absolve writers of virtual worlds from taking some of the task upon themselves however. And we'll return to the shared storytelling and character development burden peculiar to virtual worlds at that time.

The bottom line for this section is no matter how minor the character, it deserves the respect of the writer. Anyway we can help lift even servants and pets out of stereotypes or mindless automatons the better.

Merchants

We see them in most RPGS and all virtual worlds with the anomalous exception of the dead world of *Asheron's Call 2*. In an early *Ultima* RPG, merchants were portrayed as having lives and loyalties of their own. For the most part, we have lost that in MMORPGs. They are called by various names, consigners and pawnbrokers in *Horizons* for example, where they are nothing more than a menu of items to buy or sell. In *Dark Age of Camelot*, however, they are evolved a bit more. Here merchants participate in the benign half of the Chinese-menu quest system that is at the lowest rung of *DAoC's* quest hierarchy. They are either the giver of a FedEx item, or the receiver, as well as buying and selling. Occasionally, they even have non-errand quests to dole out. One step at least up the evolutionary ladder.

In *The Gryphon Tapestry*, however, merchants were inhabitants of the world, not just functionaries. In addition to buying and selling items, they handed out quests; gossiped; and sometimes trained players in new skills. This alone increases their worth as characters, but we tried to go farther, and individualize each one, so that a tavern keeper in one village had a distinct personality from his counterpart in another village. This made the world seem all the more real, and the characters in it more like living individuals than cardboard cutouts scattered across the map.

Again, even if a character's only function is that of a merchant, there is no reason whatsoever not to respect that character enough to give him a life of his own.

Trainers

As I've shown, NPCs can and should wear many hats. It's an easy aid to fleshing them out into fully realized characters. As stated earlier, mentors might be trainers. So can merchants. So can NPCs who teach their own profession like swordsmen, musicians, healers, and cooks.

In many single-player games, trainers are usually fairly limited in number, if they exist at all. If a player is able to choose the type of role she is going to play, only that type of training is necessary.

In a virtual world there can be many paths to greatness, and many trainers may be needed as a result. Individual players may choose from a smorgasbord of classes and professions. In some, players may be able to train in many different disciplines, adding to skills as necessary, or even shedding those they no longer need.

Often players just receive new skills automatically at the completion of a level or a quest. In Chapter 5 we'll explore alternatives to this bare bones approach. But it's worthwhile here to point out that dispensing with trainers robs us of the opportunity to create interesting characters and relationships to bring our stories to life.

Quest Givers

There are many functions NPCs can have. But none of them need exist only as stereotypes or as mannequins cut and pasted from town to town in a game. Writers! Don't let programmers convince your producers that cutting and pasting is a great way to save disk space. It allows the seams to show. It harms immersion. It limits storytelling and rich characters. Don't give in! *Dungeon Siege*, a very typical RPG that was famously not all that interested in depth of character or story, at least personalized characters across its large, if linear, world. If they can do it, anybody can.

Even though this topic is called Quest Givers, I include mission-assigners as well. Missions are simply the more modern version of the quest. Quests and missions are very important to us as storytellers, and I'll discuss them in detail in Chapter 10, "Charting New Territory."

Since quests are one of the most important tools at the storyteller's disposal, it should follow that quest-givers are some of the most important characters we can write. This is true because quest-givers provide us with an opportunity for consistency. And consistency helps make our worlds all the more believable to our players.

Whether single-player or multiplayer, our worlds must make some sort of logical sense or our players will be lost. If we have real pirates suddenly showing up at a high school prom, we'd better have a damn good explanation for how they got there.

We must remember to keep the quests *consistent* with the character giving them, and hopefully with the player-character as well. *Dark Age of Camelot* is set in a basic medieval/fantasy universe. Yet, in a single quest, I encountered two NPCs who used the decidedly non-medieval/fantasy phrase "do a number on." This comes to us from modern organized crime, not medieval fantasy.

Tolkien never wrote dialogue for Saruman like, "I'll gather up my orc armies and do a number on the Riders of Rohan." If it's inconceivable to the man who single-handedly codified the mythology that is the basis for *Dungeons & Dragons* to write a line of dialogue like this, it should be inconceivable to the writers of *Dark Age of Camelot*. They don't have to be as good writers as he was, but the lead writer at least should have caught this. So, even though quest givers or mission-assigners may be minor characters, they are due their author's respect. Give them some life of their own, and keep the quests they hand out consistent with their characters. Don't allow warriors to hand out mage quests, or quartermasters to hand out search and destroy missions.

Time now to move on to character traits, those that can be shared by all characters, and those specific to certain types.

CHAPTER 5

Character Traits

The player-character and the NPCs who inhabit the game world have common traits as well as qualities that are distinct. When we discuss mobility in this chapter we will be primarily talking about the mobility of non-player-characters. When we discuss character emotion and memory, only NPCs are covered. Player emotions will be examined in Chapter 11, "Story Anatomy." The remaining topics are shared equally. Skills and professions can be available to both, and both are revealed through action. In the section called "Characters in Opposition," we begin to explore relationships between characters: relationships NPCs have with each other, and between player-characters and NPCs. Here we'll confine ourselves to the reasons behind establishing relationships for dramatic purposes. In Chapter 6, "Character Encounters," we'll look at ways to bring these relationships to life within the game.

Mobility

Static NPCs, those that stand in one place throughout the entire game, are convenient for both players and programmers. Players like to know that their favorite auto mechanic or weaponsmith will always be available when they're needed. Some NPCs may not even inhabit the interactive space of the game's world, appearing only as images on communication devices within the world, or on the game's interface, although even then some contextual explanation for their presence on the interface is usually desirable. For example, if the part of the interface where the character appears represents a communication device.

Hybrid NPCs might also show up as static characters in the game world, and only become truly mobile in cut scenes. While this helps bring motion (and possibly emotion) into the world, it does so at the expense of making the player even more aware of how different cut scenes are from the rest of the game, a problem we will tackle later on.

As we saw in Chapter 4, "Character Roles," populating the world brings it alive, and while static NPCs—particularly articulate ones—can help, even those whose rightful place may be behind a store counter can feel mechanical to the player, and detrimental to immersion. Part of the solution to this is to write them as distinct characters. Another part of the solution is to also add NPCs who can move about, whether in a localized space, or throughout the world of the game.

Controlling the Space

On the surface, the two-character play *Oleanna* by David Mamet is about a charge of sexual harassment against a college professor by a female student. Actually, it is about a struggle for power. The play is set in the professor's office. As directed in the beginning, he is seated behind his desk, and the student is perched uncomfortably on a utilitarian chair. As the play progresses, the ebb and flow of the power struggle finally begins to tip decisively toward the student until at the end she is comfortably ensconced in his chair, and he is shifting uneasily in the other chair.

Figure 5.1 *Oleanna*, a struggle for control of turf.

Direction in theatre is all about positioning the characters within the space bounded by the set. The most rudimentary task facing the director is establishing sightlines so the entire audience can follow the action.

Allowing the audience to follow the natural course of the action is important in film as well. Orson Welles, concerned about producer Al Zugsmith's penchant for re-editing his directors' work, staged many scenes in *Touch of Evil*, all in single master shots or establishing shots that showed the entire scene at once. He supplied virtually no *coverage*, that is, additional shots like close-ups, or two-shots; instead, he orchestrated his actors to step in close to the camera for those angles. If the producer had tried to cut out pieces of these scenes, the result would be jarring *jump* cuts that disrupted the continuity of the scene.

Next the director must be aware of the aesthetics of composition to add visual interest to what the audience is watching. There are a lot of characters onstage when Brutus and his fellow conspirators assassinate *Julius Caesar* in Shakespeare's play, and when Marc Antony delivers his famous funeral speech:

> Friends, Romans, countrymen, lend me your ears;
> I come to bury Caesar, not to praise him.
> The evil that men do lives after them;
> The good is oft interred with their bones.

Figure 5.2 Orson Welles arranges his actors with far more precision than his tie.

The director must carefully arrange a composition that, unlike a painting, is fluid, changing from one moment to the next. Without this care, the crowd becomes a featureless rabble, and detracts rather than adds to the drama. Notice how in Figure 5.3 director Joseph Mankewicz uses the height of his set as well as depth to compose the scene in his film version of *Julius Caesar*.

Figure 5.3 Marlon Brando as Marc Antony in the film version of Julius Caesar.

We don't like stairs very much in video games. They can either add the necessity for additional character animation, or make our characters look funky going up and down if we avoid extra animations. Ramps are a slight improvement, and the opportunities for more interesting compositions make the effort to include height as well as depth of scene worthwhile. The balcony scene from *Romeo and Juliet* would be drastically changed if Juliet happened to live on the ground floor, not to mention that the physical side of their relationship might have progressed much faster!

And, as in the example from *Oleanna*, directors must also be aware of the shifting balances of emotion, and relationships between characters that can be expressed through staging. A character who stands when another sits is in a dominant position. A character who moves uncomfortably close to another is being aggressive. A character who doesn't look at those sharing the same stage is considered aloof (or may just be preparing for a soliloquy, of course!). We recognize these actions on an instinctive level. We see them often enough in real life. And there is a more primitive instinct at work buried in our unconscious. We know what it means when the defeated wolf exposes its neck for the killing bite.

We can use this instinctive awareness of the significance of certain spatial relationships between characters in games to add emotion and dramatic tension to our scenes. It is particularly important because our characters are not always as expressive as live human beings. And resorting to cutting in for close-ups can disrupt the flow of the action. Instead of relying on cut scenes to establish relationships, we can use these techniques borrowed from theatre and film to suggest those relationships even as the player remains in control of the player-character.

For example, an NPC who cowers away from us, doesn't have to tell the player he's fearful. We can see that he is. (See "Exposition in Action" in Chapter 9 for other ways to show players things they need to know without burdening them with lengthy text passages.)

An irritating NPC can attach himself to us like the talkative bore, Noober, in the village of Nashkel in Baldur's Gate. Granting the name is an immersion-damaging play on the word *n00b*, the idea is still a good one.

note

N00b: derived from the word newbie, meaning a newcomer in a multiplayer game. Newbie became noob, then evolved into n00b with the replacement of the o's with zeros in *d00dspeak*.

note

D00dspeak: a pseudo-language that has developed in multiplayer gaming and elsewhere on the internet, originally intended to get around language filters. It is now in general usage among a certain segment of the internet population. It is characterized by deliberate misspellings like "teh" instead of "the" and the use of numbers in place of letters as in "phat l00t" which means "spoils of war that are of exceptional quality."

An aggressive NPC in a first-person shooter might step in close to the player-character—even try to back us into a corner, instead of simply opening fire when he spots us.

Imagine the player is Alice, and she desperately needs information from a white rabbit who is constantly disappearing around corners and down dark holes. Here the NPC's mobility becomes a puzzle.

Leaving the Space

> . . . before her was another long passage, and the White Rabbit was still in sight, hurrying down it. There was not a moment to be lost: away went Alice like the wind, and was just in time to hear it say, as it turned a corner, 'Oh my ears and whiskers, how late it's getting!' She was close behind it when she turned the corner, but the rabbit was no longer to be seen . . .
>
> —Lewis Carroll, *Alice's Adventures in Wonderland*

The mobility of the player-character is taken for granted. This is the character we move through the game after all. We may give her all sorts of transportation options, which, if consistent with the game world, enforce the reality of that world, and the stories we mean to tell there. We can also alter her natural mobility in interesting ways.

In addition we can give insight into the character or increase suspense by removing that mobility to a greater or lesser degree. One of the most famous examples of this in films is LB Jeffries, James Stewart's character in Hitchcock's *Rear Window*, a globe-trotting photographer suddenly confined to a wheelchair by a broken leg. It is due to this temporary physical disability that his restlessness, his insatiable curiosity, and his high tech lenses turn him into a peeping tom, and witness to a possible murder. Another example is small, crippled ex-jockey, Sid Halley, in the best-selling mystery books by Dick Francis.

Figure 5.4 A cast on Jimmy Stewart's leg leads to the arrest of a killer.

Just as we saw *Ico*'s horns as a catalyst for the game's action, Princess Yorda's *lack* of mobility makes her dependent on the player-character and offers the player a unique set of challenges. In terms of story, it places her life in Ico's hands. In terms of gameplay, it offers a unique variation on physical puzzles. The player must ensure *both* Ico and Yorda surmount each hazard.

The player-character can have his mobility affected in any number of ways. It can slow him down or speed him up. He may be able to swim or not. He may be blind or corpulent or incredibly thin. Not only do these kinds of choices suggest gameplay, they obviously are a part of the physical dimension of a character.

In *Dark Age of Camelot*, Blanche, an NPC merchant of the city Tir na Nog, periodically deserts her post to go have a quick pint in a nearby pub. In that same game, NPCs called Filidhs (the name in ancient Irish law for the professional bardic class who were more schooled than ordinary bards) stroll from town to town in Hibernia, informing players who ask of various quests they have heard of in the vicinity. The game does a check on the player's list of completed quests, so that the Filidh only mentions quests new to the player. NPCs who do not remain stationary bring otherwise static areas to life; help characterize and separate game locales; and they are far easier on game engines than windblown trees and rippling water.

In the early days of *Everquest* one of the best items in the game was a pair of boots called Journeyman Boots that granted their wearer increased speed, very handy for getting across vast continents, or escaping from dangerous creatures, especially for characters who had no ability to cast speed spells. The key to the quest for obtaining the Journeyman Boots was to talk to a gnome NPC named Hasten Bootstrutter who was said to frequent the Rathe Mountains. Two problems made the quest difficult. The first was that Hasten, like many *Everquest* quest NPCs did not put in an appearance very often. And when he did, he did so swiftly, speeding from place to place, stopping only briefly, then speeding on.

This second problem was ingenious because it not only increased the difficulty of the quest, but it was in keeping with Hasten's character, as obviously was his name. So here an NPC's mobility becomes part of a puzzle. And this can be found in other puzzles and quests where an NPC will only appear at a designated place at a certain hour, or moves through the game world from location to location. We'll catch up with Hasten again in Chapter 19, "Enabling Story in Virtual Worlds," by the way.

Homer wrote epic poems, as we know, not sonnets or haiku. One of the important features of the epic style is the reappearance of characters throughout the telling of the story. And it suits games beautifully. As we move from level to level or location to location the reappearance of a character gives us:

- A sense of mobility even if the characters are essentially static. This character could still be, for the most part, static, moving only in the sense that she appears at different places in the game world at different times in the story. Here's an art-cheap solution to NPC mobility!

- An opportunity to advance the NPC's character. The more times a character appears, the more subtle can the growth or the development of the character be.

- An opportunity to advance or alter her relationship to the player-character. NPCs can show up from level to level, their relationship to the player-character altering as the player progresses. A lowly informer from level one may have his life saved by the player-character in level four, and then be driven to help the player-character for free in level seven.

- An opportunity for foreshadowing. The NPC can appear Cassandra-like to warn of dark perils ahead.

- An opportunity for recap as the NPC congratulates the player on past deeds.

- The comforting presence of a familiar face in alien surroundings. Game space can be extremely literal in small areas, but disorienting across levels or far-flung locations. The familiar NPC can help anchor or orient the player to a new setting.

- A feeling of fateful inevitability that can add to pace. In the odd pseudo-spaghetti western *Hannie Calder*, starring Raquel Welch, actor Stephen Boyd plays an enigmatic character known only as "The Man in Black" who appears at key dramatic moments. The audience knows he must be significant, but must wait until the very end of the movie to learn what that significance is. (No, he's not a film critic.) This takes us into Carl Jung symbolic territory, that shadowy realm we'll look at briefly in Chapter 8, "Respecting Story."

- A way to cut down on the number of characters in the game that must be drawn. A re-occurring character can provide the exposition and services that might have been rendered by several characters before the game started to strain the perimeter of the project budget.

In some games, NPCs can be truly mobile. This is unavoidable in the literal space of a virtual world. If an NPC needs to get somewhere, and the player-character is standing there watching, the NPC must make at least the pretext of a graceful exit before teleporting to his next appearance. In other games, NPCs can be just as literal as the world, and can be followed like Hasten in *Everquest*.

If we as designers don't want that character followed, yet still want to maintain the verisimilitude of our world, we have to find some obstacle to place in front of stalker player-characters: a door slammed in the player-character's face; NPC speed greater than the PC's, so she just out-distances him; or allowing the NPC to jump into the only cab in sight are examples of obstacles that help maintain the fiction of the game world.

So, we can use the mobility of characters in any numbers of ways. A static world is a dead world. Mobile characters bring it to life. The type of mobility can add to both character dimension and story. What other traits add to gameplay, contribute to story, and illuminate character?

Physical Skills

In simulations with story added, we get "you are a crack helicopter pilot" and then you must learn from scratch, crashing often. The same is true in many types of games, as we saw in the *Lunar Lander* example from *The Dig*. It is one of the most fiction-destroying conflicts between character and gameplay we come across. Players of simulations are much more forgiving of this paradox than players of action games who expect to be proficient with all sorts of exotic firepower as soon as they find a new weapon. We'll address the special case of simulations later, but in all other types of games we must make allowances for players' true skills, and simplify for them, or all those crashes will stop the story dead and could make them come to hate their avatar.

Once we make the choice to simplify real world mechanics in favor of gameplay mechanics we're faced with another challenge. The skills must be in character and in the context of the game world. Most games handle this well in terms of gameplay at the expense of character and immersion.

Skills are the bedrock of the development of the player-character in action games. The PC can learn special new moves as well as find new tools and weapons. Often these moves are generic, e.g. an elaborate circling kick common to martial arts. Hopefully they are in character for the PC such as Sly Cooper's special moves like sidling along a narrow ledge. They serve a double function: a reward for completing a level and almost certainly will be needed to overcome an obstacle later in the game.

In role-playing games, there are complicated trees of skills, often charted in the game or as a nicely printed insert in the box. These skills are, at first glance, vastly different from one another depending upon the type of character the player has chosen to play, his profession, and racial characteristics. We'll discuss race, as it is used in computer games in a moment.

Without doubt, some skills can be unique. A warrior in most RPGs lacks the ability to heal, and most mages cannot wear the heavy armor of warriors. Still, many skills have counterparts in all characters. In virtual worlds, this is done for play balance reasons, so that while players can appear to select a vast array of races, professions, and skills, in fact they are often selecting little more than different names and character graphics.

One way to enhance character is often overlooked when special skills are applied in most games. Story and gameplay are very different. Game designers have a natural tendency (being gamers more often than they are writers) to introduce skills only as part of gameplay. The player is told at the end of a level—often in a line of text ending in an exclamation mark—that she has learned "Critical Strike III!" or "a new language: Grislik! Now you can speak to Grisls!" This is an easy (and cheap!) way of informing the player, and usually makes sense in terms of gameplay even as it destroys the illusion that the player-character is having adventures in a real world.

It's like one of those TV commercials where a disembodied announcer suddenly speaks to a character alone in his own home. This has been a convention of commercials since advertisements first started appearing in print, and the pictured character spoke directly to the reader. It works fine in commercials—although these days the convention is often mocked even as it's being used—but has no place when we're trying to preserve the fiction of the world, and it passes up a golden opportunity for character growth or development.

Without much additional effort, the special move or skill can be tied to the player-character more closely. It can be magically granted or taught by a mentor or other character who has a relationship with the player-character. It can be an undiscovered or even better an *under-developed* talent that the player-character becomes more proficient in as it is used.

Now couple this with a delivery system that doesn't harm the fiction of the game world. Many games use NPCs as trainers already. But who wants to stop their progress in the game and go off to train someplace for even a few minutes? They shouldn't have to. A simple change of the game text from "Congratulations! You've just learned a new skill: Crêpe Making!" to "A Cordon Bleu chef has consented to teach you how to properly prepare crêpes!" works fine. In Chapter 6, "Character Encounters," we'll see how to develop this specific relationship between player-characters and "trainer" NPCs, as well as other relationships.

Skills can be added to NPCs as well as player-characters. We see this all the time in games like *Dungeon Siege* and *X-Com: UFO Defense*, where NPCs who either join the player-character or are controlled by the player gain skills and power as long as they survive in the game.

In action games, mobs get increasingly more difficult. Why? Because the challenge must be increased. But why introduce bigger monsters every level? Why can't the surviving monsters from a previous level go running to *their* mentors and demand to be taught skills to counter the player's own?

Dungeon Keeper gave an entirely new perspective to action and strategy games. It was a wicked role-reversal game where players actually controlled all those mobs we are usually mowing down. We don't need to go that far every time. But giving mobs players who have already been defeated the opportunity

Figure 5.5 Monsters finally have their day in *Dungeon Keeper*.

for revenge is far more interesting and respectful of world fiction than just re-spawning them. Allowing them to come back for more, armed with new skills, also gives us the chance to grow and develop them as characters. This personalizes the battle, and increases the tension in the same way the *Halloween* series' Michael Meyers had the ability to bounce back from axe blows, fire, hanging, and all sorts of other grisly attacks that would have finished many a good monster.

New skills can be applied to any NPC: sidekick, mentor, major or minor character; and is an easy way to add dimension to their characters.

Professions

For NPCs, roles, such as merchant that I talked about in the previous chapter, and professions are really one and the same. Quest Giver is a role, but not a profession. Trainers can be both. The teacher of a skill may do it for a living, having never actually been required to practice what he preaches. An interesting facet of LT Bonham, Tommy Lee Jones' character in *The Hunted*, is that while he was an exceptional trainer of killers, he had never killed anyone. We also have enough examples of people who weren't talented enough to be successful at a skill that they teach it instead to inspire the derogatory comment "Those who can, do. Those who can't, teach." This is attributed to that caustic observer of humankind, George Bernard Shaw, a friend of William Archer. The actual quote from *Man and Superman* reads "He who can, does. He who cannot, teaches."

Ironically, William Archer was himself a failed playwright. Archer puts it a bit more kindly: "Assuredly, if I had the power, I should write plays instead of writing about them; but one may have a great love for an art, and some insight into its principles and methods, without the innate faculty required for actual production."

Some trainers can be both teacher and practitioner. It is common to find a tennis coach or *agility* instructor who also competes. In agility, in fact, almost without exception, all trainers also run their dogs in competition.

note

AGILITY TRAINING: the form of dog training that teaches dogs to run courses of obstacles like teeter-totters and weave poles. Scores are based on speed and how well the obstacles are handled.

Some NPCs have professions to serve their characters or the story, but have no specific role in gameplay terms. Traditionally, these characters are confined in cut scenes or are limited in their interaction with the player-character. A good example is Kane from *Command & Conquer* who remains removed from the gameplay, working his villainy in cut scenes.

Electronic Arts

Figure 5.6 Kane commands in *Command and Conquer,* but only in cut scenes.

However, to segregate characters in cut scenes, or other non-functional parts of the game, makes little sense. One of the things that sets our characters apart from those in other media is that ours can serve gameplay as well as story. Writing characters who only perform one function is to not respect them. They are being wasted.

As I said in the introduction, creating a game with story in it is an adventure in balance. Both gameplay and story deserve equal attention. If one doesn't get its due, that component will feel weak. It's a vicious circle. Create enough games with weak story and people will begin to think stories in games *must* be weak. Stories need the support of characters. And since those characters can be used to support gameplay it is a shame to squander them.

Race

Race in RPGs does not mean Asian, Black, Caucasian, or Hispanic, but is used to differentiate between human and non-human sentient beings such as elves, dwarves, lizards, ants, and so on. Each race is traditionally given certain unique characteristics: both strengths and weaknesses. Traditionally, some are better suited to certain professions; for instance, elves are presumed to be better archers, thanks to J.R.R. Tokien; and ant-like creatures can be super-productive like the Klackons in the *Master of Orion* series of strategy games.

That is not to say that players cannot choose to play humanoid characters with skin color and other features to duplicate the appearance of human races. This is often allowed in RPGs, especially their multiplayer versions, so that players can differentiate how they look from one another. Some players choose to mimic how they look in real life. Detailed character selection processes—*Star Wars Galaxies* has one of the most flexible—allow for a huge range of looks.

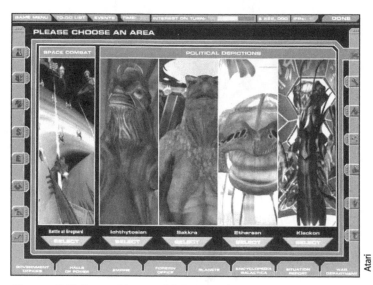

Figure 5.7 Races *Master of Orion III* style.

Relationships between races are most often carefully distanced from life here in our real world. Racial differences, even animosities, are easier to deal with when we're talking about lizards and cat people. One exception to this is *Earth & Beyond*'s racial animosities, which, even among aliens, bear more than a passing resemblance to our own troubled planet.

For most games, the argument goes that we're creating games here that are fun to play. And in virtual worlds, there are very real risks of tension between players. I remember when *World War II Online* was in beta that there was publicity and concern over the fact that some players wanted to know if they could play Nazis, and would there be concentration camps.

Pussy-footing around race in single-player games though is only to cut us writers and players off from the grand diversity that racial and cultural differences can provide us. Games often disguise the ethnic and cultural aspects of their characters, particularly when they are villains, much in the way we were censored in the 1970s in television when we attempted to portray organized crime. So we ended up with a lot of characters with New York and New Jersey accents with last names like Smith, Graham, or Robinson. I remember writing an episode of *Charlie's Angels*, and to satirize this censorship I made the criminal organization a men's club. It was changed by that episode's producer back to the typical white bread crime syndicate of the era. Of course, today we have the hit TV series *The Sopranos*, so times do change.

Grand Theft Auto: Vice City is a notable exception, but the game's developer, Rockstar, was the subject of protests from Haitian-American groups for their portrayal of Haitian gangsters. Rockstar responded that the protest was focusing on remarks made by fictional characters from a rival Cuban gang, and taken out of context. Both the protest and the defense are borderline for me. I'd like to see more genuine racial differences in games simply because of the opportunities for characterization and conflict they present. But I do think a major proviso is in order.

Avoid stereotypes! Here is another reason for taking the time to create fully rounded characters. I don't think we need to artificially balance characters, another restriction imposed on television in the past. If we have a Black villain, we don't necessarily need his exact counterpart on the side of law and order. But we need characters who live and breathe, not just function as villain or police officer.

We shouldn't make games to lecture to our audience. They are meant to entertain. But we have the ability to influence that audience in innumerable ways. I'm straying into territory covered in Chapter 20 here. I'll leave you with a last thought. Writers who think about these things must answer this question: "Do we portray society as it is, or as we might like it to be?" Each of us must answer that question in our own way. Whatever the answer, we do owe it to our characters, our audiences, and ourselves to approach the issue with the concern it deserves. And the same concern for race also occupies us when we discuss sex.

Sex

No, I'm not going to help you write better sex scenes here. Sorry. I'm talking about how games treat the sexes differently.

I'll mention stereotypes again. Don't write them! Even if they are drawn that way! A big step toward respecting characters is to respect the human beings they are modeled on.

Game publishers face a dilemma. While the demographic is changing, the primary market for video games in most game types remains young and male. Young heterosexual males like to look at sexy women. So whenever we see female characters, they are scantily clad and abundantly endowed in every ad, and on every box. Again *Star Wars Galaxies* deserves mention for allowing players to create female characters with far more diverse looks than usual. Too bad all the dancers were forced to dress like they belonged in topless bars.

Yet publishers want to grow their market. How do they do that without turning off their main constituency? Would Lara Croft have been as big a hit, if she'd looked more like Marian the Librarian? Probably not. Men and women both like to identify with preternaturally fit and attractive characters in movies, and in games they like to play them.

Figure 5.8a Lara Croft in *Tomb Raider II*.

Figure 5.8b *Lineage II*. No stereotypes here at all.

Figure 5.8c Female character in "full armor" from *Everquest II*.

Figure 5.8d Eowen's armor in *Return of the King* is a bit more practical.

It's easy to create NPCs who are not so blessed. After all "pleasantly plump" Bess was Nancy Drew's sidekick, not the lead sleuth. And we have plenty of examples of NPCs in computer games who are less than gorgeous, although they usually are mentors, sidekicks, villains, and the like. What do we do with the player-character?

We took some criticism in *Dark Side of the Moon* for our player-character Jake Wright even though it was a first person game and Jake was never seen. Some reviewers, and players too, thought he was voiced too wimpily. We wanted him to start out at least as an uncertain young man to give him room to grow, but never got him to the point where his voice matched his later heroic actions. This would not have been as much of a problem, I think, but because you can't see the character in a first person game, you are forced to rely solely on voice performance.

Any game that gives players the choice to create a male or female gives us an additional thing to think about. The male and female characters are often graphically different. But they are always functionally identical. We'll see in Chapters 18 and 19 how virtual worlds have so many things to balance. This was an easy decision to make. It meant that there would be fewer protests from either sex that their characters are being discriminated against. But single-player games could be designed so that the differences between females and males could be used to differentiate how each sex attacks the obstacles in the game.

I'm not saying Lara would be a better character if we took her guns away from her. But if a player wants to play a female character who can overcome obstacles with skills that rely more on intellect or diplomacy, why not? (And the same holds true for male characters as well.)

Other media gives us a whole range of lead female characters who are strong. Let's stay away from art and literature and focus on genre fiction since that is what most popular entertainment is all about. Genre fiction requires strong heroes, even if their strength is at first hard to find.

Films have their swordwielders like Miranda Otto, Eowen in *Return of the King*, and their gun-toters like Jodie Foster's Clarice Starling in *Silence of the Lambs*, and all the martial arts women in *Crouching Tiger, Hidden Dragon*. But these women have a lot more going for them than their abilities with weapons. Many of them also manage time for the romance often required of them, although Clarice is really just in love with her job. In contrast, look at how superficially the romance in the second Lara Croft film is handled, and how little we care about the characters in general. The film is true to its computer game roots.

The *Alien* series features tough-as-nails Ripley. But the same actress, Sigourney Weaver, was also the agoraphobic psychologist in *Copycat*, Dian Fossey in *Gorillas in the Mist*, and a strong first lady in *Dave*. Look how Jamie Lee Curtis's spunky Laurie Strode, who is basically only fighting for her life in *Halloween*, becomes the tormented woman who finally takes the fight to Michael Meyers in *Halloween H20: 20 Years Later*.

All of these female characters could find a home in computer games. Games should be able to do the same: give us female player-characters who are skilled and fun to play even if they are not superwomen. And female characters in general deserve more care than deciding how much cleavage they show. We need to ask ourselves how to make them attractive *characters* even if they are not so stereotypically conceived. The physical dimension is the easy one. That also means it's easy to rely on it too heavily. Once we make the effort to reveal their psychological and sociological dimensions, the physical dimension regains its proper stature equal to the others.

Male characters suffer from a lack of respect, too. There are no shortage of male stereotypes in games from killing machine player-characters to one-note villains, and all deserve more thinking by their creators. But there are abundant numbers of male heroes, a few women. And the wide range possible in both sexes can pave the way to fuller, richer characters.

Eowen's stand against the nasgul is all the more thrilling because we've seen what she is capable of beyond swordplay in her helping the people she will one day lead; her unquestioning defense of her sometimes less than kingly father; and her obvious love for Aragorn. Because we have been allowed to see these other facets of her character there is more at stake, and the climactic battle becomes emotionally charged on all sorts of levels beyond the visceral.

New Line Cinema

Figure 5.9 Another side of Eowen.

Character Emotion

We writers deal with two types of emotions. There is the emotion we hopefully generate in our audience. We'll talk about what our audience, the player, is feeling in Chapter 11. Here we are going to look at the emotions of our characters.

In *Earth & Beyond* there is a Jenquai quest from an NPC you've previously gone on a quest for. This time you're informed that a Progen shipment of weapons needs to be intercepted. Jenquais and Progens have a long history of conflict, and there is little love lost on either side. You go to the coordinates given and sure enough there is a ship there, but its captain claims it is not carrying weapons but children. Is he telling the truth? If he is, then do you withdraw, or blow him out of the sky anyway? I chose to let him go and returned to the NPC who was furious with me, calling the children of our enemies "weapons." It is a beautiful example of an NPC revealing character through emotion in response to a player's actions.

As we saw in *Lara Croft II: The Cradle of Life*, just going through the motion of emotion is not enough. Emotion doesn't just happen in our characters. We can't pick and choose from a shopping list of emotions and expect them to feel real. This leads to stereotypes and clichés. Emotion must be prepared for in a character's creation, and invoke the actions that character takes.

Sometimes the lack of emotion can be equally compelling. We have the extreme of the heartless, soulless killer in dead teenager movies because relentless evil is, on the surface at least, more dramatic than the petty evil of an embezzler. Yet when such evil is combined with the mundane character, the result is even more gripping. In *Devil in the White City*,

Erik Larson's bestselling account of the 1893 Chicago World's Fair, we meet H.H. Holmes, one of the most prolific serial killers of all time. Larson contrasts the remarkable architectural and construction effort that went into creating this wonder of the age with Holmes' methodical building of his hotel complete with private gas chamber and crematorium. Holmes was no flamboyant Hannibal the Cannibal. He was a pharmacist, fussy, quiet, and reserved; and he went about his business with a deliberate precision that matched the fair's builders.

When more emotion is called for, it cannot be dragged out of the bleachers just because the story demands it. The characters, if three-dimensional, have the seeds of emotion planted within them. The emotion is inevitable because of who they are. The film *Mystic River* proceeds with an inevitability that is overtly on display for most characters, and for the most part, they work beautifully, with the possible exception of Annabeth Marcus, played by Laura Linney. She has a chilling turn at the end of the film that while it may explain why she stays with her husband (Sean Penn), still feels like little more than a shocking surprise.

Emotion is prepared for not only with character growth, but with its development too. A character can hold the emotion inside longer and longer, letting it build until it must erupt like lava from a dormant volcano. I wrote earlier about a character on *Edge of Night* who I killed off. Her name was Nicole Cavanaugh. Her husband Miles did not allow himself to grieve for her, keeping his emotions locked inside for a week's worth of shows at least. He fends off his friends who offer various shoulders to cry upon. The audience was thrown by this usually compassionate doctor who could get very emotional about helping his patients, but who seemingly refused to mourn his dead wife. He remains as unmoved as a head on Mount Rushmore until one night, alone on his apartment's balcony, his emotion bursts forth as *anger* at Nicole's leaving him. Once he could deal with his anger, and all the conflicting emotions it produced in him, he could begin the process of mourning and healing.

With the proper background, growth, and development, a character is finally ready to experience the emotions that draw an audience, our players, into the story of our game. They can't then just occur. There is still another step, and that is we must choose the correct moment for their release. Mistimed emotion can be as ugly as unprepared–for emotion.

Characters in Opposition

Characters can experience a range of emotions in solitude. But drama is most often achieved when characters collide.

Conflict

Conflict has several definitions, all of them relevant.

note

CONFLICT: Webster says conflict is 1) A state of open, prolonged fighting: warfare. 2) A state of disharmony: clash. 3) The opposition or simultaneous functioning of mutually exclusive impulses, desires or tendencies. 4) A collision.

That third definition is interesting. Conflict can occur *within* characters as well as *between* them. For the most part we'll be considering conflict between characters, but it is good to be aware of the potential for interior conflict, as *Hamlet* has shown us.

Lajos Egri states "Conflict is the heartbeat of all writing." And "Since most of us . . . hide our true selves from the world, we are interested in witnessing the things happening to those who are forced to reveal their true characters under the stress of conflict."

William Archer is blunter: ". . . we need go no further than the simple psychological observation that human nature loves a fight, whether it be with clubs or with swords, with tongues or with brains." (Games have the first one down anyway!)

It is not enough to set up a single conflict and let the player-character bang up against it over and over again. Conflict is seeded through the story in much the same way that clouds are seeded to provide rain. As the characters progress, the stakes of each conflict should rise. This can't be done artificially. "Oh! Almost at the end of the fourth level! Time for another conflict!" Egri calls unmotivated conflicts like these "jumps." Conflict jumps are as distracting to an audience as jump cuts are in a film. Rising conflict grows naturally as strong characters grow in the intensity of their opposition toward one another.

Figure 5.10 Characters at war in Edward Albee's *Who's Afraid of Virginia Woolf?*

Egri: "In a play, each conflict causes the one after it. Each is more intense than the one before. The play moves, propelled by the conflict created by the characters in their desire to reach their goal."

Here is another solid reason to develop characters and story along with the gameplay. Now narrative and gameplay are not at war with one another, but working in concert. If they are created together, puzzles don't appear out of thin air; NPCs won't arbitrarily show up as obstacles, and boss mobs won't just attack because it is the end of a level.

Again we see story and gameplay complementing each other. This is great for a game design, but we don't want all our characters getting along so well! How do we prevent that and ensure there will be plenty of opportunity for conflict?

Orchestration

Egri uses this term to describe the selection of characters writers make to ensure conflict in their story. He says, "When you are ready to select characters for your play, be careful to orchestrate them right. If all the characters are the same type—for instance, if all of them are bullies—it will be like an orchestra of nothing but drums."

That we should populate the world of a game with a range of characters is self-evident. Without diversity they would all get very monotonous. But simple diversity is not enough. The characters should not only be different, but orchestrated as well.

Characters can be of similar professions, religions, political persuasions, races, sexes, anything; but they shouldn't be the same *type* of people. One could be dedicated to her job, another indifferent. One could be a Mother Teresa, another a hate-filled fanatic. Both could be Republicans. One might be moderate, another a right wing ideologue. Both could be Asian. One teenager might be very traditional, another might be indistinguishable from teenagers of other races. One businesswoman might be Estée Lauder, another might be Martha Stewart.

Once we've established potential conflict, we should remember to keep the characters equally strong, as we've discussed. Strong in mind, strong in purpose. Worthy adversaries create drama in games as on the playing field. A soccer game with a winning score of 1 to 0 is much more exciting than a game with a score of 14 to 1. In the end, one side may win, or it may even be a draw. It is the getting to that inevitable conclusion that gives us our drama.

"Orchestration," Egri says, "demands well-defined and uncompromising characters in opposition, moving from one pole toward another through conflict."

Those poles are character growth. As our player-character battles the villain, the player must adapt because the villain changes. I'm not talking about artificial intelligence, but scripted adjustments that alter the playing field as the game progresses. In such a dynamic environment the possibilities for tension and surprise are infinite. And these are qualities the best stories share with the best games.

Memory

"There's rosemary, that's for remembrance."

—*William Shakespeare*

"It doesn't matter who my father was; it matters who I remember he was."

—*Anne Sexton*

Each writer has his or her own favorite theme. We come back to it as inevitably as the tide returns to shore. "Favorite" may be the wrong word. We are compelled toward these themes by all that makes us who we are. We have no choice in the matter. My theme is memory. The past and my characters' recollections of it haunts them throughout my stories.

I call such moments of memory in my writing "echoes." They can be the verbal reminiscences of characters; flashbacks; symbols; flashes of déjà vu. When Tim Robbins climbs into the wrong car for the second time in his life in *Mystic River* and turns to look out the rear window, it is a powerful echo that the audience hears on a Jungian level.

It shouldn't be surprising that I'm most generally regarded as a mystery writer since mysteries often concern themselves with buried secrets, some literally. A play I wrote, *The Man Who Came to Murder*, concerns a 1950 Plymouth resurrected by workers digging a pool in the backyard of a modern Hollywood Hills home. There is a corpse inside. My personal favorite of the episodes I wrote for *Charlie's Angels* is called "Rosemary for Remembrance." It begins in a cemetery where the above Shakespearean quote is carved on a tombstone, and that story also features the literal unearthing of an important object from the past. Fifteen years later I wrote an episode of *Star Trek: Next Generation* called "Remember Me." An epidemic of disappearances strikes the Enterprise and only one character can remember those gone, including some characters' closest friends, and most of the regular cast members.

In the computer game *The Riddle of Master Lu*, the player-character Robert Ripley visits lost civilizations, and must solve their many secrets of the past in order to survive. I've already mentioned how the mystery of Jake's past in *Dark Side of the Moon* drives him. Even in media as collaborative as TV and computer games, writers and designers can explore those themes closest to our souls.

I don't mean to suggest that everybody—or anybody!—should adapt memory as their own. But memory is an excellent way to expose backstory, reveal character, and create emotion.

I was designing a new adventure game called *Sideshow* when we decided *The Riddle of Master Lu* deserved a sequel. *Sideshow* was set aside, and financial difficulties of the company resulted in neither game being completed.

The story of *Sideshow* concerned a player-character who suffers horrific nightmare flashbacks of a childhood friend who fell to his death from a roller coaster ride. After an opening nightmare, the player-character, now an adult, arrives back in his hometown, which he has not visited in many years, to try and come to terms with the original incident, and to figure out why the nightmares have returned after so long a time.

The amusement park that made the town a tourist attraction closed soon after that accident, and the town is now struggling to stay alive. So here I had an opportunity to contrast the town of the past with the town of the present. For this purpose, I designed a button on the interface that I called a Memory Key. At any location in the game that the player-character knew, the button would glow. When the player clicked on the button he heard a voice over memory of what the location used to look like.

*   *   *

```
A1. LOOK AT DOOR OR BUILDING

                DAVID (v.o.)
Willow Falls Public Library. Growing up in a small town
like this, the only ticket we had to the rest of the
world was through that door.
```

*   *   *

This device gave me several opportunities for character, story and gameplay:

- The memories were useful in creating the contrast of the two towns, past and present.
- They provided needed exposition.
- They provoked an emotional response in both PC and player that grew over time as the player became more invested in the character.
- I could contrast the boy character with his dreams and the adult character with his nightmares, revealing character growth and development in the perspective he brought to these memories.

- Other characters would have a different recollection of past events. The player, armed with knowledge from the Memory Key, could recognize those differences.

- I was also able to include clues and items from the town's past to solve various present-day puzzles. For example, the hidden cache beneath the hideaway the boys used to play in (based on a similar hideaway I played in as a boy—write what you know!) provided the player-character with several useful tools.

One single-player design that I later adapted for a possible virtual world included generations. In essence, the player played not one, but multiple characters, three in the single-player version. In the multiplayer version, it allowed for true player death. The player really could live through his children.

This idea, of being able to play succeeding generations in the same family, fascinated me. The rites of passage . . . the memories. . . . In both designs the game engine took screen-shots of the significant moments of a player-character's life such as the battle with a spectacular opponent or the completion of an epic quest. Then in the next generation, a family album could be accessed to relive those moments and, in the multiplayer version, share them with friends.

Memories evoke powerful emotions. Whether or not your theme has anything at all to do with memory or the past—though many do it seems—memory can be an invaluable tool for writers of games.

Revealing Character Through Action

As I said in the introduction, games are an action medium. Every time we stop to make players read text, or listen to long speeches, we are essentially hitting the pause button for them. Sometimes pauses are a good thing. We want to design natural breakpoints into the game in the same way chapters break up a book or commercials divide network television into acts. Breaks between levels or rewards like the cut scenes that appear when players complete special quests in *Final Fantasy XI*, even the pause key itself, can provide a needed break in the action for those other needs gamers occasionally have like food and rest and real life.

Mostly though, a gamer whose gameplay is interrupted is an impatient gamer, and impatient gamers are unhappy gamers. A lot of writers in all media wrestle with this issue. And it's important enough that I'm focusing on it twice: once here with characters, and again in Chapter 10, "Charting New Territory," when we're studying story. It may not be possible to reveal character solely in action, but every chance we can, we should take.

In his sidebar, Noah Falstein, producer and game designer for LucasArts, Dreamworks, and many others, takes a look at revealing characters through the action of gameplay.

Noah Falstein, Writer/Designer

Do, don't show.

Every freshman writing class reiterates the admonition, "Show, don't tell". This is solid advice; it is much more engrossing to read an account that shows a character doing something interesting than to have a character or narrator simply tell the reader what happened. This applies to stories in the interactive realm as well. Some early adventure games would simply tell you that you needed to kill the evil wizard because he was—well, evil! And plus, he will enslave the world if you don't stop him! And then probably destroy it, or other evil stuff. . . . Gradually this progressed to actually show the evil wizard in an evil act, usually kidnapping a princess who was betrothed to the character you control. But with interactive storytelling, there's a transcendent principle: *do, don't show*. Build the relationships into the actions the

Figure 5.11 Noah Falstein.

player takes and the direct relationships that the player experiences through the game, not in the backstory. If you're told that a princess is in love with a dashing young adventurer, it's weak. If you're shown that she loves him in a flashback of moonlit nights of romance, or a cut-scene with her silhouetted by flickering firelight, that's a little better. But if you have her demonstrate her love by sacrificing her own freedom to save you from capture and defeat in the game, then in the parlance of Hollywood, "now it's personal." By aligning the story with the gameplay, you evoke the emotions in the player directly, without having to appeal to a sometimes vain hope of sympathy.

Examples range from the classic "Death of Floyd" in *Planetfall*, where a selfless robot helps your character—you—directly, to more recent games like *Starcraft* or *Jak & Daxter*. One of my favorites is in the first segment of *Starcraft*'s single player campaign. The player controls a character who reports to a General. The General is clearly not to be trusted, but there's no choice as the player must follow his orders. Then he abandons you at a critical moment—not in a cut scene, but in the midst of a tough battle—and you are left to fend for yourself against what seems like impossible odds. The creators of *Starcraft* could simply have told you that the General was a bad guy, or shown him strangling underlings in classic Darth Vader fashion, but it was much more effective to have him betray your proxy in the midst of gameplay, and let you suffer the effects directly by having to fight your way out of the situation. Then later in the game when the General returns to the field of battle and you're given the chance to get your revenge it is a ruthlessly satisfying resolution. By building the story arc into the gameplay itself and having the repercussions of the General's actions affect the main character that you control, the Blizzard designers and writers achieve a powerful impact. Go thou and do likewise!

First let's make sure we understand what we mean when we say action. It is not synonymous with physical activity, its common definition. Physical activity, such as sports, fighting a fire, chases, combat and so on, are action, but they are not the only type of action. We also call making a decisive decision "taking action." A commentator can describe a chess match as filled with action: two minds battling it out with move and countermove. A sharp exchange of dialogue in a courtroom drama is action.

Any one of these is an opportunity to reveal character. Let's start with physical activity since that's what action consists most of in games. In sports, we see character, or the lack of it, in every contest: the gracious victor or the player who throws his racket against a wall; the linebacker who helps up the quarterback he's just sacked or the tackler who deliberately tries to injure an opponent to take him out of the game; the boxer who waits for his opponent to climb to his feet or the one who hits below the belt; the enforcer in hockey; the cheat; the team player; the braggart; the encouraging teammate; the taunter. The list is long.

How characters face danger reveals much about them. As I write this, a firefighter in Wyoming was sentenced to ten years in prison for setting fires to create work. Contrast this with the heroism of 9/11. Compare the dead serious faces of both the pursuer and the pursued in the classic car chase in *Bullitt* with the clownish expressions of Jackie Chan in any number of chases on foot, bicycle, or in cars. Every war movie ever made fills its squad of soldiers or sailors or pilots with characters who will approach combat in many diverse ways.

We don't need monologues, voice overs, or comments from other characters. "Hey, Jim Bob! Lookit that dude drive! He really knows what he's doin'!" We can *see* he knows what he's doing. Or not. Walter Hill, writer and/or director of action movies like *48 Hours*, *Streets of Fire*, and *The Warriors* is reputed to have answered a reporter's question on character like this: "How do I write character? I have somebody stick a gun in his face and see how long it takes him to blink." Whether you agree with him or not, that's revealing character in action!

There is no need to waste a physical action scene with just action. Look at *Die Hard*, then look at all the direct-to-video clones over the years. One of the differences is in how John McClane (Bruce Willis) reveals character in almost every scene whether he is crawling through one of those ubiquitous air ducts, or pounding a terrorist to a pulp.

What about the other cases? The Cuban missile crisis reveals character in *Thirteen Days* in scene after scene of anger, fear, conflict, and decisive decisions, many of which take place in rooms with paneled walls. We want to keep our character revelation short and sweet. Remember our impatient gamer? Remember too the moment at the very beginning of the

Figure 5.12 "Enough of this running s**t." *The Warriors,* directed by Walter Hill.

movie *Air Force One* when Harrison Ford gives his speech, and the reactions of his Chief of Staff and Secretary of Defense when he diverges from his prepared remarks. A startled look and two lines of dialogue establish something very important is happening, and these two characters don't like it very much.

The battling of two minds can be full of action, little of it physical. Long before *L.A. Confidential,* Curtis Hanson wrote *The Silent Partner,* a nifty little thriller set at Christmas time in a bank at the Eaton Centre in Toronto. It so captivated me I sat through it twice in a row. The story concerns a bank teller (Elliot Gould) who realizes that a Santa Claus (Christopher Plummer) ringing a bell for charitable donations is actually casing the bank. Gould decides to rob the bank *before* Plummer can, so that Plummer will get away with only a small portion of the swag, and Gould can pocket the rest.

This happens quite early on in the movie. The rest of the film is devoted to a battle of wits between the two with remarkably little physical action. Although there are a couple of shockingly violent scenes, most of the physical action deals with sticking fingers into marmalade jars and running after garbage trucks. The true action of the film concentrates on the increasingly ingenious mind games the two play on one another once Plummer realizes what has happened; and the character layers revealed, especially in Gould's bank teller.

We don't need to eliminate physical action. Far from it. But we can certainly intersperse other types of action amidst the mayhem, and *all* action gives us a chance to reveal character.

I conclude this examination of character in the next chapter where we discuss ways to handle the encounters between player-characters and NPCs.

CHAPTER 6

CHARACTER ENCOUNTERS

It's easy to create a Chatty Cathy doll character who doesn't move, only speaks when you click on it, and serves only one function. It takes a bit more thought to create highly mobile three-dimensional characters of purpose and service. We need to do it though. We need to respect our characters enough and give them the attention they deserve so that they are as entertaining as any other feature of our games.

In the previous chapters I've tried to suggest some ways to bring these characters to life. Let's say we've succeeded, and our game world is now populated with interesting NPCs instead of dolls, NPCs with the potential to touch our hearts as much as characters in any other entertainment medium. Our players will want to interact with them!

Perception

> "There is no truth. There is only perception."
>
> —*Gustave Flaubert*

To begin with I'm going to talk about perception. It will help the discussion if we look at a third psychiatrist, not as well known as Freud or Jung, but one who spent a lot of time studying perception and communication.

His name was R.D. Laing (1927–1989), and his views on mental illness were shaped by existential philosophy and were often very different from mainstream psychiatry. His best known book, published in 1960, is *The Divided Self,* an effort to make the inner world of the mentally ill—in particular schizophrenics—comprehensible to the rest of us. My mother was a schizophrenic, and reading this book was my first attempt to try and understand the woman who had given birth to me and raised me.

A lesser known book, written in collaboration with H. Phillipson and A.R. Lee, was *Interpersonal Perception* published in 1966. Laing was not only interested in individuals, but the interactions between people. I'm not going to try and explain all of the complex concepts in the book, but want to share with you a synthesis I made of one central point.

Figure 6.1 R.D. Laing as we perceive him.

When two people talk to one another, miscommunications happen even when both are trying to pay attention. Our perceptions of a single conversation are affected by any number of factors from momentary distractions to outright psychosis. Basically what the speaker thinks she said and what the listener thinks he heard can be radically different. The truth floats somewhere in mid-air between them. Perception is fluid and transitory. We can use that.

There was an interesting scrap of text that showed up on the Internet late in 2003. Its attribution is doubtful, but it gives us another look at perception.

> "Aoccdrnig to a rscheearch at Cmabrigde Uinervtisy, it deosn't mttaer in waht oredr the ltteers in a wrod are, the olny iprmoetnt tihng is taht the frist and lsat ltteer be at the rghit pclae. The rset can be a toatl mses and you can sitll raed it wouthit porbelm. Tihs is bcuseae the huamn mnid deos not raed ervey lteter by istlef, but the wrod as a wlohe."

Notice that the thesis of the paragraph is proven by the way the material is presented. Very cool! What is really going on when we read the paragraph? The brain is making connections for us. We can use that too.

Our last example of perception is well known to most of us who have directed or edited film. It's called the Kuleshov effect, named for pioneer Russian filmmaker Lev Kuleshov (1899–1970).

In 1919 Kuleshov intercut a rather lengthy shot of an actor named Ivan Mozhukhin with the shots of the bowl of soup, the corpse, and the woman in the bed you see here.

Mozhukhin's expression is carefully neutral. Yet when intercut with the soup, an audience sees a hungry man. When intercut with the corpse, the audience sees remorse or maybe satisfaction at a job well done. When intercut with the woman, the audience sees lust; or a man pleased he has satisfied his lover; or a man dealing with rejection. Kuleshov's purpose was to illustrate the power of *montage*. The lesson was not lost on his more famous colleague, Sergei Eisenstein, whose seminal montage sequence on the Odessa harbor steps in the 1925 film *Battleship Potemkin* inspired Brian DePalma's homage in *The Untouchables* in 1987. Those who remember the past are destined to repeat it.

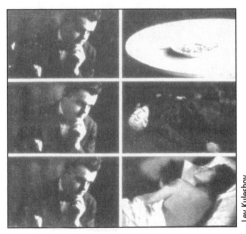

Figure 6.2 The Kuleshov effect.

Lev Kuleshov

note

MONTAGE: is the film technique of conveying ideas or emotions by juxtaposing different images.

To understand how to communicate with computer-driven characters, it helps to understand how human beings communicate with each other. We don't have the luxury of all the nuances of expression that the human face can reveal. When it is rendered and animated in our games, we see a broad parody, carefully modeled on the muscle contractions that occur when humans feel emotion, but soulless. We can help the illusion with astute voice acting, but it remains a construct and nothing more.

But it's okay. It seems to work pretty well at times. Why? Because human beings fill in the blanks. Automatically.

If we don't hear part of a comment, our brain attempts to fill in the missing bits. If we don't understand something, our brain searches for possible paths to that understanding. We make connections even where there are none. Our lives are a series of attempts to communicate. Schizophrenics are an extreme example, according to Laing, of people attempting to communicate, however inappropriately, filling in square blanks with round ideas. When I was a child and my mother spoke to me, I had to try to look beyond what she was saying to what she thought she was saying, and parse the difference.

Drama is not reality, remember? Writers don't have the knowledge or perception to duplicate reality, nor should we try. Reality isn't very dramatic most of the time. Luckily, we don't have to duplicate it. What we *can* do when writing characters is to approximate human behavior and stop there, just as an animator takes it as far as he can, then stops.

Just knowing that the player is going to fill in the blanks is key to how he will respond to our characters, and interact with them. We can take shortcuts and choose which characteristics (traits or qualities) to highlight. If our choices are good enough, the character will be three-dimensional even with surprisingly few characteristics. A rich character is not an overly explained character. You don't create a Scarlet O'Hara with three physical characteristics (raven hair, sparkling eyes, 18-inch waist), two sociological characteristics (southern belle, spoiled rotten), and four psychological characteristics (haughty, flirtatious, determined, brave). The lists are as mechanical as the numbers are meaningless. It's which ones you as a writer choose to emphasize that are important.

Laing's studies of perception and Kuleshov's experiments with montage are two good places to start to learn *how* the player will fill in the blanks. We want our characters to interact, not realistically, but as naturally as is possible.

Perspective (First Person Versus Third Person)

From perception it is a natural transition to *Point of View*, or POV. We talked about using POV when writing a screenplay to mean the camera is seeing a scene through a character's eyes. This perspective is also called First Person in literature, one of three major perspectives from which a story is told. The other two perspectives are second person and third person. There are even sub-variations of these such as first person narrator, first person reporter, limited omniscient, objective, and so on, but these are not applicable in visual media.

Most shots in movies are in third person with only occasional POV shots to draw attention to a particular feature of a scene, or to heighten suspense. One of the rare exceptions to this is *The Lady of the Lake*, a film adaptation of Raymond Chandler's mystery novel directed by and starring Robert Montgomery as Phillip Marlowe. Except for brief glimpses in mirrors, and hands that appear at the bottom of the frame as in first person shooters, the camera is firmly in Marlowe's POV.

Warner Home Video (originally MGM)

Figure 6.3 Marlowe's face puts in a rare appearance in *The Lady in the Lake*.

The effect is gimmicky, and off-putting, yet it showed up in several "interactive movies" and live action video games over the past decade.

note

> AXIS: An imaginary line drawn between the subjects of two intercut shots. Both should normally be photographed by a camera on the same side of that line or they will appear to be looking in the same direction, and not at each other.

The conceit is more successful when it is only one aspect of a computer game where the game action is in first person as well. When the POV is split, the effect can be jarring, as in the adventure game *Under a Killing Moon* where the game action is in first person. But when it's time for dialogue, the detective, Tex Murphy, steps into frame, portrayed by Chris Jones, who also happened to be the Chief Financial Officer of the developer! Unlike film, where the POV is changed very deliberately to create certain effects, splitting POV arbitrarily was one of those classic mistakes like crossing the axis. The player may not notice that anything is "wrong," but that part of the brain raised on the language of film is momentarily distracted.

Figure 6.4 Cirque de Soleil's magical *La Nouba*.

Live theatre is always third person, whether the play is seen through the traditional proscenium arch; in the round (where the audience surrounds the stage); or where the actors move among the audience as in *Cats*, Cirque de Soleil's *La Nouba*, or *Tamara*, an interesting experiment from the late 80s that attempted branching storylines in live theatre, first produced in many rooms of an American Legion Hall in Hollywood.

Novels are generally third person, also known as omniscient view, although there are large bodies of work in first person. Many detective novels are written in first person so that the reader can follow the unraveling of the crime. This is one of the reasons Montgomery chose a Phillip Marlowe novel by Chandler for his first person experiment. The books are written in first person.

I haven't done any actual counting, but perspective in games today seems to be split about the same way as novels. More are designed as third person, but first person is a healthy minority. Virtual worlds routinely offer both perspectives, and allow the switching of perspective by hitting a key.

Second person perspective games, as mentioned earlier, are easily identifiable by use of the pronoun "you." This perspective was dominant from the very beginning of text adventures. A well known example from *Zork* is "You are in an open field west of a big white house with a boarded front door." As graphics became more and more sophisticated, second person usage declined. One major exception is those games that use scrolling text to tell the player what is happening: "You pick up a red power pill!" "You've found the key to the vault!" "You hit the dragon for **34** points of damage!" These types of messages use more than their quota of exclamation points. They're not very immersive, but certainly informative.

How do we make the choice between first and third person? Or should we even worry about it when we try to bring our characters to life? Sometimes the game engine or the type of game makes the decision for us. Real time strategy games require an omniscient third person POV to see as much of the game action as possible at any one time. First person shooters of course want to place the player inside the player-character.

First person shows us the game world as if we were seeing it with our own eyes. This gives the world an almost tangible sense of place. And, theoretically at least, when NPCs turn to look directly at the player, it heightens the immersion, as long as we don't break the spell by jumping back and forth between two different points of view.

Immersion is not a new word, nor is our usage of it new. In addition to meaning "sinking within a fluid," it turns up in the 1913 edition of Webster's Unabridged Dictionary as "The state of being overwhelmed or deeply absorbed; deep engagedness."

Third person, since we're comfortable with its place in our collective film language unconscious, would seem to be a comfortable choice, if we want to create empathy. It means that when we interact with NPCs or other player-characters the interaction will appear on the screen much as it would in a movie. But empathy isn't dependent upon perspective. As Webster's tells us, it's an identification with or understanding of *another's* feelings or situation or motives.

If the first narrative movies had not emulated live theatre's necessary third person point of view, but to distinguish themselves from stage plays had decided to tell their stories in first person POV, empathy would be just as natural for us today in first person. Remember the gun firing at the camera in *The Great Train Robbery*, and how effective it was? Here's the shot of the shot seen round the world.

Figure 6.5 The first first-person shooter in *The Great Train Robbery*.

VCI Entertainment

So if empathy is not dependent on perspective, is immersion? It is caused by a whole range of factors from fascinating characters (our goal of course) to size of images, and many more in between. I'd argue that all of them can create immersion regardless of perspective. We can become immersed in a book as fully as a game or a hot bath. We become unconscious of the turning of the pages. Each chapter ending gives us a moment to catch our breath. Time stops for us. Later we have to catch back up to the rest of the world that went on its merry way while we were lost to it.

I'll suggest that it isn't the perspective—however much we seem to debate it—that matters at all in the end, it's the craft with which we make use of it. Non-player characters can be written the same for either first person or third.

There is one more character we need to look at before we move on. Empathy is identification with another. What about our identification with the player-character? Perspective would seem to play a big role in that. In first person, we can't see our avatar, or maybe only its hands. In third person, we see our representation right there on the screen. Is there a difference in how we write the player-character?

Only one of the three dimensions of character would seem to be primarily affected: the physical. In third person point of view, graphics can give us a lot of the details. In first person we need to rely on the opinions of NPCs and voice acting. These can illuminate all three dimensions. Remembering to steer clear of stereotypes in the character himself a deeper voice can convey size and authority; vocabulary or a public-school British accent can suggest education; vocal quality can suggest timidity, sexiness, and so on. Writers, of course, are most concerned with the NPC dialogue, word choices of the player-character e.g. vocabulary, and the rhythms of accents.

Dialogue

You guide your PC along the street. You come to a large Victorian house with a sign out front. You click on the sign and learn the house is not only a residence, but a doctor's office. You go in. Standing inside a small waiting room is an elderly man: Dr. Adams. You click on Dr. Adams.

* * *

```
                ADAMS
I love watching all the children I brought into this
world smoking or drinking or cholesterolling themselves
into early graves. Piling into trees at ninety miles an
hour. Ingesting chemicals that turn brain cells to
jelly. Fascinating profession: medicine. We learn far
too much! And the thing we learn that cuts the deepest
is that we'll never know enough to stop them. Or
ourselves. We're all on the same ride...to oblivion...
and we're all determined to make that ride as short as
possible!
```

* * *

Does this game mechanic sound familiar? The player-character comes upon an NPC, clicks on the NPC to "activate" it, the NPC obligingly spits out exposition, its life story, its function in the game, or some other important information. It does this without thought to any passing stranger.

This is not respecting the character. This is reducing it to a game convenience, no more. It is ignoring all sorts of possible opportunities to create a real character with a life of his own within the game. However well-written the actual speech may be, the writer/designer has already limited herself as well as the character.

People don't respond on command. They have reasons for talking to us, and they choose what they want to say. If we remember Laing, we'll see that there are more layers to any conversation than one, just as there are more dimensions than just one to a character.

How can we begin to bring the character to life? We might walk in on a conversation between two NPCs. We don't need to click on anybody. The conversation is triggered by the PC's entrance, and is written to indicate we've interrupted it. It doesn't have to start at the beginning. We will fill in the blanks.

So let's add the doctor's daughter, Nancy, to the encounter. Adams, a retired doctor, is bitter that he's brought too many babies into the world only to sign their death certificates long before their time. Nancy is also a doctor. She has taken over his practice. She still possesses an idealism all doctors must hold on to, if they are to minister to the ill, and not just apply treatment.

* * *

                        NANCY
    Dad, you love this town, and you know it!

                        ADAMS
    That's right, my dear. I love watching all the children
    I brought into this world smoking or drinking or
    cholesterolling themselves into early graves. Piling
    into trees at ninety miles an hour. Ingesting chemicals
    that turn brain cells to jelly. Fascinating profession:
    medicine. We learn far too much! And the thing we learn
    that cuts the deepest is that we'll never know enough to
    stop them. Or ourselves. We're all on the same ride ...
    to oblivion ...and we're all determined to make that
    ride as short as possible!

* * *

The two might break off now as they realize they aren't alone. Note that this isn't a cut scene, but a moment of interaction between two NPCs while the player-character, let's call him David, looks on. If the writer is uncomfortable about the chore of having two NPCs to talk to, Adams might exit angrily. If not, Nancy can be embarrassed at being overheard; and Adams can be aggressive, demanding to know what the PC is doing there. Or Adams might be unhappy about hearing his private opinions aired to a stranger, and Nancy might step into the breach with a word of welcome or inquiry.

But let's stay with the small piece of an encounter we started with. How has it improved? To begin with, of course, by giving him someone to talk to, someone he may actually love and respect, Adams has motivation to voice his frustrations. He's no longer Chatty Cathy. Next we're plunged into the middle of a real scene. We didn't cut away from the action for it, even if for a moment we snuck control away from the player to ensure she witnesses the exchange. If the moment is short enough, compelling enough, *entertaining* enough, equal to such scenes in other media, the player shouldn't mind.

But there's still a problem. Thanks to the human ego, we all think the stories we have to tell to others are fascinating, and we will ramble on. But drama is not reality. Drama reserves its speeches for special moments, and gives them special names like *monologue* and *soliloquy*. Drama is much more at home, particularly these days, with the give-and-take of two characters in conversation. Our shortened attention spans—created in part by the fact that with only 23 or 47 minutes to tell stories, television must pare dialogue to the bone—are significantly different from more leisurely times when speeches were in general longer. Audiences used to have more patience!

In the two decades I wrote television and movie scripts—from 1974 to 1994—the average length of a scene in scripts shrank from five pages to two and a half. We don't just cut out the beginnings and ends of scenes these days. Those have been gone from the very beginning of drama. See the "Point of Attack" section in Chapter 9, "Bringing the Story to Life." We fillet scenes until there is nothing left but meat. And with rare, important exceptions, the dialogue is an exchange, not a single speech.

Dialogue in games is much more similar to film than it is to plays or books. Or it should be. Games share with film the ability to pitch the action at a very fast pace. Leaner dialogue, delivered in spurts punctuating the action, is far more effective in not interrupting the action than long-winded passages. Yet here we are in games, writing these lengthy speeches. If we try to emulate the exchange of dialogue in movies or TV shows, we ghettoize it in a cut scene. Why?

One reason may be technical. Usually the speeches in an ingame encounter are chopped into separate files, whereas a single long speech would only need to be in one file. But in the various games I've written and designed I've never seen a game engine that balked at multiple files.

Another reason might be it's easier. As soon as you add an extra character to an encounter you jump from one possibility to three: The PC and one NPC can interact. The PC and the other NPC can interact. The two NPCs can interact. But if those interactions bring the encounter and its characters to life, we're shortchanging it not to allow it. No wonder players get so tired of the dialogue and characters and storytelling in games that we're forced to program the ESC key to allow them to jump through it, or ignore it altogether. No wonder players and developers alike may come to the conclusion that fully realized characters and rich stories are impossible in games, if the player's interactions with characters are reduced to pulling Chatty Cathy's string.

Here is the encounter as it was written for *Sideshow* in 1995:

* * *

                    NANCY
Dad, you love this town, and you know it!

                    ADAMS
That's right, my dear. I love watching all the children
I brought into this world smoking or drinking or
cholesterolling themselves into early graves.

                    NANCY
                 (to David)
This is an ongoing debate . . .

                    ADAMS
Piling into trees at ninety miles an hour. Ingesting
chemicals that turn brain cells to jelly. Fascinating
profession: medicine.

                    NANCY
We save lives.

                    ADAMS
We learn far too much! And the thing we learn that cuts
the deepest is that we'll never know enough to stop
them. Or ourselves. We're all on the same ride . . . to
oblivion . . . and we're all determined to make that
ride as short as possible!

* * *

One more point: it may look like I've just doubled the length of the scene, and it does take up more space on paper. In fact, the time it plays out in the three versions is identical. We haven't interrupted gameplay any longer just to create an exchange instead of a monologue. The reason is the same reason TV and movies prefer short exchanges to long speeches: they move faster. Whether the player reads the text or listens to an actor speak it, the words pick up pace when they're broken into smaller speeches. Plus, with the addition of a *character in opposition* to Adams, we've also increased the drama, and that increases pace.

Try it. Get a stopwatch. Act the first monologue aloud. Don't just read it, act it. Notice how you have to not only pause for breaths, but to make the moments happen. By this we mean taking the time to separate all the individual thoughts in a long speech, so that each one is comprehensible to the listener. Remember my anecdote in Chapter 1, "Myths and Equations," about Keith Michel in *Crucifer of Blood*? When he sped up his delivery of his lines, he deliberately stopped making the moments.

Watch any of Kenneth Brannagh's film adaptations of Shakespearean plays to see how the director and his other actors find the meaning in each Elizabethan line and especially the long speeches. They don't just recite them.

We'll get to cut scenes later on, but with more attention to encounters within the gameplay, fewer cut scenes will be needed.

What else can we do with dialogue? We can be self-conscious about how we as writers talk. Do all the characters sound like us? Usually a bad thing if we're writing a variety of characters from different cultures or walks of life. If they all share a similar background, they can share similarities, but differences in word choice, favorite expression, and so on, should be found. And this shouldn't be a mechanical process. Instead of lists of accents or slang expressions or stock phrases in foreign tongues, if we start with three-dimensional characters, those characters inform us how they will talk.

Let's look at accents for a second. Writers and designers, to make their characters sound different when they're voiced, often give them accents. When actors, whether professional voice actors or those used to being in front of the camera, are asked to voice characters the demands on their performances change.

First of all, the professional voice actors have a repertoire of different-sounding voices with a variety of accents. This is necessary because often a single *voice actor* can voice many characters just as they do in animated TV shows and films. But one way they differentiate between character voices is with accents. And if you're not careful, you can get a variety of immersion-breaking accents in your game. How many times have we heard dwarves voiced as Scotsmen and rogues with distinct New York accents?

note

VOICE OVER ANNOUNCERS: train themselves to talk in over-modulated speech patterns so that their message is clear.

VOICE ACTORS: retain a naturalistic quality that stresses character. Make sure you know which one you're getting for your game. Some actors can do both, but unless you want your scenes to sound like CNN, hire voice actors, not voice over announcers.

Some developers will justify such choices by saying they're adding comedy. The player is aware she's hearing a jokey accent. Well, as we'll see in Chapter 10, "Charting New Territory," there is comedy that enhances immersion, and comedy that fights it.

How about writing accents in text speech that players must read? Ever notice the difficulties role-players online get into when trying to do character in text? It was fun to add an accent to your character at the kitchen table playing *Dungeons & Dragons*. It's a lot harder to duplicate that accent in a chat window and make it comprehensible. If the other players can't read it, you're breaking their *immersion*.

Writers face the same dilemma. We do need to know accents and regional slang. But we shouldn't try to precisely replicate them on the page. Remember people fill in the blanks. Writing an accent is catching its rhythm and inflections, not its spelling. Use spelling of accented words sparingly, as no more than the occasional garnish on an entrée, or you will lose your reader.

Before we get into various ways to handle interactive game dialogue, I want to look at the most important thing you can do to bring your dialogue to life. Get beyond "how people talk," what we call colloquial speech. We're doing drama, not reality!

Don't even stop with writing characters in different voices with their own rhythms and inflections. Take colloquial speech and add an edge to it. Twist it. David Mametize it.

The dialogue of writer David Mamet (1947–) is so distinctive it has its own word to describe it: Mametspeak. It is anything but colloquial. Listen to the characters in movies Mamet has written and directed such as *House of Games, Oleanna, The Spanish Prisoner, State and Main* and *Spartan*, as well as those he's just written, such as *The Untouchables, Ronin* and of course the film adaptation of his Pulitzer Prize-winning play, *Glengarry Glen Ross*, where salesmen, desperate to do anything to close a deal are treated to a little motivational speech. Alan Arkin is Moss. Blake is Alec Baldwin.

www.bacjrr.org

Figure 6.6 Playwright, screenwriter, director David Mamet.

Artisan Entertainment

Figure 6.7 Ferocious dialogue in *Glengarry Glen Ross.*

* * *

Moss: What's your name?

Blake: *F**k you!* That's my name!

[Moss laughs.]

Blake: You know why, mister? 'Cause you drove a Hyundai to get here tonight, I drove an eighty thousand dollar BMW. *That's* my name. You see this watch. This watch cost more than your car. I made $970,000 dollars last year; how much did you make? You see pal, that's who I am and you're nothing. Nice guy? I don't give a s**t. Good father? F**k you. Go home and play with your kids. You wanna work here—close.

—*Glengarry Glen Ross*

* * *

Mamet isn't afraid of long speeches, but he knows when to use them.

I am by no means suggesting we try to emulate Mamet's dialogue. It is extremely stylized, sort of an amalgamation of street colloquial and the staccato delivery of early Harold Pinter in *The Birthday Party* or *The Caretaker. Filmmakers Magazine* calls it "a 'poetic' impression of streetwise jargon." There is a reason Mamet reuses actors in the films he directs. Some, like William H. Macy, can bring the dialogue to life. Others make it sound arch and mechanical.

The key to Mamet's dialogue is it is impossible *not* to listen to it. It's close enough to the way we've heard people speak, we can buy into it, yet we are startled by its cadences, and that forces us to listen even closer. Read—and listen to—the language of Studs Turkel's Chicago, Flannery O'Conner's south; and the prose poetry of Ray Bradbury and John Le Carré.

In 1984 I was writer-producer of a TV series called *Blacke's Magic*, a mystery show starring Hal Linden and Harry Morgan. One of the episodes took magician Alexander Blacke (Linden) and his con-artist father (Morgan) to a small town whose entire population vanishes during the night. They were visiting the town for sentimental reasons. It was at the fairgrounds here where Morgan had wooed and won Alex's mother, now dead for many years. Morgan finds a tree where he carved "Lenny Loves Lizbeth" decades before, and traces the heart surrounding the words with his finger.

* * *

> LEONARD
> Her eyes sparkled...catchin' the light from the Ferris wheel...I close my eyes, an' I can see her so clear...

> *And faintly, soft as memory, CALLIOPE MUSIC sneaks in beneath the scene, and the echoes of delighted children SCREAMING in make-believe fright.*

> LEONARD
> She'd joined up with us in Fresno, dancin' as parta Big Ed Twiliger's troupe. But she was no hootchie-kootch. She moved like a brightly colored curtain brushed by the wind along an open window...or like the long slow curl of an emerald wave.... She was gonna dance on the Great White Way, and I...

> *The memories and music FADE.*

> ALEX
> What, Pop?

> LEONARD
> For the first time in my life, I had no ambitions, 'cept one. To love her, cherish her, grow old in her arms...Never made it to Broadway...I always regretted...

> ALEX
> No, Pop. No regrets. It was a wonderful life, and she loved you for it. We both did.

* * *

Harry Morgan's wife of many years had died recently. I wrote the scene for him, and he played it beautifully. I broke up the speech with sound cues and Alex's one interjection when Leonard arranges what he's trying to say. It was television after all. But its rhythms are deliberately the rhythms of poetry. We both knew it wasn't colloquial. Neither of us cared.

We should not be afraid of the poetic richness of our language. We hear colloquial language all around us. We tune it out. To write it is to invite our player, whether she be listener or reader, to tune it out. Take the time to transform it into something the player is compelled to listen to, and he won't mind taking his hand off the mouse for a short while.

Dialogue Systems

There have been a lot of different systems developed to facilitate conversation between the player-character and NPCs in games. All are compromises. While an NPC can "speak" either in voice or text, players are, for the most part, forced to talk with the same devices they use for all game mechanics: the keyboard or control pad. There are exceptions. The recent PlayStation 2 game *Lifeline* from Konami allows the player to issue vocal commands to the player-character. The results are mixed as they are whenever parsers or voice recognition systems are employed.

The range of these systems are great from the non-existent—in *Riven* you watch other characters, you don't interact—to elaborate AI-based systems like Chris Crawford's Erasmatron. We'll spend most of our time between these two extremes. Some of the systems listed here may have only an historical value since we seem to have settled into a few favorite ones, but even the most arcane seem to reappear from time to time.

NPC dialogue can be text or spoken aloud. More games on personal computers use spoken responses than on consoles. They're obviously more naturalistic. Consoles still use mostly text. It's a storage issue as well as a cost issue. Sound files are larger than text files. Actors must be paid. As the storage space increases on consoles however, more and more are moving to speech.

Virtual worlds also use text almost exclusively. There are usually a *lot* of NPCs, and voicing them all can be prohibitively expensive. There is also the issue of communication between server and client. Large sound files take longer than long text files to travel between the two, and not all can reside on the client where computer-savvy players can take a peek at them before they should. Finally, text is a more private medium of communication. It allows multiple players to interact with NPCs simultaneously without disturbing one another.

The systems are listed in order of increased sophistication. The more sophisticated the system, the more natural it can be and the more opportunity for character revelation and storytelling we have; but it can also be more difficult to pull off.

Canned Speeches

Canned speeches are the first logical step beyond not interacting at all, and are without doubt the easiest conversation system we have.

Half-Life, Legend of Zelda, Goldeneye, Diablo: many games have used this system, and many still do today. The player-character doesn't speak. The player selects the NPC. The NPC may begin to speak, or a menu may appear if the NPC performs multiple functions. The NPC then spouts a predetermined response. This response can be a single speech repeated each time the player chooses to speak with the character; a series of repetitive responses; or a long speech.

If the speech is in text, it can open in a chat window on the UI, or appear in its own window, masking the action, and forcing the player to pay attention. If the speech is long, its window may have scroll bars, or it may be cut into pieces accessed in sequence by hitting the X button or clicking the mouse. The speech may be broken up like this to provide more easily digestible chunks; so the text will fit easily on the screen; or to not-so-cleverly hide the fact it's one of those long text passages again.

Many console games fall back on canned speeches for a good reason. No one in his right mind is going to attempt a parser-driven text conversation system on a console. Even beyond the limited nature of parsers, attempting to enter words on a game pad is like trying to build a flagpole by gluing dimes together in a stack. Eventually you'll get there, but it's much better to just buy the flagpole, and fly your flag.

Some designers, more comfortable with gameplay than writing, may choose canned speeches as the simplest method to get all that talking out of the way. If parsers are mentioned by some enthusiastic programmer, the designer can also argue that even typing on the keyboard is immersion-breaking. The reason we have experiments in voice communication and control from time to time is to get away from the cumbersome keyboard. Choosing menu items may be too much work, and while they are a convention we often accept, they need not be so overt as pop-up windows.

If an NPC has multiple possible interactions, we can create a less jarring way of choosing than a pop-up window. For example, if the NPC is static, we can use the environment she inhabits. If she's a merchant who's also a quest giver, gossip, and trainer, we can place hotspots on various objects in her shop. If we want to buy something, we select the merchandise counter or a display of garden tools. If we want a quest, we might select a Help

Wanted notice board that could display errands she needs doing, or could trigger her to ask the player-character if he's looking for a job. Selecting her directly would give us a greeting and exposition determined by our relationship to her, if any. We'll examine relationships shortly. Selecting the prized golden hoe she has prominently displayed on the wall behind her might prompt her to ask if we'd like to learn gardening.

Canned speeches need all the help they can get to keep the player in the world. Removing other immersion-harming reminders like basic menus can only help them.

Story is usually preserved by canned speeches, allowing little variation. It needn't be. If the underlying philosophy of the storytelling is non-linear, then even canned speeches can be adapted to it. But I'm getting ahead of myself. We'll get to story. There's often no mechanism for handling the reality of a repeat visit with canned speeches. Once that single file is in place, everybody is happy and moves on. We'll take a look at an alternative in the following "Entrances and Exits" section.

Canned Conversations

The player-character carries on a single preordained conversation, but this time the player gets to witness the PC's side of it. Instead of just hitting the X button to hear the next part of the canned speech, the player-character interjects questions or comments in the way I added Alex's "What, Pop?" to the scene from *Blacke's Magic.* This system was all but dead on the PC, replaced by canned speeches, probably for the sake of simplicity, until virtual worlds like *Everquest* and *Asheron's Call* resurrected it. Console games still must be concerned with storage space. We're adding files after all. But again text files are tiny, and we see canned conversations making a comeback in console games too.

The reason is obvious. It feels more natural to respond to an NPC than to just poke him to continue talking. Sure the player-character's speeches are just as canned as the NPC responses, but it is a step toward more natural conversation. The player may now have menu choices that go beyond TALK TO, BUY, SELL, REQUEST TRAINING, and ATTACK. There may be an indication of subject matter for discussion the player can select from.

The NPC usually inhabits the game world. Although he can appear on the interface for convenience, he is not really at home there. That's why we try to find in-game mechanisms to prompt him. But players have a foot in both the world of the game and the real world. Once the player starts directing the speech of the player-character, interface mechanisms can be more easily used. Players use them to move the PC and direct him in how to manipulate the in-game environment. For this reason, it seems less immersion breaking to allow the player to choose interface-based replies to the NPC. We've seen several of these.

Mood Meter

Games like *Return to Zork* and *Necropolis* gave players choices on how to respond in conversations. In a conversation, the player could choose from an array of emotions, graphically represented, and then the player-character spoke dialogue based on the choice. I've seen this used elsewhere as well, but it is not very common.

This was obviously an attempt to streamline conversations by avoiding the need to read and then select dialogue choices from menus. It had the added "advantage" that the player wouldn't know what the player-character was about to say, only whether he would respond belligerently, diplomatically, or whatever. My feeling is this solved a problem that didn't really exist. Players were used to selecting choices from menus (we'll get to this system shortly), and surprising them with dialogue is not always a good thing as we'll see in the next example as well.

Attitude Chart

A variation on the mood meter was the attitude chart from Tex Murphy games. The player chose from a series of player-character attitude descriptions like Play It Cool; Get Tough; Pour on the Charm; Dazzle with your Wit, and so forth.

The danger here, of course, was the player's idea of pouring on the charm or being witty may not correspond to the writer's. The player's surprise at hearing the line of dialogue might include annoyance that the reply wasn't all that charming or witty. The game also toyed with the player's expectations by deliberately giving the player-character Tex Murphy lines the character thought were charming and witty, but obviously weren't. This added humor—the Tex Murphy games were tongue-in-cheek—but really amounted to playing a game with the player, reminding her that she was not really Murphy, or a part of the game world.

Neither the attitude chart nor the mood meter enjoyed much popularity. The interest the player may have in seeing what dialogue her selection triggered was at the expense of the integrity of the game world. They are offered here as interesting experiments in communication. They may give designers ideas for variations on the systems or, at the very least, save designers before they stray too far down a dead end path.

Iconic Choices

This was an attempt at a short-handed topic list that keeps the choices visual. *Circle of Blood* used icons to represent topic choices and NPCs available to talk to. Instead of the topics being listed as "Tell me about George." Or "Do you, Henri?," the icons replaced the words with faces of the individuals in question.

This removes the pitfalls of the attitude chart, and some of the immersion-breaking game aspects of both it and the mood meter. However, it is still vague where vagueness is unnec-

Figure 6.8 The player clicked on icons in *Circle of Blood.*

essary. Icons in general are frustrating challenges we face every time we design the UI. How do we make sure an icon's function is simple to recognize, and not misinterpreted? Do we use the same old icons, or at least variations on them, much in that way international symbols are used? Icon design is an art all its own, and outside the scope of this book. This system is dependent on mastering it.

A sloppy icon system will disconnect the player from the game world, the exact opposite of what it is trying to achieve. It's an interesting system, however, and I expect while we may not see any mood meters or attitude charts again anytime soon, iconic conversation systems may be worth re-examination. Console games in particular, with their limited TV resolution, might be able to advance beyond canned speeches and conversations with such a system. We'll see.

Topic List

The player picks from a list of topics: this list can include generic topics as well as specific topics added as the game progresses. *Legend of Zelda* has a rare and rudimentary form of this: the fishing shack, race course, and so forth. The games *Syberia* and *Tex Murphy Overseeer* move the list halfway into the world by presenting it off to one side as if their protagonists were glancing at notepads.

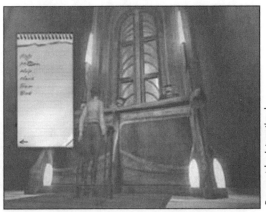

Figure 6.9 A Topic List from *Syberia.*

Topic lists do show up in more recent games, having survived the previous attempts to do away with them. At their best, they're simple and straightforward, cut down on verbiage, and, when integrated even partially into the game world, are not as immersion-breaking as they could be.

There are a couple of ways to handle the topic list. The topics can disappear after they've been chosen. If the information gleaned from the NPC's response is important, it can be automatically added to some memory-jogging device like a player journal.

The topics may remain on this list, perhaps grayed out, but still selectable. This allows the player to go back over topics to immediately refresh his memory, but at the expense of immersion when the NPC responses are rote.

Whereas icons, mood meters, or attitude charts rarely led to anything more than a single reply or brief exchange, true topic lists actually can be the interface into a simple branching dialogue structure, or even a web-like structure. These will be studied in more detail in Chapter 14, "Modular Storytelling."

Some topic lists try to be a puzzle in themselves. The list of topics must be gone through in its entirety. Clues or puzzle elements may be hidden in the foliage.

All four of the previous conversation systems have merit, and I should add I enjoyed playing all of the games. The fewer words the player has to read the better. They are clever attempts to avoid, or at least truncate, menus that display actual dialogue, therefore limiting the amount of reading necessary. To achieve this, however, they give up clarity. We're removed one step from the natural flow of the conversation. And they can interject an immersion-harming game played between designer and player—What is my player-character going to say next?—for immersion in the actual conversation. The next group allows for even more sophisticated interaction between player-character and NPC, but at the risk of adding more words to read.

Highlighted Text

This is a conversation system that is enjoying a current popularity, especially in virtual worlds. It's basically a topic list embedded within a paragraph of NPC text dialogue. Both *Dark Age of Camelot* and *Horizons* use it. The player clicks on highlighted text and this leads to another response. This can be used in NPC quest dialogue, or if NPCs offer more than one service. Highlighted text can be **bolded**, a different color, [in brackets], and so on.

This variation allows for the topic list choices to be within the context of the conversation. The examples I've seen have used it only to select canned speeches. Like them, it requires no dialogue from the player-character, although in *Dark Age of Camelot* the NPCs sometimes attempt to voice the player-character's thoughts: "Now, I know what you're thinking, enchanter . . ." An awkward conceit.

Highlighted text works quite well in gameplay, which explains its popularity. It doesn't avoid any of the limitations of canned speeches in general, but also doesn't have to be used only to access them either. While there is no give-and-take between characters, it could be used, as other topics lists can be, as a way into a simple branching or web dialogue structure.

Dialogue Menu

The dialogue menu can be found in a number of single-player personal computer games, and has been around a long time. While it gives the writer even more opportunity for character revelation, especially of the player-character, it adds more text to read—one reason it only occasionally shows up in console games, and why designers are forever trying to find ways to shorthand it.

As in topic lists, dialogue choices may disappear after being selected. They can also remain to be selected again. An even more sophisticated approach to the dialogue menu is making groups of choices disappear after the player has chosen just one. This design obviously does not belong on an in-game topic list object like Murphy's notepad. But it is the most naturalistic approach.

It flows much more like a real conversation where one topic veers off on to another, and then to another, and so on. "But!" cries the astute reader, "How do we plant exposition in the conversation, if the player does not choose the correct dialogue? Isn't that choice lost to her?"

Not really. I'm going to save most of this for Chapter 14. But let's take a worst case scenario. Let's say in any given conversation between player-character and NPC Abbott, I, the writer, have three pieces of exposition I want to get out. I also have two important character beats I'd like to establish. Now let's say I've planted one of these five "important things" in each of NPC Abbott's responses to my five dialogue choices A to E. The player selects A. B to E vanish so that a new group, F to J, can appear based on that choice. I've created variations of F to J. Once the game knows the player has chosen A, the variations of F and G include the necessary exposition from B and D. And for an encounter with Costello, a different NPC, the game will know that A, B, and D have been covered, and will therefore incorporate variations that include C and E.

Our next step, of course, is to match non-linear gameplay with non-linear story advancement, and allow the player to visit either Abbott or Costello first. We include checks, so that we know who's on first, and the appropriate variations fire as needed. Again, more of this in Chapter 14. I'm getting ahead of myself again!

"But!" the super astute reader retorts, "That's wasteful! If there are five dialogue choices and four of them vanish when we choose one, the effort that went into the NPC responses—including paying the voice actor—is wasted! All those variations? More waste!"

It takes longer to write, no question. More thought and logic testing are needed. If you're looking for the *Lazy Writer's Guide to Writing* this isn't it. Write the extra variations. You'll find the effort isn't that much greater. You'll be surprised how similar the variations can be. Cut and paste, change a couple of words, and move on.

As for those pesky voice actors who get paid by the hour? I've directed quite a few voice sessions, and once the character voice has been found, since the variations are remarkably similar, we tear through them. I have matched or beaten the time and expense budgeted for games whose authors didn't bother to seed their important exposition throughout a naturally flowing conversation.

Back on track, sorry for that natural digression. Another advantage of dialogue menus is the opportunity to share the dialogue choices with the player. The player can now intelligently choose not only topics (topic list), but ways to approach those topics (attitude chart), and how hard to hit them (mood meter). Further, one of the reasons we like characters we empathize with in other media is that they do things we can never do. They can also—through our talent—be far more witty, articulate, and wise (or boring, tongue-tied, and stupid!) than the player himself.

Here's a chance to share that with the player. We give him the chance to stand up in a conversation with Albert Einstein or Dorothy Parker or Dennis Miller and hold his own. Make the player into someone he could never be. Allow him to do things he could never do. Remember?

Player-character dialogue can be found, not surprisingly, in most of my games as well as *Grim Fandango* and Bioware games like the *Baldur's Gate* series and *Neverwinter Nights*.

In some of my games, from the single-player *The Riddle of Master Lu* to the multiplayer *The Gryphon Tapestry*, I used full sentences. *Grim Fandango* used sentence snippets to good advantage. Bioware games use full sentences that provoke text speeches partially voiced.

Natural Language/AI-Based Conversations

At the far end of the spectrum from no conversation we have natural language/AI-Based conversations like Chris Crawford's *Le Morte D'Arthur*. They are outside the scope of this book, but are fascinating. We're nowhere near ready to turn over conversations with major characters to AI, but one interesting line of investigation is creating more natural-feeling minor characters. I invite you to explore their many possibilities.

From the preceding, you might assume the only system I like is the dialogue menu. You would be wrong. I have used canned speeches, canned conversations, topic lists, and highlighted text too. Sometimes more than one type within a single product. A topic list might suffice for a merchant who has no other function. Highlighted text might work fine for a quest NPC. A canned speech or conversation might be perfect for an encounter with a minor character. We should keep our interfaces consistent, but we can't possibly put in the effort with our minor conversations we do with our major conflicts anymore than we have the time to treat all characters, great and small, equally.

Some game designs require little character interaction, and canned conversations may suffice. Just as some movies emphasize action over character, so do some games.(Well, actually most games. We need to get beyond that.) We don't want to overwhelm the rest of the game with our conversation system anymore than we want to overwhelm story with gameplay. All the elements of the entertainment experience must work in harmony. Save the conflict for the characters themselves.

Entrances and Exits

Whatever conversation system we choose, a few variations will help enormously to preserve the fiction of the world and the naturalism of the conversations. It is easy to introduce some variation into the moments we first encounter NPCs, and when we leave them. It is the first opportunity we have to begin to establish a relationship between player-character and NPC, and should be embraced for that, not avoided.

Let's look again at Aristotle's unities: Time, Place and Action, and how they can affect entrances and exits.

Time

In real life, conversations don't necessarily begin at the beginning, progress through to the end, then stop. We come in on the middle of them, pick them up later, decide we want to talk about something other than what the person we're talking to does, and so on. To replicate these possibilities in game conversation, we identify natural entrance and exit points, paying close attention to the passage of time, as the player-character experiences it in the game. Again, compromises must be considered, particularly concerning the art necessary to cover more than a few possibilities, but we can strive to address at least three variations:

1. If the player concludes the conversation, then immediately reopens it without doing anything else.
2. If the player remains in the area, but does other things, or briefly leaves the area and returns.
3. If the player is gone for some time before returning.

The player-character can handle these. Or the NPC. It doesn't matter.

Place

Whether the NPC is static or mobile, the locale affects our meeting and departure. If the NPC can see the player approach, she might want to comment on the sword he's carrying in his hand. The player-character might interrupt her if she can't see him arrive. The NPC can turn to face the player-character when the PC comes within range as in *Star Wars Galaxies*, not just when the player pokes her with a mouse click.

Action

If the meeting between PC and NPC is cordial, the PC may earn a friendly farewell. If the meeting goes poorly, a hail of bullets might chase the PC out the door.

All of these are simply examples of writing and programming NPCs who are *aware* of their surroundings, the player-character, and how they feel about her. Entrances and exits in real life are extremely important, often accompanied by elaborate, centuries old ritual. The handshake evolved from an approaching person holding out his hands to show he wasn't carrying a weapon. Nuances like these are easy to do, and the rewards can be great: more actions to draw upon to illuminate our characters.

Return Visits

Many games succumb to what some designers consider a necessary evil: the repetition of repeat visits. Players don't always know they have exhausted an NPC of whatever primary use it had in the game, and that revisiting the NPC will not further the plot or provide additional gameplay. Most writers will be asked to provide a single generic line an NPC can say in response to a return visit. One thing that destroys for me the illusion that the game is anything other than a game is when NPCs repeat the same old stock phrases over and over when you return to them. Simply because their utility is over doesn't mean we can abandon them, acknowledge they were simply tools, and move on. Their responses during return visits should make as much sense as possible within the fiction of the game.

In most cases, we get simple repetition. In some there is a little variety built into a few characters, but only of canned speeches. A few basic variations wouldn't add all that much disc space, or art production.

Another trick is to choose a generic series of remarks, hopefully related to the character or situation, but that don't require specific game-affecting responses. Then choose a generic series of responses to the *type* of remarks chosen. You can then mix and match these in any number of ways, creating the illusion of continuing small talk.

We successfully applied this system that we dubbed CHAOS Intelligent Conversation Modules to create hundreds of different "small-talk" combinations in *The Riddle of Master Lu* back in 1994. We were expanding it to player-character voice-overs in the uncompleted sequel *The Siberian Cipher*.

In the location Sikkim whenever Ripley (the player-driven character), having exhausted all of a certain temple guard's pertinent information, returns to talk to the guard, he can still do so. And the guard will not answer him with a single repeated phrase typical to many games such as, "I have no more time to waste on you, begone!" When the player clicked on the guard, the engine "shuffled" (more on this in a moment) a "deck" of five possibilities, then pulled one of the following lines of dialogue for Ripley to speak:

Figure 6.10 Ripley questions the philosophical guard.

"Can you tell me more about the temple?"

"I'd like to hear what those of the temple believe."

"If an outsider were interested in the sect, what would you tell him?"

"Can you tell me some of the key doctrines of the Temple of the Hidden Way?"

"Numerous westerners are facinated by Eastern religion. What would you tell them about your beliefs?"

The following lines of dialogue were *not* simply shuffled. They could be called as single lines; two lines could be given together, or three, or four, all the way up to all eight. And *any* of the lines could be said by the guard *in any order*.

These lines, like Ripley's, were voiced by an actor. I directed the actor to deliver them so that they could be combined in any of the previously mentioned ways. The actor only recorded each line once. The combinations were then built by the game engine on the fly. Here were the separate lines:

"We believe in the testing of the faithful."

"We believe only through questioning can we find answers to that which puzzles us."

"We believe that to learn one must study."

"We believe one may not reach true enlightenment until one has found the Hidden Way."

"We do not believe in trial and error."

"We believe in method and reason."

"We believe anyone who proves himself worthy, by throwing off the trappings of the outer world, may join us."

"We welcome questors from all lands."

Just be sure to shuffle the stacks of remarks and responses, and put aside each as it is used. Don't randomize them. Shuffling guarantees two things. One, while you'll begin to hear at least partial repetitions, they won't be in the same order. Two, you'll hear *all* of the possible combinations before there will be any exact duplicates. How many unique combinations are there in the above example?

One colleague has pointed out to me that the methodology behind CHAOS is the same used when character animations are drawn to begin and end at neutral positions so they can be seamlessly connected to one another. Another noted the similarity to "tiling" in graphics where the geography of an area is built up using terrain tiles with edges drawn to connect to other tiles in what is called a tileset.

It's not a full conversation. It will never compete with a fully scripted conversation. But it makes reasonable sense no matter how it is constructed by the game engine. It's not much harder to write than "Take a hike, Mike," repeated over and over. And the additional database, and recording costs are negligible.

We must also consider a number of other variables. If we solve a problem for an NPC that gains us a necessary clue or item, gameplay may be satisfied, but narrative often isn't. In *Return to Zork* (1993), one of two games that were frustrating enough for me as a player to be a catalyst for me becoming a designer, there was a puzzle that involved the reuniting of two lovers, a ferryman and a witch. Another puzzle involved finding the lost child of a club owner. In both cases, once the puzzles are solved, there is no acknowledgement by the NPCs that the player-character has affected them in any way. The reunited lovers treat the player-character as a stranger. The only state that has changed is the puzzle is no longer available. At the very least, there should be a simple recognition of the player's actions. We must respect the characters!

Relationships

Creating characters in isolation only takes us so far. As we populate our worlds, we place NPCs in close proximity to one another, give them similar professions, and different opinions. It's only natural that these NPCs begin to develop relationships with one another, and with the player-character.

First we'll look at large groups whose structure and relationships with each other can resemble religions, political parties, and racial and cultural groups in the real world. When we want to orchestrate how these groups interact, we can lump all of them under the heading of Factions.

Factions

"When you're a Jet,
You're a Jet all the way
From your first cigarette
To your last dyin' day"

—*West Side Story*

When you're a Jet, you're a Jet all the way. Unless you're in a virtual world of course. If they made a virtual world based on *West Side Story*, the Jets and the Sharks would be two factions the player could choose from. Asking the player to choose between two or more groups early on in a single-player game can alter the entire experience. The most basic factions we can construct are the broadest like good and evil. If the player chooses the dark side of the force, the challenges she faces in the game, and the tools she has at her disposal to overcome them will be different than if she'd chosen the good side. The areas of the game where her player-character is safe or at risk can be reversed. And the NPCs she encounters, if they know of her choice, should respond accordingly.

Figure 6.11 Tony and Riff, members in the Jets "faction" in *West Side Story*.

The player-character's faction may be visible for all to see, or secret. Whether the player-character's faction is in the majority or minority; ruling class or oppressed slaves; respected or suspect; in effect which passport the player-character carries can shift story, relationships, and gameplay as a result. In *Morrowind* an NPC's attitude towards the player can change depending upon a player's faction and reputation.

In virtual worlds, factions play an equally strong role. Dark elves who enter the town of Freeport in *Everquest* are at risk. They will be attacked by the guards. If you're an overt rebel in *Star Wars Galaxies*, you will be attacked by Imperial storm troopers. If you keep your rebel affiliation secret, they will not suspect you. We'll take a look at virtual world factions again in Chapter 18, and how factions are used when there are many player-characters.

Whether we're creating a single player game or a multiplayer game, major factions can be extremely helpful, and allowing the player to change his allegiances adds another dimension. In the strategy game *Heroes of Might and Magic III*, there is a moment in a scenario where players are given the opportunity to switch sides in the conflict that has overtaken the world. If a player chooses to go over to the opposition, that particular scenario is much easier to complete. But then the player discovers that later scenarios are more difficult. Switching sides isn't as easy as trotting across a battlefield to shake hands with your enemy, and it can be equally challenging in games. A traitor once, a traitor twice? Suspicion often follows such a choice. An interesting, if dangerous, game might be built around a character perched precariously between two opposing factions. We can call the game *Double Agent*.

Factions don't need to be huge groups either. As in *West Side Story* or *Grand Theft Auto: Vice City*, factions may be gangs fighting for control of their turf, either a physical neighborhood or a source of income. The important thing to remember is to orchestrate factions just like characters. If the factions aren't in opposition, opportunities for conflict and drama are limited.

One final interesting thing to note is that factions, unlike individual characters, don't necessarily have to be balanced in power. Whereas the best games in sports come from two strong opponents, there are also fans of the game, without a real stake in either side, who will root for the underdog. And there is, of course, the grand delight audiences or readers take when their heroes start out on what appears to be an obvious losing side.

The film *Independence Day*, or the arrival of the Borg in *Star Trek: Next Generation*, forces the characters we empathize with to confront a seemingly undefeatable enemy, and the triumph is all the more sweet when that enemy is finally vanquished. The second part of "Best of Both Worlds" the two-part episode that introduced the Borg was the first episode I worked on. Interestingly, Mike Pillar's script features a forcible shift in allegiances from the Federation to the Borg when Captain of the Enterprise, Jean-Luc Picard, is "assimilated" by the Borg. After his rescue, he still retains certain residue of his time as a Borg, and there is the suspicion, among his closest shipmates and even himself, that he might revert.

The Player-Character and NPCs

In addition to group relationships, we of course have relationships between the player-character and the NPCs who share his world. In single-player games, these can be closely scripted, or constructed with choice built into the gameplay. In either case, relationships should grow and develop just as individual characters do. Remember our decision on *Edge of Night* to kill Nicole? Her relationship with her husband, Miles, had become static. Most possible relationship changes between them had been played out over the years. To repeat them was to be redundant, a trap soap operas that have been on for years often fall into. Every "bad girl" will eventually seduce every "good man." Every character will be accused of a crime she didn't commit. Every man will fall in love with his best friend's sweetheart.

A game world populated with interesting NPCs is only the first step. Whether the player-character is in opposition with an NPC or in love with him, relationships are an opportunity to reveal both characters, and to carry the story forward. The player-character's relationships with those NPCs make the player feel that her avatar inhabits that world, and is not simply playing a game set there. The distinction is vital. It is the difference between a game that relies solely on its gameplay for success, and a game that has all the elements of popular entertainment in other media.

While we can construct every step in the ebb and flow of multiple relationships between a player-character and NPCs in single-player games quite easily, it's harder to track them in virtual worlds. Like soap operas, virtual worlds have no true end. They run until they die. Thousands of player-characters can inhabit them. One solution is to create a few factions and leave it at that. Very simple, and if only a few major interactions are possible, we can set flags to keep track.

If a Jet wants to buy a candy bar on the Shark's turf, it may cost him more, and the storekeeper may be fearful or hostile. If a Shark strolls down a dark alley on the Jet's turf, he may find himself under attack simply because of his gang affiliation. But what about Tony and Maria? Or all the thousands of Tonys and Marias who inhabit the *West Side Story* virtual world? What if the Tonys are player-characters and the Marias are NPCs?

Okay, so it's really the movie, and that's Richard Beymer and Natalie Wood. It *could* be a virtual world, and she *could* be an NPC!

Figure 6.12 Tony and Maria from the *West Side Story* virtual world. Maria is the NPC.

Writers can and should fall back on programming to help them manage the infinite numbers of variables that occur when all those player-characters interact with all those NPCs. You don't have to be a programmer. I'm not a programmer. But you do have to think like one. Programmers love simple, elegant solutions where only a small chunk of code with a few variables to pop in can drive an entire system in a game. The dark side of this thinking is a quest system that is only Chinese menu-type errands with no opportunity for character revelation or story. The bright side is reflected in the relationship system that follows.

One of our primary goals for NPCs in *The Gryphon Tapestry* was to make NPCs as real as possible, granting them multiple functions—reasons for being in the world besides just roles as merchants and trainers and so on. We wanted them to have lives and relationships of their own. It was relatively easy to construct a web of relationships between the NPC inhabitants of a town, and large relationships and factions between towns. But we wanted a system that would allow player-characters to have ever-changing relationships with NPCs as well.

The visible result of the system could mean an NPC would trust a player-character enough to gossip with her. A tidbit an NPC confided to one player-character might be the truth if the NPC was well-disposed toward him, but another tidbit could just as easily be a lie if she didn't much like how he behaved. An NPC merchant might be grateful to a player-character and give him a discount on his next sword. A trainer might refuse to help a player-character who had wronged an NPC friend of the trainer's. This wrong should be subjective of course. In this last example, we see NPC relationships and player-character and NPC relationships working in concert. Once scripted but changeable relationships between NPCs were in place, we needed a player-character/NPC relationship system to keep track of how NPCs would react to the way players chose to live their lives in the world.

Here is what we came up with. The TGT Full System that follows was my first pass at it. Dorion Newcomb, artist and co-designer on *TGT*, took my version, broke it down, and decided it was more complex than it needed to be, particularly given the time we had to implement it. Instead he came up with a much more simplified system that we ultimately decided to adopt. Our feeling was that players would be so amazed by the changing relationships with NPCs that even the simplified system provided, they wouldn't miss the full system, and we could always revisit that system when the game had been live for awhile and the concept had been stress tested. This was in 1999. Nothing like it had been tried before in a massively multiplayer game. To the best of my knowledge to this day it remains unique.

TGT Full System

The NPC Base score is determined by assigning a rough score to the NPC in six areas: Like, Respect, Loyalty, Trust, Admiration, and Love. The rough score in each of the three categories is added up, and an average is determined. This then becomes the NPC's Base Score. The area in gray is the suggested range of values that should be assigned to any NPC for a specific interaction.

NPC Personality Chart

Positive Descriptor							Scale							Negative Descriptor
Love	6	5	4	3	2	1	0	−1	−2	−3	−4	−5	−6	Hate
Admiration	6	5	4	3	2	1	0	−1	−2	−3	−4	−5	−6	Contempt
Trust	6	5	4	3	2	1	0	−1	−2	−3	−4	−5	−6	Mistrust
Loyalty	6	5	4	3	2	1	0	−1	−2	−3	−4	−5	−6	Disloyal
Respect	6	5	4	3	2	1	0	−1	−2	−3	−4	−5	−6	Disrespect
Like	6	5	4	3	2	1	0	−1	−2	−3	−4	−5	−6	Dislike

Next is a table that represents the base personality that an NPC could be assigned. This would represent an NPC who has a general dislike of other people.

Calculating the NPC Personality Values

Positive Descriptor	Value	Negative Descriptor
Love	−2	Hate
Admiration	−1	Contempt
Trust	1	Mistrust
Loyalty	2	Disloyal
Respect	−2	Disrespect
Like	−2	Dislike
Generalized Value	**−4**	

Next is the chart that represents the maximum values that can be assigned for each category according to each player. Each player has a default of null in each category, and it is only through interactions with the NPC that these values are modified. For example, if a player successfully completes a difficult task for the NPC, he may receive an additional positive point in both the Like and the Trust categories.

Player Relationship Modifier

Positive Descriptor						Scale							Negative Descriptor
Love	6	5	4	3	2	1	0	−1	−2	−3	−4	−5	−6	Hate
Admiration	6	5	4	3	2	1	0	−1	−2	−3	−4	−5	−6	Contempt
Trust	6	5	4	3	2	1	0	−1	−2	−3	−4	−5	−6	Mistrust
Loyalty	6	5	4	3	2	1	0	−1	−2	−3	−4	−5	−6	Disloyal
Respect	6	5	4	3	2	1	0	−1	−2	−3	−4	−5	−6	Disrespect
Like	6	5	4	3	2	1	0	−1	−2	−3	−4	−5	−6	Dislike

The following chart shows an example of how the player to NPC relationship value is generated, and how these specific categories are added together to generate a generalized relationship value.

Calculating the Player to NPC Relationship Value

Category	NPC Personality	Player Relationship Modifier	Player to NPC Relationship Value
Love(Hate)	−2	+3	1
Admiration(Contempt)	−1	+2	1
Trust(Distrust)	1	−2	−1
Loyalty(Disloyalty)	2	0	2
Respect(Disrespect)	−2	−1	−3
Like(Dislike)	−2	−4	−6
Generalized NPC to Player Relationship Value			**−6**

The last chart shows the values and their meanings behind the generalized NPC to Player Relationship Value. These categories are guidelines behind understanding the relationship, and these values can be tested instead of more specific category tests.

Generalized NPC to Player Relationship Value	
Score Range	Descriptor
25 to 36	Adores
10 to 24	Amiable
9 to –9	Neutral
–10 to –24	Strained
–25 to –36	Despises

TGT Simplified System

This is Dorion's version. It allows for easier implementation, and quicker customization. Some depth is lost, but the variety of possible relationships remains fairly high. The rough score in each of the three categories is added up, and an average is determined. This then becomes the NPC's Base Score. The area in gray is the suggested range of values that should be assigned to any NPC for a specific interaction.

NPC Personality

Positive Descriptor	Scale																					Negative Descriptor
Like	10	9	8	7	6	5	4	3	2	1	0	–1	–2	–3	–4	–5	–6	–7	–8	–9	–10	Dislike
Trust	10	9	8	7	6	5	4	3	2	1	0	–1	–2	–3	–4	–5	–6	–7	–8	–9	–10	Distrust
Respect	10	9	8	7	6	5	4	3	2	1	0	–1	–2	–3	–4	–5	–6	–7	–8	–9	–10	Disrespect

Like(Dislike)

This represents the emotional feelings that an NPC has towards the player. An NPC may increase his like (dislike) value for the following reasons: the player listens, and provides good council; the player does favors for the NPC; the player compliments the NPC; the player helps others in times of need, and so forth. An NPC may decrease his like(dislike) value for the following reasons: the player lies to the NPC; the player refuses to help the NPC; the player displays cruelty to the NPC; or the player performs selfish actions which hurt others.

Trust(Distrust)

This represents the amount of responsibility that the NPC would place on the player. An NPC may increase his trust(distrust) value for the following reasons: the player successfully completes a task that the NPC assigned to them; the player keeps her word, and does not reveal private information to other NPCs; the player demonstrates honesty in her relationship to the NPC. An NPC may decrease his trust(distrust) value for the following reasons: the player receives a task for the NPC but does not complete it; the player breaks a confidence, or reveals private information about the NPC; the player lies to the NPC.

Respect(Disrespect)

This represents the amount of admiration the NPC has for the player's abilities. An NPC may increase his respect(disrespect) value for the following reasons: the player has developed a high skill level in a skill that the NPC values; the player provides meaningful help or services to other NPCs that this NPC knows; when the player has to make a decision, it is one that is harmonious with the NPC's world view. An NPC may decrease his respect(disrespect) value for the following reasons: the player has no skills that an NPC values; the player has avoided helping other NPCs that this NPC knows; the player makes decisions that are discordant with the NPC's worldview.

This table represents the base personality that an NPC could be assigned. This would represent an NPC who has a general dislike of other people.

Calculating the NPC Personality Values

Positive Descriptor	Value	Negative Descriptor
Like	−2	Dislike
Trust	1	Mistrust
Respect	−2	Disrespect
Generalized Value	**−3**	

The following chart represents the maximum values that can be assigned for each category according to each player. Each player has a default of null in each category, and it is only through interactions with the NPC that these values are modified. For example, if a Player successfully completes a difficult task for the NPC, she may receive an additional positive point in both the Like and the Trust categories.

Player Relationship Modifier

Positive Descriptor	Scale	Negative Descriptor
Like	10 9 8 7 6 5 4 3 2 1 0 −1 −2 −3 −4 −5 −6 −7 −8 −9 −10	Dislike
Trust	10 9 8 7 6 5 4 3 2 1 0 −1 −2 −3 −4 −5 −6 −7 −8 −9 −10	Distrust
Respect	10 9 8 7 6 5 4 3 2 1 0 −1 −2 −3 −4 −5 −6 −7 −8 −9 −10	Disrespect

The next chart shows an example of how the Player to NPC relationship value is generated, and how these specific categories are added together to generate a generalized relationship value.

Calculating the Player to NPC Relationship Value

Category	NPC Personality	Player Relationship Modifier	Player to NPC Relationship Value
Like(Dislike)	-2	-2	-4
Trust(Distrust)	1	2	3
Respect(Disrespect)	-2	-1	-3
Generalized NPC to Player Relationship Value			−4

The last chart shows the values and their meanings behind the generalized NPC to Player Relationship Value. These categories are guidelines behind understanding the relationship, and these values can be tested instead of more specific category tests.

Generalized NPC to Player Relationship Value	
Score Range	**Descriptor**
19 to 30	Adores
6 to 18	Amiable
5 to 5	Neutral
–6 to –18	Strained
–19 to –30	Despises

These are by no means all of the issues involved when we write character encounters. For example, one of my sidebar contributors, Hal Barwood, notes that a variation on simply repeating canned conversations is having three variations of the same material for return visits: "First encounter with the specialized NPC, hear (or read) the long version. Second encounter, get a quick summary. Third encounter, get an even quicker brusque summary to enforce the idea that possibilities have been exhausted." This is a simple and reasonable compromise between story and gameplay that can also add a couple of relationship beats in how the NPC reacts to each return visit.

The important thing to realize here is that we have not exhausted all of the ways of handling encounters. There is no reason to keep repeating the few we're most familiar with. Before the design document turns to iron take the time to experiment with your own.

PART III

TELLING THE STORY

Interlude on the Way to San Jose

It happened that, on a rainy day in March, as I lay
In Chicago, at O'Hare, grounded by a long delay,
Ready to resume my pilgrimage and start
To San Jose, fervent gamer at heart,
There came at night's core to that airport
Some nine and twenty of a motley sort
Of sundry folk who had failed to reach
Connecting flights, stranded pilgrims were they each
That toward San Jose town would fly.
The benches were narrow, but at least they were dry.
And fairly well we there were eased, every one
Full of Starbucks, pizza, or a sweet Cinnabon.
And shortly, when midnight had gone to rest,
So had I spoken with them, each companion guest.
A fellow pilgrim in me perceived,
I was of their fellowship received.
We made agreement that we'd early rise
To catch the first available flight, as I will to you apprise.

But none the less, whilst I have time and space,
Before yet further in this tale I pace,
If it may be in accord with you
To describe the shape of this accidental crew.
Whether short and stout or lean and tall,
Of the fairer sex, or not fair at all;
In truth how their characters appeared to me
Whence they came and their psychology,
And even what clothes they were dressed in.
And with a writer thus will I begin.
Grey-haired and without apparent means,
Unshaven in sweatshirt and worn blue jeans.
After his description, and you know him full well,
We'll hear what tale he perchance can tell.
In hope that it will speed the night,
Distracting us from our communal plight.
For as we know stories hath ways
To pass such nights and ease our days.

CHAPTER 7

Once Upon a Time

In the last four chapters we have discussed the writing of characters. Characters came first in this book and in its title because we can't begin to tell our stories without them. Our themes grow from character. The most brilliantly written story will not move us unless characters we empathize are a part of it. We're not going to abandon our characters as we turn to stories, the topic of Part III. We're going to add story to the mix. Character and story should be developed together, and as we're about to see, so should stories and games.

Building a Home for Characters

Geoffrey Chaucer (1342–1400) was a minor diplomat as well as a poet, and his years spent traveling about Europe on various errands for King Edward III gave him much background for his most famous work, *The Canterbury Tales*. The tales are the first selection of short stories in English, and have earned him the title of "Father of English Literature." As I started this book with characters before moving to stories, so did Chaucer.

His original plan was for a total of 124 stories, but in 13 years of writing, he completed only 24, about a group of middle-class pilgrims who have stopped at an inn in Southwark while on their way to Canterbury. The Middle English in which the tales were composed was a patchwork of the Anglo-Saxon's Old English, and Norman French, courtesy of William the Conqueror. Don't feel bad if you find it difficult to piece together the recognizable words that have survived to this day. Old English was already on the way out when Chaucer was writing. My pastiche of the tale's prologue is modernized pseudo Middle English that owes more to *The Adventures of Robin Hood* with Errol Flynn (Yay Warner Brothers!) than any actual version of the language.

Figure 7.1 Geoffrey Chaucer was once held for ransom by the French.

There are plenty of scholars who have done interlinear and side-by-side translations of *The Canterbury Tales* and to them we owe a debt of gratitude, because they deserve to be read. Things don't become classics by accident. The characters, everybody from church officials to con artists, are vividly and realistically drawn. The stories deal with themes as contemporary today as they were in Chaucer's time: marriage, sex, infidelity, greed, church corruption, and more.

The tales are a perfect transition from our study of characters in games to stories. Chaucer was intensely interested in his characters as individuals, more than just "types." His stories are built on their characters.

There is another reason to take a fresh look at the tales. They are written in a format that will seem familiar to writers of games. There is a frame to the tales: the pilgrimage, a traditional structure Chaucer was familiar with from *The Arabian Nights* and *The Decameron*; a similar structure to television shows like *The Practice, The Sopranos,* and *Sex and the City* where each episode is complete in itself, but framed by the ongoing story.

Figure 7.2 Chaucer would have loved *Sex and the City*.

Most games that include story are broken down exactly the same way into levels or quests that are separate episodes with an over-arcing story. For this reason, *The Canterbury Tales* holds an honored place in the evolution of episodic storytelling that began with Homer, and that is a brick in the foundation of the new storytelling I'll explore in Chapters 13, "The Roots of a New Storytelling," and 14, "Modular Storytelling."

Chaucer recognized that characters alone are not enough. They must inhabit stories. He also realized stories without due attention paid to characters were unlikely to touch the reader. It seems obvious today, but this was a revolutionary concept back then. Previous to Chaucer, storytelling in England was confined to romances of high-born men and women whose entire characters could usually be described in one word: either "beautiful" or "handsome." Oh and possibly "brave" for the men. Women were done at "beautiful."

Story or Game: Which Comes First?

All those three-dimensional characters you're now inspired to create for your games need stories to live and breathe in. At what point in the development process do we need to concern ourselves with story? There are three possible scenarios.

While showering one morning I may be struck with a great original never-done-before idea for a game. Instead of the typical console treasure hunt action game where the player searches for pieces to a larger puzzle, or batteries to power a machine that will defeat evil, what if we reverse it? The player must deposit something in receptacles guarded by fearsome beasts. And . . . and . . . these somethings must be built by all these other creatures who the player has to convince to do the job by performing tasks for them, or maybe bribing or blackmailing them, but that isn't important. What is important is to flesh out that game mechanic as quickly as possible into a design, start to think about levels, get a prototype up and running, oh and we'll call the land where this all takes place Grayaria, and the player-character will be called Murk and he'll be handsome . . . and brave!

Those of you who ply your trade writing for games already know where I'm headed with this. How many times have you been hired on a project after the design is well under way? It often seems to be the norm. The scenario usually runs something like the following.

The developers have been sitting around in conference rooms for weeks coming up with one great original never-done-before idea for gameplay after another, watching each build of the prototype on the plasma screen on the wall, and all of a sudden one of them realizes, "Hey, we haven't spent a lot of time on the story . . ." All eyes turn to Norm who's been building complicated structures out of paperclips down there at the end of the table. "Norm, didn't you once take a writing class in college?"

Norm immediately brightens, knocks over his paperclips and admits it's true, and he didn't take any old writing class in college, it was called *creative* writing. Norm has a new action item to take away from the meeting, and everybody gets back to the real work designing the game. Cut to four months later in that same conference room. The first two levels are marginally playable on the plasma screen, and Norm's first six-page draft of the story has been read, and is now being discussed. The producer glances at his Gantt chart, exchanges a look with the lead designer and says, "Norm, this is great, but I think we need to bring in an outside writer. . . ."

Another variation on this theme is the lead designer who decides he will write as well. Four months later in that same conference room the designer's first six-page draft of the story has been read, and everybody in the conference room is either squirmy or slunk down in a chair. Nobody wants to say to their boss, "Norm, this is great, but I think we need to bring in an outside writer. . . ."

Sometimes the realization never hits. Sometimes months into the design process, the freelance writer is brought in to add story to the game. The characters are already drawn, so they don't need any character stuff.

The second scenario goes something like this. A writer comes into a meeting with the developers. They hand him a story, usually by Phillip K. Dick. "This guy's written a lot of stories that have become great movies. We can't afford to option any, but we want you to write us a story that will feel like a Phillip K. Dick story that we can build a great game around." The writer packs up her laptop, heads off to catch her plane, and returns four weeks later with a story that reads as if it were written by Dick himself. She's thanked, promised that the check is in the mail, and leaves to catch her plane.

Freelance game writers know I'm not making these two examples up. How many times have you been hired on a project after the design is well under way? How many times have you been hired at the very beginning, then sent packing with a, "Thanks a lot! We'll take it from here!" Both don't just happen; they happen all the time, even if the writer is on staff. *Both* scenarios happened to different projects at a certain company where I once worked. In one case I had to pick up the pieces. In the other, after a huge amount of wasted money the game was never released.

Gameplay and story work best together when developed together. Trying to tack a story on to an already existing game design, or attempting to cram gameplay into a solid story structure are recipes for mediocrity, if not outright disaster. If each element in a game is to share equal importance in the entertainment experience, it needs to be constantly balanced with the others. We need to develop the story and gameplay together so that each creative process can feed off the other.

Characterization and concept art collaborate in this way. How many times has an artist been inspired by the first lines of prose describing a character? How many times has a writer been inspired by seeing a sketch of the character? It is a two-way street that results in a synergy of two separate but equal crafts creating something that is greater than both of them.

One of the first questions we face before sitting down to write the story of a game is its origin. It should come as no surprise that games based on original ideas are the most attractive to designers—we get to use our own ideas. Developers and publishers like sequels because engines and assets may be reused; teams start with a leg up on the material; and if the first game attracted a following, the sequel's future is rosier. Publishers like adaptations from other media for the same reason they like sequels. The franchise is established in the public eye. Of course, in all cases a great game must follow!

If the developer is lucky enough to have all three options available, what issues should writers and designers be aware of as they begin? Let's start with story that springs from imagination alone.

Original Material

In the ten years I've been writing, designing, and producing games I've rarely been given the opportunity to work on my original ideas. The games have been based on other media; franchises; sequels; designs already in progress; or someone else's sketchy concept.

The only game design I ever worked on which was my idea from the beginning was *Sideshow*, and that was shelved so I could work on the Ripley's sequel. One game I'm about to begin work on is based on material from another medium. Another waiting in the wings is still seeking funding, but is based on material from another medium. Even

Figure 7.3 *Dark Side of the Moon*: the closest I've come to starting from scratch.

those where I had the most freedom like *The Riddle of Master Lu* and *Dark Side of the Moon*, the initial concepts were not my own.

I think every writer must want to do original work, or why be a writer at all? Of course, even in 20 years writing series television, I rarely had that chance either. Even pilots I wrote were sequels or based on other media, with a single exception. So what is the writer to do? I try to bring myself to each project with an open mind. I find within it elements that hook me and that I can make my own: a character, an aspect of the arena, the theme, a twist, a surprise or two. And I find original ideas that work within whatever parameters are laid out for me.

Being able to realize your own dreams by writing something that is your vision from start to publication is a holy grail in collaborative media. And if you get the opportunity, don't squander it. Books are different, of course. My last book, a mystery novel, this book you now hold in your hands, and my next book after this, are entirely my own vision from start to finish. What luxury!

Where does the writer begin? It can be almost anywhere: an engaging character, a one-line story hook, an exciting gameplay element. If you don't start with a theme from the outset one better present itself very early on. But not all ideas, even great ones, are meant to be games.

Every story can't work identically well in all media. When the idea for a story starts to percolate around in my brain it doesn't take long for me to see what form of expression it wants to take: novel, game, play, film, TV pilot, and so on. I've written all of them. Each has its own distinct needs. Some ideas, of course, do cross media, as we'll see in the next section.

What about an idea makes it suitable for a game? Games are an action medium, not a cerebral one. A story that deals with the inner workings of a mind *can* be a game, but only if the game visualizes those thoughts and desires. More probably the game idea should immediately associate itself with activity as well as action, which is why, like films and television, games fall readily into certain genres of crime, fantasy, and science-fiction. The cerebral sides of these genres show up most often and to best advantage in prose. Most successful examples of these genres in action media emphasize the physical action.

Another key point, which I bring up throughout the book, is that games don't do complex stories well. But as I've already mentioned, mystery writers know the best approach is to offer a simple story disguised as a complex story. It isn't necessary that the game story be like this, but it makes it easier to come by story twists and turns that add to the story and give it the weight to balance it with the gameplay. A simple story without surprise or twists can be excruciatingly dull, no matter how well crafted. The *only* exception to this is tragedy, where fate's hand is clearly shown, and events march inexorably towards doom. As we've seen, games don't do tragedy much, so that simple type of story is lost to us.

The trick is to make sure that, even with twists and turns, the story remains clear to the player without vast amounts of exposition. That is why the underlying McGuffin is simple, even if the chasing after it appears complex. Less is more.

Creating a simple story is a big help. Creating an action-filled story is a big help. We must make certain however that both are conducive to gameplay. In the 1970s Hollywood made many so-called multiple jeopardy movies like *The Poseidon Adventure, Earthquake,* and *The Towering Inferno. Independence Day* is structured the same way. These films are filled with action, but not single-player action. Games have been made from *Independence Day,* of course, but allowing the player to play many avatars did not survive the adaptation.

The director Robert Altman, in films like *Mash, Nashville, A Wedding,* and *Gosford Park,* brilliantly weaves characters around events or locations (the Korean War, the city of Nashville and its music, a wedding, and an English country house party). This style of multi-character drama has influenced directors like Quentin Tarentino (*Pulp Fiction*), Alan Rudolph (*Welcome to L.A.*), John Herzfeld (*2 Days in the Valley*), and Stephen Soderburgh (*Traffic*). Keep this type of movie structure in mind though. We'll revisit it when we come to virtual worlds where gameplay *is* experienced by more than one player-character.

I love this structure. It remains popular. It's full of action. But such a structure does not work in single-player games. We've seen some examples in games where the player can shift between two player-characters like Gabriel and Grace in *Gabriel Knight: The Beast Within* and *Gabriel Knight: Blood of the Sacred, Blood of the Damned,* and my generation idea would give players multiple avatars, one after the other. But I've never seen a story-based single-player game with 20 player-characters. I make the story-based distinction because arguably in a strategy or war game the player can control hundreds of "player-characters," but as we'll see, when we get to these types of games in Chapter 15, they are more properly thought of as units, rather than characters, and are manipulated in batches. There's a reason for that ability to lasso a bunch of units together.

It would be an interesting exercise to create a single-player game with multiple player-characters the player could switch between at will, and the result might be as entertaining as it would be unique. The hook would have to be a strong one. The film *Identity* comes to . . . mind. . . . But if you're embarking on an original game idea you won't find much encouragement among those who pay you for such a revolutionary idea. And since I'm looking out for your interests here, unless you have the clout to push it through, you will want to stick with a story idea that focuses on the actions of a single player-character.

A major component a game idea needs is the opportunity for interactivity. The arena should, by its nature, provide the player with gadgets, weapons, locks, characters, vehicles, and all sorts of other elements the player can interact with or manipulate.

The idea must make sense, not only for games, but the type of game too. If we want to portray World War II in a game, and want the player to see the big picture, it would be better to make a strategy game or a virtual world like *World War II Online*. A squad-based combat game could move from engagement to engagement through the course of the war, but some of the big picture will be lost except in the background briefings between missions. If we want to drill down farther, a single-character shooter like the *Medal of Honor* series gives us lots to do as a soldier, but the major developments of the war are usually lost to us, much like they would be to a soldier in actual combat.

The first-person shooter *Call of Duty* does a good job of establishing context with cinematics, but the first-person shooter gameplay cannot focus on the big picture. It shouldn't have to. The point is: choose the style of game to match the scope of your storytelling.

Figure 7.4 This sequence from *Call of Duty* is reminiscent of a scene in the film *Where Eagles Dare*.

Another choice to make is genre. You may be an ardent bug collector, and have found an exciting game mechanic for creating a virtual killing jar, and great cursor control for piercing those frail little bodies with big pins. But you do have to know something about the marketplace before you expend the next year or more of your life, and a few million dollars, to base a game on your passion. (Force the player to collect those same bugs in a vast swamp full of alligators, poisonous reptiles, piranhas, and poachers though, and you may have something.)

I'm so tired of seeing the same old genres made into games over and over again: fantasy, science-fiction, post-apocalyptic, crime. . . . But the fact is that these are the easiest genres to do because they have many of the elements that a) appeal to the demographic and b) lend themselves to gameplay. A worse offense than a hackneyed genre is a me-too product, which essentially duplicates games already on the market.

We're in a catch-22 here. Until developers spend the time and energy to bring exciting products in other genres to market, we seem stuck in the same old ruts. Yet the same old ruts are hard to get out of because well-selling products can still be found in them. If we're going to do an established genre in an established type game-like fantasy RPG or anti-terrorist shooter, we start with two strikes against us in the originality department. Two strikes also in the marketing department, since we'll need something better than cooler explosions to reach the radars of gamers.

We need to assume latest-generation graphics and animation and smooth gameplay. What can set our product apart, therefore, is context, and context is story and character. If we can make these compelling enough, we can be noticed in the mass of other games with the same stalwart male or busty female with an automatic pistol on the box. And yes, even if you avoid stereotypes in the writing, the marketing department hasn't read this book, and will still slap them on your game.

If we're going to try a new genre, or one rarely explored like romance, or a western, or bug collecting, it's all in the execution. The player will accept just about anything if the experience is entertaining. *Roller Coaster Tycoon* had a chance. *Garment Sweatshop Tycoon?* Maybe not, unless the tycoon is also a hip-hop artist or supermodel, but that's [ahem] another genre. *Black & White* attempted to stake out some new territory, but it wasn't much fun to play.

Unfortunately, we cannot create original games in a vacuum. We must be aware of the market. If we're lucky, there's somebody a few cubicles over whose job it is to gather that research. If we're luckier, the research will support a genre and type of game that we enjoy. Writing or designing a pet project without taking externals like demographics into account is irresponsible, a waste of time and money.

These are all issues the writer/designer should consider when creating original material. And there are more. The abilities of the team can affect the decision. Before you embark on that virtual world, it might be a good idea to see who on the team has made one before, or even played one.

Knowing the type of game you want to make is essential. Don't be afraid that your baby may get infected by knowledge. If you don't want to create a game like all the others, at least play those others; study them, and learn how they were built.

This is how we learn: from others' mistakes as well as their successes, from our own mistakes and successes. I worked for a previously successful company that was making a type of game with which they were unfamiliar. It was a brave attempt. But the design lead was very leery of having his ideas influenced by the game establishment. He knew what his vision was, and was determined to see it through no matter what might be happening at other game companies; an understanding of the new player base he wanted to reach; or what the market realities were. That game was in development for years, cost millions of dollars, and ultimately was only released as the type the developer was most comfortable with.

The new game that was going to revolutionize its type never saw the light of day because of the designer's fear of being overly influenced. If you believe strongly enough in your original vision, have the courage to confront and learn from the visions of others, however much you may disagree with them, and be willing to seek a win-win situation by adapting some elements while discarding others. To hide from the game establishment will end in your game remaining hidden as well. A continuing theme of this book is learn the rules before you break them.

Adaptations from Other Media

The major reason we do video game adaptations of material from other media is the success it has already enjoyed that will hopefully result in more sales of our game. Of course, this doesn't always work. Take films for example.

Due to the lengthy development cycle of games, the video versions are best started as soon in the production cycle of a film as possible. Unfortunately, the best cast or most talented director cannot guarantee a hit movie.

I faced exactly this predicament when I was working on *Wild Wild West: The Steel Assassin.* Even with our game slated to be released at the same time as the video version of the film staring Will Smith, Kevin Kline, Salma Hayek, and Kenneth Brannagh and directed by Barry Sonnenfeld (*The Addams Family, Get Shorty, Men in Black*), we had no choice but to press on even after the film opened to terrible reviews and mediocre business. Money had been spent and contracts signed.

Figure 7.5 *Wild Wild West,* a game with the characters from the film, but the spirit of the TV series.

Also, even when a movie is good and does good business, it is painfully obvious that that doesn't guarantee a game's success. Maybe the film's subject matter is simply not suited to another medium, and the gameplay suffers. Or maybe the game developers just drop the ball. As I said above: Not all ideas, even great ones, are meant to be games.

Sometimes there is simply no crossover interest between the audiences that loved a movie and gamers who might want to play in the same fictional setting. This is why we see most adaptations are genres like fantasy or science-fiction. The crossover audience has been well demonstrated. This is also one of the reasons why, despite numerous efforts over a number of years, a romance-themed massively multiplayer game still remains unproduced.

The audience of a soap opera, I was told by an advertising executive as I was about to become head writer on *Edge of Night,* consisted in the main of housewives, college students, law enforcement professionals, and incarcerated felons. Obviously, some of these had access to computers and an interest in computer games, but the largest group, housewives, did not, at least in 1983. Today many more do, but the vast majority of them is playing cards or socializing in chat rooms.

The next issue we face when adapting is staying true to the material. First of all, the very crossover audience we're trying to reach has definite expectations about how the subject matter will be handled. It would be dangerous to take James Bond and plunk him down into a story about starting a shelter for homeless dogs; or change his character to the co-owner of *La Cage aux Folles.*

It's dangerous, but not impossible! Take a look at Charlie Kaufman's wildly different take on the bestselling non-fiction book *The Orchid Thief* by Susan Orleans when he adapted it as a motion picture. The end

Figure 7.6 Nicholas Cage as Charlie Kaufman and his fictitious brother in *Adaptation.*

result, *Adaptation,* is a free-wheeling fantasy about the nature of the job he undertook, hence the title. He put himself at the center of the story and invented a brother, Donald, who also shares screenplay credit (both Charlie and Donald are played by Nicholas Cage). The fictional Donald is actually the commercial side of Charlie's ego, and a critical scene in a hotel room sets up the bizarre shift in tone of the film that baffled many moviegoers.

note

Adaptation also skewers screenwriting guru Robert McKee (acidly portrayed by Brian Cox), and all the other cult leaders of writing who profess to have templates to writing success. If you're reading this book to find such a template, you're doomed to disappointment. There's no such thing.

Staying true to the material does not mean a literal adaptation. It can't. Margaret Mitchell's novel *Gone with the Wind* was made into a classic motion picture, but the film is not a literal adaptation. It would have been impossibly long, impossibly expensive, unwieldy, and far less thrilling. The screenwriters (Sidney Howard credited; Jo Swerling, Charles MacArthur & Ben Hecht, and several more uncredited) under David O. Selznick's guidance faithfully preserved the major incidents of the book, rightly concentrating on the most visual moments from the ball to the burning of Atlanta, but more importantly captured the spirit of the novel.

Television mini-series have much more time to tell a story, but even then changes must be made when adapting prose to film. Even with three motion pictures to adapt the *Lord of the Rings* trilogy, Peter Jackson was forced to make some cuts (like Tom Bombadil), and build up some relationships (like Aragorn and his women) that annoyed purists, but were forgiven by the general audience because the spirit of the books has been so ably captured. Perhaps if the *Matrix* trilogy had been based on 1200 pages of prose, its one-trick pony might have been an equally thrilling ride.

In *Runaway Jury*, the film based on John Grisham's bestseller, the industry targeted by the trial was changed from tobacco to firearms since tobacco is already on its knees and gasping and the firearms industry has yet to be successfully brought to task. Also, of course, it isn't cynical to point out that firearms made for a much more visual opening to the picture. The story moves remained similar, and the twist on the two characters who promised to "deliver" the jury remained the same in spirit, even with the change of culprit.

So, trying to capture the spirit of work from another medium is the safest route. But again there are exceptions. A classic bit of Hollywood folklore tells us that John Huston handed his secretary Dashiell Hammett's novel *The Maltese Falcon* and told her to take out all the description and type up the dialogue in screenplay format. That was the first draft of his adaptation. Of course, it may have helped that Hammett's style was lean enough and his page count low enough to make the exercise possible. I doubt if the secretary would have had the same success with James Joyce's *Ulysses*.

Next we need to decide whether to tell the exact same story; borrowing characters and set pieces, but altering the action to suit gameplay; or start from scratch with the same characters in the same world, but with an entirely new storyline.

Telling the exact same story is difficult for a number of reasons. Action that works well in a film may not translate to gameplay. The story moves when analyzed may turn out to be unaffected by the central character's action, or happen in scenes where the protagonist is not present. To adapt them literally we'd need to use cut scenes without the player-character to advance the story. It can be done, but it removes the player from the game action.

Another reason literal adaptations are tricky is that games are puzzles, and players advance through them by solving those puzzles, whether they're mind-benders like François Robillard's laboratory puzzle from *The Riddle of Master Lu* or simply gunning down a Nazi soldier. Adapting the exact plot of a movie, particularly the resolution, means that the player knows the ending already.

This isn't such a problem when adapting a book to film, or a movie to the stage. The audience goes to see it to relive memories, as well as seeing a favorite story in a new form. Even then, adapters often make changes, again to endings, to retain a surprise or two.

Hal Barwood is a fellow Hollywood immigrant. He cowrote the first feature film Steven Spielburg directed, *The Sugarland Express*, and cowrote as well as produced *Dragonslayer* before becoming a project lead at LucasArts. There Hal had a lot of experience adapting both the *Indiana Jones* and *Star Wars* franchises to games. He shares some of the challenges in adaptations with us in his sidebar.

Hal Barwood, Writer/Designer

I've built three Jones games. Successfully adapting Indy's character to interactivity meant paying attention to four key ideas:

First of all, in a game there is no Harrison Ford to admire, and it wouldn't matter if there were—the player is the star, and Jones is merely his avatar. Instead of basking in reflected glory, the player is asked to roll up his sleeves and go to work; to understand and solve exactly the kinds of problems that movie heroes solve for us. This means that a lot of the fun is to be found in the world around Indy. Special care must be taken to make it a rich and varied experience, and to explain his situation in it.

Figure 7.7 Hal Barwood.

Second, the twists and turns of a good story can easily seem like rococo decoration in an environment where action speaks much louder than words. Plots must be lean. Games are ten times longer than movies, however, so there's still time and space for a lot to happen.

Third, character means one thing in a movie, and something else in a game. On the silver screen, the hero's most important attributes are his dramatic characteristics—for example, Indy's burning desire to investigate the mysteries of antiquity, his eye for women, his greed. In a game, his most important attributes are his fists, his whip, and his revolver. Players care little about who Indy is, and a lot about what he can do. In designing *Fate of Atlantis*, a puzzle game, I was careful to include action elements. On his way to the fabled city, the player had to evade Indy's enemies while riding a camel, win a car chase, operate a balloon and a submarine, and use his fists.

Finally, games are good at creating a different emotional experience than movies. Conventional feelings like love, hate, and sorrow, the emotions of literature and drama, give way to frustration, determination and fiero, the emotions of sport. Accordingly, in designing *The Infernal Machine*, I included a lot of dangerous stunts, some pretty fierce combat, and a series of exotic boss monsters. After each challenge, the game offered substantial rewards in the form of cool powerups and wild new territory to explore.

As evidenced by his games, Hal chooses to adapt the franchise and its characters, and not the literal plots of specific films. This did not prevent him from respecting both the characters and the spirit of the franchise, even as he put them into original stories.

My first adaptation was *Once upon a Forest*, based on a Twentieth Century-Fox animated film. I stayed close to the source material, condensing it and altering it for gameplay, but staying true to the characters and the ecological theme of the film. Later when I adapted *Wild Wild West*, I created an entirely new story. I was not enamored of the screenplay. It took a winking, smug, ultra-hip approach to the original. How do you spoof a show that was already a spoof? The same arch treatment of my favorite television series, *The Avengers*, also ruined that movie for me. (Boo, Warner Brothers, for both remakes!)

The screenplay was all I had to go on when I began writing. I retained the updated train of the film because it made a great base of operations with plenty of cool gadgets for players to use, and we based our design on photographs of the film's sets. But I decided to remain true to the spirit of the original television series even though my James West and Artemus Gordon were obviously based on Will Smith and Kevin Kline.

Having tried both approaches, I much prefer adapting a character or a franchise. The design has a much better chance to be a good game than when tied to a linear story developed for another medium. And because the gameplay and story are developed in concert, the balance between the two is more easily maintained.

Sequels

Congratulations! The first game was a hit! Now what? There is no fixed rule that sequels will be worse than the originals. The sequels to the film versions of *Charlie's Angels* and *Lara Croft: Tomb Raider* were. Yet *Godfather II* and *Aliens* were at least equal to, and in my mind anyway, superior to the originals. Why do some sequels work and others don't?

Games have a built-in bonus for sequels: improved graphics. More pixels, more polygons, and better lighting effects all help sequels to look "better" than the originals.

There are several different ways to approach sequels. The most obvious one is the worst: rehash the original. Neither of my first two examples added anything to the mix, deciding to play it safe and just go with what had worked before. *Godfather II* built on its predecessor, creating an epic story that cut between a prologue to the first film: Vito Corleone's (Robert de Niro) rise to power, and the assimilation of Michael Corleone (Al Pacino) into the family business after the deaths of his father Vito, and brother Sonny in the first film. *Aliens* took a single character, Ripley (Sigourney Weaver), and the acid-blooded antagonist from the original film, took them out of the haunted house sub-genre of *Alien* and successfully dropped them into another sub-genre: the squad-level combat movie. Some ideas just don't support sequels, as the *Matrix* proved with its one-line "what if?" premise.

All the filmmakers had to work with were variations on a theme that grew thinner with each of two sequels.

"We blew up a chicken coop in our first game. Let's blow up a barn in this one!" Bigger does not necessarily translate into better. That's a second danger to be wary of in sequels. Recognizing that an identical rehash may appeal to hardcore fans, but not bring in any new customers, we can try for the Roman approach. "Fights between bears and lions sold tickets at the coliseum last season, but I'm seeing some empty seats out there now, any suggestions? Yes, Flailius?" "How about we toss a few Christians in there, boss?"

Motion pictures go down this same rocky path every time there is a new technical achievement. CGI creatures were pretty cool the first 50 times we saw them, but each iteration must be even better than the last. The ogre in *The Fellowship of the Ring* was impressive when it attacked in the Mines of Moria. There are more ogres in *Return of the King*, and they're given a larger role to play. Nevertheless, they are easily eclipsed by Gollum. The irony is that Gollum's success owes as much to Andy Serkis, as to advances in CGI.

A successful sequel needs its own identity. The aliens carried on the way the alien did in the first film, and there were more of them, but the context in which they were placed would have made a good film *even if it had not been a sequel*. The sequel must stand on its own merits as a complete entertainment product. And that's how it is best to approach it.

We can be grateful that some of the work has already been done for us. If we can add some more polygons to our characters, and smooth out some rough spots in the animations, it's much easier than starting from scratch. The player expects similar game play, and hopefully we don't need to rebuild the engine from scratch. If we already have bullet-time, all we need to do is find ways to tweak it, or find different situations where it can be used in new, spectacular ways. We begin as writers knowing any returning characters, and we can welcome the opportunity the sequel gives us to explore them in even more depth. And while we don't want to do the same plot, it should have similar elements.

It becomes pretty clear what players are enjoying in a game. The important thing is to give them more, plus making sure the game can stand on its own and be entertaining without thought to how the original was. Again, it's a matter of finding the balance between characters we already like, and new characters that are equally compelling; story and style (see the next section) that is reminiscent of the previous success, but not just a copy of it; and gameplay that adds new features the same way the first game did that set it apart from the crowd.

Finding a Style That Fits

Finding the correct style for the story we want to tell seems like a no-brainer. A squad-level counter-terrorist game like those in the *Rainbow Six* series requires a hard-edged style to action and dialogue that would be as wildly out of place in the wacky side-scroller

Super Mario Bros. series, as the Marx Brothers would have been playing the leads in *Saving Private Ryan*. But it actually isn't as cut and dried as that.

In every tragedy Shakespeare ever wrote, there is humor: the drunken porter in Macbeth.

Or Hamlet's flirtatious teasing of Ophelia.

> "Lady, shall I lie in your lap?" (A double-entendre meaning to have sexual intercourse.)
>
> "No, my lord."
>
> "I mean, my head upon your lap." (Surprisingly not a similar double-entendre.)
>
> "Ay, my lord."

As we learn in high school English class, the humor is used to give the audience some relief from all the carnage and angst. Any game can benefit from not taking even serious subject matter *always* seriously. One of the things we haven't done enough in games is comedy-drama. Our genres may not appear to lend themselves to such subtleties, but *Star Trek* always featured the sparring between the cantankerous McCoy and unflappable Spock even at the most dire moments. And comedies have been built around otherwise tragic situations. The doomed bride Shelby in *Steel Magnolias* (Julia Roberts's star-making role) is the center around which the other very human but very comic characters swirl.

Poor old poisoned Nicole from *Edge of Night!* I need to resurrect her again. I deliberately intercut the shocking scenes of her death during a live broadcast at the fictional TV station—Nicole was a newscaster—with comedy scenes of always frazzled Mitzi at her restaurant trying to enlist the aid of the thuggish chauffeur Gunther after her cook has walked out during the dinner rush. So as Nicole dies, and the broadcast is disrupted, Gunther is busily burning hamburgers and barking at customers. This was *not* done to give the audience any relief at all. I wrote it that way to keep them off-balance, to make the death all the more shocking when played off against the humor of the restaurant scenes.

We'll talk about comedy more in Chapter 11. There are some other points about style to consider. It should be:

- True to the material. Every so often people will try to upgrade a Shakespearean play. Kenneth Brannagh's *Hamlet* was set in the early 1900s. *West Side Story* and *Romeo + Juliet* update *Romeo and Juliet* to New York and L.A. street gangs. But all remain essentially true to the material. However in the 60s, that breeding ground for experimentation in all walks of life, there was an off-Broadway production of *Hamlet* performed on roller-skates. Hmmm.

- The best style to tell the story. *Pork Chop Hill* and *M.A.S.H* are both films set during the Korean war, but whereas the first film is grimly realistic in its depiction of war, *M.A.S.H* is irreverent and hilarious, even as gouts of blood are hitting the roof of the surgical tent. It's not the setting or arena that suggests the style, but the story told within it.

- A style that makes sense for our medium. I'd love to do a musical game. It's one of my favorite genres. The second play I had produced was a musical. But it would have to make sense as a game as well. The musical genre alone shouldn't prohibit it from being a game, but unless it was hip-hop it might not work as a first-person shooter. Remember the bug collector idea? It's all in the execution.

- Finally, whatever the style we settle on, that style should remain consistent throughout the game. If we interject drama into a comedy game it should still be a legitimate part of the story and the world, and spring naturally from our characters. Remember Laing told us that even schizophrenics are not just crazy. They have an interior reality which may be at odds with the rest of the world, but it isn't a box of isolated tics. It is a consistent reality.

Linear Versus Non-Linear

One of the great misconceptions many writers and designers have when they sit down to write story for a game is that they think the story must be linear. I hear this time and time again from writers who should really know better. I can understand it, if the person holding this view is a writer newly arrived to our industry from other media. I can understand if it's another member of the development team that knows little about how storytelling developed. It makes no sense to me when someone who understands that games can be non-linear doesn't see how to make a story game that way.

This misconception is used all the time as an excuse for seemingly intelligent people, and well known designers, to say things like, "Story must be linear. That's why story and games don't really go well together." Or "Story forces the game to be linear, but I want the player to be able to do whatever she likes in any order, so I won't have story, just backstory or context."

In one sense progression through all games is linear. Every time a player moves from level to level in an action game, she is following a linear path. In fact, in the strictest sense, each game *experience* is linear because the player makes only one set of choices on what to do. Let's say a player reaches an obstacle she can't get past, so she backtracks in the level to find something that will help her: a hint, an item, or another obstacle that must be overcome first.

As we see in Figure 7.8 even if the player returns again and again to the first obstacle, then goes off in multiple directions until she figures out how to get past it, she is following a linear path of her own making. That path can end up looking like 100 feet of tangled string tossed in a drawer, but as long as you recognize that the player is always moving forward through the game (even if she appears to be retracing her steps), the experience must be linear.

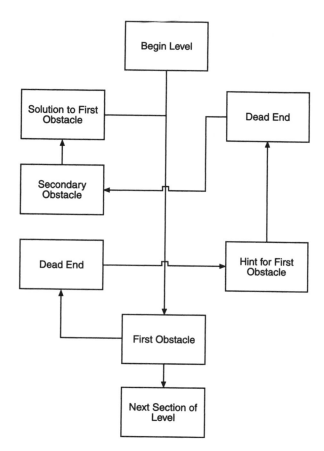

Figure 7.8 Linear Experience in Non-Linear Space.

The *gameplay* however can be as non-linear as we want. This is obvious in a treasure hunt game where players can access many discrete areas, and may move from one to another and back again.

Both examples would seem to make any coherent storytelling impossible. Yet in fact it's perfectly possible, even desirable, because it is storytelling that doesn't get in the way of the player experiencing the game in whatever order she chooses.

The Riddle of Master Lu was non-linear, but many reviewers didn't notice because they thought they'd cleverly discovered the *golden path*. There wasn't one.

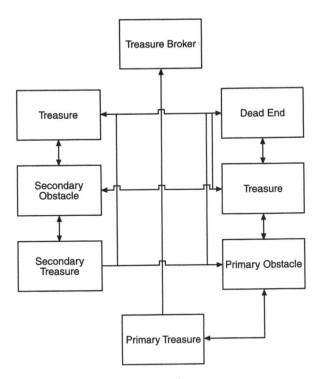

Figure 7.9 Non-linear gameplay.

We game designers sure are an eclectic bunch. We use the word *mana* to describe a measurable amount of energy that powers our magic spells in RPGs. The word mana means a supernatural or spiritual power, and comes to us from various Melanesian and Polynesian religions. In New Zealand today, highly regarded individuals are said to possess mana.

The word *avatar* we often use to describe the player-character was used in the *Ultima* series of RPGs and popularized in Neal Stephenson's science fiction novel *Snow Crash* where it referred to a representation of someone in a virtual reality where that person could interact with his surroundings. It actually comes from Hindu mythology, where it meant the temporary body or incarnation a God adopted when visiting earth.

Golden path comes from Zen Buddhism, and refers to the Buddha's eight-fold path to nirvana or enlightenment:

1. The four noble truths (life is suffering, suffering is caused by desire, desire can be broken, travel the eight-fold path)
2. Right intention
3. Right speech
4. Right action
5. Rights means of livelihood
6. Right effort
7. Right awareness
8. Right meditation

Unfortunately, the accepted wisdom of a "golden path" in game design forces linear thinking on game designers as much as any story might. Thinking in terms of paths at all is misleading. Non-linear doesn't mean many paths. It means *no* paths. There are not two, but three, possibilities open to us.

We can place the player in a long, narrow tunnel. A side-scroller action game is essentially a long tunnel viewed in sections from the side. The player-character can move forward or back, maybe even up and down, but side to side movement is limited by two-dimensional space pretending to be three-dimensional. When action games first moved into 3D space, designers would still try and keep players on tracks or "rails" so they couldn't stray too far. The RPG *Dungeon Siege* is a perfect example of this design philosophy where the player has the illusion of some freedom of movement, but really the walls are only a bit farther apart, and the path is just as linear.

We can place the player in a twisty maze of passageways where there may be many side passages and dead ends. Some of those side passages may eventually find their way to our destination, but a golden path is the "best" choice, even if without a map it isn't clear what the exact steps along that golden path may be.

Or we can place the player in an open space dotted here and there with interactions: mobs to kill, merchants to trade with, treasures to locate, and quests to undertake. This is the truest non-linear game space. It can also be the most difficult to manage.

The PS2 game *Baldur's Gate: Dark Alliance* uses all three possibilities. It narrows its world to literal paths in the mountains; gives players many passages to explore in the sewers beneath the city; and even provides open spaces like the swamp. Yet the storytelling is strictly linear. The game's levels can only be played in one order, despite the lesser or greater degrees of freedom of movement in each level.

This is the popular "python" approach to providing the player freedom of movement, yet still forcing him through a linear storyline. Think of the game's structure as that of a python who has swallowed several animals. He might look like this:

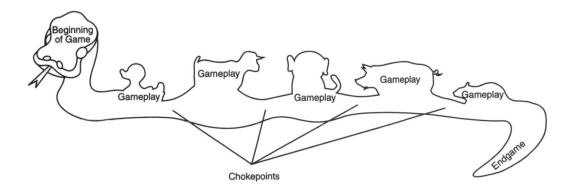

Figure 7.10 Linear structure with big bites of non-linear gameplay.

The narrow sections are called chokepoints. They can be levels, but they don't have to be extracurricular to the game world. They can be locked doors, bridges that collapse behind the player-character, palace guards, a boat that has run out of fuel, and so on. In his book, *Game Design: The Art and Business of Creating Games*, Bob Bates defines them as "points beyond which the player can't go back, other than by restoring a saved game." There can be a practical technical reason for this that has nothing to do with storytelling. Bob points out that "If you design a multiple-disc game with a huge world and allow the player complete access to the entire world at any time, you are designing in the problem of annoying disc swaps for the player."

This was certainly true for me in *Dark Side of the Moon*. The non-linear structure of both game and story led to way too much disc swapping. We tried to break the disks up by "levels" of the huge mining colony, but anytime the player hopped on an elevator, or took the mystical shortcut of a "river of light," he swapped discs. That was a few years ago, however, and hard drive capacity continues to grow and grow. These days, single-player games on personal computers load entirely on to a hard drive with the occasional exception or option of leaving large cinematics on disc.

Of course, all virtual worlds load the bulk of their graphics on to the player's computer, the client, because one of their draws is worlds where players do have access to the entire world at any time. Sometimes they break up contiguous space into zones that have to be loaded separately. These zones can be cleverly disguised as dungeons or planets, but there is still no disc swapping involved, just hard drive grinding.

The python structure creates the illusion of non-linearity for the game, while only needing it at certain spots. It can be very comforting to writers who think game stories must be linear.

But there is no need for writers and designers to try and wrestle the game structure into a linear form just because they want stories in their games. Any of the three forms (tunnel, maze, or open space) lend themselves to storytelling as much as they do gameplay. The first happily accommodates linear story. The second requires some branching or web structure. The third requires a modular approach to storytelling. We've certainly seen our share of the first structure, and even some of the second. The third we will explore in detail in Chapters 13 and 14 when we look at game stories that have no need to be linear at all.

Avoiding Clichés

We've talked about avoiding stereotypes when writing characters. Now it's time to look at the similar damage clichés can do to our stories. Just as our shared unconscious understanding of film language sends up a warning flare when the camera axis is crossed or exposition freezes the action and warns the audience something has gone wrong, the game player's antennae begin to itch if either story or gameplay is stale and derivative.

Clichés are a recipe for boredom. Yet so many game stories are dependent upon cliché! Some writers, when working within a genre, are scared of it. Genre writing can be a crock pot of cliché. Some inexperienced writers just dive in head first, assuming genre writing must be clichéd. Others decide to cop an attitude toward the genre. The clichés still remain, but now there's a lot of winking and chuckling behind the scenes as if to say, "Yeah, we know this stuff is pretty bad, but that's what we're stuck with when we do film noir."

Here is another reason people think stories in games don't work. How unfair it is to assume that because some writers cannot get beyond clichés that game writing can only be clichéd, and therefore boring! How many times have we heard a reviewer say about the story in a game, "It's about what you'd expect from a game." I don't care if the reviewers are willing to shrug it off. Writers can't. Game stories deserve as much respect as character.

How do we avoid clichés? By learning to recognize them when we see them. How do we do that? There are three ways.

The first should be obvious. Stories are built on characters. Build a story on stereotypes, and you will most likely end up with clichés. Stereotypes tend to speak in clichés, make clichéd decisions, and act in clichéd ways.

The second is to make the story our own. Our truest characters are part ourselves and part observed behavior. Sometimes they can be the same. Sometimes we can't tell if they are or not. Our truest stories are combinations of our life experience; observed bits of reality that are "dramatic" even if they are not truly drama; and stories that are drama because they are translations of life seen through the eyes of our fellow writers.

The third is to know how the story we're writing relates to all those other stories people have already told. We *can* learn from studying and analyzing the work of other writers. We will see how they successfully handled a love scene or an action sequence. But if we start to break them down into their component parts, we run the risk of discovering lists. You know the ones I mean, those lists writing gurus are so fond of making up: 10 Potent Conflicts To Ensure Dramatic Stories, 25 Plot Moves Network Executives Love, 50 Emotions that Will Bring Your Characters to Life.

You can find such lists in *Cosmopolitan* ("10 Things Men Don't Want to Say, but Want You to Do!" "15 Erogenous Zones Men Need to Know about Now!"). Those lists won't actually make anyone a better lover. Lovemaking takes heart as much as it does technique. It's the same with lists for budding writers. They do not guarantee that drama, exciting plot moves, or human emotion will ever be a part of your story. Without context, they only increase the chances the unwary writer will end up neck deep in clichés.

There is no guarantee. All we can do is learn enough about literature (read a lot of books!), drama (see a lot of plays, or read them if we have to!), and film (see a lot of movies and TV!) to help us begin to recognize clichés. Then we must bring our own life experience to the equation: *our* emotions, *our* dreams, the poetry of *our* souls. If we don't succeed—and even great writers fail often—we at least will have tried. If we don't try, we are doomed to a Sartre-like hell where our efforts at storytelling continue to be shrugged off with the words, "It's only a game."

CHAPTER 8

RESPECTING STORY

When I discussed the importance of respecting the characters we create, I mentioned that granting characters purpose beyond the designer's convenience makes it easier for us to tell our stories. By the same token, respecting the story makes it easier for us to design our games. I've already suggested some ways of respecting story even before we reached this chapter, and want to briefly recap them before we move on.

- Give the story a reason for existing by providing it with a compelling theme. Start with that theme or discover it early.
- Develop the story in concert with gameplay. Don't try to tack either one on to the other like an afterthought.
- Balance the story with the gameplay. The same amount of player time needn't be spent on both, but both should be built with the same craft and care.
- Ensure that the story fits our medium.
- Make the story worthy of its characters.

Now let's examine some more ways to respect story and make it as gripping and entertaining as our gameplay.

Willing Suspension of Disbelief

"Water, water every where
And all the boards did shrink;
Water, water every where,
Nor any drop to drink."
　　　　　　—Samuel Taylor Coleridge, *The Rime of the Ancient Mariner*

There's no better place to start respecting story than respecting the audience we tell it to. The player who hits the ESC key to skip the story in a game may be able to sit for hours watching a movie in a theatre. He's a captive audience. He's paid money, and unless the film in his opinion is excruciatingly unworthy of his time, he's liable to forgive quite a few lapses in entertainment.

Watching TV, on the other hand, he may hit the channel buttons (a remote control's escape key) just as much, and he's doing it for the same reason he does in a game. The material is unable to capture his attention. Maybe the exposition is too long, or too wordy. Maybe the characters are stereotypes or the story is a quagmire of clichés, so he doesn't have to watch. He already knows what's going to happen.

We need to give the player some credit though. If he finds a TV show worthy of his time, the remote is put down and the popcorn is picked up. If he finds story in games worth following, he might actually enjoy it enough to keep his finger off ESC. What can we do to ensure this? Absolutely nothing. What can we do to at least make it possible? Understand our responsibilities as authors to the concept of "willing suspension of disbelief." We try very hard to provoke our audience/player into willingly suspending her disbelief. It is important to know, or at least sense ways to help players suspend disbelief; and conversely when we're doing something that fights against that desire.

Often erroneously shortened, leaving off that all important first word "willing," the phrase "willing suspension of disbelief" comes to us from Samuel Taylor Coleridge (1772–1834). Coleridge was a maverick. Abandoning Cambridge University, he and his friend, fellow poet Robert Southey, attempted to found a

Figure 8.1 Coleridge was more than willing to suspend his disbelief.

commune in Pennsylvania, but the effort failed. Before long, Coleridge put radical politics on a back burner and settled down to doing what he did best: writing poetry.

The poems Coleridge is most remembered for are "The Rime of the Ancient Mariner" and "Kublai Khan," both written when he was 26. He suffered facial pain most of his life and, as was the fashion of the day, was prescribed opium for the pain. His inspiration for "Kublai Khan" reportedly came to him in an opium dream. Along with another friend, William Wordsworth, Coleridge is considered one of the founders of the Romantic Movement in poetry. In his middle age, opium addiction consumed Coleridge and drove away all who were dear to him. He still managed to work, turning out a book of prose dissertations called *Biographia Literaria* that included literary critiques and theory and in which he writes about how the volume of poetry copublished with Wordsworth that contained "The Rime of the Ancient Mariner" came about.

Their plan was to cowrite and publish a book that represented what they considered "the two cardinal points of poetry, the power exciting the sympathy of the reader by a faithful adherence to the truth of nature, and the power of giving the interest of novelty by modifying colours of imagination." Wordsworth, not surprisingly, chose subjects from ordinary life. Coleridge goes on:

"In this idea originated the plan of the 'Lyrical Ballads'; in which it was agreed, that my endeavours should be directed to persons and characters supernatural, or at least romantic, yet so as to transfer from our inward nature a human interest and a semblance of truth sufficient to procure for these shadows of imagination that willing suspension of disbelief for the moment, which constitutes poetic faith."

Today almost 200 years later many who know the origins of "willing suspension of disbelief" think Coleridge was speaking of drama. He wasn't. He was talking about a depiction of events outside the norm that is still persuasive enough to capture a reader or audience. Appreciation of reality is replaced by faith.

How do we approach this when writing events set outside the world an audience or player knows to be real?

We need to believe in the world we create and respect it. Make sure its laws are consistent and logical. Aspects of the game world should all feel like they belong in the same universe together. If we take care to do this, the player has enough points of reference in the world and its fiction to latch on to that she is more willing to accept those points that are alien to her.

This approach encourages us to immerse the experience in as much real-world detail as possible. See the section later in this chapter on verisimilitude for other ways these details can help our stories. We should also try—as much fun as we think it may be—not to break what we call *the fourth wall*.

The Fourth Wall

note

THE FOURTH WALL: a theatrical reference alluding to the fact that traditional theatre sets have three walls: upstage and one on either side. The audience views the play through the invisible fourth wall while the actors perform as if it is as solid as the other three.

In live theatre, sets are built, furnishings placed, and props arranged to create the illusion that a fourth wall exists to the actors, but the audience is permitted to see through it. If we were to physically place the fourth wall there, the audience couldn't see the play and would demand their money back. Movie and television sets are built on the same principle, although sometimes adding the ability to fly any of the four walls in and out, that is to remove or replace them to allow camera and lights to be able to cover the action from any angle.

www.rialtosquare.com

Figure 8.2 The traditional proscenium arch.

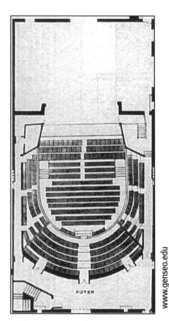

www.genseo.edu

Figure 8.3 The line between the world of the play and the world of the audience is clear.

Thrust stages, so called because they are built out into the audience and arena stages for "theatre-in-the-round" where the audience surrounds the stage, have no proscenium. The term fourth wall has easily migrated to other entertainment media. Early film directors framed their action as if viewed through a proscenium, and movie theatres were traditionally built with prosceniums and curtains. Today, even though the arch may survive only in older theatres, the fourth wall is easily defined by the movie screen, the screen of a television set, or the monitor.

When it first came into vogue, this invisible fourth wall was framed by the proscenium arch. The proscenium arch takes its name from the construction of playhouses in ancient Rome, the word *proscenium* translating as "in front of the stage." The modern stage version developed during the Italian renaissance which explains the elaborate carving that surrounded the arch, emulating an ornate picture frame.

Edge of Night was one of the last daytime dramas to be shot as if it were live action, even though we were recording onto one-inch video tape. Approximately six sets were built on the soundstage, circling three cameras, lights, sound boom, and so forth in the center. Actors would wait patiently on their sets while the camera men and boom man would move from set to set, shooting the scenes in continuity, unlike movies, where you shoot out of continuity, doing all the work needed at a single location or set before moving on to the next.

While we could, of course, stop tape and re-record if there was a glitch in the scene, we attempted to shoot the show every day in a single take. Even so, there was still the occasional disconcerting crack in our fourth wall. I remember one taping where it was supposed to be snowing outside. Cornstarch was floating charmingly down beyond the windows of an interior set. An actor entered from outside, enthusiastically stomping the snow from his boots, and slamming the door to keep out the imaginary cold. The door slam dislodged a few flakes from the top of the set. Just for a moment it snowed inside! We broke the fourth wall, but we left it in.

In the two years I was head writer, we succeeded in a complete run-through only a couple of times, and it was a cause for pride and celebration. It gives one a real appreciation of how hard live television must have been.

I gave that example because it shows how the fourth wall remains metaphorically important when we discuss "breaking" it. Here we are speaking of breaking the illusion that the characters are unaware of our observation, or interference in the case of games; or that the fiction's creators are unaware that their work is being performed for an audience.

There are, of course, times when the fourth wall is purposely broken. For example soliloquies spoken directly to the audience like this (one of my favorite Shakesperean speeches to quote), the opening to *The Life of King Henry the Fifth*:

> "O for a Muse of fire, that would ascend
> The brightest heaven of invention,
> A kingdom for a stage, princes to act
> And monarchs to behold the swelling scene!
> Then should the warlike Harry, like himself,
> Assume the port of Mars; and at his heels,

Leash'd in like hounds, should famine, sword and fire
Crouch for employment. But **pardon,** and gentles all,
The flat unraised spirits that have dared
On this unworthy scaffold to bring forth
So great an object: can this cockpit hold
The vasty fields of France? or may we cram
Within this wooden O the very casques
That did affright the air at Agincourt?
O, pardon! since a crooked figure may
Attest in little place a million;
And let us, ciphers to this great accompt,
On **your imaginary forces** work.
Suppose within the girdle of these walls
Are now confined two mighty monarchies,
Whose high upreared and abutting fronts
The perilous narrow ocean parts asunder:
Piece out our imperfections with your thoughts;
Into a thousand parts divide on man,
And **make imaginary puissance;**
Think when we talk of horses, that you see them
Printing their proud hoofs i' the receiving earth;
For 'tis **your thoughts** that now must deck our kings,
Carry them here and there; jumping o'er times,
Turning the accomplishment of many years
Into an hour-glass: for the which supply,
Admit me Chorus to this history;
Who prologue-like **your humble patience pray,**
Gently to hear, kindly to judge, our play."

This exhortation is aimed directly at the audience, bemoaning the fact that the play they are about to see may not quite live up to the ideal, but promising that the actors will give it their best, and if the audience is willing to suspend its disbelief, things may not turn out too badly after all. I bolded parts to highlight how many times the *willingness* of the audience to use their imaginations is hoped for. Shakespeare, a pretty good writer actually, knew the importance of immersion.

And there are other ways the fourth wall may be broken by intent. Where the characters in the classic Walt Disney animated features would rarely (never?) break the fourth wall, other cartoon characters, particularly the equally classic creations of Chuck Jones like Bugs Bunny and Wile E. Coyote would often directly address the motion picture audience or the TV viewer.

This style of allowing characters to comment on the action carried over from cartoons to live actors in the occasional movie, usually always comedies. There is a delightful short sequence in François Truffault's celebration of children, *Small Change*, where a boy is followed by the camera. Every few steps he turns and mischievously glances back directly at his pursuer. This works because of the freeform New Wave style of Truffault's filmmaking.

Another such memorable moment occurs in Truffault's *Shoot the Piano Player*, a tragicomedy where a hardened criminal swears he's telling the truth on his mother's life. Quick cut to the poor old lady keeling over in her bedroom. Then right back to the scene. The audience fell out of their seats laughing.

The TV series *Moonlighting* that made Bruce Willis a star, and later series like *Hercules: The Legendary Journeys* and *Xena: Warrior Princess* all broke the fourth wall with comments directed to the camera. While this style works in certain situations, there is a very good reason why the vast majority of films, TV shows, and plays choose to maintain the illusion of the fourth wall. The illusion aids the audience in its willing suspension of disbelief.

Figure 8.4 Autolycus, played by Bruce Campbell, would acknowledge the camera on *Xena: Warrior Princess*.

Every time we break the wall, we should have a very good reason for doing it. Often it's just a bad idea. In computer games there is a tradition of breaking the fourth wall. The earliest text adventures encouraged it, mainly because they were written in second-person: "You open the door and walk into the next room." Whenever there is a "you," it suggests there also is an "I." The creator of one of these games would therefore, unlike the Wizard of Oz, step out from behind his curtain, and wink at the player.

As I pointed out in Chapter 3, in Steve Meretsky's *Planetfall* whenever the player chose to save the game, Floyd would respond, "Are we going to do something dangerous?" Funny? Absolutely. But for the moment at least the fourth wall is gone. Floyd is no longer a sidekick of the player-character within the game fiction, but exhibiting knowledge that they are both within a game, and knowledge that saving games is an established convention.

This remains a popular type of game writing, and it crops up in all types and genres of games. Remember when you click on one of your minions in *Warcraft* too many times without giving him his marching orders, he'll get annoyed and shout, "Stop poking me!" There's not much problem if the type of game is not dependent on story like a real time strategy game. *Warcraft* was one of the earliest. It works fine here because the character isn't as much a character as he is a unit.

Another reason writers of games break the fourth wall I mentioned earlier. They often seem fearful of genre material. This manifests itself as an attitude of superiority where the writer feels the need to reassure the gamer that he knows it's all nonsense. Here's one way the writer can reassure the gamer that, like he, the writer is far hipper than the material he's writing. He isn't, of course. Those that feel themselves above the material come and go, but genres endure.

It's all dependent on tone. If the tone of the game is wildly comedic, and the world of the game is a place where anything can happen, then such asides work fine. Unless you're doing an out-and-out spoof like Mel Brooks' *Young Frankenstein, Blazing Saddles*, and many more, try to refrain from copping an attitude. Stay true to the material.

It's far more difficult to create immersion in a game than it is in a film. The player is constantly busy, interacting with the game through game pad, mouse, or keyboard. When we say we want to make the interface as transparent as possible, we are speaking of the fourth wall. We mean keep it as simple as possible, so as to interrupt the immersion as little as possible. In a game where we want the player as engaged in the characters and story as much as the gameplay, going for a laugh at the expense of the fourth wall is going for a cheap laugh at the expense of character and story. It's difficult enough to immerse the player in our story and characters; why choose to make it harder? If we're going to break the fourth wall, we'd better know what we're doing, and have a damn good reason for doing it.

Let's look at three other traps the writer of games can fall into when he doesn't respect the story.

The Trap of Cut Scenes

I've alluded to this first trap before because it is so common. What are cut scenes? They are those sequences in the game, removed from, yet purporting to represent, the same world and its fiction. They can be an opportunity to switch modes from animation to live actors, or at least upgrade the quality of the graphics. They are used extensively as connective tissue between levels or missions and as eye candy rewards at the completion of a hard challenge, such as the defeat of a boss mob. Boss mobs rightly deserve a death worthy of their difficulty.

Many designers of games seem to think cut scenes are the only way to tell story and reveal character. The writers they hire, particularly if they're refugees from Hollywood, are more than happy to agree with them. Cut scenes are exactly what they're used to. A movie is nothing more than a series of cut scenes. And we've seen over and over again that movies can be great at telling stories.

Let's first examine the good points of cut scenes. They do have much to recommend them.

- First, as stated earlier, when we write cut scenes we're on familiar territory. They follow the conventions of film language without the need for interpretation or translation into interactivity.
- Cut scenes are easily accessible to players who are familiar with this type of storytelling, having grown up with it in television and the movies.
- They can be produced independently of the rest of the game and by a separate team. This can free up resources and help keep development time down.
- Technically, all cut scenes need to run is a multimedia player and codec (coder/decoder), both of which are routinely licensed from third-party developers and dropped into the game code.
- They allow video in the game, and because they don't require interactivity, the limitations of video aren't an issue.
- If they're animated, the animations and graphics can be much richer.

The *Wing Commander* games were a pioneering effort in advancing story through cut scenes. As can be seen, the very nature of cut scenes requires them to be segregated from the rest of the game. This is their greatest strength and, in terms of storytelling, their greatest weakness. It's difficult enough molding story and gameplay into a single entertainment experience without this segregation. Separating story and gameplay because it may seem easier to do than integrating them hurts storytelling in a number of ways.

Figure 8.5 The two worlds of *Wing Commander*. Story.

- As we've discussed, it requires the player to shift gears to enjoy both. Gameplay is an active experience; storytelling in cut scenes becomes passive, just like other media.

- The sequences don't just feel different in delivery; they look different because the game designers are able to ramp up the graphic quality in cut scenes.

- It reinforces Myth #2, games and stories don't mix, from Chapter 1, "Myths and Equations."

- It discourages the search for ways to tell story within the gameplay. If a writer convinces herself that cut scenes are the answer, why try other methods?

- It fosters the belief that story and gameplay don't need to be developed simultaneously,

Figure 8.6 The two worlds of *Wing Commander*. Gameplay.

that story can be added later to gameplay, or gameplay to story, with impunity. This makes balancing the two all the more difficult.

Let's take it in stages, and see if we can wean ourselves from the trap of cut scenes. To answer the first point, remember that I wrote earlier about the shortening of attention spans of passive audiences? Does anyone think the same isn't true of game players? Yet cut scenes, because they are more expensive—that second team isn't cheap—can become bloated in length to justify the time, money, and effort put into them.

Many writers and designers recognize the dangers of cut scenes, but it is a rare few who are able to eliminate them. Take a look at games designed by Tim Schafer like *Monkey Island* and *Grim Fandango*. Tim is very proud of the fact the stories are told without cut scenes.

Just as we often force players to read paragraphs of text in some games, with cut scenes we can force them to sit through sequences that are drawn out to justify their inclusion in the game. By making a special case of the cut scene, we encourage producers to ask, "Why, if we're spending all this money on well-known actors and big production values, are the cut scenes so short?"

Why indeed? Snagging an ensemble of stars like Pierce Brosnan, John Cleese, and Judy Densch to voice their characters adds immeasurably to the illusion that *Everything or Nothing* is another big-budget addition to the James Bond franchise (as do all the vehicles and Bond moves—at last a Bond game that feels like a Bond film!). One of the reasons it works is they don't just show up in cut scenes. And, lo and behold, storyline and dialogue almost measure up to a real Bond movie. That shouldn't be surprising since they were written by Bruce Feirstein, cowriter on three Bond feature films.

This game is an absolute rarity. It still relies on cut scenes where we find the story, but at least the voice actors and dialogue cross over into the game. If you're using their voices anyway, the first step on the road to recovery is to create cut sequences that resemble cut scenes but are sandwiched into the action with the same game engine that drives gameplay.

The *Metal Gear Solid* games, notable for their attention to story, rely heavily on cut scenes as well as long game engine non-interactive passages that pull gameplay to a halt, still segregating it from the storytelling. The *Final Fantasy* series uses both cut scenes and game engine scenes as well to advance story.

Using the game engine alone is the route many Japanese console games like *The Legend of Zelda, Ocarina of Time* take. It may be from necessity. They have less memory to work with than games on personal computers. But it immediately answers the second difficulty on our list. While the player may be forced to stop play for the same length of time as with a regular cut scene, the sequence is within the same game world as gameplay. Also, it is much easier to limit the length of the scenes because no additional team is nec-

Figure 8.7 Every time Link played his ocarina we got a game engine cut scene.

essary to create the sequences. Shorter scenes equal less player fidgeting. This is a good thing! It means they may keep those fingers off the ESC key!

There are no real cut scenes at all in the *Riddle of Master Lu.* Instead there are cinematic moments built with the game engine, such as exchanges of dialogue, or eye candy rewards for the completion of puzzles like a building blowing up and a flood of mercury inundating a villain. There are also brief windowed close-ups of characters, their use mandated by the slim video capabilities of 1994 when game production began.

Figure 8.8 There were no cut scenes at all in *The Riddle of Master Lu.*

Whenever possible, these sequences are mercifully short. There were exceptions, and I should have known better: a couple of excruciatingly long exposition scenes, one in particular between Ripley and the Baron where they sit still almost the entire time. This broke so many of my personal rules: put exposition in action; or at least keep the characters moving; keep such scenes short; don't write wordy paragraphs . . . on and on, why didn't I know better? And if I knew better, why didn't I do something about it? Ah well, every time we sit down to write, it's a learning experience.

So the next step is to keep our cut scene or game engine sequences short. Just like the other media we're emulating. *Half-Life* uses game engine-driven sequences that are little more than a brief appearance of a character, or an overheard snatch of dialogue to support the game's story. When we use the game engine to drive them, sequences can be no more than a split second long: a Spockian raised eyebrow on the part of an NPC, or a shouted command. Once we pare them down this far we should notice something else.

The next step is to create a continuum of scene length from full sequences to single cuts. At the short end of that vast range we have scripted moments that barely interrupt gameplay at all: moments of character revelation like a quick frown the NPC thinks we haven't noticed; moments of storytelling like a sidekick remembering the legend of the haunted castle while you are both swinging across the moat on a rope; moments of storytelling *and* character revelation like an NPC choosing door number two before the player-character decides which of three doors to open.

And once we've noticed this, the next step is to put as much of our storytelling and character revelation into game moments as we can. This is the ideal. Right now we haven't discovered enough ways to put the entire story there, because we've been distracted by cut scenes. But it's okay. Writers of movies and television don't always discover the perfect attack to every scene. We will explore a few approaches to integrating storytelling and gameplay in the next chapter. I expect the readers of this book will find more. Some of you probably have already.

It's a worthy goal. Every time we try to reach this ideal, we're rewarded by story and gameplay that are not at odds with each other, but that complement each other and are balanced. This won't work if you try to add on story to gameplay already developed. It won't work if you try to sandwich gameplay into a locked down story structure. It works beautifully if story and characters and gameplay are developed simultaneously.

Abandon cut scenes? No. I frequently use cut scenes as teasers, or at least cut scene-like game engine sequences. They can still function to provide some context and continuity in games where levels are rigidly separated, for then the gameplay is as segmented as the story. But one day we may see a game where there are no discrete levels; where the only pauses in the action are those chosen by the player; where the immersion is as complete as the best films and books. Story integrated into gameplay will take us there, not story stuck in the ghetto of cut scenes.

When players become accustomed to these cut moments, they will relax and expect them. Then the longer cut sequences will seem all the more palatable. Design and write them with the same care that the gameplay is designed, and there is only one entertainment experience waiting on that disc, not two.

The Trap of Too Much Backstory

The heading of this section must sound so unfair! After all the trouble we've taken to create three-dimensional characters with psychological and sociological dimensions; and all our efforts to create a consistent game world that is logical and faithful to its own rules; how can we fall into a trap of too much backstory?

It's far too easy. One of the telltale signs of amateur writers is that once all the research is done; once the character profiles are written; they can't abandon all that work, trying to shove as much of it as they can into the product it is meant to support. This can be as deadly in a game as it is in a screenplay or book. The only writer I've ever seen who was able to successfully bring off this approach was Jane Jensen in her Gabriel Knight games like *Gabriel Knight: The Beast Within* where *if* the player wants to, he can seek out all the research material in appropriate places inside the game world, but if not, he can move on with his hunt to find the werewolf. Remember the interactive news in the film *Starship Troopers*? "Want to find out more?" Same principle.

For the rest of us, it's better to follow the advice of screenwriter and novelist William Goldman (1931– —). Goldman is the screenwriter of many great films including *All the President's Men, Butch Cassidy and the Sundance Kid,* and *The Princess Bride.* He is also the author of the non-fiction *Adventures in the Screen Trade,* a book in my bibliography that contains a now famous quote about Hollywood: "Nobody Knows Anything."

After doing the research for a project, Goldman cuts away all the fat from his screenplays, leaving only what is essential to the telling of the story. If the characters don't reveal themselves in dialogue and action, paragraphs of description won't help. If convoluted explanations of events the player has been a part of are necessary, we've failed to expose the story. Once we've done the research for the game world our characters will inhabit and where our story will play itself out, it will come alive on its own, or it's fundamentally flawed.

There is a second trap of too much backstory. That is the mistaken belief that backstory and story are the same thing. For all its virtues, the adventure game *Myst* does not have a story. It has a backstory that is gradually revealed through the gameplay. The only effect the player can have on the "story" is to decide the fates of the two brothers. This is only a problem when we mistake backstory and story. As long as we can recognize the difference, a game may get along just fine with only backstory, as *Myst* did. Notice it's an adventure game though, not an action game.

Backstory is often added to single-player games to explain all the shooting and running around. It establishes the antagonist, and what he's been up to. Just as in the Golden Age mysteries where most of the story is a static unraveling of a murder committed early on, the player spends her time in the game making things right again. The much better approach is to establish the antagonist who has an ongoing plan for evil that must be foiled. Villains who wait for the hero to come after them are not worthy antagonists in an action game, and by their inactivity they weaken the protagonist.

Some designers and writers of massively multiplayer worlds recognized fairly early on that if they rely only on backstory, worlds are static and gameplay is repetitive. *Asheron's Call*, the recently cancelled *Earth & Beyond*, and *Horizons* all attempt to feature ongoing story. Games like *Everquest* and *Dark Age of Camelot* that did not recognize this in their initial designs were faced with finding other, often more expensive, means to retain player's interest like additional creatures, higher loot, and more locations to explore. These worlds are much more likely to depend on expansion packs than those that incorporate ongoing story. We'll explore this in more detail in Chapters 18 and 19.

The Trap of Letting Players "Discover" the Story

This trap can be found in single-player games, although because of their size, it is most egregious in virtual worlds. For that reason, my main example will be taken from a virtual world.

I remember several years ago then *Everquest* lead designer Bill Trost was quoted at one of the game's official fan get-togethers that he was frustrated that players were complaining about the lack of story in the game, insisting there was a full, rich "storyline" in *Everquest*, and that people were simply failing to uncover it. Bill was the keeper of the lore (backstory) of Norrath, the world where *Everquest* was set, and he, with the help of others, put a lot of work into that lore. No wonder he was frustrated. What went wrong?

When I left *Everquest* after playing it for almost two years, I wrote a critique of the game signed by my character name, Skyrain Dreamweaver, the same character I've played in most of my adventures in virtual worlds since then. I understood Bill's frustration and was sympathetic, but this was my response.

> This is such a page from the amateur writer's scrapbook, it needs to be mentioned. Successful writing is 1) inspiration and talent and 2) the ability to present the work to the audience so that it can experience it. If you fail at number two, one is meaningless. Stop blaming your audience if they don't get it!
>
> People are simply playing the game you designed. If it isn't the one you wanted to design, or thought you designed, then change it.

I'd only recently begun work on my first virtual world, *The Gryphon Tapestry*, and in retrospect, my comments may have been phrased a bit too harshly, but I was speaking as a player who had his own frustrations about the game, and as a writer who knew better than to hide his story from his audience. The full critique can still be found on several Internet sites, if you're curious.

Games that rely only on lore or backstory fall easily into this trap. As game designers, we realize everything we can make interactive, such as an obstacle or puzzle; everything we can give the player to do, instead of just being told, is a good thing. Virtual worlds in particular need all the "content" they can get to feed the voracious appetites of players. Therefore, on the surface it seems logical to treat backstory the same way, like the clues in some great mystery that must be unraveled, or the extra backstory Jane Jensen made available for the inquisitive to peruse.

There are a couple of differences. Gabriel Knight's game world was much more contained than the vast continents of Norrath. And Jane didn't make an attempt to hide where that backstory was located. By planting bits and pieces of the lore on NPCs and in books scattered through the game world, the *Everquest* designers were deliberately hiding it from players. They assumed players would be interested enough to track it down. And a few were. I remember a couple of fan sites where the collected lore was slowly being gathered.

Unfortunately, as we'll discuss in Chapter 17, not every player of a virtual world is an explorer. Some are just there to kill things and acquire phat l00t. I *am* an explorer, and I couldn't find enough of the lore to make much sense of it. I had to go to those fan sites outside of the game world to fill in what gaps I could.

This is similar to a blunder designers of adventure games can make. We called this a *pixel* hunt and strove mightily to avoid falling into *that* trap.

note

PIXEL: an abbreviation of the term *picture element*, describes the smallest component of a digital image.

Some adventure game designers have the mistaken belief that they can add complexity to their games by adding the step of *finding* the puzzle, forcing players to move their cursors ever so slowly over almost every pixel that a scene was composed of. This practice does not create the anticipated complexity or depth of gameplay. It succeeds only in frustrating players. One solution is the "smart" cursor that changes in some way to indicate it's hovering above an interactive element on the screen.

Another, even more player friendly, is used in *Horizons*. In that game, crafters are required to gather the materials they need from the world in order to make goods. This includes mining, chopping down trees, and harvesting plants, among other activities. Not all rocks or trees or plants are harvestable. Some are permanent fixtures of the background. Every one that *is* useable highlights entirely as the cursor passes over it. This is true of other interactive features in that world as well.

The disconnect comes from turning the exploration or puzzle-solving or interaction that should occur *after* the material is located into impediments in the search. If we're afraid our puzzle or obstacle might be too easily overcome; or that our backstory may be too thin; we may be tempted to add such "complexity." We not only run the risk of obscuring our story, we may fail to expose it to players at all.

The best solution is to reveal backstory through exposition brought to light during the action of an ongoing story. If we have no real ongoing story, it's far better to at least provide pointers to where the backstory can be found. Instead of hiding it, make a big deal of it! Have your three-dimensional NPCs tell players that historians discovered a book previously thought lost, or that archaeologists have excavated some ancient ruins. This does not have to be an added element. These may just be static pointers to locations and objects that have always been, and always will be, part of the game world.

Verisimilitude

note

VERISIMILITUDE: the appearance of truth or the quality of seeming to be true. It mimics reality enough to be perceived as real.

The setting of your game can be a mining colony in the far reaches of space, but we can people it with characters whose motives and desires match our own or those around us. If we propose a land where pigs fly we can still be aware of gravity. No matter how outlandish the conception of our world may be, it is essential that we give the player enough hooks to create the illusion of reality that we refer to as verisimilitude. If we don't, we leave the player floundering without a point of reference she can grab on to.

Maintaining verisimilitude forces us to avoid creating our worlds and stories on the fly, a sign of weak writing in any medium. I've met more than my share of writers who are convinced this style of writing is the only way to go. I was one of them once upon a time. I'll admit it's the most fun. My first plays and screenplays were written this way, and they were vastly entertaining. To me. I was constantly being surprised by the twists and turns in my own stories, and delighted by the unusual choices my characters made. But how indulgent! And how contemptuous of your *other* audience!

We don't want to get hung up on reality. We can't duplicate it, and we shouldn't want to anyway. Moment to moment reality is dull. It's not drama. But we must apply verisimilitude to every aspect of our games to give them the necessary veneer of reality the player requires. He will thank us for it, because it allows him to hit the ground running—and playing—in any world we devise.

Expressionism

note

EXPRESSIONISM: a 20th-century art movement begun in Europe that stresses the expression of emotion and the inner vision of the artist rather than the exact representation of nature.

My favorite movie of all time is expressionist. No, the film is not *The Cabinet of Dr. Caligari* or *Nosferatu*, classics of German expressionism from the days of silent movies.

It is *Night of the Hunter*, the only film ever directed by actor Charles Laughton (1899–1962). Released in 1955, it is a gothic fairytale starring Robert Mitchum and Shelley Winters. Written by noted film critic and novelist James Agee, the story is set in the depression. A Bible-quoting serial killer kills a woman, then pursues her two children for some bank robbery money. That's the plot.

Figure 8.9 Robert Mitchum is a wolf in sheep's clothing in *Night of the Hunter*.

The film is an allegory of good and evil. Check out Mitchum's knuckles in the photograph.

The movie is composed of one haunting image after another: the car at the bottom of the river with its ghastly passenger; the journey of the children down-river in the skiff with the various wild creatures in the foreground of the shots; the silhouettes of farmhouse and a lone rider on a mule. It is also one of the scariest motion pictures ever made.

It was adapted by Agee from a novel by Davis Grubb, and transformed by Laughton into imagery so vivid it is almost unique in filmmaking. It isn't literal. It's far from realistic. Audiences often have difficulty knowing what to make of it. What I bring away is the completeness of its vision in every frame: theme, style, performance, photography, music. If its spell touches you, there's no letting go. It's something I strive for in every game I work on, even if it's only a moment or two where the player is transported from this world, oblivious to time passing, captured heart and mind.

[Agee deserves his own mention as a writer who loved the English language and wrote prose that flows like poetry. His novel "A Death in the Family" won a Pulitzer Prize.]

Symbolism

note

SYMBOLISM: a movement in art at the beginning of the 20th-century. More generally it means infusing objects or actions with significance beyond the literal.

Both Joseph Campbell and Carl Jung tell me they would be delighted if your game writing used symbols. They are a shortcut to the human heart and mind I just spoke about capturing. It allows us to do great chunks of storytelling in the composition of a single scene or the objects within it. No need to be all that subtle. Just as great stories are wasted if nobody can find them, symbols should be accessible.

In *Mirage*, a movie written by Peter Stone, a psychiatrist washes his hands of Gregory Peck's plight as he apparently does the plights of all his patients, by . . . washing his hands. Bond arch-villain Ernst Stavro Blofeld doesn't just happen to have those Siamese fighting fish in *From Russia with Love*. The arrogant mastermind of the plot to compromise Bond, and steal the decoding device is not a gardener, he's a chess player.

But if we're going to use symbols, we must respect them, the same as we should genres. If we laugh at them, they lose their potency. Symbolism isn't just for high art and literature, as the above examples should prove. It is another storytelling tool waiting to be utilized by the writer of games.

Consistency of the World

This isn't the first time I've mentioned consistency, and it won't be the last. It's so important that, even though the concept is woven throughout this book, it deserves its own heading. We've talked about consistency of character and of style. It is a key to helping the player become willing to suspend his disbelief; to preserving the fourth wall; and creating verisimilitude.

It also helps us as writers. Once we settle on a theme, or a group of characters or a story or a style, everything else falls into place, if we're faithful to that element. And when all the elements are consistent with one another, we don't sit staring at the blank page on the monitor hoping for an idea. They suggest themselves thanks to the consistent structure we have built and are maintaining.

Tim Schafer's *Grim Fandango* and *Full Throttle* are examples of beautifully consistent writing and game design.

Arena, story, incidents, characters, puzzles, artwork, and music all combine to create and heighten the unique moods. In the first, the player-character is Manny Calavera, travel agent to newly arrived souls in the Land of the Dead from Mexican folklore. The second is the game version of a biker movie, funny and deliberately lowbrow.

Many of the games we remember most fondly win a place in our hearts because of consistency. Whether it is the theme or story or characters that we remember most, we remember them because they are reflected in all aspects of the game. Consistency can make good games unforgettable.

Lucasarts

Figure 8.10 The consistency of *Grim Fandango's* bizarre setting helps bring it to life.

Setting

"Two households, both alike in dignity,
In fair Verona, where we lay our scene,
From ancient grudge break to new mutiny,
Where civil blood makes civil hands unclean.
From forth the fatal loins of these two foes
A pair of star-cross'd lovers take their life;
Whose misadventur'd piteous overthrows
Doth with their death bury their parents' strife.
The fearful passage of their death-mark'd love,
And the continuance of their parents' rage,
Which, but their children's end, naught could remove,
Is now the two hours' traffic of our stage;
The which if you with patient ears attend,
What here shall miss, our toil shall strive to mend."

—William Shakespeare, *Romeo and Juliet*

The classic example of the importance of setting in literature is the heath, a vast expanse of fallow rolling hills, sudden steep defiles, and rugged coastline that made up the fictional county of Wessex in England's west country that is as much a character of the novels of Thomas Hardy (1840–1928) as Bathsheba Everdene of *Far from the Madding Crowd* or Tess in *Tess of the d'Urbervilles*. Hardy, a master of setting, is said to have written his settings as if they were major characters in his stories.

This is the same general location as the famous moors of detective fiction on display in *The Hound of the Baskervilles* by Arthur Conan Doyle (1859–1930) with its windswept tors, fog-gripped hollows, and bogs that can suck a horse under in seconds.

In drama we "set the stage" for the action of a play with every bit as much care as a gleaming diamond is set in a golden ring. Today Broadway audiences applaud the set as the curtain rises on a play with the same enthusiasm they applaud the actors after the curtain's final fall. The baroque setting of Andrew Lloyd Webber's *Phantom of the Opera* is a faithful adaptation of its source novel, recreating the Paris Opera House down to the massive crystal chandelier that swings menacingly out over the audience and plays its own role in the musical's climax.

But the setting need not be so elaborate. In the play *Waiting for Godot* by Samuel Beckett, we have a stage empty except for a withered tree. In his adaptation of Herman Melville's *Moby Dick*, Orson Welles was faced with recreating an epic chase at sea on a live stage. Wisely understanding he could never hope to duplicate the scope of the action the way a film can, Welles used minimalist sets, such as a series of hanging ropes that swayed back and forth to indicate the pitch and yaw of the whaling vessel *Peaquod* rolling in the waves. He then directed his actors to sway in concert with the ropes. The effect was almost mesmerizing, and apparently *too* realistic since several theatergoers reportedly became queasy during the performance!

In films we have countless examples of setting being instrumental: the Italian village of *Il Postino*; the tiny town invaded by a Hollywood film company in David Mamet's *State and Main*; John Ford's favorite location, Monument Valley, lovingly rediscovered by Sergio Leone in *Once Upon a Time in the West*; and the very different cornfields we get in *Field of Dreams* and *Signs*.

A setting is not necessarily only geography. It can be a time, such as the depression, beautifully realized in John Steinbeck's *The Grapes of Wrath* and the film *Seabiscuit*; or Elizabethan England brought to rowdy life in *Shakespeare in Love*; or the time of Christ in *Ben Hur*.

A setting can be an event like the title celebration in *A Wedding* directed by Robert Altman; or the violence surrounding the 1968 Democratic National Convention that became the backdrop for *Medium Cool*, directed by cinematographer Haskell Wexler. In *The*

Figure 8.11 *Seabiscuit*'s setting supports its story, characters, and theme.

Good, the Bad and the Ugly, the American Civil War is no more than a constant irritation to the three men intent on recovering a fortune in buried gold coins.

There is another term I've mentioned before that encompasses all of these different types of settings. That's an arena, used by Hollywood writers and producers to immediately communicate setting, types of characters, even the style of a story. The arena of *Full Throttle* is not just its seedy bar, junk yard or demolition derby racetrack. Those are settings. But the arena for that game provides hints to the writer about where Ben, the biker player-character, will feel most at home. Arena is the complete milieu or environment of a story.

Another setting that deserves its own heading is weather.

Weather

"A lot of people like snow. I find it to be an unnecessary freezing of water."

—*Carl Reiner*

What would a murder mystery set in a gloomy old mansion be without a thunderstorm raging outside? Think of the blizzard that traps the handful of scientists and military men fighting off the bloodthirsty alien in *The Thing from Another World*. Weather is often used as an obstacle as well as a setting. The plane that can't take off due to a storm; the ship that is lost at sea; or the Victorian gentleman lost in a London fog, so major a weather phenomenon in England they named a raincoat after it.

It doesn't show up much in games. Games will use snow as a change of scenery as in the PlayStation game *Goldeneye*, but neither it nor the cold affects the player-character at all. Weather is not just present in *Everquest*, but can affect gameplay when inclement weather limits the player's field of vision. This was so successful that in the first few weeks after the game's release, players complained bitterly they were getting jumped by mobs or losing their way—surely the idea!—but their complaints were heeded, and the effect was rolled back. I liked the added danger, but others were more vocal.

Why isn't there more weather in our games? One of the reasons parallels the reason weather doesn't figure in a lot of movies or TV shows. "It was a dark and stormy night" is easy to write, more difficult to film. Movies are shot over long stretches of time. *Die Hard II* supposedly takes place during a blizzard one night before Christmas. The filmmakers were forced to travel all over the country looking for snow for the snowmobile chase, and manufacturing a lot of it around the airport themselves. To get the necessary control over the

Figure 8.12 The *Andrea Gail* runs headlong into *The Perfect Storm*.

Warner Home Video

rainstorm that pounds the desert motel in *Identity*, the set was built twice: in the desert and on a soundstage. And weather plays such a large factor in *A Perfect Storm* and *Twister* it's the title character.

We don't have the problems with real world weather in games. Our technical hurdle for a long time was any moving pixels on the screen could slow down our game action. That's not really true any longer. *Star Wars Galaxies* does some nice dust storms.

Also it does add one more thing for the artists and sound effects teams to deal with. I've worked on two games where weather was placed suspiciously late in the production schedule, and eventually dropped due to time constraints. You thought I didn't notice, huh guys?

I think the real problem for us writers though is that unless the genre or arena suggests it: haunted house mystery, ski-lodge, desert, it doesn't occur to us to add weather to enhance our stories. It's obvious what a great obstacle it can be, but weather can also affect the mood of a story in more subtle ways.

A storm on a distant horizon can be symbolic. Steaming tropical jungle, high humidity and afternoon tropical rain squalls are used to great effect to heighten the romance between Guy Hamilton (Mel Gibson) and Jillian Bryant (Sigourney Weaver) in *The Year of Living Dangerously*. Nothing like khaki shirts stained with sweat to conjure up all sorts of images, not all unpleasant.

Raymond Chandler (1888–1959) evokes the hot dry wind that blows westward over Los Angeles in this famous passage from the story "Red Wind":

"There was a desert wind blowing that night. It was one of those hot dry Santa Anas that come down through the mountain passes and curl your hair and make your nerves jump and your skin itch. On nights like that every booze party ends in a fight. Meek little wives feel the edge of the carving knife and study their husbands' necks. Anything can happen. You can even get a full glass of beer at a cocktail lounge."

Throughout the course of a game, weather can be used simply to alter the look of the graphics for a change of visual. It is a setting, just like a physical location, a time, or an event. It can become an obstacle or plot point. It can create different moods and evoke emotion. Weather is the writer's friend.

Scope and Scale

I saved the biggest for last. Just as the correct style is important to a player's buying into a story, the correct scope helps too. Direct-to-video movies often betray their low budgets when they attempt to tackle subject matter too broad in scope for them to handle. We wrestled with this in *The Riddle of Master Lu*, trying with very flavorful, if limited locations, to recreate the feel of Ripley's continent-hopping adventures.

Some stories work best in intimate settings, and can get buried beneath the spectacle of an epic. *Doctor Zhivago*, the film directed by David Lean, and adapted from Boris Pasternak's best-selling novel by Robert Bolt is set against the backdrop of the Russian Revolution. But it is not about that revolution. It is a love story. For that reason the massacre of the students and the cavalry charge across the ice—sequences that were featured in the trailers—are actually very brief. Lean and Bolt took great pains to keep the revolution in the background so that it did not overwhelm the love triangle of Zhivago (Omar Shariff), Lara (Julie Christie), and Tonya (Geraldine Chaplin).

Contrast that with *Enemy at the Gates*, the Jean-Jacques Annaud film that opens with the epic scenes of the battle of Stalingrad in World War II. The scope and scale of that film overwhelm and render inconsequential the love story between Vasili Zaitsev (Jude Law) and Tania Chernova (Rachel Weisz). Tonya and Tania are both nurses with their own stories, but the characters are worlds apart in how well-served Tonya is over Tania.

Figure 8.13 Pearl Harbor, but not in the movie. This is a game, *Medal of Honor: Rising Sun*.

Scope was another aspect of game production that was for a long time hampered by technical limitations, and certainly it still requires a lot of effort. But one look at *Medal of Honor*'s impressive depiction of Omaha beach during the invasion of Normandy or the attack on Pearl Harbor in *Medal of Honor: Rising Sun* show us game engines these days can handle just about anything.

Scope and scale still bring up technical issues that must be dealt with in virtual worlds. The massive, beautifully rendered cities in games like *Star Wars Galaxies* and *Horizons* can slow movement to a few frames a second. *Dark Age of Camelot*'s artifact raids with dozens of attackers and defenders could be equally punishing. This is due more to the communication between game servers and player's computers.

A single-player game like *Return of the King* can be much more selective in the parts of the world it needs to create for the player, than a virtual world. One of the draws of virtual worlds is the huge areas they give players to explore.

Scope and scale are also big draws in strategy games where the player's omniscient god-like view over vast distances has even given rise to the sub-type of strategy games called god-games like *Civilization*, *Populous*, and *Black and White*.

Not all games require great scope and scale. Single-player shooters and squad-level games work far better in more restricted surroundings. Today, many technical considerations that limited us even a few years ago have been overcome. That's no reason to choose a scope of game that doesn't fit our story or gamplay however. Our choice should be based on the same things that inform our other choices like style and setting. Choose the appropriate scope or scale to tell the story and bring the gameplay to life, no more and no less.

CHAPTER 9

BRINGING THE STORY TO LIFE

Now that we have a respect for the story we are telling; have learned some traps to avoid; and have looked at some of the issues that should be taken into account as we write, it's time to take those stories and bring them to life. We'll be looking at drama again, and our friends William Archer and Lajos Egri will offer guidance. And we'll explore opportunities within the game design to tell story.

Foreshadowing

FORESHADOWING: the practice of hinting about action or revelations to come.

Foreshadowing is used to create anticipation and suspense. The idea is that whether or not something exciting is happening at the moment we foreshadow, there are exciting things to come.

> "Had I but known then what I do now, I might never have married a man I didn't really know, and settled down to domestic life with him in that fog-bound house of stone . . ."

So many gothic romances from the late 18th and early 19th centuries began with similar words that they became known as the "Had I But Known" school of writing, shortened to HIBK. And of course, modern *bodice-rippers* (one of my favorite euphemisms for a sub-genre of period romance novels) are not immune to HIBK either.

This is foreshadowing at its most obvious, a hook telling the reader flat out that however many pages of sunlight and roses the book may start out with, sooner or later there are going to be bumps in the night and a plucky, nightgown-clad young woman, holding her candle aloft, will haltingly descend into a dank family crypt; climb a creaky stairway to a high, windblown gable room; or timidly tip-toe into a sealed-off wing, there to confront even danker and creakier family secrets whose florid descriptions are guaranteed to run on as much as this sentence.

Most television shows and some movies start with what we call in screenwriting the *teaser*.

The teaser can be direct action, without foreshadowing other than it promises the entire story will contain such action. It can also be more subtle, as we see the wheels set in motion for what is to follow.

Figure 9.1 is not only a great place for a producer to stick his name, the drag race on an abandoned runway creates the climate for the even more dramatic landing of a plane with no one on board. Both elements foreshadow the bizarre nature of the mystery to follow and contain the clues to its solution.

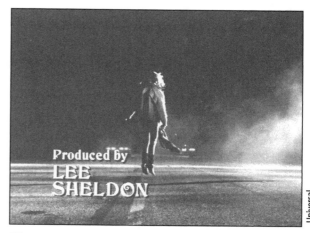

Figure 9.1 Teaser to a *Blacke's Magic* episode.

William Archer in *Play-making* stresses the importance of "carrying forward the interest of the audience . . ." and lays out this principle: "A good first act should never end in a blank wall. There should always be a window in it, with at least a glimpse of something attractive beyond." When he uses the word "attractive," he doesn't mean "pretty." He is using the word in its basic sense of something that will attract the audience enough so that they don't pack up and leave when the first act curtain falls.

Archer uses an excellent example of foreshadowing from the end of the first act of Oscar Wilde's *Lady Windermere's Fan*. Lady Windermere has discovered that her husband has been calling on a certain Mrs. Erlynne, and then discovers Lord Windermere has written many large checks made out to Mrs. Erlynne. Her husband then enters, and asks her to add Mrs. Erlynne to the guest list of a party they are giving. When she refuses, he fills out the invitation himself. Archer points out that this alone foreshadows trouble ahead when the two women meet, but the act isn't over yet.

The first act of the play is set on Lady Windermere's birthday, and at the beginning of the act, her husband has given her an ostrich-feather fan. When he sends a messenger off with the invitation, she announces, "If that woman crosses my threshold, I shall strike her across the face with this fan." Foreshadowing in spades, but the curtain still doesn't fall.

Lady Windermere rings for her butler, and instructs him: "Parker, be sure you pronounce the names of the guests very distinctly to-night. Sometimes you speak so fast that I miss them. I am particularly anxious to hear the names quite clearly, so as to make no mistake."

Archer admits, ". . . for my own part, I can aver that, when the curtain fell on the first act a five-pound note would not have bribed me to leave the theatre . . ."

If it occurs at the beginning of our story, it can be Campbell's "call to adventure." The reason for the call will have been dramatic enough already. Both the setup and the call foreshadow the excitement to come.

Of course, there is no rule that says foreshadowing needs to be confined to teasers or first acts. Just like the old movie serials we'll be looking at later, every act of a TV show ends on a cliffhanger that tries to ensure we'll still be watching after the commercial. Characters may share "What if?" speculations on what may happen if certain actions are carried out. Or some character will make the obvious mistake of relaxing. "Well, looks like the worst is behind us!" Not.

In games, we want the player to keep playing after the first level is solved, so we don't end with the defeat of the boss mob for that level. We want to reveal to the player, or remind her, that this opponent, as tough as it was, is only the minion of a more dangerous foe. We can do this in many ways, such as through the dying threats of this lesser villain; a message that is triggered upon his death to "bring out the big guns"; our sidekick or mentor announcing he's just received word that the antagonist has already made his countermove: killing, kidnapping, or besmirching the character of someone; revealing that the prize we sought at the end of this level has already been sent on; or any number of other escalations of the conflict that foreshadow more and bigger conflicts to come.

There are other types of foreshadowing. I'll foreshadow where I'm going with the next few paragraphs. One of these types is our new best friend from the last chapter: symbolism.

In 1922 a mild-mannered former campaign manager for President Warren G. Harding named Will Hays was picked to head the newly formed Motion Pictures Producers and Distributors Association that is the forerunner of today's Motion Picture Association of America (MPAA), run for the past 38 years by a more feisty Jack Valenti, who has finally announced he will step down at age 82. The association was created to counter public indignation at immorality in Hollywood as well as its movies; and to clean up the image of both that had led to local censorship laws all across the country. The association did little to clean up Hollywood's act, and film became increasingly risqué with the arrival of sound in 1929.

In 1930 the association created the Production Code that remained in effect until 1967 when it was replaced by the MPAA's ratings system that remains with us only slightly modified today. But it wasn't until 1934 when an amendment to the code established the Production Code Administration, and required all motion pictures to get a certificate of approval before they could be released. Hays appointed Joseph Breen, a gentleman with an enthusiasm for censorship, to head up the new office. One of Breen's first acts was to force cuts in *Tarzan and His Mate* that featured a body double for Maureen O'Sullivan who played Jane skinny dipping. You'll be happy to learn the sequence has since been restored.

Universal

Figure 9.2 Mae West at her pre-code peak in 1933's *She Done Him Wrong.*

The new code was also responsible for all those twin beds seen in movies after 1934 and all through 50s television to try and discourage audiences from wondering what all those squeaky clean couples got up to after the lights went out. We're just lucky it didn't prevent future generations from being born. I'm proud to report that I was responsible for removing one of the last sets of those twin beds from the bedroom of Mike and Nancy Kerr on *Edge of Night* in 1983.

As with all censorship attempts, the creative forces immediately set to finding ways around the Production Code. One of the most obvious was the lovers' clench where the camera would discreetly tilt up, and off of the action, but we were meant to assume that they didn't stop there. And believe it or not, here's where symbolic foreshadowing comes in. The writers and directors of the time were not content to infer that the couple had sex. They wanted to indicate whether it was good for both participants.

They did this by tacking something on to that tilt up. If the lovers were stretched out on a soft bed of grass beneath a tree, wind would detach a leaf from that tree. The leaf would eventually flutter down towards earth. If it landed in a bed of blossoming flowers, the audience knew there were rosy times ahead for the young lovers. If it landed in a mud puddle, it suggested the coupling had not gone as well as expected. If the wind picked it up and blew it away in the face of darkening storm clouds, watch out! The approaching storm is often used to foreshadow dark times ahead metaphorically as well as literally.

Foreshadowing may be accomplished through simple action: the discovery that the door behind which we earlier heard disconcerting growls is found to be mysteriously unlocked. All the dogs starting to bark before an earthquake. The bubbles that roil the surface of the Black Lagoon before the creature pops his head out to grin at Julia Adams.

In the opening teaser to an early film directed by Sam Peckinpaw, the foreshadowing doesn't occur until the very end when the leader of a band of renegade Indians looks over the scene of a massacre he ordered, and shouts to the surrounding hills: "Who will you bring against me now?!" The answer is a thunder of music and the film's title in letters 20 feet high: *Major Dundee*.

Notice that in some of these examples foreshadowing can be used to excite anticipation for something that will immediately occur just as well as events that may be a long time in coming. You and I know we have great conflict and action coming in our games, foreshadowing is a way to let the player in on the secret.

Point of Attack

note

POINT OF ATTACK: the term we use to mark the moment that we pick as the opening to our story or a scene. It is *never* at the very beginning of the plot.

". . . the curtain rises when at least one character has reached a *turning point in his life*." states Lajos Egri. "We must start a play at a point of decision, because that is the point at which the conflict starts and the characters are given a chance to expose themselves and the premise." Remember when Egri speaks of "premise" to translate it to "theme."

The Fellowship of the Ring appears to begin at the beginning. All is quiet in Hobbiton. War clouds do not loom. Yet Sauron is already rebuilding his power base and has dispatched his nazgul to search for the ring. It doesn't begin on an average day either. Bilbo has already planned his disappearance from his birthday party. A turning point in his life has been reached. A decision has been made.

It might seem like Campbell's hero's journey always begins at the beginning. And in fact the quest often does start here when the hero answers the call to adventure. There may be the "refusal of the call" as when *Shane* declines to help the homesteaders, but we know that sooner or later heroes must face their destinies. The quest may be beginning, but the plot is already in motion. A village is raided, a spell is cast, the Holy Grail is already missing. Evil forces are gathering behind the scenes. Calamity has struck, or the decision of a character will cause it to strike.

Sony Computer Entertainment

Figure 9.3 Sly Cooper doing what he does best.

The story of *Sly Cooper and the Thievius Raccoonus* does not begin when the Thievius Raccoonus is stolen, or even when Sly has decided to get it back. It begins after he has begun his quest. We don't find him sitting around with his sidekicks, working himself up into a lather over the theft, and vowing to right the wrong. We discover him on the rooftop of police headquarters, about to do what he does best: break and enter. There *is* a montage of still pictures that precedes this that does explain some of the backstory. This exposition could just as easily have come out during the early action.

In almost every action game, the first moves of the villain have already been executed before the player picks up his gamepad. The player may know little of the details of the villain's plans, but something is obviously afoot. It's not all that difficult for us to find the appropriate point of attack for our game. It's much harder to do to find the best point of attack for a scene.

The second script I wrote for *Charlie's Angels* was an episode called "The Jade Trap." I received a copy of my first draft back from producer Leonard Goldberg with the following note written in the margin: "Make this scene more witty, clever and sophisticated." After much consternation and gnashing of teeth, I finally removed the entrance of a character at the top of the scene, and all exits at the end. The scene now started in the middle and ended still in the middle. Simply by changing the point of attack, and leaving off the goodbye, the scene became wittier, cleverer, and definitely more sophisticated. Leonard caught that the scene was dragging, and his note reflected that, even if its admonition was a bit vague. He was pleased with the rewrite. If only all rewrites were that easy!

This solution worked because in film we can choose the entrance and exit points for our scenes with great care. We can cut in to a scene and out of it again. We can remove all sorts of pace-deadening material like waiting for characters to enter a room, or exit it. Unfortunately when writing games we are often forced to begin at the beginning of scenes, even if it's unnecessary and un-dramatic. In graphical games we are at the mercy of contiguous space. Stage productions can turn the lights off or drop the curtain to accomplish the same thing as a cut, but Egri's take on transitions in drama is worth repeating. Here he is speaking about all sorts of transitions: changes in characters and relationships or from scene to scene:

> Shall we record every movement of a transition? The answer is no. It is not necessary. If you suggest a movement in transition, and this suggestion throws a light on the working of the character's mind, we think it is sufficient. It depends on the dramatist's ability, how successfully he can compress his material in transition, giving—or suggesting—the whole movement.

Remember? The audience fills in the blanks.

When adventure games jumped from text to graphics, players explicitly guided the player-character from room to room. We opened all the doors, walked the PC through them, encountered an NPC loitering there only to discuss story or puzzles, then walked all the way back across the room, and out the door again. This exists today in almost every game. Cuts do occur in single-player games as we transition from level to level, but in general we must traverse the virtual space of a level in the same way that we do in real life. As we know, drama does not equal life. How then can we capture the dramatic urgency that point of attack can give us? By not taking the space or the progression of our game story quite so literally.

I remember in one of the earliest of the Star Trek graphic adventure games once players had explored an area they were able to use the point-and-click interface to jump to distant locations as long as they could see them. This shortcut successfully removed at least some of the literal traversing of the space. Some games like *Syberia* add a run mode to speed things along.

When a player-character transitions between two rooms, we do not have to see every step that she takes. Film directors have three main choices when deciding how to cut between scenes. The first is the establishing shot, a wide angle that gives the audience a feel for the next location where the action will take place. Another is to cut to a close-up of a significant object in the next scene, for example a hand turning on a light, a significant *objet d'art*, or prop. The last is a matching cut that can be literal or simply thematic such as a cut between two identical actions—a book slamming shut to one being opened—or a waterfall to a shot glass being filled in a bar.

Since we try not to dictate the direction a player must look, preferring to give him more freedom of movement, the matching cut is most difficult. The establishing shot doesn't do much for us since the majority of exploration and action in games takes place in wide angles, so we'd expect to see our character enter a new room. But the second, the close-up, has possibilities.

It is a perfectly reasonable jump in a game to move from directing the PC to open a door, to a brief cut of that same PC's hand flicking on a light switch. In this case, if the room were in darkness, it is the next step in a progression the player must take anyway, and would not be jarring provided such cuts were used consistently throughout the game.

In an action game, as soon as a player-character moves into a new area, an immediate attack by an enemy serves to thrust the player directly into the scene. It shouldn't be such a fierce attack that the player has no chance of survival, but a lower-level enemy that can be dispatched after the player has gained his bearings is a good way to cut literally to the point of attack.

Massively multiplayer games face the exact same dilemma, and it is not so easily overcome as in single-player games. The problem lies in one of perception. All massively multiplayer games are thought of as virtual worlds with a very literal geography. Opportunities for cutting are few and far between. Yet transitions between zones, entering or leaving cities or buildings, modes of transportation such as teleports and vehicles, all give us chances to cut out non-essential movement. The key is a more flexible view of the virtual world that allows for dramatic license.

We can also use NPCs to help us cut to the point of attack of a new scene or encounter. In real life, we drop phrases like "Let's cut to the chase," or, "I'll get right to the point," into our conversations, if time is limited or our need to say something is urgent. An NPC can replace the usual pleasantries of "Hi, how are you, brave adventurer?" and "I have many fine baked goods for sale today," with "I'm sorry if I seem distracted, but my dog disappeared," or "Aren't you the bold adventurer who rid the village of those werewolves awhile back?" We are "cutting" to the point of attack.

As Egri concludes, "It is imperative that your story starts in the middle, and not under any circumstances, at the beginning." I would only add that we can say the same thing for our scenes and encounters too.

The Obligatory Scene

note
***
THE OBLIGATORY SCENE: a scene that must be written, otherwise the audience will feel extremely dissatisfied.
***

William Archer suggests it may have been Francisque Sarcey (1827–1899), a French journalist and drama critic who may have invented the phrase *scène à faire*, or obligatory scene. Another possibility is Augustin Eugene Scribe (1791–1861), French playwright, librettist, and founder of the Society of Authors, generally credited with perfecting and popularizing the "well-made play" as well as perfecting and popularizing author's royalties, an achievement that made him rich. And yes, his name really was Scribe.

Sarcey describes the obligatory scene in a play called *Les Fourchambault* by Emile Augier: "... it is precisely this *expectation mingled with uncertainty* that is one of the charms of the theatre. I say to myself, 'Ah, they will have an encounter! What will come of it?' And that this is the state of mind of the whole audience is proved by the fact that when the two characters of the *scène à faire* stand face to face, a thrill of anticipation runs round the whole theatre."

Whoever came up with it first, Archer likes it a lot. His own definition is "a scene which, for one reason or another, an audience expects and ardently desires." It is currently considered to be an old-fashioned notion. Egri dismisses the concept of an obligatory scene with "every scene in a play is obligatory." He's right in one sense. Every scene, every character, we write should move the story forward, and as Egri says, "prove the premise." Certainly in a television series we quickly learned to write only critical scenes. We had little time in our 22 minutes (half-hour show) or 47 minutes (hour show) as it was to indulge in the luxury of writing scenes that weren't essential to the story or character revelation. Better to do both in every scene.

I agree that no moment in our story should fail to support theme, story, character, or all three at once. However, *some* scenes are far more important than others, and we do notice their absence. One of my favorite American authors is William Faulkner, and *Intruder in the Dust* is one of my favorites of his novels (*Absolom, Absolom* is the other). While in general I dislike unnecessary remakes of movies, I've always wanted to do a remake of the 1949 film version of the book. Faulkner is said to have written the entire novel over one long, drunken weekend. It is for this reason I forgive him for leaving out an obligatory scene.

The scene in question is two old ladies standing off a lynch mob bent on hanging an innocent Black man accused of murder. That the lynch mob will be coming is foreshadowed, as is the timely disappearance of law officers. Yet because the story is told through the eyes of a young boy not present to witness it, it happens offstage like action in a Greek tragedy.

It would have been easy to put the boy at the scene to witness it. It is a major dramatic confrontation the reader has been prepared for and is expecting.

You probably remember the similar scene from the film version of Harper Lee's equally superb novel *To Kill a Mockingbird* when Gregory Peck waits in the rocking chair for a similar mob on a similar mission. In that story, also told from the point of view of children, the kids *do* witness the confrontation.

Figure 9.4 *To Kill a Mockingbird:* Gregory Peck's finest hour.

If we're going to go to the trouble of foreshadowing a critical moment in a story, we'd better deliver it. If we're going to create two characters in opposition, they had better clash. This need is so deeply felt by writers and their audiences that to not deliver the scene is to betray the audience's need even more than the stories. In movies as diverse as *The Towering Inferno*, *Heat*, and *Runaway Jury*, the same obligatory scene in each is not a necessity for the story or the theme, but because of the casting. Paul Newman and Steve McQueen, the two reigning stars of the time, were only in one movie together, *The Towering Inferno*. To not have a scene between them (there were two) would have betrayed audience expectations. The same holds true for Robert DeNiro and Al Pacino in *Heat* (They were both in *Godfather II*, of course, but could never have met) and Gene Hackman and Dustin Hoffman in *Runaway Jury*.

General Gordon and the Mahdi never met face to face during the siege at Khartoum, but in the film of *Khartoum* they do. It was felt necessary to place these two characters in opposition in the same room (or in this case tent) at least once, even if it meant altering history.

It's easy to spot obligatory scenes. They are the high points of drama and conflict in a story. And they're usually easy to spot. Is there any question what the obligatory scene is in *Rocky*? If Rocky and Apollo Creed never got into that ring together, the movie screen would have been studded with Milk Duds and Jujubes.

Inherit the Wind's obligatory scene is historically accurate. William Jennings Bryan (Matthew Harrison Brady in the play) did take the stand to be questioned by Clarence Darrow (Henry Drummond in the play), although there is much debate over the difference between the play and the actual trial transcript. But it was an obligatory scene the entire play was leading up to.

The obligatory scene benefits from not being exactly what the audience expects. Because it is so highly anticipated, any twist we throw into it is all the more powerful, as long as it doesn't violate the reason the scene is obligatory to begin with. At the end of the western *The Professionals*, written and directed by Richard Brooks (who received academy award nominations for both), protagonist Henry 'Rico' Fardan (Lee Marvin) learns his mission to rescue the kidnapped wife of powerful land baron Joe Grant (Ralph

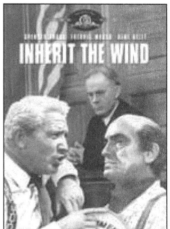

Figure 9.5 The obligatory scene was so important in *Inherit the Wind*, it's in the poster and box art.

Bellamy) has been a lie, and it is Grant who is the true villain from whom his wife was only trying to escape. The confrontation between Fardan and Grant is the final obligatory scene in the film. Up until now, this being an action movie, obligatory scenes were primarily resolved in gunplay and explosions, and a movie with less on its mind might have ended with a shootout. Instead of taking the gold offered as his reward, Fardan sends Grant's wife off with her lover again.

* * *

```
                GRANT
    You bastard!

                FARDAN
    Yes, sir.  In my case an accident of birth.
                (he swings up into his saddle)
    But you, sir, you are a self-made man.
```

* * *

And Fardan with his wounded comrades rides off into at least a metaphorical sunset. Brooks chose to punctuate his obligatory scene not with bloodshed, but a memorable exchange of dialogue, one of my favorite ending lines in a movie.

We are faced with including obligatory scenes in every game we make. If, like the casting examples on the previous page we promise something on the box, it better be in the game, or players will revolt. Protagonist and antagonist inevitably must meet for the final showdown. In *Dark Side of the Moon*, there were two chief villains going about their nefarious deeds with entirely different agendas. Both were responsible for the loss of many lives, although only the first did any actual murdering. He is dispatched in the old-fashioned way with the expected confrontation, final exposition, and resulting fireworks. The second villain is only encountered in passing as Jake tries to escape the unstable moon. The player is given a moral choice of effectively executing this man, or permitting him to live, and letting justice take its course. Both scenes were obligatory.

Obligatory scenes occur in every level and every quest we write, not just in the endgame. Yes, as Egri argues, *every* scene should be necessary, but some are more so than others. Those are the true obligatory scenes. We set them up like jokes. Every joke has an A and a B side. The A is the set-up. The B is the punchline. Leaving out an obligatory scene is like forgetting the punchline of a joke.

Crisis, Climax, and Resolution

Lajos Egri defines crisis as "a state of things in which a decisive change one way or the other is impending." Archer, distinguishing drama from fiction, says the "essence of drama is *crisis*." He argues that the dramatist "deals in rapid and startling changes," what our old friends the Greeks call the *peripeties*, and what we today call reversals (see the following "Reversals" section). He then goes on to defend drama in what is my favorite quote of his:

> It may be thought a point of inferiority in dramatic art that it should deal so largely in shocks to the nerves, and should appeal by preference, wherever it is reasonably possible, to the cheap emotions of curiosity and surprise. But this is a criticism, not of dramatic art, but of human nature.

Writing in 1912, he sums up precisely why we writers of games have more to learn from drama than prose fiction. Because if there's anything we're good at, it's "shocks to the nerves," and I'm not talking about vibrators built into our gamepads. We already begin with the ability to provoke the adrenal gland through the intensity of gameplay, something other media must work harder to achieve. But all mammals have adrenal glands. It's up to us to take that ability, and add to it with something a bit more profound and human.

We have our crisis then. A major change is going to occur. Only one? No. As we move through the story, crisis follows crisis, each one escalating tension and suspense. Every one of these crises needs an additional element: a climax. Egri says, "crisis and climax follow each other, the last one always on a higher plane than the one before."

The word climax does not refer to the very end of a story that is followed by the denouement. The actual word is taken from the Greek and means stair. That gives us the hint about its meaning. Each crises demands a climax, a point where the rubber band of crisis has been stretched excruciatingly taut, and finally snaps: that moment of confrontation, accusation, conflict, violence. And that climax then begs resolution, the final stage begun with crises.

Resolution is simply the outcome of the climax that is a result of the crisis. The story is built from this three-step dance. Every one of these crises has reached a climax and has been resolved, only to have the stakes raised higher, and the next crisis always looming as even more profound.

Now, they don't have to follow one another in lockstep fashion, one immediately after the other: Crisis A followed by Climax A followed by Resolution A followed by Crisis B followed by Climax B followed by Resolution B as in Figure 9.6.

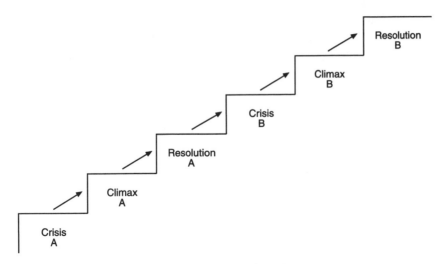

Figure 9.6 The stairway of crisis, climax, and resolution.

There can be a great deal of time between a crisis and the moment it reaches a climax, and the same between climax and resolution as in Figure 9.7.

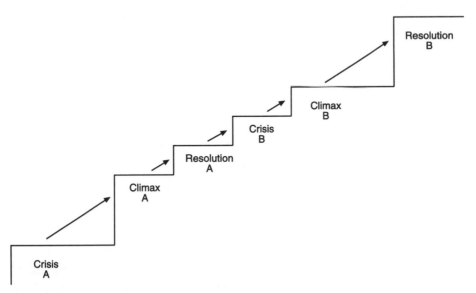

Figure 9.7 The stairway with time expanded.

Even more interesting is that multiple crises may play out in parallel with one or more great crises stretching past many smaller crises, climaxes, and resolutions, as in Figure 9.8.

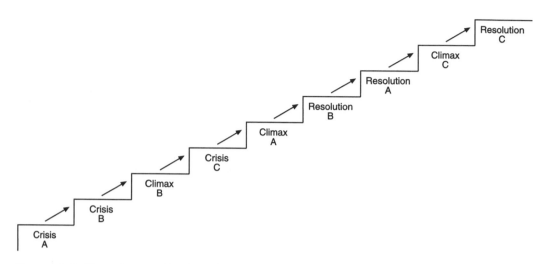

Figure 9.8 The stairway with crises, climaxes, and resolutions of different lengths.

This overlapping of different lines of crisis, climax, and resolution is at the heart of soap opera structure. You never finish all your stories on the same day if you want to seduce viewers to tune in the next. Overlapping of stories like this can be at odds with distinct levels in single-player games and monthly episodes of new content in virtual worlds, and care must be taken that the levels and episodes are not too formally presented. We'll discuss the latter problem more in Chapter 18, "Bringing Virtual Worlds to Life," when we examine "The Trap of Episodic Structure." Once the needs and limitations of the structure are understood, however, many variations and combinations are possible in a single game story.

Watch how novelist and screenwriter Alistair MacLean tightens the screws by piling crisis upon crisis in *The Guns of Navarone* or *Where Eagles Dare*. Both are textbook examples of this style of action writing.

However the dance plays out, we know by the end of the game the player's protagonist character will have triumphed time and again against ever fiercer obstacles. And still all the player's best laid plans; all the new skills and gadgets the player-character has acquired; all of the allies she may have recruited will still not seem to be enough to defeat the strong antagonist we've set in opposition against her. Sound familiar? It should. This is the essence of single-player game balance, and player versus environment (PvE) balance in virtual worlds.

Story and gameplay are not at odds here. They complement one another. Gameplay and story working together with one goal in mind: to take the player and wring her dry of energy and emotion.

Reversals

note

REVERSAL: when the defensive wrestler comes from underneath and gains control of his opponent, either on the mat or in a standing position, while inbounds.

It's as good a definition as any. I was a pretty scrawny kid in high school. I was six feet two and weighed less than 140 pounds. But I wasn't all that bad at reversals when we wrestled in Mr. Brown's gym class!

In storytelling, of course, it is a sudden turn of events or fortunes. In writing television and movies, we focus on what we call the third-act reversal, borrowing the three-act structure from drama. Alan Ball, academy-award winning writer of *American Beauty*, sums up his feelings about such things when discussing network meetings he endured getting notes for three sitcoms he wrote and produced (*Grace under Fire*, *Cybil*, and *Oh Grow Up*):

> There always seem to be twice as many people as needed at every meeting. The networks have so many people who have to justify their jobs that they sit in on meetings, trying to come up with some kind of accepted feedback. They use all of these recycled buzzwords they learned in some storytelling seminar that I don't even understand: 'We need a third-act reversal here' or 'Let's telescope the action here.'

I mention them because, yes, they can be used to good effect. It was a deliberate parody of the third-act reversal in *The Riddle of Master Lu* when a villain knocks Ripley down, then empties his inventory. But just throwing a reversal into the third-act guarantees nothing. In fact, it has become so formulaic in screenwriting (thanks, I suppose, to those same damn seminars) that audiences can pretty much feel one 'a comin' in sort of the way birds get skittish when a storm approaches. How do we use reversals without their becoming clichés? Carefully set them up with the barest of clues, clues that are big enough, however, for the audience to remember and not feel cheated.

The great thing about our audience, the player, is that he isn't inundated with third-act reversals enough to spot 'em when they're coming, because *games don't have third acts*. Or at least not as we think of the term. I'm not going to go into all the business of breaking stories down into three acts. Enough people do it already. You won't see a special heading for it in this book. Just know that what is meant by a three-act structure is this:

- Act One: Introduction
- Act Two: Complication
- Act Three: Resolution

Ah, there's a word we know! The odd thing is that drama, where the notion of three-act structure originated, has long since wised up and gone to two acts, something network executives, the occasional aspiring writer, and other seminar attendees (even game company executives now unfortunately) are never told. Plays used to be five acts.

In the broadest sense, yes, game stories have an introduction. It's usually that cut scene up front. Then for the rest of the game all we have is Act Two. Finally, we have the endgame: Act Three. My act three reversal in *Master Lu* actually occurs right before the endgame, so I guess I cheated.

A game's structure cannot productively be defined by acts. Or if it is, every level should be one. And what are the acts in a virtual world? The introduction is hidden somewhere in the backstory. Complications are littered about the world waiting for players to trip over them, and there is never, ever, a third act. If we need three things to define story structure, we already have crisis, climax, and resolution. We start in the *middle* of our stories. We start with a crisis. We don't need no stinkin' acts!

This gives us far more freedom than those hapless screenwriters! We can have reversals in every level if we want. We can throw planet-shaking reversals at thousands of players at once in virtual worlds any time we damn well please. In a single-player game, we set-up an expectation, then reverse it.. Things are finally going the player-character's way when all of a sudden the plot slaps him upside the head. Reversal. Or the converse: that new horde of mobs descending to finish off the PC actually turn out to be needed allies. Reversal. Call it a twist if you like (I know I do) although twists can be other things besides absolute reversals of fortune: a plot turn that sends us still forward, but in an entirely new direction; a character revelation that changes our perception of the character; a dance popularized by Chubby Checker.

Arcs

This term gets bandied about in seminars as well, but it has more merit. It is a good visualization for story and character tracked over the life of a game. Character arcs describe the growth and development of the character. Nothing too surprising there. Story arcs, however, are each one composed of crisis, climax, and resolution. And like those three building blocks, arcs can be found in any structure, three-act or thirty-act.

Egri, talking about the theatre of over fifty years ago, tells us that "The shortest scene contains all the elements of a three-act play. It has its own premise which is exposed through conflict between the characters. The conflict grows through transition from crisis and climax. Crisis and climax are as periodical in a play as exposition is constant."

Periodical is a great word. Look again at the staircase in Figure 9.6. Let's add the arcs like gravity-defying Slinkies. Periodically a new step is mounted. Exposition occurs on all. And over that staircase of crisis, climax, and resolution, we can draw our story arcs, as in Figure 9.9.

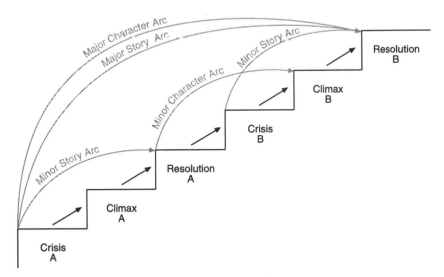

Figure 9.9 Story arcs climbing the stairway to drama.

They overlap beautifully. And that's what we need through our thirty levels or never-ending escalator of virtual worlds. Be sure you can track all the character arcs for your major characters. Minor characters may not need them. Be sure you can lay out on a chart all the overlapping story arcs of your game. If you can do that, all the levels or chapters or episodes in the world can't disrupt the player's interest.

Exposition in Action

My mentor at CalArts, Sandy MacKendrick, had a cousin named Roger McDougall who was a writer (*The Man in the White Suit, The Mouse that Roared*) and composer.

(Roger is also known, by the way, for having been diagnosed with multiple sclerosis in the 1950s, but his doctors decided not to tell him what he had. He was bedridden by the time he learned the truth, did a lot of reading, put himself on his own strict diet, and recovered. Sandy used to chuckle and shake his head in amazement every time he told the story. Notice how this paragraph of exposition stopped *my* story.)

Sandy told us that Roger had a simple definition for "exposition in action." Every time a character walked into a room, he should have a gun in his hand. Sandy used *Odd Man Out*, the film that made James Mason a star, as an example where this rule was followed almost literally. Mason plays an IRA leader on the run, and he does wave a gun around quite a bit while trying to explain himself.

A kinder, gentler definition of "exposition in action" is exposition that doesn't stop the forward movement of the story. Mystery writers have it pretty easy. The investigation of a crime is both exposition and the story's primary action (not necessarily physical action remember). We also get to save the biggest barrel of exposition to empty at the very end.

Figure 9.10 Lee follows his mentor's advice: *Dark Side of the Moon.*

Action movies (now it means physical action!), on the other hand, can survive on very little exposition; and we can extend Roger's definition from "gun in hand" to include "cars in chase," "bombs being defused," "monsters on the prowl," and many more situations that give us a nice cover of suspense or adrenaline rush to sneak some plot in. Drama with non-physical action like courtrooms, medical operations, corporate takeovers and the like can use exposition in action in precisely the same way.

How can we keep the exposition from interfering with the action?

- Reserve it for cut scenes. You can, but you still run the risk of bogging down your cut scenes with it. Besides we like to tell our stories as part of the gameplay and that is our action.

- Stick it into the action as a game engine sequence. Better, but the risk is still there.

- Keep it to the point. Even if there is important secondary exposition, save it. Tell only what absolutely needs to be told for the player to understand what's happening.

- Keep it brief. A few lines interjected here and there. No action, however rousing, will cover paragraphs of exposition.

- Break it up. Create "cuts" with action, comments from another character, or a lapse of time. Let's assume a player-character, a knight named Edmund. Let's give him a sidekick named Baldrick, and primary antagonist, a villain named Melchett. In the game they inhabit, we can lay in one piece of a chunk of exposition at a time. Start with a scout who declares, "Someone who looked like Melchett was seen on the battlements of Level's End Castle!" Then as player-character and sidekick ride out (player is steering the horses): "If it is Melchett in that castle, he'll be guarded." They fight their way through an ambush on the forest road (player is actively fighting). "Funny, these aren't Melchett's's men. I wonder if Lord Percy has interested himself in the affair." As they approach the castle (steering horses): "We can't just ride up and knock on the gate, Sir Edmund. We need a cunning plan." "I have it, Baldrick. The moat is swimmable." Upon breaking into Melchett's bedchamber (player clicks on a crumpled form on the bed): "Melchett!" "He's been strangled!" "He wasn't master here, but a prisoner! But whose . . . ?" In the same breath: "Lord Percy!"

See how the common practice of having NPCs spew out information in paragraphs not only cheapens the potential for the character as we discussed, but fights against the pace of the game?

And exposition does not have to be in dialogue. No, I'm not suggesting essential exposition be stuck into long paragraphs in a book or journal either. Let's follow Edmund and his sidekick's adventures *without* dialogue: A dying messenger hands the player-character a blood-stained note. It reads "Someone who looks like Melchett has been seen on his castle's battlements." As the player-character prepares to mount up, his sidekick appears with extra weapons. A hanged man swings from a gibbet at the entrance to the forest with a sign on his chest that reads "Death to all brigands!" The ambushers are wearing the Lord Percy family crest. The player-character and sidekick must kill two guards at the bedchamber door, both wearing that same crest. A portrait on the wall bears the name Melchett. The dead man on the bed is the same.

Sure no dialogue at all is stretching it. But study Hitchcock's mastery of exposition without dialogue for many clues on how to accomplish it. Remember the playground scene from *The Birds*? Exposition is fluttering down on to the jungle gym behind Tippi Hedren. In the same film, the sequence where she sees the man lighting a cigarette while gasoline spreads at his feet doesn't need the brief dialogue it contains.

Look for opportunities for exposition in geography (length of journey, possible hazards, time elapsed), weather (clothing needed, obstacles), body language (fear, aggression, love, hate), décor (wealth, a character's self-esteem, interests, hobbies, professions), wardrobe (wear and tear, armor or no, elegant, seductive), and any other non-verbal cues that will not stop action. This is one way where having three-dimensional characters really pays off.

Don't stop the story or the action sounds obvious. Yet it is one of those concepts, like "Your uncle the Duke" exposition, that often seem to get lost in the shuffle when the writer actually writes. "Your uncle the Duke" is another gift to me from Sandy MacKendrick. It is a phrase that describes exposition artificially shared between two characters only for the benefit of the audience. The characters should both already know the information.

Sandy's example went like this: "You know your uncle the Duke?" to which the only reasonable reply is "Of course I do. He's my uncle." But we see this all the time. "Remember when I told you . . . ?" "When we started this venture you promised me . . ." "Don't try to back out now. You told me . . ." And on and on and on.

In the next chapter we'll move from concepts games share with other entertainment media to a few that are quintessentially our own.

CHAPTER 10

GAMES: CHARTING NEW TERRITORY

Many of the ideas we've been discussing come to us from other media, mainly the theatre, television, and film. Some of these thoughts needed translation; others could be used as is. Now we're going to turn our attention to a few of the new concepts that games bring to the table. Here no translation is necessary, since the concepts were developed while writing game stories.

What about characters? Did computer games add nothing new to writing characters? Actually we did, so we're going to first jump back in time to the section of the book where we looked at characters, and affix the following addendum.

Characters Revisited

The most obvious new idea the computer brought to characters was the ability for the audience to become the player, and take part in the action. That is the entire point of computer game entertainment. It is not passive. It is active. Until now the closest thing to this experience other media have provided has been the actor playing a role. The audience usually has had no part in this. There are exceptions.

Earlier I mentioned *Tamara*, a play set in an Italian villa before World War II where the "theatre" was an American Legion hall on Vine Street in Hollywood, and a number of rooms had been dressed to recreate the rooms in the villa. The audience had "passports" stamped upon entering the building, were eyed suspiciously by actors playing customs agents, and questioned. Unfortunately, the audience's part in the play ended there.

Once inside, the actors moved freely from room to room, followed by the audience. Several scenes took place simultaneously. The audience could choose to follow any characters they wished, but were asked not to interrupt the scenes. Another problem was that the play had been written with a golden path. Audience members following the "correct" actors got more of the central story.

Most audience members knew which scenes to witness, either though word-of-mouth or repeat visits. I went back a second time and deliberately chose the path less traveled, and it did make all the difference. I saw some interesting vignettes, but missed most of the main action of the play.

The Mystery of Edwin Drood, the mystery novel that remained incomplete at Dickens' death, has been completed by others many times. Most are novels that take up the tale where he left off in a pastiche of Dickens' style. In 1985 a musical version of *Drood* debuted. Not only did it break the fourth wall repeatedly, by allowing actors to step out of character and address the audience, but at the end the audience was asked to vote for whom they thought the killer was.

The idea of allowing the audience to vote on the outcome of a mystery or courtroom drama had been used before several times. The best known example is *The Night of January 16th* by Ayn Rand. Rand is best

Figure 10.1 *The Mystery of Edwin Drood.*

known for *The Fountainhead* and *Atlas Shrugged,* and the school of philosophy that is called objectivism. Even in this minor effort though, her favorite theme of the individualist versus collectivist is in evidence. Otherwise it's a very ordinary mystery. The audience was invited to vote on the guilt or innocence of the accused. It was made into an even more ordinary movie in 1941 that dropped that gimmick.

Audience members shout sketch ideas to improvisational theatre troupes. The late 60s and early 70s gave us Guerilla theatre, spoofed by Brian DePalma in the "Be Black Baby" sequence from *Hi Mom!,* where a battered and brutalized uptown couple stagger out afterwards, praise the play, and vow to tell all their friends to come see it. Performance art too can drag audience members into becoming a part of it.

Films, of course, have also dabbled in game-like structures, alternate plotlines, and so on, such as *Sliding Doors, Groundhog Day,* and my favorite *Run Lola Run,* but true audience

Columbia Tri-Star

Figure 10.2 Lola runs, watched by nuns.

participation has been limited to a few failed experiments like *Mr. Payback* and *Ride for your Life* where audiences pushed buttons to vote on which branch of the story to follow next.

TV has even gotten into the act with numerous unsold pilots and short-lived game shows like *Whodunnit?* with Ed McMahon. My only limousine ride ever with Dick Clark occurred when we went to pitch one of these interactive mystery ideas to CBS. You've never heard of it, trust me. I suppose even today's "reality" shows have something in common with the earlier attempts.

But none of these comes close to what we do. The player becomes—or at least drives—the player-character. Audience and actor are one.

Another aspect of characters that computer games didn't invent, but have embraced, comes to us from tabletop role-playing games like *Dungeons & Dragons, Call of Cthulhu, Vampire: The Masquerade,* and countless others. In these games and their progeny, computer role-playing games (CRPGs, shortened these days to RPGs) players build their characters using attributes like strength, dexterity, and intelligence. Each attribute, represented by a number indicating the points in that attribute the character has, affects the character's ability at certain skills like swinging a sword, dodging bullets, or casting magic spells. A Game Master, the person in charge of storytelling, would determine the outcome of gameplay with die rolls, adjusting to decisions made by the players.

In tabletop games, these were the only aspects of character the Game Master determined. The rest, accents, character traits, and so on, were added by the players themselves. This explains why RPGs for a long time did no more with characters either unless they were

NPCs. Gradually, more and more of the character work we've been studying in other media was adopted.

The most interesting idea computer games can call their own evolved out of this. We can allow our other characters, the actors not played by the player, whom we call NPCs, to react to the player's actions. I've given numerous examples of this from the funny rejoinders voiced by units in *Warcraft* when we click on them too many times to the programmable charts that can track subtle changes in the ebb and flow of relationships between player-characters and NPCs.

What do we have to look forward to? Interesting experiments by Chris Crawford, Barbara Hayes-Roth, and Joe Bates suggest there are very real benefits to using even the limited artificial intelligence available to us today. It's a lot of work to write interesting character and dialogue for every one of possibly hundreds of NPCs. And NPCs who mouth identical phrases throughout a game are at odds with encouraging the player's willing suspension of disbelief. But minor characters, even with limited AI routines like *Eliza* and *Julia* could flesh out our lesser characters without the tedious task of writing each one individually. Something to keep in mind the next time you face those hundreds of blank pages.

Time now to step out of the Way Back Machine and return to our present topic of storytelling.

Puzzling Developments

Obstacles are common to all dramatic media, and puzzles, as Bob Bates points out in his sidebar, are one of the obstacles gamers face. The difference is that puzzles the audience must solve are the province of interactivity alone. We might think that mystery novels share puzzles with us; and it's true when we talk about the game the writer plays with the reader, and the puzzle of the crime. Clichéd dialogue like "There's still a piece missing." and "It all fits!" refer explicitly to the puzzle aspects of a mystery story.

But the enjoyment of the mystery is not only that "game." The reader need not figure out the puzzle of "Whodunnit?" at all to enjoy it. Even more significantly, the reader can continue from the beginning to the end of the story without hindrance, whether she solves anything or just enjoys going along for the ride.

Puzzles remain underutilized as a means for telling story and revealing character. Too often, they are obstacles to story progression, but bear little resemblance to dramatic obstacles. There's no reason they can't be both.

Bob Bates started writing Infocom text adventures in 1986, and was the cofounder of Legend Entertainment. I've already quoted from his book *Game Design: The Art and Business of Creating Games*. Bob knows puzzles.

Bob Bates, Writer/Designer

In traditional media, the hero of a story has obstacles to overcome. In games, these obstacles become puzzles.

Good puzzles contribute both to plot and character development. They draw the players further into the fictional world by encouraging them to explore the environment and to delve below the surface of the people they encounter.

Imagine, for example, that the player enters a room and discovers a door blocked by a teenage boy who is sitting cross-legged on the floor, his eyes staring vacantly into space, tears streaming down his cheeks.

To get through the door, the player will have to get past the boy. But who is he? Why is he crying? What will it take to get him to stop? To learn the answers, players

Figure 10.3 Bob Bates.

will have to talk with the boy, or with someone else, or learn something about his background, or look around the setting to find something that might make him feel better. All these activities enhance the story. The backbone of good fiction is character, and the best puzzles are those that involve the desires and motivations of the characters who populate the game.

As you approach the problem of puzzle design, think about the hero you have created and about what he or she needs to accomplish. Then think of reasonable obstacles that the villainous forces of the game might place in the hero's path. When you create puzzles that spring naturally from the characters and settings of the game, and when players learn the solutions through exploration and conversation, you'll find yourself with puzzles that contribute to, rather than hinder, the flow of your story.

Another way to write character is to create puzzles that, like dramatic obstacles, grow your player-character by revealing nuances of her character. It's done in a similar fashion to other media. The most obvious is to offer a moral choice to the player as part of the puzzle, as in *Dark Side of the Moon*, where the player decides whether to watch the villain die, or rescue him and hope the courts punish him as he deserves.

Another obvious possibility is to require some skill or knowledge the player-character may be known to possess, but that has not been utilized before. If that skill or knowledge is detrimental to another character, the player must decide whether to use it or not. And that can affect the relationship between PC and NPC. It's often an interesting idea to offer an alternative solution to the puzzle so that there is no real right or wrong solution.

A bit more subtle puzzle would be one where all the repercussions of solving it are not immediately apparent. The player only learns after she is past the puzzle that while opening the water valve has helped her, it has drowned some creatures she was trying to help. Reversal! Then present her with a similar puzzle where the result might be the same!

The puzzle can provide exposition. A series of bombs are constructed in such a way that provides clues to the manufacturer or his whereabouts. An ingenious trap suggests engineering skills the villain may have that were previously unknown. The player can now be on the lookout for similar traps. Foreshadowing!

Every good story puzzle is a crisis that leads to a climax, and a resolution. Back to those bombs for the obvious example. The player knows: "If I don't defuse this, that house nearby will be utterly destroyed!" Crisis. Climax follows: "The player chooses the blue wire!" Wrong one. The player runs for his life and makes it to safety just as the bomb explodes . . . causing a landslide . . . that buries an entire town.

Other story elements puzzles can expose include the fleshing out of backstory: "Ah! So that's where that stolen concrete truck went!" More foreshadowing: "Notice anything odd about that demolished bridge? It wasn't blown up. It was *chewed.*" Symbolism: "Every obstacle that Hitler fellow throws in my path reeks of his belief in Aryan supremacy."

The point is once puzzles are recognized for the excellent character revelation and storytelling tools they are, a whole other set of options are opened up for the writer of games. Imagine the joy when you can remove great masses of exposition that swell your cut scenes and scatter them among a few puzzles.

Quests

Quests, missions, tasks, errands . . . they go by many names, but they are one of the primary means we have for telling our stories in games. And we're going to look at them in detail. They are structured like stories, or at least story acts. And as Egri says of scenes in the quote in the "Arcs" section in the previous chapter, they should each contain all the elements of the larger story. There is no need to demote the storytelling to a cut scene when you can play it out in the action of the game.

All quests share common elements that reveal themselves in a series of steps. In parentheses I'll tie them to Campbell's hero's journey.

- A request is made to the player that she accomplish something. (Departure: the call to adventure)
- The player decides whether she'll accept. She often *does* have a choice. She can turn down the request. (Departure: refusal of the call)

- She *may* be handed a special weapon or device or spell. In *Dark Age of Camelot* there is a Hibernian quest called Treasure Hunt whose ultimate goal is a hidden gem. From components collected by the player, an enchantress fashions a Necklace of Finding that will pulse with power when the player nears the hidden gem. (Departure: supernatural aid)

- The player sets out. (Departure: crossing the first threshold)

- The player *may* experience a variety of adventures. (Departure: Belly of the Whale and most of Initiation)

- The player accomplishes her goal. (Initiation: the ultimate boon)

- The player returns to the NPC or to other aspects of the game that were put on hold. (Return: all subheadings)

Quests can be given to players in all sorts of ways: a mission assigned in a pre-level cut scene; an NPC within the game who may offer it when the player selects him, or may accost the player on his own; an entry found in a journal; a looted object. There are more, but they all fall into two categories: pull and push. Pull quests are uncovered by an overt action of the player. Push quests are thrust upon the player while she's going merrily about her own business.

Push is used to solve the challenge of making sure the player is aware of content, and does not rely on her stumbling over it, or force her to go looking. The quest should not be to find the quest. At one of my tutorials my guest Chris Klug of *Earth & Beyond* shared a subtle push technique that I like a lot. Here are several variations on the principle.

Part of the routine in virtually every virtual world is killing mobs and looting them. Players then make use of what loot they can, give away what they can't, or sell it. They can sell it to other players in virtual worlds. Both single-player games and virtual worlds can also provide merchants. So a game could introduce a special item or class of items not seen before. When taken to a merchant the looted item would trigger a result beyond the usual "I'll give you 10 silver pieces for that." Instead, the merchant can become interested in the special loot, and might relate a snippet of story; suggest someplace the player-character might look for more information; or ask the player if she'll take on a quest to find similar items, or learn more about the looted item.

This idea offers a surprising twist to the normal routine of the player. Any twists in the routine can make gameplay less repetitive. It also offers the possibility of more unique adventure to follow.

Tasks and Errands

Let's first look at the differences between these. Definitions are not standard from game to game, so I'm flying by the seat of my pants here. The simplest of quests are called tasks or errands because of the trivial nature of the work involved. Not all of the above steps are included.

These tasks and errands are usually *Fed Ex quests*. Fed Ex quests are the most straightforward and prevalent of *all* quests in computer games.

note

FED EX QUESTS: get their name because they resemble how Federal Express and other delivery services work in real life.

They are divided into two similar types:

■ The errand is a straightforward delivery or pickup. In one variation the player is told by NPC1 to pick up an item from NPC2. In the second variation the player receives an item from NPC1 and is told to deliver it to NPC2. In both variations either or both of the NPCs may give the player a reward.

■ The second type involves combat. NPC1 asks the player to slaughter a specific creature to receive a reward. There is no NPC2. The player proves to NPC1 that he has completed his task by looting (removing from the mob's carcass) a possession, or a body part such as a hide or tooth.

The item in both cases is called a *token* by designers.

note

TOKEN: a piece of data used to measure the player's progress in a game.

When the item—such as a letter or a box of chocolates in a delivery errand, or the looted tooth of the great white tiger in a kill task—is given to the player-character we say the token has been passed to the PC. This tells the game engine that the PC has it in inventory. When the player hands over the item, the token is passed to the NPC and a reward is given to the PC.

We can also track a player's progress by flipping *flags* rather than tracking tokens.

note

FLAG: a signal, symbol, character, or digit that is used as an indicator of the player's progress in the game.

Once the player arrives at a certain physical location in the game, for example, the state of the flag is changed to indicate that. This may trigger an encounter or other happening in the game world, but it may also just be filed away by the program code for later use.

The virtual world *Horizons* contains an early quest for scouts where the player-character is asked to go "scout" for enemy activity at a series of locations. The player goes to a location and a flag is flipped to let the program know that when the player returns to the quest giver, a reward is to be paid out or the player is to be given the next in the series of assignments.

Figure 10.4 *Horizons* is one of the more recent MMORPGs.

We also find in *Horizons* an interesting *suite* of *one-off* tasks under the umbrella title "Trials of the Gifted." Like the scout example listed earlier these tasks cleverly teach various gameplay mechanics to players within the fiction of the world.

note

SUITE: a word taken from music to describe a group of connected puzzles or quests.

note

ONE-OFF: a term borrowed from manufacturing where it means a fabrication process where only a single part is produced. I use one-off to indicate that they are meant to be played only once.

In one, the Test of Endurance, the player-character is weighted down so she can barely move, then asked to walk a certain distance. In a second test the player is required to use a sprint command to speed the player-character's progress. A third test involves the use of a resurrection command. The Test of Knowledge only required that the player visit several NPCs to learn about the history of the world. The final test involved solving riddles.

Whether tokens or flags were used to track progress, none of these are Fed Ex in structure. I mention that because I recently had a brief online debate in an email list I belong to with another game designer who believes there is only one type of quest because the mechanism for tracking progress by the game engine is virtually identical in every quest; and it's important to understand quests at that minute level. I remember having a similar discussion with another game designer some years ago (aboard the Queen Mary actually). He insisted that all puzzles were "lock-and-key."

Both observations are correct as far as they go. But they are as counter-productive to the creation of quests and puzzles as stating that there is only one plot, a variation on "Boy meets Girl. Boy gets Girl. Boy loses Girl." To me this is like saying you've detected that words are made up of letters, and that discovery of this fact will somehow make you a better writer.

As I wrote during the exchange of posts, "it leeches out all meaning and context; gets us nowhere in finding new ways of doing things; and makes it look like there are none." And "to reduce all quests to the same simple mechanism is to follow a postmodern reductionist path where there is no reward at the end but an empty canvas: not art, not life."

It is far more valuable to writers and designers to go the other direction, expanding instead of contracting, categorizing tasks and errands like these as "activities" (scouting), "trials" (endurance, speed), "knowledge" (game mechanics, history), "*mini-games*" (riddles) and so on. Finding unique qualities in various quests and giving them workable descriptions is far likelier to produce a greater variety of more interesting quests.

note

MINI-GAMES: complete little games within the world of the larger game.

In general, tasks and errands are composed of only two or three steps. Whether they're one-offs or repeatable even in this basic form they can be used in storytelling in a variety of ways.

- Backstory on the world of the game, its history and historical figures can provide a context for tasks and errands. *Everquest* and *Dark Age of Camelot* have some quests that refer to backstory.

- Exposition on a region and its inhabitants can be revealed. When the player enters a new location or level, the tasks she's offered can reflect the interests of the new characters she meets, the culture of the area, primary concerns the inhabitants have, and so forth.

- Characters can be introduced, and play different roles in different quests, becoming more fleshed-out in the process. An NPC who has an item another NPC wants the player to pick up (Task1) might also need alligator shoes for his store (Task2). That same NPC may be a neo-Nazi (Task3) and a spy for alien invaders (Task4) who is unfaithful to his wife who wants him killed (Task 5), so that she'll reveal the whereabouts of the plans for the new rail-gun design she stole from her lover's briefcase (Task 6) . . . These are not quest suites, but *intersecting simple tasks*. Look how much you've learned about the character of the NPC in the process of doing a few.

■ The items obtained can have more than one use, and can lead to other quests, or some other form of storytelling. The Better-than-Average Grail may be used in a later task to heal a wounded soldier.

Tasks and errands are not always one-offs even in single-player games. Players can repeat simple errands for cash in order to purchase better supplies, for example.

In *The Riddle of Master Lu*, one of our mini-games required the player to hunt down curious exhibits to stock Ripley's *Odditorium* in New York, the forerunner of the *Ripley's Believe it or Not! Museums* found all over the world from Orlando to Hong Kong.

Chinese Menus

Speaking of Hong Kong. . . . In virtual worlds the number of quests is astronomical when compared to single-player games. We'll deal with specifically multiplayer quests in Chapter 18, "Bringing Virtual Worlds to Life," but I want to describe a popular low-level mechanism for quests that can create the illusion of "many" quests with a lot less effort than one-offs.

I call it a Chinese Menu quest system because it is built using a simple matrix that resembles the menus in Chinese restaurants where diners choose items from several columns or categories to make up a meal. The difference is that in games the engine chooses the dishes (details) for the customer (player).

Figure 10.5 The Odditorium is in constant need of new exhibits.

While they are very helpful for quickly adding a lot of content, Chinese menus should not be relied upon as the entire quest system in a multiplayer game. Even with random variables, they can quickly become redundant and boring, and players soon figure out what is going on. Once they do, willing suspension of disbelief, and the immersion that should follow, suffer.

In structure, Chinese Menu quests are simple Fed Ex type quests, either delivery or kill. Both types of quest are built on the same matrix. Here is one for delivery quests:

Any NPC from Column A gives a player any item from Column B to deliver to any NPC from Column C.

Column A	Column B	Column C
NPC1	Item1	NPC5
NPC2	Item2	NPC6
NPC3	Item3	NPC7
NPC4	Item4	NPC8

The engine doesn't choose until the player queries it for a quest. Even a dozen NPCs or items in each column provide a reasonable number of permutations. A basic system will simply randomize the variables, but this could mean that the game engine chooses the same NPC and item many times in a row, immediately revealing the shallowness of the enterprise. Shuffling variables so that the result NPC1/Item3/NPC6 for example, will not occur again until all other permutations have been exhausted goes farther to preserve the illusion of there being many "new" and "different" quests.

In *Dark Age of Camelot* they are called tasks. In *Star Wars Galaxies* they are called missions. Similar to other science fiction MMORPGs like *Anarchy Online* and *Earth & Beyond* the missions in SWG are given by mission computers as well as NPCs. These should not be confused with missions in single-player action games that correspond to the more elaborate quests we'll look at shortly.

[A more detailed comparison and critique of Chinese menu quest systems in *Dark Age of Camelot* and *Star Wars Galaxies* can be found on my Web site www.anti-linearlogic.com.]

There is absolutely no reason storytelling can't occur in Chinese Menu quests. Enough permutations, artfully conceived and written, can conceal the underlying structure. Chinese menus sophisticated enough to replace one-offs haven't appeared yet, and keeping them bare bones will reveal their repetitive structure. Unfortunately, *Horizons*, despite the excellent quests mentioned earlier, suffers from this in its simple tasks.

Chinese menu quests can be given more variety simply by creating different matrixes depending on the profession of the player-character, or the region where the quest givers can be found.

Multiple Chinese menus can have crossovers to interconnect them with each other. In soap operas we have what are known as "crossover sets." These are sets of public places where our many characters, dragging their own storylines with them, can run into each other to exchange exposition or complicate each other's stories. In games, crossover locations can include NPCs in some proximity to one another who can actually access different menus. A single NPC can be a character in several different tasks.

The more variations we can incorporate, the better chance we have of disguising the simple structure of Chinese menus, and we can still benefit from the ease with which we can increase the content of virtual worlds.

Quests and Missions

True quests or missions are more elaborate, and can be of varying lengths, number of steps, and styles. The missions of a combat game are intricate quests to secure or hold strategic objectives, rescue hostages, uncover nefarious plots, and so on. An epic quest in an RPG can be a series of tasks stretched across an entire continent.

Quests and missions can come in all sorts of interesting shapes and forms. Here are some examples from real life: Run with the bulls in Pamplona; play bingo for cash; return home from the Trojan Wars; win the hand of a fair maiden; help Jews escape Hitler; prove that chivalry isn't dead (*Don Quixote's* quest); agree to face your personal demons on *Oprah*; finish this book. Each has a reward for overcoming one or more challenges.

Knowledge can be more important than items in a quest. Story, backstory, secrets, geography, ethics, character traits, universal themes, and so forth can all be tracked the same way we track items with tokens and flags. "Secrets?! But wait, Lee! Hours after a game is released, walkthroughs are available on the Web!" If the knowledge is untracked and can be used by anyone, you're out of luck. But obtaining the combination to a safe from a Web site wouldn't be enough if the combination was random. Players can't skip steps if those steps are flagged.

It's trickier in virtual worlds to protect secrets, but still possible. In *The Gryphon Tapestry*, we had a system for trading game secrets. The trick is to take what is thought of as intangible—in this case knowledge—and make it tangible. An analogy would be an attribute like strength. In real life we can measure someone's strength by making them bench press weights, adding more until they can no longer lift them. We simplify this in games by assigned numerical values.

Figure 10.6 *The Gryphon Tapestry* used a system for trading secrets.

In real life, we gauge knowledge by testing, and scoring those tests. In games, we simplify this by assigning values to discrete bits of knowledge. The *TGT* system used tokens masquerading as knowledge. First of all, they were attached to various skills, so not everyone could use all secrets. And there were levels of rarity. Some secrets could be shared by many people. Others, once learned, were the player's for life, and the token was no longer tradable. Still others could not be permanently learned. They required the secret (token) to be possessed by the player-character, just like the Journeyman Boots in *Everquest*, for example.

Once secrets are formalized in a single system, the rarest grow in stature and can be coveted and sought as much as uber loot drops. They can be as ordinary as magic spells, and as unusual as evidence. Hearing gossip that an NPC might be a smuggler isn't proof of anything. But a piece of evidence proving it can be used. It can be held over the NPC as blackmail, or delivered to the police.

Types of Quests

To populate our game world with quests or missions, we use a variety of types; otherwise the quest system is repetitive and boring. Single-player games can offer any type of quest without fear, so the writer of single-player quests can view the following types only with an eye to increasing variety. Virtual worlds have to be a bit more thoughtful about their use. The ramifications can be earthshaking. For this reason, I'll be going into more detail about virtual world applications.

Quests can be categorized in many ways:

- Number of steps or length of the quest.
- Unique components, such as activities, knowledge, or mini-games.
- Overall complexity or difficulty. The difficulty may be due to how hard individual puzzles are, or the sheer number of them.
- Ease of execution by the writer/designer: how fast they can be constructed. This is obviously affected by all of the three above bullets.
- Repeatability. In the sense that a single player can replay the quest more than once; multiple players can do it; or both.
- Single or multiplayer. This is different from the previous bullet and refers to whether the quest is designed for a single-player or multiplayer game. A more special consideration is whether the quest is truly multiplayer. Just because it's in a multiplayer game doesn't make it so. We'll look at that in Chapter 18.
- Usefulness in storytelling and character revelation, of primary interest to writers.
- Affect on the world. An important factor that can influence all aspects of the quest design.

■ Value or effort versus reward for the writer/designer. A group of quests that are easy to execute, but have little impact on the game might have equal value to a single massive quest that significantly alters the game world.

Given all these possible ways to sort our quests, I'm faced with a challenge: how to create some sort of hierarchy that makes sense. I'm going to hedge my bets and stay flexible, but you'll see there is something of a hierarchy from "small" to "large." For each class of quest, I'll highlight as many of the above features that the level supports. I'm indebted to discussions I had a few years ago with Chris Foster, now a designer on *Middle Earth Online*, that helped me begin to refine classes of quests.

1. We've talked about the simplest class of quests: tasks or errands. One-offs are simple delivery or kill tasks of only two or three steps. Example: "Take this cloth to the weaver in the next village, then return to me for your reward." They also can be infinitely replayable and fill out the content of the game. Example: "The entire town is plagued by rats. I'll give you a copper piece for every one you kill!" Writing each individual task is a huge waste of time. Virtual worlds often supplement these with Chinese menu type systems. The danger is in relying on them too heavily, or presenting them so baldly that their structure is revealed. In virtual worlds, the only affect on the game world is the player's acquisition of a reward. These tiny quests can deliver story, background, and character in small bites.

2. The second class is comprised of variable quests. They can save us some time in single-player games. Example: "Find the members of the rebel forces trying to assassinate the mayor of the village and eliminate them." Each target is a quest or level in itself with different challenges that must be overcome in different ways, but all follow a similar structure. In virtual worlds, the scope of the quest can be expanded without changing the structure. Example: "Find the Romulans who have invaded Middle Earth disguised as elves and eliminate them!" These quests may be replayable or not, but at the very least provide enough targets and variables they almost seem to be. Also in virtual worlds, they will not affect the world if they can be repeated, except for player rewards. These can be more ambitious in character and storytelling *because* they aren't infinitely replayable. Example: We could set kill limits. When the player kills 10 pointy-eared invaders, more of the Romulan plans might be revealed; they might retaliate; somehow the stakes can be escalated.

3. The third class of quests is restricted in some way. The particular skill or faction the player chose at the beginning of the game may determine which side of a battle he finds himself on. Example: *Star Wars* games differ in gameplay and story depending upon which side of the force the player chooses. There may be entirely unique quests offered. Example: If you chose to play a Ninja you may get the quest to assassinate a warlord, but shouldn't be surprised if you're not asked to participate in palace politics. This can add to the replayability of the game by offering

unique gameplay for different initial choices. In virtual worlds, these quests are routine. Examples: "A wily wolf is killing the local livestock. No swordsman can catch up to it. Maybe your arrows will be faster!" or "The space station is holding a baking contest, but to enter you must be able to at least bake fruit tarts" where fruit tarts require a skill level of 10 in baking. These quests generally can be a step backwards in complexity from the second class because they already have the unique feature that restricts participation; and to lessen the impact that some resources may go unused in single-player games. In virtual worlds, they are usually variations on lower level quests because designers may not want to limit access to major plot points or unique characters. Deliberately restricting access to story points and characters can make for some lively player discussions at the pub, so I would do it with pleasure. They may affect other players if the quest involves a competition, but need not affect the world at large.

4. The fourth class of quests is an advance in complexity on the first three levels. They may still be repeatable, but are more commonly seen as one-offs, the staple for non-repeatable quests in many virtual worlds, they offer as reward a unique item: gun, spell, whatever. Whether repeatable or not, these can delve more deeply into story and characterization than the first three levels because of their additional complexity and length. These quests can get very involved, if we'd like. Instead of a straightforward path for the player, there can be twists and turns. An NPC encountered later in the quest may require a subquest before he'll aid the player. Another may insist the initial quest giver lied, and try to get the player to switch allegiance. The nature of the quest object might be unknown. In the movie *Romancing the Stone*, the stone was a huge emerald. In the sequel, *Jewel of the Nile*, the jewel was a person. More sophisticated structures also exist. The quest may not be linear, but modular, allowing the player to experience the steps in any order. When you think of a quest with many steps, perhaps dozens, this is the level. It is the most complex of non-world affecting quests.

5. The fifth class of quests adds interest because it is the first to affect the world beyond the player, if only in a limited way. Here the focus is on rewards that are not just transient items, but become temporary or permanent fixtures of the world such as plaques commemorating player accomplishments; souvenirs players can display in their homes; articles about player achievements in ingame news reports; or town criers announcing the deeds out loud. While these affect the world, they do nothing to really change story or gameplay. These rewards can be attached to either one-off or repeatable quests, although to avoid clutter the world-affecting reward should probably be limited to the first time a player completes the quest. The benefit is of high value because the quest complexity level should be higher than the preceding levels. The rewards may not be entirely unique, but everyone won't have one because everyone won't finish the quest, and the player achieve-

ment can be shared. Either the player can call attention to it, or even better, the *world* calls attention to it. Opportunities for ongoing storytelling are limited deliberately because the player is able to take the stage instead. We'll discuss this more in Chapter 18.

6. The sixth quest class is similar to number five. The world affect is somewhat larger, but temporary. This could be a quest for a single player-character, or a group. We call this a "flip-flop" quest because the game state is not permanently changed. One questor completes the quest, setting State A to State B. Another questor completes the quest and State B is reset to State A. For example, a player aligned with the green faction might free a green NPC from the blue jail. Celebration in Greenland, outrage in Bluesville. The quest is in context with the game world and can provide additional limited storytelling and character revelation, but won't contribute anything to an ongoing story.

7. The seventh class of quest is the big brother to six. Here the world affect can be much larger, but is still temporary and flip-flop. To maintain imbalance, the key to this situation, there should always be an odd number of opposing factions. A good example of this is *Dark Age of Camelot* where players are divided into three realms in opposition: Avalon, Hibernia, and Midgard. Players of each realm periodically take over the castles of their enemies, and steal artifacts to increase their powers at the expense of their foes. This "capture the flag" gameplay can only swing back and forth with power ebbing and flowing. This swing can take months, but it will happen. No realm can ever completely conquer the other two, or both game and revenue stream would end. Unfortunately, just like its smaller sibling, this class of quest does not contribute to ongoing story. It's just as well. The game structure is actually static. There is no ongoing story to tell.

8. The eighth class of quest is important to us because it is created specifically to support ongoing story. These quests may be added as part of the opening of a new playable area; in an expansion product sold separately; or as a part of monthly episodes in games like *Asheron's Call* and *Earth & Beyond*. *Horizons* features weekly episodes although they do not all contain quests. The distinction between this class and number nine is that the quest does not trigger new content. The new content is given to players as part of the episodic update, and the quests tied to it are a part of that. It is obviously a great way to contribute to the advancement of story and character. And while I consider this type of episodic update a trap for writers and designers (see Chapter 18), it is certainly putting focus on story and character, and for that we can be grateful. The game world can be affected, but again, it isn't so much the quest or the players doing the affecting. There are some exceptions to this, but this formal presentation of new material can lessen player immersion. Far superior is our next class.

9. The ninth quest class is the event quest, the first to allow players to affect the game world in a big way. It is a tremendous opportunity for telling ongoing story that lies along that large arc we drew in Chapter 9, "Bringing the Story to Life." These quests alter the world, not just for a single player or a small group, but everyone. These quests are not replayable unless the new state achieved can be added to. In *Disney's Virtual Kingdom*, I created Class 5 quests where players received a brick with their character name on it as a reward. That brick could be used to rebuild a castle, or build a bridge to a new island. That new island was a new playable zone. If there had been other zones created off of the first, more bridges might need to have been built. I first proposed this idea several years ago in an internet newsgroup in a discussion on storytelling in virtual worlds. I suggested that instead of just bringing a server down for a few hours, updating the content, then when it came back up there was a new zone where none had been the day before that the world change could be brought about by the actions of the players. We know we're going to have to add new content, why not give the players the chance to do it? I gave as an example a huge quest *Dark Age of Camelot* could implement that would require players with varying skills weeks to accomplish, but at the end of it the players would have released the content, not the developers. Nothing came of that suggestion, although earlier this year I was able as a player to see the concept in action in *Horizons*. I was part of an effort contributed to by hundreds of players that opened four new zones, and freed the race of satyrs. That race became a playable race. The selling of the idea to players was problematic, and the execution of the idea was rocky, but the concept was proven with flying colors. It was the most profound sense of community I have felt so far in one of the massive worlds. And the excitement with which players entered into the quest to free the satyrs was intense. In theory, players were moving the ongoing story of the game forward. The event need not be on that grand a stage. Any new content developers want to add to the virtual world can be done in a similar manner.

10. The tenth and last quest class I'm going to talk about is the ultimate quest of the virtual world, and hopefully the neverending quest. Here the journey is more important. The Holy Grail is never found (or lost again as in the third Indiana Jones movie), but the experience is fulfilling and entertaining nonetheless. Most massively multiplayer games have neverending quests because to complete the quest would essentially end the game. Yet games like *Asheron's Call*, because they provide ongoing story, can ride on neverending quests the way soap operas ride on neverending stories. In *Horizons*, players are involved in an ongoing struggle with the Withered Aegis, an undead army that threatens to overrun player-controlled lands. But I expect the Withered Aegis will never be defeated. *Asheron's Call* might allow players to defeat one enemy at the end of a story arc, but would then

introduce a new one. As long as the quests and the stories that drive them overlap (again like soap operas) multiple huge story arcs can survive just as long. Remember some soap operas have been running for *decades*.

Puzzles, learning skills, quests . . . killing stuff, forming clans or guilds, politics, achieving wealth or fame . . . any of these can form the foundation that we can build story upon. We'll look at some more of these in Chapters 18 and 19.

Imagine your surprise if, by clever use of puzzles and quests and other gameplay mechanisms, you can remove *all* of the character development and exposition from your cut scenes and then cut the cut scenes.

Rewards

Just a further note about rewards. They've come up more than once already. Rewards add to the "fun" factor of the experience. These rewards can be eye candy, a cool dramatic scene, a plot or character twist that launches us into the next act. . . . Action games are full of such rewards, if often limited to the visceral: cool explosions and deaths. They give the player the satisfaction of victory that compels him to play more. Just as we sprinkle reminders to players throughout the game about what they need to accomplish, we sprinkle rewards to pat them on their backs and push them back into the game with renewed energy. Accomplishments are marked in *Jak & Daxter* with a shuffled selection of cute (and short!) animated celebrations.

Rewards can be plot devices on their own as we've seen: loot that propels us into a new story or quest; or increased faction with an NPC who will now share with the player new revelations. They are another tool writers of games can pull out of our hats to reveal our characters and tell our stories.

The Story Up Till Now

"What did that NPC say to me back at the hamburger stand?" "How many objectives of this mission have I completed?" "What was the town the villain threatened with destruction next?"

Over the years we've come up with several ways to remind the player what she's done. I introduced a couple of these earlier: journals, diaries, a tape recorder or notebook that are often a part of the interface. I prefer to use a "game world" place to stash them. The journal might rest on my desk in my home. The tape recorder is a part of my inventory. But however it is done, it is much less likely to break the fourth wall than the player-character returning to an NPC and having the NPC repeat a conversation, as if it hadn't occurred.

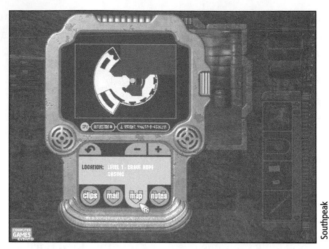

Southpeak

Figure 10.7 The Video Digital Assistant from *Dark Side of the Moon*.

In one of the early games I worked on, *Once upon a Forest*, important clues are noted in a journal one of the characters keeps. In another, *Dark Side of the Moon*, this is handled by the V-Clips (V for Video) in the VDA, the Video Digital Assistant, an extrapolation of the PDA of today.

The method used is not nearly as important as the concept of keeping it within the context of the game fiction. Anything we can do to preserve the fourth wall and aid in the player's willing suspension of disbelief, however small, is worth doing!

CHAPTER 11

STORY ANATOMY

Here are three topics that didn't precisely fit in any of the chapters, but that bear thinking about as we write our games. We'll take a look at the other side of emotional game moments; sort through some ideas on how to share our themes with players without beating them over their heads; and look at the many and varied roles comedy can perform in games.

Heart: Player Emotion

"I think the guys who are really controlling their emotions . . . are going to win; the guy who is controlling his emotions is going to win!"

—Tiger Woods

In sports that's very true, Tiger. Entertainment in games though can spring both from the gameplay and the heart.

Remember the example I gave in Chapter 5, "Character Traits," when I talked about the emotions our characters feel? It was the quest from *Earth & Beyond* where a Jenquai NPC you've previously helped offers a new opportunity to intercept a Progen shipment of weapons. You go to the coordinates given, but the ship there is carrying children, not weapons. I chose not to blow the ship up, and returned to the NPC, who was furious with me, calling the children of our enemies "weapons."

We discussed the NPC who gave out the quest and his revelation of character through emotion. The quest evoked emotions in me, the player, as well: surprise and sympathy upon learning what the ship's true cargo was; the consternation aroused trying to decide what to do; and my anger at the NPC's response. His remark about the children of our enemies being weapons resonates with echoes of our own planet's troubled politics; conflicts between peoples that have been going on for centuries, and seem today as far from being resolved as ever. That sent a chill down my spine. All those emotions in a short one-off (non-repeatable) quest.

That quest in *Earth & Beyond* will stay with me as long as Floyd's death in *Planetfall*, and another moment from another Infocom text adventure game, Brian Moriarty's *Trinity*. Very early in the game an elderly woman, crippled and deformed, handed my player-character an umbrella in Hyde Park that would be of critical use later on. Hours of gameplay later, my player-character traveled back in time to Hiroshima right before the atomic bomb is dropped. There I met a little girl, and I realized that she would become the old woman who gave me the umbrella in Hyde Park. I was shaken. Shock, pity, a feeling of helplessness over what was about to happen to her and what it would mean, sadness, all washed over me in a second or two.

Emotion lies at the core of all great literature; classic drama and films; and the best of TV. What touches us . . . what illuminates a truth about the human condition . . . is at the heart of what entertains us. Mark Barrett, whom I've worked with more than once, has done a lot of thinking about emotion in computer games, as his sidebar will indicate.

Most game designers to date have shied away from emotion, or failed at delivering it when they've tried. Everybody has emotions with the exception of asocial personalities who can only mimic them. But the ability to communicate these emotions, so that an audience may feel them, is a talent. It's the same with story ideas. Everyone has them because everyone has an imagination to a greater or lesser degree. Story ideas are a part of children's make-believe. But bringing those ideas to life for others to enjoy is a talent.

Why is emotion in computer games so elusive? I've been told it's because gaming attracts people who aren't very in touch with their emotions to begin with. Players and creators alike are suspicious of emotion, and fearful of it. All stereotypes may start with a grain of truth, and the computer geek is no different. But it *is* a stereotype, and therefore no more valid an observation than all actors are immoral or all writers drink way too much bourbon. (I never drank bourbon. When I drank whiskey, I drank scotch!).

A more plausible answer may be that performing artists are trained to lose their inhibitions. They learn to infuse their art with their personalities, as in music; or strip away their own characters, so they can inhabit the personas of others as actors. Writing, the fine arts, two of the main creative pillars of the games we make, are far less social pursuits, but they too require a dialogue between the artist and her emotional center. But the making of games is dominated by the third pillar, the technical foundation, and experts here are never given training to get in touch with their emotions.

Another possibility is that the nature of collaboration in the computer games industry is somewhat different from other collaborative mediums. There are two models in music

Mark Barrett, Writer/Designer

Too often, in even the best big-budget titles, interactive works play out on the screen in front of us and not in our minds. We watch the moments, we don't live them.

That's ironic because, unlike movies and other passive mediums, interactivity offers us the chance to experience emotional involvement not simply by witnessing events, but by participating in them. As game designers, this immediacy and intimacy give us an advantage over passive mediums, but despite exponential leaps in computing power, graphics capabilities, and production budgets, we haven't made much progress.

Figure 11.1 Mark Barrett.

What is emotional involvement? It's believing in a false reality, the same way you believe in a movie when you watch it, or a novel when you read it. Books are a collection of paper pages that you hold in your hand. That's reality. The Lord of the Rings novels are fantastic journeys you take in your head. That's emotional involvement.

Linear games like Splinter Cell can often create moments of compelling emotional involvement. By combining freedom of movement with the capability to move quietly, then placing the player-character in a world full of shadows and heavily armed guards, the player can be induced to experience the same sense of exposure, risk, and fear that the in-game character would be experiencing in that narrative context. When an audio cue sounds, notifying the player that a guard has been alerted to the onscreen character's presence, that sound alone can provoke an emotional response that goes well beyond rational game-related concerns about what may happen to the character depicted on the screen. The player may in fact actually experience the raw fear of being caught.

A game like The Sims creates emotional involvement, not by asking the player to take on the role of a specific character, but by encouraging the player to take responsibility for the welfare of onscreen characters. The player's investment of time and energy creates an emotional bond between the player and those in-game characters in the same way caring for a child or a pet or even a plant creates a bond. Once the bond is strong enough, in-game events and threats that impact the health or welfare of the in-game characters can produce a wide range of emotional responses in the player.

Combining these two techniques, games like ICO (and several missions in Splinter Cell), give the player both an in-game character to play as well as an NPC to take care of with that player-character. Add additional narrative context or more simulated elements to the game world and the potential for even greater emotional involvement is clearly real.

This potential is rarely, and often only briefly, reached, however, for two reasons. First, it's damn hard to do. Second, during the design of most interactive works, game goals still trump emotional involvement. Given the choice between allowing the player-character to be killed or protecting the player's emotional involvement, most game designers blindly follow tradition.

The question we all have to ask is: do we care?

worth looking at: the orchestra and the rock band. Both are collaborative, but approach their collaborations very differently.

An orchestra is highly structured. There is a conductor, a strict hierarchy of musicians such as first violin, second violin, and so on. Even if the orchestra is going to perform an original work, the music is written down. The various members are allowed to interpret it for the instruments, but they are guided by the conductor who always has the last word for the sake of the overall presentation.

A rock band is a far looser collaboration. Paul McCartney and John Lennon wrote the bulk of the Beatles' songs, but George Harrison and Ringo Starr both composed as well. The essence of collaboration in a rock band is everybody has the chance to inter-

Figure 11.2 The tight structure of a symphony orchestra extends to the seating.

ject ideas. They are tried, wrangled over, ultimately accepted or discarded. The process can lead to music every bit as successful as a symphony written by a single composer on his Steinway grand. One of the hottest developers out there right now is called Rockstar after all. But it requires a spectacular amount of talent or talents not often found. It is also fraught with pitfalls the tighter structure of the orchestra attempts to avoid. With talent comes ego. With great talent often comes great ego. McCartney's solid populist approach and Lennon's far more eclectic tastes finally clashed once too often, and the Beatles were no more. Rock bands break up over differences of opinion on the type of music to play, the style of play, and so on, whether they write their own material or just perform songs written by others.

Figure 11.3 Fairly well known rock band of a few decades ago.

The film and television industry is firmly orchestral in the structure of its collaborations. But the game industry is a young industry, both in terms of the average age of its members, and its short time on the planet, and you'll find far more posters of Nickelback on the walls of cubicles than you will Loren Maazel, the music director of the New York Philharmonic. So it shouldn't be any surprise that computer game collaboration is a lot more reminiscent of rock bands.

In film, every artist or technician knows his or her job. They each create and contribute in their own little niche within the structure of the production. A costume designer is usually content to design costumes. Of course, he may move on to write, produce, or direct. He earns those opportunities based on additional skills he displayed on a production apart from his regular duties. He is not rewarded for his efforts as a costume designer by being given the chance to try his hand at a job he may be interested in, but for which he has no talent. Pay, benefits, and rewards are focused on advancement and recognition as a costume designer.

In games, everybody wants to help with the fun stuff. And developers, bless 'em, are often happy to comply. In our industry, we have the concept that everybody needs to buy into the idea before an original game can be built. This often means allowing everyone to contribute directly to the vision in all areas, not just those for which they are qualified. I remember my first job at a game studio, coming out of a meeting and being told in absolute seriousness by one of the programmers that he thought it was the duty of management to see that he had a good time. In movies, if you don't buy into the director's or producer's or (rarely!) writer's vision, you are gone.

I need to stress here that writers and designers shouldn't stifle input from anyone. I try to listen to every idea that comes my way while I'm designing. If the interest is there, I'll use the idea as a teaching tool to help that person grow into writing or design, and mentor them in any way I can. But it is dangerous when everybody on a new production team *assumes* they will have an equal say in its development.

This rock band approach to game design can result in good games. But with all those different personalities squeezed into the conference room for hours at a time, all having a voice in what the game will be in order to commit to it; it should be obvious that a lot of emotion can emerge. Whether it makes it into the game though is another thing. And any overriding vision that we may find in creation (expressionism) or interpretation (an orchestra) will have difficulty surviving.

Whatever the explanation, emotion that touches players is so hard to find in games—and here I mean the *range* of emotions found in other media—it is a major reason games are treated by critics as well as the general public kind of like *The Beverly Hillbillies*: tolerated because they make a lot of money, but laughed at or ignored by the majority.

I'm not going to try and make a list of ways to mechanically insert emotion into games. I don't work from such lists as I write. The lists are a part of me *in context*, and ready to be drawn upon, because the emotions are mine. Read the lists if you have to jumpstart your memory. Better to make up your own list. Read books, watch films and television. Watch as other humans interact with each other, and how you interact with other human beings. When you are moved in a way that is meaningful to you, a way you might like to move others, remember it.

Lee Sheldon

Figure 11.4 Peppy at play.

If you aren't having any luck sharing the emotions you feel through your writing, you might do well to get some professional help. "Wait," the outraged reader will cry. "Is he saying I need therapy?" Not necessarily. Try an acting workshop at your local college instead. Most workshops will include training in improvisation, as well as exercises in funny faces and making yourself cry on cue. I've been an actor on-and-off for many years.

To cry on cue I think of the dog I grew up with, Peppy: a half-Dalmatian, half Labrador who was jet black except for a splash of white on his chest. When I use that image of Peppy (called in acting *sense memory*), I'm not pretending to cry. The emotion is absolutely real. And it is mine.

note

SENSE MEMORY: recalling an object not present to create its reality for an actor.

I remember how Peppy looked; how he felt when I petted him; how he smelled. Then I use a second technique called *emotional memory*.

note

EMOTIONAL MEMORY: recalling significant events that evoked emotions at the time to recreate those emotions in a performance.

I grew up in a small town called Olmsted Falls, Ohio. There were no leash laws in those days. Dogs ran free. I remember I was around 10 or 11 the night Peppy didn't come home. He was gone for hours. At last, very late he finally came limping and stumbling up to the door, bloody and whimpering. He'd been hit by a car. The vet was close. He bandaged a broken leg, and cleaned some other cuts. I sat on the floor with Peppy the rest of the night, his head in my lap. That's the night I invoke when I want to cry on cue as an actor.

Marriage and having kids can be two more great ways to get in touch with our emotions, and to force us to examine them. The emotions can surprise and overwhelm us. Whether we can learn from them, and translate them into our work, is something else. If you can't find any emotional moments in other media, or life, or aren't interested enough to try looking for them, writing is probably not for you.

Once we can draw upon our own emotions and can make others feel them, we aren't tied to the themes and interests of the present day or even this planet. If we can write three-dimensional characters and interesting stories, we can take on any subject matter set in any time or in any place real or unreal. All that's left is researching the details, or imagining what it would be like.

Games are very good at capturing the mood of their intended audience, their interests, and their outlooks on life. It's a direct copying from life in the present. Little interpretation is necessary. They are fast, slick, and more often than not, relentlessly hip and cool. But individual games will last only as long as they hit that ever-moving target. What is hip and cool today isn't tomorrow. To pursue the present is to get lost in the past, a past only hanging on as nostalgia.

If we want our work to endure as *Hamlet* endures, it is absolutely essential that we attempt to get beyond what is hip and cool at the moment, and tackle some more lasting human values. Emotion is a good place to start.

Mind: Sharing the Theme

Okay, we've settled on a theme we want to explore in our game. We write characters orchestrated to illuminate the theme. We allow it to drive our story. But how do we prevent turning our entertainment into pedantry?

We can't forget that our first and foremost goal is to entertain. As soon as we lose sight of that, all of our good intentions mean nothing. It's also not enough to let the gameplay be the fun part while we teach. Edutainment is littered with enough learning games that try to combine gameplay with obvious teaching; we can safely leave that rocky marriage to them.

It's easy enough to say that we should support the theme with every character and story situation, but how do we put that into practice? Few TV series rely on a single storyline to carry an episode. There is always a main story, what we call the A story. Our A story may not be able to sustain itself for the entire episode, and some padding may be required. Also, there are often other cast members who must be serviced, but who are not prominently featured in every story. For them, we write B stories, smaller stories that play out in only two or three scenes in an hour, or "runners," brief story moments that are scattered throughout the show.

Rarely do all of these relate to one another except incidentally. There are exceptions, of which the British courtroom comedy-drama *Rumple of the Bailey*, written by John Mortimer, is a textbook case in point. Mortimer wrote *all* of the episodes for the series, and every one had a central theme. Mortimer knew he had a limited time in which to expose the theme, yet he faced the same problems all series writers do in servicing all of the characters every week. His solution was to ensure that every story—A, B, or simple runner—supported a single theme.

Figure 11.5 Leo McKern, born to play the brilliant, irascible Rumpole.

If the main criminal case Rumpole was involved in centered on infidelity as a motive for murder, Mortimer's theme might be that infidelity can be destructive to everyone involved, no matter how peripherally. You can bet that at least the temptation of an extramarital affair would be highlighted elsewhere in the same episode, perhaps involving one of Rumpole's fellow barristers in chambers. Rumpole's wife Hilda might be angry at Rumpole defending a philanderer because her best friend suspects her husband of having an affair. The barmaid at Rumpole's favorite pub might lay into her husband the barman over his flirting with a customer.

I've mentioned how *Seabiscuit* explores its theme that every one has value in just about every scene in the film. The dozen or so stories in Richard Curtis' *Love Actually* openly revel in the fact that they are explorations of the many facets of love. It's not enough—and in fact way too unsubtle—to have a single character sum up a theme for the audience. It's like those awkward moments when the title of a film is disingenuously dropped into the middle of a defenseless conversation in order to explain it.

Figure 11.6 The theme is the title: *Love Actually.*

But when we have the luxury of all of the characters (at least the major ones), and all of our plot points (at least the major ones) reflecting our theme, our job is done for us. We don't have to worry about the player getting it. She can't avoid it. And as long as it is subtle enough, she won't mind.

Let's look at *Sideshow* again. I named the player-character, David's best friend, Joel, after my own childhood best friend, Joel, who committed suicide in his early 20s. I felt guilt over that, as well as sorrow. My guilt was not that I could have prevented it, but that we'd allowed ourselves to grow so far apart, I didn't know why Joel took his own life. I only had stories, a few bits and pieces that seemed to explain it, but didn't really. The loss was all the greater for my inability to understand it, and therefore come to terms with it.

Even though my favorite theme memory and the past's influence on the present is in abundant display in *Sideshow*, the main theme is of guilt, and what it can do to us. I made it more explicit. David feels guilt over his best friend's death when they were kids because he is present at Joel's death, and feels cowardice prevented him from saving his friend.

The very first scene (Yes, a cut scene, but this was nine years ago! I've learned!) shows the accident as David and Joel ride on a roller coaster. Joel's showing off causes him to lose his balance. David watches as he plummets to his death. Might he have helped? Was he a coward? The moment is ambiguous.

So we start with the incident that inspired the guilt, then see it is a reoccurring nightmare of David's. We soon see he has returned to his boyhood town. These moments, without any dialogue referencing David's guilt, still strongly suggest a motive for his current actions. But David's is not the only guilt. It is partially guilt that has turned Dr. Adams into a bitter old man. Guilt plays a part in why another character, Kathy, has transformed herself into the stereotypical old-maid librarian. A more recent and ongoing guilt haunts the chief of police.

Sounds like we have enough guilt to satisfy any jury. But the key is not to bury the player in it. I give him enough things to do, including thwarting an attempt to take over the world. I don't dwell on the theme, but it crops up enough that an accumulation of moments is enough to get the point across. Here David is telling his old friend about his writing career.

*   *   *

```
                    DAVID
I do mostly local stuff for a couple of weeklies. In
Boston. That's where I live now.

                    KATHY
Gee, I never would've thought you'd be a writer. Joel
was the storyteller. You liked to take things apart, see
what made them work...

                    DAVID
People change.
```

*   *   *

People don't change, of course. Not that much. David has become a writer more because it was Joel's aspiration than his own. We talked about using NPCs to reveal character. As in *Sideshow*, we can simultaneously reveal the theme to both the player and the player-character through the comments and observations NPCs make. Those comments may not even refer directly to the PC, but if we've layered in enough hints, the player will take the comments to heart.

And, of course, as the plot reaches a crescendo, you know David will be faced with a similar moment to the one we saw in the opening scene, and will be given the chance to redeem himself. Character is revealed through action more than words.

We don't have to be serious when we treat serious themes. Comedy is another road to the same destination.

Funny Bone: ROFLMAO!

"Something familiar,
Something peculiar,
Something for everyone:
A comedy tonight!"

— Stephen Sondheim, *A Funny Thing Happened on the Way to the Forum*

Communication between human beings in Internet chat rooms and online games is still predominantly accomplished with text. Many ways to streamline all that keyboarding have been developed, such as acronyms like the elaborate ROFLMAO which stands for Rolling On Floor Laughing My Ass Off. This indicates to those reading that whatever remark prompted it was even funnier than a remark that prompted only LOL (Laughing Out Loud). We love our comedy in entertainment. And games are no exception.

Comedy games are not as common as action games. Often they are aimed at younger audiences. But we have had our share of great comedy games like *Planetfall* and *Monkey Island*. Console games with their younger demographic, of course, do more comedy than personal computers.

We've talked about comedy quite a bit so far here and there, but how games treat comedy deserves some closer study. Self-referential and anachronistic comedy are both popular. As we've seen, winking at the player is fashionable regardless of context or the fourth wall. And we have lots of examples of wacky, off-the-wall comedy.

Comedy can be liberating to the writer/ designer, which explains its appeal beyond the obvious. Hal Barwood calls this the "Three Stooges take on design" because the player is invited to settle into the mindset of a game world where its internal logic is illogical. We then can get away with all sorts of situations and obstacles and puzzles that wouldn't work at all in more straight-laced games. Hal points out that "the skateboarding, plum-bouncing, chair-riding, and pirate–ship-flying sequences in *Rayman II*" are great examples of the freedom comedy can give us.

Figure 11.7 The liberating world of *Rayman*.

Ubisoft

In Chapter 7, "Once Upon a Time," I discussed comedy as a counterpoint to heavier material to either give the player some relief from flying body parts, or to provide a contrast that highlights the non-comedic action of the game by placing it in stark contrast to the comedy. No matter how grim a game's premise, there is usually room for the appropriate kind of comedy, one that doesn't break the fourth wall. Players will welcome it.

I mentioned in my text bite on Aristophanes that he wrote very edgy comedy, prickly social satire that makes plays like *Lysistrata* work for audiences centuries later. We have little of this in computer games. We seem to leave the edgier humor to other media. It is comedy with a sharp point. It cuts the mighty down to size; gets in the face of its audience; and enthusiastically breaks taboos.

Figure 11.8 Riding an A-Bomb to glory in *Dr. Strangelove*.

Comedy doesn't get much edgier than the satire *Dr. Strangelove, or How I Learned to Stop Worrying and Love the Bomb*. From the Nazi scientist's arm with a will of its own to mad General Ripper trying to start World War III because he believes commies made him impotent through fluoridation to its uncompromising finale pictured here, the film shoves the audience's face into the absurdity and horror of nuclear war. Memorable one-liner from writer Terry Southern: "Gentlemen, you can't fight in here! This is the war room!"

We aren't going to find the searing humor of *Dr. Strangelove* or even *Lysistrata* in games yet. Just as we avoid tragedy, we don't set our sights on comedy so intense. To do so could alienate players who might be thrown by it.

But earlier I did give a few examples of provocative humor that are found in games. They are worth looking at more closely. In Steve Meretzky's adventure game *Space Bar*, in addition to the main player-character, players drive several different avatars in flashbacks. As Steve explains:

> You play an incredibly *incredibly* wealthy and jaded alien businessman who is putting together a consortium to buy an entire planet. One entity is interested in minerals; one in harvesting the oceans for fish; one in lumber rights; etc. Once the deal is done, the entire population of the planet will be relocated and the planet completely broken up for its component parts. In addition to being a really interesting puzzle (putting together the best possible consortium to make the highest possible offer) it was supposed to be an indictment of out-of-control corporate capitalism, and its complete disinterest in human suffering while trying to max the bottom line."

We can see some of this same greed and exploitation at work in *Tropico*, where the player is again invited to play the role of unblushing capitalist pig.

In *Space Bar*, the main player-character is Alex Node, a human being on a planet where humans are a minority. In a reverse twist on the film *Alien Nation*, the PC is a police officer partnered with a Marmali, one of the majority race. Alex's partner is a friend, and treats him with respect. But as Steve says, "every other Marmali you meet (including your Marmali boss, the police chief) consider humans to be incapable idiots—whereas it's the Marmali who are a bit on the dim and lazy side. It's played for humor but with the hope of getting people not used to being a member of a minority group to think about what it would be like."

And there, as we'll see in the next section, is the crux of the matter. Steve hoped the player might think of more than how to solve the puzzles, or to complete the game.

Another example is *Grim Fandango*, set in the Land of the Dead. Writer/Designer Tim Schafer has said it was inspired by a folklore class at Santa Cruz and film noir, such as *Double Indemnity* and *Gilda*. *Grim Fandango* isn't the only game to use film noir as its inspiration, but it is the only one to date to go beyond a superficial copy of the genre. Mimicry is not mastery. It looks at its subject from the outside, without respect or understanding. Even in its fantastic setting, *Grim Fandango* succeeds where others failed because it gets at the human core, the small, mundane victories and evils that film noir loves to explore.

Figure 11.9 *Grim Fandango.*

A more recent game to explore comedy with an edge is the controversial *Grand Theft Auto: Vice City* from Rockstar. This is not a comedy game, but an example of using some sharply-observed parodies of American culture to both heighten the impact of its violent themes, and to provide some relief from them.

Comedy can be used in many ways to help us in our writing, and to tickle our players. Cheap laughs are easy though. It's much more important to take the time to mold the comedy until it fits the fiction of the game world. A wacky, anachronistic game world can mean freedom for us and fun for the player. The wrong kind of comedy can destroy all our efforts at immersion.

We also run the risk of slipping into ruts in the types of comedy we use. Meaningful themes that make the player think about the world around her can be present in comedy as well as any other genre. We just have to decide to do it.

CHAPTER 12

EDITING

When I was producing *Blacke's Magic,* I wrote a first draft script in two and a half days. The notes I received took half an hour to address. The episode was nominated by the Mystery Writers of America for an Edgar Award.

A 45–47 page half-hour script for *Edge of Night* took me on average two and three-quarter hours to write. Many times, there were few notes; sometimes no notes at all. They were often shot exactly as written.

A few years before that, I'd worked for a producer who made me do 13 drafts of an hour-long script. He was having his dream house built. His wife was overseeing the work. The tennis court contractor moved into the house with his wife. I looked like the contractor.

On more than one other show, I was summoned to the set to find shooting halted and everyone standing around. An actor or the director or someone else had found a problem in the scene that needed to be addressed. In each case I found the most comfortable chair I could and rewrote on the spot with the dollars ticking by.

As Old Lodge Skins, played by Native American actor Chief Dan George, said in *Little Big Man,* "Sometimes the magic works and sometimes it doesn't."

Most situations that we writers face fall somewhere in between. Rewriting will be necessary for a whole host of reasons ranging from the creative to the technical. Often a creative solution won't be possible technically or a technical solution will require a compromise that harms the original material.

Writers have brushes with reality when we write our first drafts. Experience teaches us to keep one ear cocked at the Victrola's horn like the pooch in the old RCA ads, to hear as much reality as we write even then. Later drafts require the cold harsh light of reality to illuminate our thinking. Editing is essential. And even more than writing a first draft, editing requires craft as much as it does talent.

Figure 12.1 The dogged writer tries to keep one ear tuned to reality.

(For the dog lovers amongst us: the name of the dog was Nipper, first immortalized in an oil painting in 1895. Check out his interesting history sometime, and win a few bets in bars.)

We need to start with some sense of what is achievable to minimize the rewriting later on. In TV we learned to write to the limitations of the show. The budget for *Charlie's Angels* allowed us, on average, a guest cast of only seven. *Edge of Night* had six standing sets circling the soundstage. Given the time the production crew had to work between the end of shooting one day and the beginning of rehearsal the next morning, I was allowed a change of only one or two sets per day.

The same is true in games. This is where that knowledge of programming and art comes in handy. Writing something that cannot be created with our technology, or at least can't be in the time we have to produce the game, is a waste. We shouldn't trust other team members to do our jobs for us. We need to learn what is possible, what is probable, and what is impossible, or at least know who we should ask.

Sometimes we get it right the first time. Sometimes we don't. Editing a game design is no different than debugging program code. Creativity counts, but knowledge and craft come into their own. This chapter will address some of the issues writers face when we take off our creative writer hats and put on our craftsman editor hats. We'll start with collaboration. Without it, we would never be forced to edit at all.

Collaboration

Making games is a collaborative process. It is often a different type of collaborative process than movies or television, much more indulgent and freeform. Movie and TV production teams are orchestras. Game developers are rock bands. It's "everybody into the pool" collaboration.

At no point is this more dangerous than when the design is being written. We've had all the blue sky meetings. We've marked up the whiteboards for weeks. Notes have been diligently typed and grudgingly agreed upon. Now it's time for all those less fun details to be hammered out.

There are two ways this can occur. One writer/designer can create a design document based on the notes, supplementing them with one-on-one discussions with the leads responsible for various parts of the design. The other is for design leads to write up their own sections, and hand them off to a writer/designer to mold into a single document.

I've worked at game developers who prefer the first and game developers who prefer the second. The first is the quickest and the safest. Almost everyone wants the second. Why? Well, the writer thinks he's getting help with the writing. Everybody else thinks they are writers. It looks like a match made in heaven.

It isn't until the non-writers face that blank screen that all those great ideas dry up and the words form themselves into sentences that don't quite mean what they meant to say. This is the point at which the writer/designer—in the worst cases just a poor staffer who is expected to do little more than collate—is forced to go from lead to lead with either hat or whip in hand and try to get the material out of them.

In either case, as the design morphs over the months of production, the keeper of the design document will be tasked with maintaining it, and distributing updates back to the rest of the team. At one developer I introduced the system of colored pages we use in television and film so that team members could tell at a glance which updates were the most recent. All the team members had to do was insert the new pages into their copies of the design document. This created very colorful stacks of paper on desks, file cabinets, and floors.

No one wanted to take the time to insert new pages into binders. This baffled me at first until I realized that what no one really wanted to do was take the time to read the changes. Coming from an industry where this task was accepted as essential, I was astounded. I watched as various teams went their merry ways, creating assets that no longer matched the current design requirements, then calling acrimonious meetings to blame each other for the wasted time and effort. I spent my time answering question after question that was already answered in the design document.

I tried e-mailing executive summaries highlighting design changes. Nobody read them. The changes continued to be hashed out in large, time-consuming, face-to-face meetings, or by people poking their heads into my office. If they didn't come to me, I hunted them down, and checked to see if what they were working on resembled the design in any way.

In TV and film, we at least have a continuity person, a script supervisor, whose job it is to see that all work was indeed part of the whole. I've seen a similar position at only a single developer in the past decade. She also answered phones, did copying and distribution, kept the break room stocked, and distributed T-shirts.

These days our design documents are often in HTML, easy to search online, extensively linked, and every section can be selectively printed out, or in Excel so we can follow and debug our game logic. We're saving a lot of pink and blue trees. Nobody reads these either. Games get made with things in them lead designers are surprised to find. Senior creative leads face player questions with, "I'm not sure how that works. Let me ask."

What can we as writers do about it? Nothing. It has to be a top down decision in a company that can put aside for the moment the thrill of finally getting that first lump of VC capital deposited. That there is a structure to the team and procedures that will be followed has to be communicated to each interviewee before they are hired. The interviewee must then sign in his own blood that he will respect the structure and follow the procedures, and understands that failure to do so means he can be summarily shot and killed.

Otherwise, executives and publishers better just shrug and go with the flow. Stop wondering why so many deadlines are missed, games don't resemble their specs, features don't work or are missing. It's the culture. Rock 'n roll.

In addition to collaboration between all team members, we can look at the special collaboration between writers or designers. Just as there should be a single keeper of the design document to at least attempt continuity and consistency, there needs to be a "keeper of the vision." The creative buck must stop someplace, or different opinions and disputes can cause the process to grind to a halt. When a final decision has to be made, the keeper of the vision makes it.

This keeper of the vision can be a single individual, or it can be collaborators. In the fluid nature of such things, writers, producers, programmers, and artists may all be designers. The important thing is to establish a hierarchy with checks and balances built in. If your keeper of the vision owns the company, all the writers, designers, and producers in the world may not be able to provide any checks and balances unless she is enlightened enough to welcome them.

In recent years, Hollywood has seen teams of brothers like the Coens (*Blood Simple, Fargo, The Ladykillers* remake); the Wachowskis (the *Matrix* movies); the Farrellys (*There's Something about Mary, Dumb and Dumber*), and the Hughes (*Dead Presidents, From Hell*) sharing various jobs on films including direction, a fairly rare collaboration. But writers have collaborated for centuries.

Remember drug-addicted Sam Coleridge who gave us the phrase "willing suspension of disbelief?" Here's the longer passage in *Biographia Literaria* the earlier quote was taken from. It's a rather long quote. You may be tempted to hit the ESC key, but I thought it was an interesting view into collaboration between writers two hundred years ago.

"During the first year that Mr. Wordsworth and I were neighbours, our conversations turned frequently on the two cardinal points of poetry, the power of exciting the sympathy of the reader by a faithful adherence to the truth of nature, and the power of giving the interest of novelty by the modifying colours of imagination. The sudden charm, which accidents of light and shade, which moon-light or sun-set diffused over a known and familiar landscape, appeared to represent the practicability of combining both. These are the poetry of nature. The thought suggested itself (to which of us I do not recollect) that a series of poems might be composed of two sorts. In the one, the incidents and agents were to be, in part at least, supernatural; and the excellence aimed at was to consist in the interesting of the affections by the dramatic truth of such emotions as would naturally accompany such situations, supposing them real. And real in this sense they have been to every human being who, from whatever source of delusion, has at any time believed himself under supernatural agency. For the second class, subjects were to be chosen from ordinary life; the characters and incidents were to be such, as will be found in every village and its vicinity, where there is a meditative and feeling mind to seek after them, or to notice them, when they present themselves.

In this idea originated the plan of the 'Lyrical Ballads'; in which it was agreed, that my endeavours should be directed to persons and characters supernatural, or at least romantic, yet so as to transfer from our inward nature a human interest and a semblance of truth sufficient to procure for these shadows of imagination that willing suspension of disbelief for the moment, which constitutes poetic faith. Mr. Wordsworth on the other hand was to propose to himself as his object, to give the charm of novelty to things of every day, and to excite a feeling analogous to the supernatural, by awakening the mind's attention from the lethargy of custom, and directing it to the loveliness and the wonders of the world before us; an inexhaustible treasure, but for which in consequence of the film of familiarity and selfish solicitude we have eyes, yet see not, ears that hear not, and hearts that neither feel nor understand.

With this view I wrote the 'Ancient Mariner,' and was preparing among other poems, the 'Dark Ladie,' and the 'Christabel,' in which I should have more nearly realized my ideal, than I had done in my first attempt. But Mr. Wordsworth's industry had proved so much more successful, and the number of his poems so much greater, that my compositions, instead of forming a balance, appeared rather an interpolation of heterogeneous matter. Mr. Wordsworth added two or three poems written in his own character, in the impassioned, lofty, and sustained diction, which is characteristic of his genius. In this form the 'Lyrical Ballads' were published; and were presented by him as an *experiment*, whether subjects, which from their nature rejected the usual ornaments and extra-colloquial style of poems in general, might not be so managed in the language of ordinary life as to produce the pleasurable interest, which it is the peculiar business of poetry to impart."

Figure 12.2 I.A.L. Diamond and Billy Wilder.

One of the best directors ever was Billy Wilder (1906–2002). In 1934, Wilder came to Hollywood from Galacia, an Austro-Hungarian province now a part of Poland. He arrived with little knowledge of English. Yet while neglected by film critics because of his deliberately unobtrusive directorial style, he became known for films featuring acerbic wit and riveting dialogue. It was suggested at first by those who didn't know him that since English was a second language, his collaborators provided the verbal brilliance. But Billy was a writer himself. And the wit was every bit as much his.

Billy gave us: "Let me get out of these wet clothes and into a dry martini," a line sometimes mistakenly attributed to humorist Robert Benchley. He told actor Walter Matthau after a take, "That's fine. We're on the track of something absolutely mediocre." To his fiancée: "I'd worship the ground you walked on if you lived in a better neighborhood." When producer Sam Goldwyn asked him to arbitrate (settle a dispute) on a film directed by Otto Preminger, Billy replied, "I'm sorry, Sam, but I wouldn't dare disagree with Otto. I still have relatives in Germany."

With the possible exception of Raymond Chandler (*Double Indemnity*) who annoyed Billy by trying to think up complicated camera angles instead of writing dialogue, Billy's collaborations were a meeting of two minds. His two major collaborations were 12 years with Leigh Brackett (*Sunset Boulevard*, *The Lost Weekend*), and 25 years with I.A.L. Diamond (*Some Like It Hot, The Apartment, Witness for the Prosecution, The Private Life of Sherlock Holmes*). In an American Film Institute interview, he and I.A.L. Diamond were asked how they collaborated. Billy said this:

> I'm already very gratified if anybody asks that question, because most people think the actors make up the words. . . . We meet at, say, 9:30 in the morning and open shop, like bank tellers, and we sit there in one room. We read Hollywood Reporter and Variety, exchange the trades, and then we just stare at each other. Sometimes nothing happens. Sometimes it goes on until 12:30, and then I'll ask him, "How about a drink?" And he nods, and then we have a drink and go to lunch. Or sometimes we come full of ideas. This is not the muse coming through the windows and kissing our brows. It's very hard work . . .

I highly recommend seeking out the American Film Institute interview for an informative and very witty look at one of Hollywood's most famous and successful writing teams. It's called A Dialogue with Billy Wilder and I.A.L. Diamond. It can be found at www.fathom.com/feature/122029 in .pdf format.

My primary mentors in my days as a writer in Hollywood were both writing teams. The first were Ron Austin and Jim Buchanan (*Mission Impossible, Harry in Your Pocket*) who were one of two production teams on the second season of *Charlie's Angels*. My second pair of mentors were Dick Levinson and Bill Link (*Columbo, Murder She Wrote*) who watched over me like guardian angels on *Blacke's Magic*. Dick passed away in 1987 at the young age of 52. Ron, Jim, and Bill have remained my friends to this day.

Jim and Ron would work in different ways. Particularly in the beginning of their career they would write together. Jim suggests this was due to "insecurity." He says, "For most the togetherness eventually drives you both bonkers." They preferred to support each other in whatever way was necessary at the time. Jim would be writing one episode while Ron directed another. They would toss around some story ideas, then one would go off and write the script, the other acting as critic or rewrite person. On the next script they would reverse the roles.

I also talked with Bill Link while preparing for this chapter. He began with a quote from Oscar Hammerstein: "Collaboration is the same as marriage only without the sex." Bill and Dick wrote together. As he put it, "Every sentence came out of the two of us. It was a ping-pong game." This was true no matter what medium they were writing in.

"Dick typed and I paced. Luckily, we were both morning people. We'd write from 10 a.m. to 1 p.m., then spend the afternoon producing. We were happy if we turned out five good pages of screenplay in a morning." If they hit a rough patch, they would go to their separate homes and sleep on it.

Great believers in the power of the unconscious mind, as I am, they knew that if the creative mind tries too hard, it gets stressed. And when you are filled with stress, there is no room for creativity. Bill says that one of his best times for solving writing problems is 3 a.m. He'll wake up with the problem on the tip of his brain, roll it around a bit, write down the solution, and go back to sleep.

Some collaborations are between very different types of writers who complement each other. For example, one may be strong on dialogue, and the other is very visual and good with action. He and Dick were different. They were like two halves of the same coin, both working on every aspect of the project with one exception. When they went into a meeting to pitch an idea, Dick would do the talking.

Bill had two other thoughts. He believes very strongly that the earlier in life two writers begin their collaboration, the stronger it will be: "We met on the first day of junior high school. We evolved as people together. We were best friends from the day we met until the day Dick died."

Bill and Dick were lucky in another regard too. When Dick married, then later Bill, both of their wives liked the other writing partner. But it isn't always like that, Bill warns. If one partner gets married and if the single partner and the new mate don't get along, trouble can arise. He's seen it many times. The new husband or wife can become jealous of the time the collaborators spend together. He or she can decide that the spouse is doing all the real work for only half the money. Divorce can follow, or what's worse the breakup of the writing partnership. Or . . . doesn't this sound like a situation for a *Colombo* episode you might have seen?

Don't look for only one way to do it. There isn't one. Every team must reach its own style of collaboration, and writers who are not part of the same team from game to game must be flexible enough to adapt to one another. It helps to immediately establish some ground rules. Some of these will help with full team collaboration as well.

- If the keeper of the vision is not an individual, keep the core group as small as possible. The more people you add with the ability to veto or filibuster, the more likely your progress will keep grinding to a halt just like politics. Unless they really screw up, governments know they're around for years. Your team may only have a year or 18 months to get it right.

- Create a hierarchy. Everyone must understand the hierarchy, and abide by it. Respect chains of command. Don't wander into a junior artist's cubicle to ask a question unless you have established with her lead that it's okay to do so. This isn't just polite; it facilitates communication, and prevents nasty surprises.

- Establish procedures. What form will the design document take? How will revisions be tracked? How many rewrites before a draft is submitted to the rest of the team? Who gets to make the final edit? Who gets to read what? How are notes produced and shared? Strict procedures actually do not limit you. They provide security. They guarantee that the fluid creative process can continue smoothly because at the end of the day you always know what the next step is.

- Assign roles. Respect those roles. There will always be overlap. Roles may shift and change with time. But keep them clear. A junior programmer who's been with the team for two days needs to know his decisions are subject to review. The keeper of the vision has to remember that creating the game is above all else a collaborative effort. He is not the commandant of a POW camp.

- No matter how passionate the creative wrangling becomes, don't make it personal. Keep it courteous. We live in an increasingly rude world. Whatever culture or environment you have been brought up in, don't carry it intact into a collaboration like Pigpen with his dust cloud. Be willing to adjust to the temper of your colleagues. It's the difference between being perceived as a professional or a candidate for day care.

- When the keeper of the vision says it's time to move on in the discussion, everybody needs to move on. Right then. And with no hard feelings. Leave the inevitable but non-productive anger and frustration in the room. Take the passion with you, and apply it to your work.

- Assign a single individual or tiny team to maintain the design document. They will have to ride herd on all those leads who need to contribute to the document in one form or the other. Give them the authority to do so.

All, *all*, of the structure we may balk at in the beginning of pre-production will free us during the production. It's not a paradox. Everyone will know her job, and what to expect. Even in rock bands the lead guitarist would think twice about banging on the drummer's drums.

Adapting to the Engine You End Up With

There's a lot of enthusiasm at the beginning of a new game. If it's the first one, we know we want to be competitive, but we may not be quite sure what we're capable of. If it's yet another in a long string of hits, we know the customers will want us to top our previous efforts. In those halcyon blue sky days, we sit around that long conference table and decide what it is we want to do, and then try to figure out if we can do it. We never get it quite right.

In the world of the personal computer, video cards get more powerful every year and CPU speeds increase every quarter. We know we want to take advantage of those advances. Sometimes we are working from specs that have been proposed, knowing we'll have to tweak once they are finalized.

If we're designing for the next generation of a PlayStation, Xbox, or Gamecube, the problem is the same. The time between new hardware releases in consoles is approximately three years. That relative stability can give us some breathing room if we're aiming at the current machines. But even then we are constantly trying to squeeze as much out of our target machine's capabilities as we can.

In order to cope with intricate and ever-changing technology, developers enter the twilight zone of educated guesswork. It is a realm of imagination. There are signposts up ahead, but who can tell for sure where they point?

There are many potholes in the road called production. Capital dries up. Personnel changes. The bar is set too high. Promises, based on wishful thinking, are made, but are unable to be realized. In the cubicle by the window, the tech director starts to sweat.

Meanwhile, in the corner office, the lead designer is focused on the backside of the dental hygienist who works down on the first floor as she walks to her Mazda. The producer (who also has a nice office, but is never in it) swings by to see the tech director and after a brief conversation whispered at the tops of their lungs, he heads for the lead designer's office, smile fixed firmly in place.

The writer in her converted utility closet is happily scanning the blue skies of the sequel. Suddenly there's a knock on the utility closet door. The writer, brain deep in alien worlds, for a moment assumes someone has forgotten the room is no longer a utility closet. She never gets knocks on her door this far into production. Then she realizes that if someone were looking for a mop, they wouldn't knock. Sure enough, it's the producer. He wonders if she'd mind joining him in the lead designer's office.

It's been awhile since she's been in an office with windows, but finally the writer tears herself away from the view, and focuses. The game has been designed for an engine that cannot be completed in the remaining development time. The writer is a professional. She's heard this all before and never contemplates jumping out the window to see the view closer up.

This type of editing is difficult because a game engine's influence is felt in every aspect of the game. As illustrated in Figure 12.3 the editing process is going to feel like correcting a mistake in knitting where you must pick apart rows of interlocking loops one at a time. For example, let's say you were planning on letting the player-character swallow an occasional flying pill, but now the aerodynamics are never going to happen. For every spot where flying occurred, a substitute, and dialogue and action must be rewritten for it.

www.nicolaiwallner.com

Figure 12.3 Rewriting to accommodate changes in the game engine.

It may require multiple solutions. If you already have the animation for climbing a ladder, that impassable cliff can be made climbable, maybe with the addition of special climbing shoes. Getting from the roof of a tall building to a room several floors below may now require lowering a window washer platform. Whatever alternatives you come up with, if you can keep within the spirit of the story and the character, you should be okay.

Faced with a technical reversal, like a scaled-back game engine, is no time for the writer to panic. It's a time for invention, or re-invention. And it's as inevitable as breathing.

Stopping the Bleeding When You Cut Levels and Areas

Another gotcha that will getcha sooner or later is the need to cut entire blocks out of your game. While it may be an aesthetic decision only, this more often occurs when it becomes apparent that a key milestone will not be met. The only alternatives to such radical surgery are beyond the writer's job description: extending the deadline and adding more people. Both cost more.

Luckily adjusting the amount of content is a challenge television writers face on a daily basis. We've talked about how shows sometimes need to be padded. There's an infamous episode of *Moonlighting*, which was so short actors Bruce Willis and Cybill Shepherd were filmed seated on stools talking to fill out the time at the end of the program.

More often shows need to be cut. When I first started writing *Edge of Night*, it was necessary that I write the first two weeks of the transition between the former head writer's ongoing storylines, and the beginnings of my own. Overlap, remember? There was no time to learn how daytime scripts differed from nighttime. They have very different formats. One developed from live television. Nighttime scripts evolved from movies. I had a few examples to work from. That was it. I wrote two weeks of scripts and shipped them off even before I moved to New York.

Something went horribly wrong. Nick Nicholson, the show's executive producer was not only talented and experienced, but a very courtly gentleman. I can imagine how he truly felt when he phoned me the morning they were rehearsing the first of my shows, but what I heard was:

"How are you, Lee?"

"Great, Nick! How are you? Shooting my first script today, aren't you?"

"I'm splendid, thank you! Yes, yes. Thank you for getting the scripts to us so quickly. We're looking forward to welcoming you properly to the show next week."

"I'm looking forward to that too."

"Oh, there was one thing. . . . The scripts you sent us are somewhat long."

"Somewhat? What is somewhat?"

"Oh, this show we're rehearsing right now is about one-third too long. . . . Think you could cut it a bit before we tape this afternoon?"

One third too long. Cut two weeks of episodes by 33 percent. Make sure it all still flows, characters are properly introduced, exposition is not lost, and do that all on the first show, the one all the others depend on in the next few minutes . . .

"Sure, Nick . . . Um. . . . May I get back to you?"

"Of course, of course. Soon as you can, my boy. I appreciate it!"

So, while Nick probably turned to the Writers Guild Directory and called the show's attorneys to see how solid my contract was, I set to work. It wasn't that hard. Here's why:

I had been a story editor and writing producer enough to know that there's very little time in television to get sentimental about your own work. If you don't cut it, somebody else will. And writers are like auto wrecking yards. We never throw anything away. If a good part gets lost among the stacks of rusting Pintos, it'll eventually find its way back into a working vehicle. I transfer the passion I put into the scenes to begin with into the gusto with which I make swooping big X's through page after page like Xorro.

Craft plays a huge part in cutting entire levels or areas or characters in a game, because if the game has been solidly constructed, every element supports and is supported by others. Pull one out and the structure can collapse entirely. This is something non-writing producers and executives have trouble understanding. All they know is it's cheaper to cut pages than any other solution to meeting milestones.

But the experienced writer knows the most important task is to determine what can be removed entirely and what should be re-purposed elsewhere. Again, we must be ruthless. But we also need to not cut away too much until there are gaps in story or character development.

Let's look at a fairly simple example. We faced the challenge of losing an entire level in *Wild Wild West: The Steel Assassin*. It was an elaborate variation on PacMan where the player uncovers critical exposition by completing puzzles while avoiding guards in a warehouse full of theatre and circus props and costumes. Because of the patrolling guards, puzzles could only be finished in bits and pieces. Learning the guards' routine was essential to figuring out in what sequence to do which steps. Part of the exposition uncovered led to the next major section of the game: a rundown mining town in Nevada. Figure 12.5 illustrates the place in the overall game structure of this one level.

By disassembling the level into its components I saw that the cut was not as disastrous as people thought. None of the gameplay could be used because just transferring assets

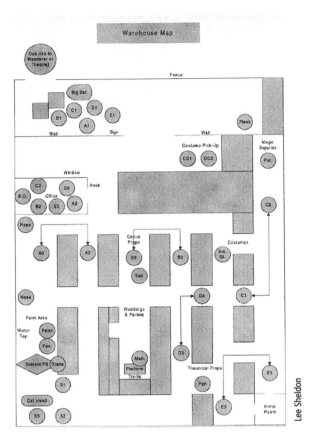

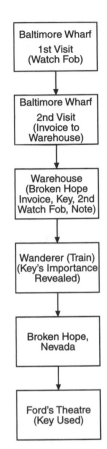

Figure 12.4 The level that never was in *Wild Wild West: The Steel Assassin*.

Figure 12.5 Game structure with warehouse level intact.

wasn't going to help our time and resource crunch. So that was filed away in my junkyard for possible use in another game. A look at the characters in the level revealed there were no major characters beyond Artemus Gordon, the player's current avatar, present and nothing critical to Artemus's character was discovered, so no character arcs were affected. I knew we couldn't cut a block of exposition and simply insert it in another level because that would only inflate the storytelling there. So I next sifted the exposition. I identified two pieces of critical exposition, and two pieces of important exposition. All else was discarded. This left me with:

1. Broken Hope, Nevada, the name of the town where the shipment Artemus was following was headed. (This was critical. It pointed the player to where the investigation should go next.)

2. An item (key) indicating the gang has access to Ford's Theatre where President Grant is scheduled to appear. (This was critical. This showed that the gang was much farther along in their plans than was suspected, and would provide a possible way into the theatre for Jim West.)

3. A note revealing that the guards know about Artemus, and have orders to kill him. (This was important because it indicated that Artemus could not con his way past the guards here. They would shoot first and ask questions later.)

4. An item (watch fob) linking the guards to the assassin of Lincoln known as "The Bull." (This was important because it meant the guards were not just a bit more zealous than some, but received their orders from the criminal organization.)

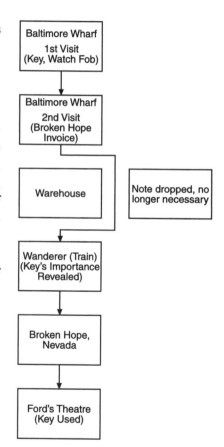

Figure 12.6 Game structure now bypasses the warehouse level.

The first important item, the note, was dropped. No more level, no more reason to warn the player. The second important item was duplicated elsewhere in the game, and could be dropped. The second critical item, the key, was transferred to the pocket of another bad guy earlier in the game, but not *identified* until the same spot later on where it already was. The first critical item, the shipment's destination, was moved to an office safe in the second wharf level, effectively bypassing the need for the warehouse level between that one and Nevada. Figure 12.6 shows the game structure after bypassing the warehouse level.

I deliberately chose an easy example here. The more a level or area of the game is connected to the others, the more work there is to be done. The more discrete the areas of the game are (meaning they are independent of one another) the easier. We want both though, and we'll explore this idea when we talk about game modules in Chapter 14, "Modular Storytelling." Whatever, the modus operandi for the editing process is exactly the same:

■ First trim all excess fat. We instinctively know what some of it is: a joke or character beat or subplot that stands on its own, or only reinforces other material. That goes easily.

- Preserve any genuinely entertaining moments, if possible, even if they aren't entirely necessary. Entertainment is entertainment after all. If you can't, save them in your junkyard.

- Gameplay can sometimes be moved. If you have a level a bit lighter than others, see if you can work it in there. No place to put it? Save it in the junkyard.

- Identify how the level affects character arcs. Look at the moments of character revelation with the level removed. If there is a jump in the growth or development of that character, that jump needs to be fixed either in the level before, or the level after.

- Separate out all the specific points of exposition. Determine which are critical, and which are expendable.

- Don't treat the exposition as a single block that must be shoved into another level, doubling its expository load. Remember how the prisoners of war in *The Great Escape* mixed the darker tunnel soil into the gardens so it wouldn't be noticed? Do the same thing. Spread the exposition out over several levels. Even if there are two or three points tied to a specific moment or object, break them down. Don't assume they all must be moved as a group. It is much less disruptive on other levels to spread them out just like any others.

Happily, not all editing is the result of calamity or outside pressure. There is actual rewriting and editing we could and should do on our own.

Polishing Dialogue

"The search for the *mot juste* is not a pedantic fad but a vital necessity. Words are our precision tools. Imprecision engenders ambiguity and hours are wasted in removing verbal misunderstandings before the argument of substance can begin."

—*Anonymous Civil Servant*

As is often the case with these things *le mot juste* is not the entire term. It drops an important word. The complete phrase is *le seul mot juste*. And that gives us its true definition.

note

LE SEUL MOT JUSTE: describes the one correct word to express meaning, or to prompt the desired reaction.

If a description of action or line of dialogue is not clear to reader or audience, or does not affect them as it was intended, it usually means the writer has failed to find *le seul mot juste*. An amateur writer may not notice that what is in his brain failed to make it to the page. He thinks he's expressed himself fine, and can become defensive when someone questions him as to his intent.

A professional knows, even if no one has given him a note, when a word or phrase is not exactly right. When writing dialogue, we will recognize that a joke can be funnier; an argument more intense; an expression of love more passionate; a putdown more savage; an apology more heartfelt. That's when we rewrite, or to use a kinder, gentler word, we polish. All writers polish. It can happen at three different moments while writing: instantaneously, immediately, and revisiting.

I expect that because I have written for most of my career to extremely tight deadlines, the moment I begin transferring thought to page I'm already polishing it. It's instantaneous. When I try to picture what I do, I think of password cracking programs, and how they're portrayed in movies. Sometimes recognizable words or at other times random characters are displayed on a computer screen, then replaced at a dizzying speed to suggest it is only a matter of time before the program comes up with the correct password. Of course as speedy as this is, our brains work far faster. I'll start to type the word, stop, delete it halfway through, then type its replacement, barely aware of the steps my brain took me through to prompt the substitution.

Once I manage to get the line of dialogue or a sentence in this book on the screen in front of me, I'm already re-reading it, even as I begin to construct the next line in my mind. This parallel processing means that I can actually be writing something new at the same time I'm polishing both instantaneously and immediately. If I see a better choice, I make the change, then start writing the next sentence.

If I sense a change is needed but *le seul mot juste* still eludes me I may leave the word out or throw in an approximation, write for awhile, then return to it. Revisiting can occur when I know a polish is needed, or not. In the latter case, it is a part of the natural process of re-reading an entire scene or chapter to make sure I'm saying what I want to say. This revisitation can occur moments, minutes, hours, days, weeks, months or even years later, if I've put the entire project aside. Remember the piece of dialogue between Dr. Adams and his daughter from *Sideshow*? Here's how it *really* went in the original:

* * *

```
                    NANCY
      Dad, you love this town, and you know it.

                    ADAMS
      That's right, my dear. I love watching all the children
      I brought into this world smoking or drinking or
      cholesterolling themselves into early graves.
```

```
                         NANCY
                      (to David)
        This is an ongoing debate...

                         ADAMS
        Or piling into trees at 90 miles an hour. Or ingesting
        chemicals that turn their brains to jelly. Fascinating
        profession: medicine.

                         NANCY
        We save lives.

                         ADAMS
        And we learn far too much! And the thing we learn that
        cuts the deepest is that we'll never know enough to stop
        them. Or ourselves. We're all on the same ride...to
        oblivion...and we're all determined to make that ride
        as short as possible!

                        *  *  *
```

I count at least five edits: three conjunctions dropped to increase the intensity; a punctuation mark changed to indicate more emotion; and an extra space deleted as a copy edit. There are also two spaces after periods instead of just one, a holdover from my typewriter days. If you don't know what a typewriter was, you'll have to look up that definition on your own.

One trick to help you recognize that le seul mot juste has not been found is to watch out for *tombstoning* when you're polishing.

note

TOMBSTONING: refers to the over-repetition of individual words or phrases in a sentence or paragraph.

The word was originally a printer term referring to a mistake in laying out a page. If all the stories and illustrations are laid out in identical columns one next to the other, the repetition makes the layout boring. Don't confuse tombstoning with deliberate repetition to drive home a point. In the next paragraph, tombstoned phrases are in italics:

George W. Firtree told us there were weapons of mass destruction in Iraq. *John Contrary told us* there was never any evidence of that. *George W. Firtree told us* Saddam Hussein had ties to Al Quaeda. *John Contrary told us* there was never any evidence of that.

This is repetition for effect (again follow the italics):

> George W. Firtree said there were weapons of mass destruction in Iraq. *There were none.* He told the American people Saddam Hussein had ties to Al Quaeda. *There were none.* He promised to create six million new jobs. *He didn't.*

Here the repeated phrase is used like a hammer. Even when the words change in the last sentence, the rhythm of the hammer is well established.

Don't get hung up on correct English in dialogue. You may have noticed how little discussion of "correct English" there is in this book. The *seul mot juste* has nothing to do with it. In the opening voice-over to the various *Star Trek* series "to boldly go" is a split infinitive, but it *sounds* stronger than "to go boldly." Complete sentences can slow pace to a crawl. Find the point of attack the same way you would in a scene. Cut away the connective tissue as I did the conjunctions in Dr. Adams's dialogue.

The search for *le seul mot juste* is as critical to writing as the search for the North Pole was to scientists. But unlike scientific exploration, the search can be rewarding even if we never make it. Just making the attempt, digging out the dictionary or thesaurus if we have to, can be worthwhile. Even if we fail to find the *best* word, we may find a *better* word. And every time we do that, we're one step closer to clarity and emotional impact. We just need to know when to stop searching.

No discussion of *le seul mot juste* would be complete without mention of Gustave Flaubert (1821–1880), its most famous stalker. Flaubert would spend days searching for a single word. *Madame Bovary*, his best-known work (and a very readable novel), took five years to write. Part of learning to be a writer is learning when to stop searching and move on. Maybe the reason Flaubert suffered from nervous ailments, drank heavily, and frequented prostitutes was that he realized his search was endless.

Figure 12.7 If Flaubert had tried to paint a self-portrait, we'd never know what he looked like.

Once upon a time in my former life, I found myself at a party in the Malibu Beach Colony. I was searching for a glass of drinkable chardonnay when I fell into conversation with a blow-dried, deeply tanned man in his 30s who introduced himself as a fellow screenwriter. This is the moment during most Hollywood parties where strangers begin the profoundly religious Credit Ritual Dance. "I'm writing/directing/acting in that new buddy cop flick over at Warner's. What have you written/directed/appeared in lately?" He told me he had been working on his first screenplay for the past three years. That was the extent of his writing career. I realized then I was either talking to somebody with a trust fund or one of the waiters. I wanted to shake him, but instead I smiled politely and nodded my head a lot as he detailed the adventures in writing he was experiencing week in and week out. I did ask one question, "When will you know it's done?" "Oh!" he assured me, "I'll know!"

Maybe it's the relentless search for le seul balance juste when game developers say they'll "release it when it's done." Instead of the implied perfectionism, it feels more like a self-indulgent excuse for missing milestones. It certainly is no more a guarantee of quality than a product that actually ships on schedule.

I don't think I've ever had that much freedom, so maybe that's why I'm not more tolerant of it. From the mini-plays I used to write at Boston University for my fellow actors to perform and my fellow directors to direct in our classes to the tight and unrelenting deadlines in television, I've always known that there comes a time to stick a fork in it and give thanks you have something to eat.

As you polish your dialogue, imagine David Mamet sitting on the pallid bust of Pallus by your chamber door. This is your last chance to take it beyond the colloquial to something that rivets the attention. Write words that pierce the brain, not those that go in one ear and out the other.

Less is more. In this day and age, unless a character is written to be wordy, keep the dialogue lean. Then when you want a character to burst forth into an impassioned speech it is all the more compelling because of the contrast.

Actor John Crispin Blake in my play *The Man Who Came to Murder* is entirely too fond of hearing himself talk:

* * *

BLAKE
Language is so much a part of my life I must try to
remember that to most mortals speaking is merely a
hurdle in the race to make one's needs public, whereas
to me a single word is a banquet in and of itself.

MILLIGAN
I get it. The word's your oyster.

* * *

His male nurse, Milligan, jumps his small hurdle and is content.

Even if dialogue seems in character, mix up the length of the individual lines. In a long speech, or only three or four lines, if each sentence is close in length to the others, it creates a monotonous rhythm. If you missed it in the polish, a good voice actor will instinctively try to break it up for you. Let her.

Remember not to allow your characters to be too self-aware, or to explain themselves in too much detail. Show them in action. If a character's dialogue is reminiscent of a patient on a psychiatrist's couch, you're in trouble.

Copy Editing

"The dialogue itself is better than in most adventures, although it reads as if it was translated from another language by a non-native English speaker. Also (a pet peeve of mine) it's poorly proofread; when a game company spends presumably hundreds of thousands of dollars developing a title, why can't they pay a professional sub-editor a few bucks to look over the text?"

—*PC Gameworld review of* Post Mortem *(2003)*

Language evolves. Words become extinct or their meanings change. At any given point in time, however, there are distinct rules for language usage. To ignore them is to surrender in the battle for communication without firing a shot.

note

COPY EDITING: proofreading: the review of style, spelling, grammar, and punctuation in a written document.

Copy editing is obviously important in a book. (Right, Sandy? I'll bet this is the first book you've ever copy edited that includes a pitch for your profession!) But there is a feeling in the games industry that it's not important. There appear to be several reasons for this.

- People think computer spelling and grammar checkers catch everything. They don't. They're particularly bad at sensing context. My apologies to Bill Gates, but they miss tons of errors. Style sheets are just as dangerous. Human beings have built-in computers that do a far more reliable job.

- Many of our documents are seen only internally, so why bother with the time or expense?

- Just as everybody thinks they can write, they seem to feel the same thing about grammar and punctuation. They don't notice how sloppy some of the documents they produce really are.

- Internet chat rooms, e-mails, instant messaging, and yes, PvP games have increased both the volume of communications we must process and the speed required for input. Spelling and grammar suffer accordingly. Kids are being raised by the Internet just as generations ago they were raised by television. Their opinion is they're correct when they think there is only one way to spell "there."

There are three reasons copy editing should be a routine step in the production of our documents, even if they are only dialogue scripts, design and technical documents. The first is clarity. The farther our words stray from their true meanings the greater the obscurity of our pronouns; the longer our runon sentences; the more likely it is that readers will misinterpret our meaning. R.D. Laing already told us how difficult it is to communicate. Why make it worse?

The second motivation for copy editing our documents is impression. There are few stronger signals we send to those around us than our use of language, either written or spoken. Whether we like it or not we are judged by phrases like "He don't know nothing." and "Me and her went to the store." And the same holds true for all those double negatives and misspellings in our business documents. Let's give ourselves the benefit of the doubt: most are simple typos. My keyboard sticks like crazy, dropping letters all over the place. If we had more time to check our writing, we would clean it up. But we don't, and nobody takes into account how busy your schedule is if your writing is full of errors.

The third is force of habit. Let's say you still think impression isn't that important in internal documents, but do think it's vital in communications outside the company. If the bulk of your writing is only design-related, and you don't bother to copy edit and one day you're given the assignment of writing an external proposal, those same errors you unconsciously slide past in one may come back to haunt you in the other.

"All your base are belong to us" was part of a new introduction written for a U.S. port of the Japanese game *Zero Wing* on the Sega Genesis. It's become a classic of bad translation. But there are examples in many games, even those developed in English-speaking countries, of text that cries out for copy editing.

Figure 12.8 *Zero Wing*, a game that will live in infamy.

If the job is left to some poor programmer trying to insert two hundred text files into a level at 3 AM, expect mistakes. Have someone re-read the text in the game. And what happens if that design document you wrote is suddenly requested by a potential investor?

Few game developers can afford copy editors any more than they can afford a continuity person. But please when you hire someone for a position, check their written communication skills. *Read something they've written.* Having a few people who can spell or understand grammar will pay off in the long run. Not taking the time to copy edit can backfire in more than industry hilarity at your expense. It could cost you a contract with a publisher or a line of credit you need to finish the game.

CHAPTER 13

THE ROOTS OF A NEW STORYTELLING

C++ and Java are both computer languages that support *object-oriented program-ming*, a type of modular programming with more formalized rules. It may seem like a strange way to introduce a discussion of a new type of storytelling, but the paradigm is remarkably similar. In OOP, data structures become objects that include both data and functions. Functions are parts of a program that perform specific tasks.

note

OBJECT-ORIENTED PROGRAMMING (OOP): a programming paradigm in which independent mod-ules of code are built to interact with each other.

In modular storytelling, the modules are objects that include both data (story) and func-tions or tasks performed on the story, like the passing of tokens, setting of flags, and track-ing of player actions. The idea is to bring the telling of story in games into line with how gameplay is constructed. Both can be programmed as modules. Story can be written as modules.

Modular storytelling has its roots in the distant past, as we're about to see and, at its sim-plest, combines two key concepts: episodic storytelling and non-linear storytelling. In a way, it is a wedding of the two fields I know best: television and computer games. It gives us a basis for creating games where story and gameplay are never at odds with one another but complement one another. But I'm getting ahead of myself. Let's take a look at the roots of modular storytelling.

The Odyssey

Homer's *The Odyssey* is three stories in one: Odysseus, King of Ithaca, and his 20-year journey home from the Trojan wars; his ever patient and faithful wife Penelope fending off suitors for her hand; and Odysseus's son Telemachus's growth from boy to man. To keep things simple we'll focus only on the events that make up the main story that gives the epic poem its name.

- After leaving Troy, Odysseus's ships are caught in a storm and land on the island of the Lotus-Eaters where many get high by munching on the plant, and decide to just hang, rather than continuing the journey. Odysseus manages to get enough of them straight to set sail again.

- The ships stop at the land of the Cyclops, one-eyed giants. After one of the Cyclops, Polyphemus, traps them in his cave and dines on a few of the crew, Odysseus and the surviving crewmen blind him with a large stick, and escape by hanging on to sheep let out to graze. Unfortunately for Odysseus, Polyphemus is the son of Poseidon, God of the Sea.

- At the island of Aeolus, King of the Winds, Odysseus is given a bag of all the bad winds that would hamper his progress. But within sight of home, some of his crewmen (thinking the bag is filled with treasure), open it, blowing the ships far off course.

J.M.W. Turner, artist (National Gallery, London)

Figure 13.1 J.M.W. Turner's "Ulysses Deriding Polyphemus" (1829).

- The goddess Circe on the island of Aeaea turns a number of Odysseus's crewmen into pigs and falls in love with Odysseus. Odysseus, after spending only a year with her, learns from Hermes how to undo the spell, and the ships set sail again.

- Odysseus journeys to Hades to seek counsel from the prophet Tiresias, who tells him he will never reach home unless he earns Poseidon's forgiveness.

- Odysseus fills the ears of his crew with wax so they won't be seduced by the Sirens' song. He wants to hear it, so they tie him to the mast of his ship.

- Two hazards confront Odysseus simultaneously: Scylla, a six-headed monster and Charybdis, a ship-devouring whirlpool. Six crewmen are sacrificed to Scylla in order to bypass Charybdis.

- On the island of Helios, God of the Sun, crewmen give into temptation and eat some sacred cattle. A thunderbolt from Zeus kills the crew and destroys Odysseus's last ship.

- Odysseus is rescued by the sea nymph, Calypso, who wants to be his bride. With the help of Athena and Hermes, Calypso is persuaded to release Odysseus and give him a small boat.

- Poseidon unleashes a storm that demolishes Odysseus's boat. With the help of Athena he reaches the island of the Phaeacians. They transport him in one of their ships home to Ithaca where a few more adventures await.

Even though this appears to be pretty straightforward storytelling, it's easy to see how we might classify each of the separate events as a module, connected to the others and complete in itself. This is important because I have a confession to make. This isn't the way Homer told his story at all. The point of attack is far later in the story. The correct order of events goes like this:

- Odysseus is held prisoner by the sea nymph, Calypso, who wants to be his bride. With the help of Athena, Calypso is persuaded to release Odysseus and give him a small boat.

- Poseidon unleashes a storm that demolishes Odysseus's boat. With the help of Athena, he reaches the island of the Phaeacians. There he reveals his identity and recounts his adventures as follows:

- After leaving Troy, Odysseus's ships are caught in a storm and land on the island of the Lotus-Eaters where many get high by munching on the plant, and decide to just hang, rather than continuing the journey. Odysseus manages to get enough of them straight to set sail again.

- The ships stop at the land of the Cyclops, one-eyed giants. After one of the Cyclops, Polyphemus, traps them in his cave and dines on a few of the crew, Odysseus and the surviving crewmen blind him with a large stick, and escape by hanging on to sheep let out to graze. Unfortunately for Odysseus, Polyphemus is the son of Poseidon, God of the Sea.

- At the island of Aeolus, King of the Winds, Odysseus is given a bag of all the bad winds that would hamper his progress. But within sight of home, some of his crewmen (thinking the bag is filled with treasure), open it, blowing the ships far off course.

- The goddess Circe on the island of Aeaea turns a number of Odysseus's crewmen into pigs and falls in love with Odysseus. Odysseus, after spending only a year with her, learns from Hermes how to undo the spell, and the ships set sail again.

- Odysseus journeys to Hades to seek counsel from the prophet Tiresias, who tells him he will never reach home unless he earns Poseidon's forgiveness.

- Odysseus fills the ears of his crew with wax so they won't be seduced by the Sirens' song. He wants to hear it, so they tie him to the mast of his ship.

- Two hazards confront Odysseus simultaneously: Scylla, a six-headed monster and Charybdis, a ship-devouring whirlpool. Six crewmen are sacrificed to Scylla in order to bypass Charybdis.

- On the island of Helios, God of the Sun, crewmen give into temptation and eat some sacred cattle. A thunderbolt from Zeus kills the crew and destroys Odysseus's last ship.

- Odysseus is rescued by Calypso.

- After he tells his tale to the sympathetic Phaeacians, they transport Odysseus in one of their ships home to Ithaca where a few more adventures await.

Novelists often use a similar flashback structure. Instead of straightforwardly tracking the story from one incident to the next, we leap ahead in time, then describe the intervening events.

Here is the end of Chapter Sixteen from my mystery novel *Impossible Bliss*:

> "Inside, a dark shape huddled over the bookcase next to Wagner's desk. Shepard felt for a light switch, found it, and flipped it up."

The action in Chapter Seventeen continues without missing a beat:

> "Light flooded the living room. The figure whirled. Bruce Wagner glared at them, a small sheaf of papers clutched in his hand."

Chapter Thirteen in the book starts after a time lapse:

> "Wednesday morning the Carmel Valley hills were blue and green, already heated by
> an advancing sun. Shepard tried to concentrate on the phantom melody that
> refused to become a song while he drove out the valley road toward the Carmel
> Rancho Racquet Club."

In the third paragraph I begin to fill in any important events with a flashback:

> "Before he headed out to the tennis club, Shepard had tracked down Charlie Revere
> in the tiny lounge at the back of the station. Crammed with vending machines, a
> couple Formica-topped tables, and a clump of molded plastic chairs, the lounge also
> served as ready room, and general gathering place for on-duty officers.
>
> 'Any luck with the Sea Orchard Fish Company?' he asked the young, red-headed
> man."

This low level non-linearity is just a different method of beginning the chapter to interject some variety into the structure and rhythm of the storytelling. The choice of the point
of attack is critical. Choose the right spot, and the audience still experiences the story in a
natural flow. Choose the wrong point of attack and the flashback will seem gimmicky and
artificial.

One other feature of the epic poem deserves mention: this is the reappearance of characters first encountered early in the story. Poseidon sets his traps for Odysseus after learning
what Odysseus did to his son, Polyphemus, then wanders offstage for much of the voyage,
only to return, and unleash his direct fury when he sees Odysseus still afloat. Athena and
Hermes show up on more than one occasion to help Odysseus out of a tight jam. If *The
Odyssey* were a computer program instead of an epic poem Poseidon, Athena, and Hermes would be functions, not gods.

Janet Murray in her interesting book, *Hamlet on the Holodeck*, goes into some detail on
the bardic tradition supporting *The Odyssey* and *The Iliad* that I brought up in Chapter 2,
"The Story Remains the Same," and goes into some detail describing Alfred Lord's analy-
sis in *The Singer of Tales*, concluding:

> [The bards] success in combining the satisfactions of a coherent plot with the plea-
> sures of endless variation is therefore a provocative model of what we might hope to
> achieve in cyberspace. To do so we must reconceptualize authorship, in the same way
> Lord did, and think of it not as the inscribing of affixed written text but as the inven-
> tion and arrangement of the expressive patterns that constitute a multiform story.

So we can bid farewell to Odysseus, keeping in mind our first roots of a new storytelling:
stories in other media are not always linear; the modular nature of *The Odyssey*'s story;
the functional nature of reoccurring characters in the epic poem structure; and the bardic
tradition that allows for improvisation on the strict patterns and themes of its storytelling.

The Canterbury Tales

Fast forward almost 20 centuries to The Father of English Literature. Geoffrey Chaucer's *The Canterbury Tales* are separate stories within a connective framework: a pilgrimage. Each narrative is intended to be equivalent in length and stature. There is no attempt to raise the stakes in the stories from "The Knight's Tale" through the odd last tale "The Parson's Prologue" and "Chaucer's Retraction" where the author apologizes for writing of such mundane matters. The tales were unfinished remember. Chaucer intended to write a hundred more, and there is much evidence to suggest even the "completed" tales were in various stages of editing. They are divided into

Figure 13.2 *The Canterbury Tales.*

ten sections, or fragments. The most well known of these, "The Wife of Bath's Prologue and Tale" appears in the third fragment.

Because the stories are separate entities framed by the journey of the pilgrims, as opposed to the fairly linear narrative (even though much is told in flashback) of *The Odyssey*, Chaucer had much more latitude in the order in which they're presented. Of more interest in our own historical pilgrimage then is the nature of the connective tissue.

Medieval scholar G.C. Coulton wrote in 1908:

> "Even more delightful than any of the tales told by Chaucer's pilgrims is the tale which he tells us about them all: the story of their journey to Canterbury. Nowhere within so brief a compass can we realize either the life of the fourteenth century on one hand, or on the other the dramatic power in which Chaucer stands second only to Shakespeare among English poets. Forget for a while the separate tales of the pilgrims—many of which were patched up by fits and starts during such broken leisure as this man of the world could afford for indulging his poetical fancies; while many others (like the Monk's and the Parson's) are tedious to modern readers in strict proportion to their dramatic propriety at the moment—forget for once all but the Prologue and the end-links, and read these through at one sitting, from the first stirrup-cup at Southwark Tabard to that final crest of Harbledown where the weary look down at last upon the sacred city of their pilgrimage. There is no such story as this in all medieval literature; no such gallery of finished portraits, nor any drama so true both to life and to perfect art. The dramatis personae of the Decameron are mere puppets in comparison; their occasional talk seems to us insipid to the last degree of old-world fashion."

The frame for the stories, a common structure, as we saw in Chapter 7, "Once Upon a Time," is a looser example of an over-arcing story than the more complete narrative structure of *The Odyssey's* three storylines. Yet this fragile connective tissue feels familiar to our contemporary eyes. It is identical to the separate stories or episodes we see in nighttime television framed by an over-arcing story.

It is also very similar to the over-arcing stories we write for our games. What are the individual quests if not separate stories linked thematically to the overall story in an RPG? The briefings and other story beats between levels and missions in our action games, however elaborately they are produced, are just as insubstantial. They are made more so by their disconnection from the gameplay. It is in fact how this connective tissue is viewed by game writers that often *forces* the game stories to be linear, not the stories forcing the gameplay to be linear.

It should be obvious that if *The Canterbury Tales* was a game, and the stories levels, only the barest of changes in the frame would be needed no matter what order we chose for them to be played. It seems though that what we gain in flexibility of storytelling is balanced by a loss of depth in the over-arcing narrative. Let's take that concern to the next stop on our pilgrimage.

Don Quixote de la Mancha

A much smaller jump in time, a little over two centuries, brings us to what we learned in school is the first true novel in western culture. During a discussion in an Internet newsgroup a couple of years ago somebody said that a free-form, modular approach to storytelling *might* generate coherent story, but asked how could it ever approach great art or literature? I might have used *The Odyssey* as an example, or *The Canterbury Tales*. But in answer I presented *Don Quixote de la Mancha* by Miguel de Cervantes Saavedra. Written in 1605, it is rightly considered a work of immense literary and artistic achievement.

Pablo Picasso

Figure 13.3 Picasso's Don Quixote.

My first introduction to a *picaresque novel* was *Gil Blas* by Alain-Rene LeSage. Set in Spain, but originally written in French at the beginning of the 18th century, the novel was a major hit, translated into many languages, including Spanish, which explains why I stumbled across it in my fifth grade Spanish class.

note

PICARESQUE NOVELS: originated in 16th century Spain and are composed of a loosely constructed series of episodes connected by a central character. Examples also include *Tom Jones* by Henry Fielding and *Moll Flanders* by Daniel Defoe.

The episodic nature of picaresque novels make them unusually well suited to the study of storytelling in games, as well as to the more particular form called modular storytelling. Let's take a deeper look at *Don Quixote de la Mancha*.

In the book, a somewhat befuddled Don Quixote imagines himself a heroic knight, and sets off to prove that chivalry is not dead. He experiences a number of adventures in his quest, the first alone before he meets up with a servant/sidekick, Sancho Panza. Together they meet Dulcinea, a serving girl Don Quixote mistakenly believes to be a lady. The three set off together.

Up until this point in the story, the episodes follow a predictable linear path as the Don announces his intent and collects his compatriots. Compare this experience with the early stages of the hero's journey of Joseph Campbell or a player-character collecting party members in a single-player RPG. But now the episodes take on a new quality. Each is fairly equal in terms of emotional intensity, and each we will see can be considered as a module as well as an episode. No tricks this time. Here they are in the order presented in the novel.

- Don Quixote tilts at windmills, mistaking them for giants.
- Don Quixote rescues a "princess" from her two captors (actually friars).
- Don Quixote becomes involved in a tryst between a servant girl and her lover.
- Don Quixote scatters a flock of sheep, thinking they are two opposing armies.
- Don Quixote disrupts a funeral procession, imagining it to be a parade of monsters.
- Don Quixote is prevented by Sancho from fighting a monster he hears in the night (it's only the roaring of a windmill).
- Don Quixote seizes a barber's bowl, thinking it to be a famous golden helmet.
- Don Quixote encounters a chain gang on their way to the galleys.
- Don Quixote fights for Dulcinea's honor.

Now follow a series of several scenes that again work best in linear order, leading to yet another series of modules. (The book was written in two parts with ten years separating their publication.) Finally, in true epic style a character from an earlier module returns.

On his deathbed Don Quixote comes to his senses, bemoans his foolishness, and renounces chivalry. The irony and moral of the story is of course that his noble-hearted nature, however misdirected, *was* the true essence of a chivalric knight. He dies without learning the truth.

What is the best remembered moment of the novel? Tilting at windmills. The phrase (along with the word *quixotic*) entered our language and has remained for four centuries. *When* does this episode occur in the novel? It is the first module in the story. And what is the implication to us? The novel would have reached the same emotionally satisfying conclusion no matter what order the modules were in. The picaresque novel can be thought of as modular storytelling, with only one path mapped through the modules. There is no need for a golden path for the story to be enjoyed to its fullest.

If Don Quixote were a game, the modules I listed above could be played in *any* order with the tracking of variables to make sure that the dynamic world would always make sense to the player. In Figure 13.4 I've deliberately mixed up the incidents. The sequence is irrelevant.

Here we have an over-arcing story that is far more substantial than *The Canterbury Tales*. The meaningful narrative, complete with compelling theme, moving climax, and ironic conclusion, is there before us. Each episode in Don Quixote's quest supports that over-arcing story. The *order* of the modules is unimportant.

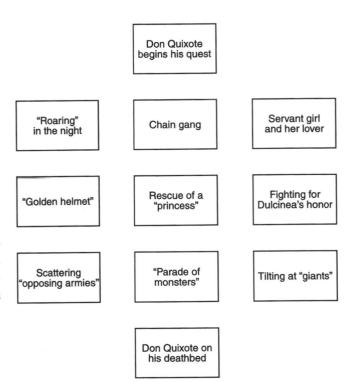

Figure 13.4 *Don Quixote* structured as modules.

Charles Dickens and Publishing in Parts

A little over two and a half centuries later our quest takes us to Victorian London where Charles Dickens polished episodic structure to gleaming art. His long novels, written as serials, have a much more defined linear structure, yet there are modules in any of them that could be experienced in different order. The Victorian novel is a far more sophisticated form than the picaresque. Its structure may not appear at first glance to suit our purposes as well as *Don Quixote*. But remember that Cervantes was there at the birth of the novel. Is it any wonder that his structure speaks most easily to us here at the birth of interactive storytelling?

Let's consider Dickens for a moment. Of immediate interest is the fact that he wrote his books in bi-weekly or monthly installments called *parts*. Dickens wrote episodically a long time before TV.

Figure 13.5 The Ghost of Christmas Present (and presents!).

note

PARTS: the first issue of many Victorian novels. They consisted of a few chapters bound in paper. *The Mystery of Edwin Drood* had seen the publication of six parts composed of 23 chapters at the time of Dickens' death.

Take Scrooge's ghostly visitors in *A Christmas Carol*, published in 1843. After we get past Marley's introductory spirit, each episode is a distinct module; each is a complete story with its own conclusion and moral; and each supports the main over-arcing story and the theme "greed is bad." With a bit of shifting around, couldn't those visitations transport us to the same satisfying conclusion in another order? Or as a game in *any* order? Scrooge could very well have been visited first by the Ghost of Christmas Present, seeing the dinner party given by his nephew, and hearing what his contemporaries really thought of him; then terrified by his grim future; and finally taken back to the moment when he made a decision that started him on his pursuit of wealth above all else.

The movie *Betrayal*, written by Harold Pinter, begins with the breakup of a relationship, and then takes us backwards, scene by scene, to the moment the characters met. Their meeting is warm and witty and full of promise, but we know where the relationship is heading; and that knowledge infuses every moment with the melancholy of lost love.

A Christmas Carol, because of its structure built around the three visitations is an easy example. Let's take a more complex Dickens novel, my favorite actually: *Bleak House*. Dickens' intent was the unmasking and ridiculing of a venerable institution of English property law called the Chancery Court, responsible for all matters pertaining to inheritance and property.

Bleak House, published in 1852, was loosely based on a case in Chancery Court involving the estate of a man who died intestate in 1798. By the way this case was still not resolved in 1915 and had by then cost over £250,000. The Chancery Court's reputation was so bad, there was even a boxing hold called "Getting in Chancery," which involved your opponent locking your head under one arm and pounding it repeatedly with his other fist. In the famous children's rhyme used by Agatha Christie in *And Then There Were None*, we find:

> "Five little Indian boys going in for law;
> One got in Chancery and then there were four."

To illustrate the dreadfulness of Chancery, Dickens introduces us to a bucket-full of characters, all affected by its insane intricacies. Each story is carefully threaded through the novel. It would appear impossible on the face of it to start rearranging things. But this novel too was written as a serial. And Dickens did not have every twist and turn plotted in advance. How he wrote is almost identical to how daytime serials are written today, as we'll see shortly.

In *Bleak House* it is possible to pluck an entire thread from one place in the book and plop it down whole in another. Here the story *threads* are the modules. They consist of multiple A stories, B stories, and runners populated by sharply drawn characters:

- Esther Summerstone, narrator of much of the book, carries the over-arcing story that ties together the others.

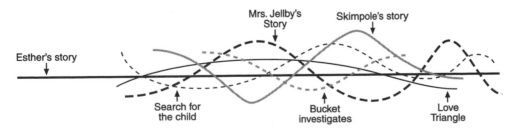

Figure 13.6 The modules of Bleak House are threads.

- Richard Carstone and Ada Clare are wards of the court, their love tested by the ongoing intricacies of the Chancery case.
- Sir Leicester Dedlock and his wife, and her search for her lost illegitimate child.
- Inspector Bucket's investigation of the mysterious death of lawyer Tulkinghorn.
- The love triangle of Esther and John Jarndyce and Doctor Woodcock.
- Selfish Harold Skimpole's luxuriating in the generosity of others.
- Mrs. Jellby's philanthropic concern for the rest of the world at the expense of her family.
- And many more.

All in some manner support the horrors of the Chancery theme. But instead of existing as discrete chunks, they are woven through the entire structure precisely the way they're woven in episodic television. We have our tokens and our flags ready in games to help us mark players' progress. With the tracking of a remarkably few variables our own story threads can be juggled in just the same way.

What is necessary is the mindset to be able to see the steps in each thread as separate from steps in the other threads. Dickens demonstrates in book after book that he was able to see his complex stories as individual strands making up the whole. It's a skill anyone writing daytime serials today must also possess. In fact, it's precisely the skill needed in editing when we have to cut a level or area, but don't want to create a jump or discontinuity in the narrative.

Often in this book modules will be depicted as separate boxes of story for the sake of clarity, but we mustn't forget that this is only the simplest form they can take. Time now for us to continue on our journey forward in time some 50 years, but to take a step backwards in terms of the sophistication of modular storytelling.

Saturday Morning at the Movies (Movie Serials)

In 1909, only 39 years after Dickens' death, the Clarendon Company of Great Britain produced what is believed to be the first movie serial, a series of one-reel episodes featuring Lieutenant Rose, RN. Four years later in 1913, an American company, Selig, released *The Adventures of Kathlyn*, the serial that established the formula that was to last for another 40 years in movies, radio, and television. *The Adventures of Kathlyn* introduced the ending we call the *cliffhanger*.

note

CLIFFHANGER: an exciting end to a chapter or episode that derives further suspense from leaving the audience uncertain of its outcome.

Characters were often literally left hanging from cliffs at the conclusion of the weekly chapter of a movie serial. The audience had to dangle for seven days before finding out their fate.

Less than a year later one of the most famous serials of all time, *The Perils of Pauline* starring Pearl White, was released.

The serial or "chapter play" became a staple of Saturday mornings, playing before the regular matinee feature, and for a reduced price. As befits a young audience out for thrills, the stories were

Figure 13.7 Pearl White, queen of silent serials.

unsophisticated and repetitious. Stretched out over 12 to 15 weekly chapters, each peppered with car chases and more fist fights than an Irish wedding, the 20-minute episodes always ended with a cliffhanger. The basic premise of the story was set up in Episode One and remained unresolved until the final wrap-up. In between the structure of the episodes was identical. The villain would unleash a dastardly deed and the hero would heroically counter it; or the hero would close in on the villain, only to have the villain slip through his fingers at the last second.

In a 12-episode serial, only 2 episodes, the first and the last, needed to be shown that way. Writers would often come up with cliffhangers before any other material for an episode. They would make lists of possible cliffhangers, even borrowing stunt footage from other serials or regular movies and tacking it on to new episodes. The cliffhangers and their resolutions were the connective tissue. If we retain the concept of their flexibility, ready to be dropped into any episode, the 10 intervening episodes could be shown in any order. Even given the linear nature of the medium, we shouldn't be surprised to hear that projectionists occasionally got the reels mixed up, but audiences often never noticed.

What made these episodes *feel* modular even if they weren't? Several things:

- The repetitive action. Watch a few serials, particularly those from Republic Studios in the 1940s. Many are now available on VHS and DVD. Even though they may differ in locations, the fistfights are virtually interchangeable, the climaxes impossible to tell apart.

- The blandness of the characters. None stand out enough in the audience's mind to overshadow any others.

- The static relationships. The banter between hero and heroine was established in the first episode and remained the same until at last they're permitted one token clench before the final fadeout.

- The infinitely spawning bad guys. Villains seemed to have an inexhaustible supply of unquestioningly loyal minions at their disposal. And just like the mobs in our games, they often looked alike. This is because the same actors played multiple parts. A clean-shaven villain killed in Episode Three would often show up again in Episode Six sporting an unconvincing moustache. And most of the action heroes were doubled by incredible stuntmen like David Sharpe. Shot with the camera pulled back to blur their features, the combatants looked like the same people from fight to fight in serial after serial because they *were* the same.

- The pendulum story moves. Neither hero nor villain ever gains an insurmountable upper hand until the finale. The balance of power simply swings back and forth like clockwork.

Yet the audience *was* entertained. And as the serial plot meandered its way towards the denouement ticket sales swelled. Something very interesting was occurring: a synergy we'll talk more of in Chapter 14, "Modular Storytelling."

The Saturday morning serials fit the modular storytelling mold as well as anything we've looked at so far. We can thrill to the Captain fighting the re-spawning forces of evil in repetitive modular episodes that, except for the first and last, really can play in just about any order. Pass a few tokens, wave a few flags and Shazam!

Republic

Figure 13.8 Captain Marvel in thrilling black and white!

Dennis Wheatley's Crime Dossiers

During the 1930s, as movie serials were beginning to reach their peak of popularity, a significant experiment in storytelling took place.

For many years, a popular form of novel had been one composed of reproduced letters or other documents supposedly written by one or more characters. Bram Stoker's *Dracula* was structured as a series of journal and diary entries. Agatha Christie's *The Murder of Roger Ackroyd* is told in the form of a journal penned by the murderer, skillfully concealing his or her identity until the very end. In 1930 Dorothy Sayers, one of the best of the Golden Age of Mystery writers, published *The Documents in the Case*, a mystery told entirely through various interview transcripts, letters, and police reports.

In 1936, prolific mystery and fantasy writer Dennis Wheatley collaborated with J.G. Links to produce four unique books: murder mysteries consisting of loosely bound documents and physical clues such as torn photographs (one was *very* racy), telegrams, locks of hair (reportedly contributed by nuns!), real matches, and even bloodstains. The solutions were sealed at the back of the book. The precise nature of the collaboration would seem to have been Wheatley plotting the mystery stories and Links fabricating the various documents and procuring clues. He must have known a lot of nuns.

The first of these, *Murder Off Miami*, barely managed to be published. The original publisher Hutchinson's had little faith in the idea. Booksellers thought it too much of a novelty to sell. Wheatley personally hawked the book to bookstore owners throughout London. Once it reached the public, the book was an immediate success, spawned three sequels, and several imitators.

In 1983, a gimmick mystery novel *Who Killed the Robbins Family?* edited by Bill Adler and written by Thomas Chastain left off the last chapter and offered a $10,000 cash prize to the first reader to solve the mystery. Later that same year, I was approached by my friend, Otto Penzler, editor, publisher, and book dealer, to write two books in the same vein for Warner Books, but patterned after the Dennis Wheatley Crime Dossiers. It would have been prohibitively expensive to produce books with actual clues, so our plan was to include reproductions of documents and photographs of clues and suspects.

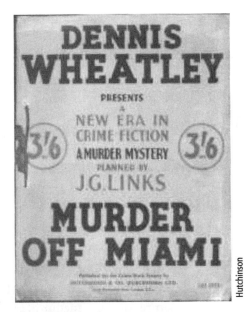

Figure 13.9 *Murder Off Miami*, interactive storytelling circa 1936.

At the time I was head writer of *Edge of Night.* I used my knowledge of soap opera production (yes, my scripts were shorter by that time!) for the first book, entitled *Death in Broad Daylight.* Unfortunately, our fortunes were tied to the success of two books in an earlier series that more directly imitated *Who Killed the Robbins Family?* Their sales were disappointing and our series was never published.

I bought back the rights to the two stories I'd written, and *Death in Broad Daylight* eventually did see the light of day as an Internet mystery in 1996 that offered a $5,000 prize for the correct solution. Surfers were able to access several Web sites, such as a fan site for my fictional soap opera, a police department Web site, and a library. More mysteries were planned framed by the search for missing photographer and amateur detective Joshua Light, whose files provided the stories. That's your humble narrator as the mislaid Mr. Light hiding behind the camera in Figure 13.10.

The Crime Dossiers by Wheatley and Links remain for me the first attempt of what we call today interactive storytelling. They presented the evidence of the case, and invited readers to construct the story in their minds. The game of solving the crime was every bit as important as the story. Even though the copies of the books were all bound identically with the pages and clues in the same order, readers flipped back and forth through the pages, rechecking alibis and studying clues.

Southpeak Interactive

This format translated beautifully to the Internet where aspiring detectives could follow dozens of links between documents and photographs. Not only was the structure not linear, the course of the story was entirely determined by the choices of the reader/player deciding where to click next. The home page of the mystery, now called *The Light Files,* deliberately gave no clue which links were considered by us to be important. Each Web page was a module, and each document or map or photograph on it were modules nested inside them.

Figure 13.10 *The Light Files: Murder Off Miami* in the Internet age.

That's the next stage of modular storytelling, and we'll examine it in Chapter 14. Because of the unique nature of our medium, we can create three-dimensional story structures just as we do three-dimensional characters. Take another look at Figures 13.4 and 13.6 above. Those are two-dimensional structures from another medium. Now imagine drilling down inside each one of those boxes to find the modules that form them, and inside those modules still others. . . . The human body is made up of cells that are made up of molecules that are made up of atoms that are made up of subatomic particles . . . modular anatomy. In the next chapter we'll take these two-dimensional roots from other media and watch them blossom into something rich and strange.

Daytime Soap Operas

The thriller wasn't the only genre of serials, or chapter plays, that evolved. Radio introduced listeners to soap operas that dared to turn Republic serial climaxes into climaxes of a very different sort. First appearing in the 1920s, radio serials blossomed in the 30s and made a successful transition to the 40s, thanks in large part to a former school teacher named Irma Phillips. Her first soap was *Painted Dreams*, unknown today. Not so another of her soaps. *The Guiding Light* is the only soap to make the transition to television. It is still running almost 70 years later. I wonder if any of our virtual worlds will top that record.

Figure 13.11 *Edge of Night* was the "Mystery Soap."

Soap operas mark a major step in my development as a writer. *Edge of Night*, debuted in 1956, was the soap known as much for its murders as its love triangles. I was head writer for its last two years. I came to *Edge* from primetime (nighttime) television where my specialty was mystery writing. I thought I was used to deadlines. Primetime television schedules were harried enough, but we at least only had to do one show a week, and every year we went on hiatus between the last episode of the season and the beginning of pre-production for the next season.

A daytime soap airs every weekday, day in and day out, 52 weeks a year. The episodes my staff and I wrote one week were shot the following week, and broadcast the week after that. There was no time to be sick. If I wanted a vacation, I wrote faster, getting at least an additional week ahead. I averaged 500 pages of writing every month. That included long term story arcs, weekly breakdowns (story outlines of episodes), and two to three scripts per week.

Our characters in primetime episodic television remain relatively static from episode to episode. They might face many different crises each week, but their roles in the show rarely changed unless there was a contract dispute. Characters in soap operas grow and develop over time. One character might be a "bad girl" for years on a soap only to evolve into a loving wife and mother. Good guys could suddenly turn rotten. Child actors grew up. Romantic leads grew old. So there is far more concentration on character.

Even with all those pages of writing, every single scene cannot move the story forward. The average viewer sees only two to three episodes every week. We need crossover sets and coffee table scenes ("More coffee, Madge?" "Thank you, Betty. Did you hear what happened between Jared and Kate last night?") to keep the audience up to date. Beyond that the sheer amount of new content necessary is enough to send you screaming away in a straightjacket. (Sound familiar, massively multiplayer world writers?) So there are far more A stories, B stories, and runners. Any given character might be integrally or peripherally involved in four or five stories at once.

The other major mistake I made in my first few weeks on *Edge* (in addition to the long scripts) was the speed with which I told the stories. I'd been hired to bring a swifter, nighttime pace to the show. I left the audience blinking in the dust. So many major incidents happened in so short a time, the producers had to force me to apply the brakes. My scenes were much shorter than what they were used to. There was much more intercutting. Easy enough to write. But it meant the crew was racing across the soundstage trundling these huge video cameras, and trying to do it silently while another scene was in progress. It took us about six weeks to settle into a pace both the audience and the crew could survive.

Daytime TV couldn't rely on matching the production values of big budget television shows, let alone movies. We might occasionally head off on location, but those times were few and far between. You know what shooting on location was called? A remote. We set one scene on the roof of a fictional TV station. We shot it on the roof of our own studio. It was 50 feet away. It was still a remote. In soaps, the story and the characters have to carry the interest of the audience. There is nothing else. That was what I loved and feared the most.

I loved it because on *Edge of Night* I was able to take a relationship from the moment a man and woman met through to their wedding night 18 months later. I could weave a score of stories together, bouncing characters off one another in unexpectedly dramatic and ironic ways. I learned that when you have that many stories running simultaneously, the best stories were the simplest. Their construction would add all the complexity I needed.

I feared it because the deadlines were daily and the need for content was relentless. The weight was all on me and my small staff of two or three people. Yes, it could be frightening, but it was also the most exhilarating writing experience of my life. One of the reasons I'm attracted to massively multiplayer games is the similarities between them and soaps. Yet even after designing several, still nothing has come close to challenging me the way soap operas did.

I'll be returning to soap operas when we get to Chapter 18, "Bringing Virtual Worlds to Life." In the meantime, here are some more roots for the new storytelling in general.

Soap operas are the most advanced model of individual modules connected by story since Charles Dickens. Unlike Dickens, we not only have story threads as modules tied to an over-arcing story, we have multiple threads tied to multiple stories; and we have the simpler episodic structure of Chaucer and Cervantes and movie serials as well. Variety is not only the spice of life; it is one of our most valuable tools. Anything we can do to hide the underlying repetitiveness of our games is good.

Soap stories can last for months, just like our games. Also, one of the points of taking the steps of a story and making them interchangeable modules is to give the player freedom of choice and movement, yet still guarantee her that the story will not only make sense, but remain compelling. Soaps give us models like coffee-table scenes; crossover sets; and simple stories woven together to make them seem more complex, yet at the same time comprehensible.

Episodic Television

By way of introduction, I should point out that designers have been playing with the concept of episodic games for a few years now. The thinking seems to settle on three ideas.

The first is a suggestion to release single-player games in smaller increments, or episodes, to provide an ongoing experience to the player. The benefits would be lower production costs and hopefully equivalent price points; the ability to reuse assets and engines without the radical overhaul the demand for next generation graphics requires; and to enable the developer in producing more product in a shorter period of time.

Television producers often make pilots that become the opening episode of a TV series. More money is lavished on these than a typical episode to make them look as good as they can, much like an original game followed by expansion packs. Since we already have expansion packs, all this episodic model seems to give us is a cheaper original game. Even with all the talk promoting this idea, I haven't seen notable successes created like this. I provide it here for completeness.

Next, we have the episodic release of content in virtual worlds. This occurs monthly in games like *Asheron's Call*, *Earth & Beyond*, and *Star Wars Galaxies*. This wholesale adoption of the episodic model of television seems so logical on the surface, and is such a big trap; I devote an entire section of Chapter 18 to it.

The third idea is of most obvious use in our discussion on the roots of a new storytelling, and I've already alluded to it: modules = episodes. Episodic television gives us the whole range of examples of modular storytelling we've been discussing:

- The individual stories loosely attached to a framing story in *The Canterbury Tales* is the model for television series that use only a premise and arena to frame weekly episodes. Most situation comedies (sitcoms) fall into this category, as well as crime shows like *Law & Order* and *Monk*. There are continuing relationships, but if there is an over-arcing story, it's kept well in the background. The stories of individual episodes take prominence.

- The more ambitious story that arcs over Don Quixote's adventures can be seen in dramatic series like *The Practice* and *ER*. Here, the individual episodes are still the focus, but there are clearly over-arcing stories that connect the episodes.

- The intricately woven story threads of Dickens are found in dramatic series that—no matter what their genre—emulate the structure of daytime soaps. These series

Figure 13.12 Cervantes would have approved of the structure of *The Practice*.

include *Sex in the City* and *The Wire*. The over-arcing story takes prominence and individual episodes are little more than steps along its course.

All of these types of episodic structures can be found in our games. The first two are mostly the province of single-player games. Our first example was the planned structure for *The Light Files* Internet mysteries with one over-arcing mystery framing the individual episodes.

There is the over-arcing story to which levels or missions are attached. The strength of the connective tissue varies. The complexity of the third example might overwhelm the game-play of many single-player games. Less is more. Simpler is better. We can make the stories seem complex, while keeping them simple. Despite their seeming complexities *The Usual Suspects* and *Identity* can easily be explained. The most prominent over-arcing stories seem to be in RPGs like *Morrowind*.

There can also be a continuing story that bonds a series of games. The only one I can think of like this is another RPG, *Baldur's Gate*. The player's search for identity and the results of that search carry through the entire series. Most series seem to start from scratch in sequels with only characters and relationships intact much as the TV series in the first example.

The third example comes into its own in massively multiplayer virtual world story structures as intricate as any daytime soap can be woven. The trick is, of course, to keep them modular enough that linearity doesn't overwhelm the non-linear world of the game. Again, we'll look at virtual worlds in Chapter 18.

Now it's time to take these roots of a new storytelling, and grow something.

CHAPTER 14

MODULAR STORYTELLING

"Indeed, naturally I think that a film should have a beginning, middle, and an end—but not necessarily in that order."

—Jean Luc Goddard (French New Wave filmmaker)

The roots of modular storytelling are deep and long. Even in linear media, there are different story structures than the one we trot out time and time again.

In Geoff Ryman's Internet novel *253* (now also published in book form) we are given brief character sketches of the riders in one car traveling between stations in the London tube. The sketches are meant to be read in any order, just as the documents in The Light Files. The writing isn't strong enough, and Ryman squeezes his narrative into a linear event near the "end," but up until then it is an interesting experiment.

Akira Kurosawa, one of the world's greatest directors, made a film in 1950 called *Rashômon*, with several of the roots we've been discussing embedded in it. It's available on DVD, and I highly recommend viewing it. (Avoid the wild west remake released in 1966 with Paul Newman & Claire Bloom.)

Several people seek cover from a rain storm at the Rashômon Gate near Kyoto, Japan. To pass the time, they discuss a shocking crime that has occurred nearby. A woman allegedly has been raped. Her husband has been killed. This story frames flashbacks told from the points of view of the three participants: the woman, a bandit, and yes, even the dead husband speaks through a medium!

The bandit claims he didn't rape the woman; it was consensual sex. He does admit killing the husband. The woman claims she was raped by the bandit, but her version suggests she may have killed her husband. The husband's spirit supports her claim of rape, but says he committed suicide. All of these stories have the ring of truth about them. And there's a fourth version. One of those gathered at the gate, a woodcutter, says he witnessed the crime. Yet his account seems to draw on parts of each version, and his version is the most suspect of all. Did he really see anything?

Figure 14.1 The bandit (Toshirô Mifune) and the wife (Machiko Kyô) in Rashômon.

Rashômon isn't a mystery story. Hercule Poirot doesn't step out of the rain and use his little grey cells to clear the matter up. Instead it is a meditation on the nature of truth and perception. No matter how much we may think we know the truth, in the end we can never be sure.

Look at what this single film gives us:

- A framing story right out of Chaucer.
- Flashbacks that relate different versions of a single incident.
- A narrative that does not move from A to B to C, but converges on a single point on the horizon. Yet no matter how fast we run towards it, it stays distant and undefined.
- Characters revealed not by self-awareness, but by the descriptions of others.
- R.D. Laing's theories of perception in action.

Quentin Tarantino's *Pulp Fiction* and the *Kill Bill* duo are examples of films where the order of the story has been rearranged to foreshadow, provide ironic juxtapositions, and to keep the level of the action rising. In *Kill Bill Vol. 1* we know early on that The Bride (Uma Thurman) will kill O-Ren Ishii (Lucy Liu). But the sequences leading to that confrontation play out on a broader canvas than her first mano a mano fight with Vernita Green (Vivica A. Fox). By mixing up the linear sequence of events Tarantino builds to that final series of spectacular battles in traditional style even while his story bounces giddily back and forth in time.

If we decide that all linear media story structures are the same just because pages follow each other in the same order in a book, or movie action is nothing more than light shown through a succession of frames all in the same order each time, we are narrowing our focus far too much—just as if we say all puzzles are lock-and-key or all quests are Fed Ex.

I'm going to propose another analogy. Imagine a set of 26 children's blocks, each with a different letter of the alphabet on it. If the child stacks the blocks in order from A to Z, we have a linear progression of the alphabet. If we allow the child to stack the blocks in any order the child wishes, the presentation of the alphabet is no longer linear. Yet the stack is the same height, and all of the letters of the alphabet are still there.

If the steps in a story progress from A to B to C and so on, it is the picture most people have when they think of linear story. If it doesn't matter what order they are presented in, the story is non-linear.

Modular story structure is new. Some people don't even recognize it as story structure at all. Like film direction that concentrates on what is in front of the camera (Billy Wilder), rather than the camera itself (Brian De Palma), modular storytelling is transparent and should go unnoticed by the player. We'll set our stage for modular storytelling by looking at the common forms narrative takes in games.

The Yoke of Narrative

In Chapter 7, "Once Upon a Time," we talked about the Golden Path, the concept of an optimum path through a computer game. The Golden Path will only seem a viable or inevitable part of a game design if it is tied to a limited definition of linear storytelling. If books, plays, and movies can break the bonds of linear storytelling, why shouldn't the most non-linear medium of them all?

This blind adherence to tradition is a result of incomplete knowledge on the part of some of the first practitioners of storytelling in games. Then those that followed them simply copied the ideas. As Richard A. Bartle says in his book Designing Virtual Worlds, "Too much virtual world design is derivative. Designers take one or more existing systems as foundations on which to build, sparing little thought as to why these earlier worlds were constructed the way they were."

This is not just true of virtual worlds, but of game design in general. You may see an echo of my comparison of Picasso's mother and daughter from Chapter 1, "Myths and Equations," as Richard goes on to say, "Question the paradigms, avoid stagnation. You have to understand a system before you can challenge it, but that doesn't mean you have to accept it."

There are two traps in game design here: parroting an idea without knowing why and discarding an idea without bothering to learn it. The first trap is, as Richard states it, pretty clear. It's like aspirant clockmakers who notice that a clock ticks and chimes, a pendulum swings, and hands move; and then try to copy it without bothering to study the gears that make it all work. The second rises from a combination of ignorance and arrogance.

The ignorance takes two forms. One is a failure to learn how other media have explored storytelling for centuries. The second is an assumption that because computer games add the additional element of interactivity or gameplay, that even if game writers and designers knew the old rules, they can't possibly apply to games.

The arrogance also takes two forms. The first is that games—even with shoddy storytelling techniques, cardboard characters, and clichéd plots—have sold quite well thanks. There wouldn't appear to be any need to improve. The other is that because a designer who is not an experienced writer can't see the trap in discarding concepts he hasn't bothered to learn, or even knew existed, no one else can either. This middle-management style of arrogance that forces creators to work within the limited imaginations of their employers has been the bane of artists from Mozart to Orson Welles. If employers don't understand, or can't do something, they assume it can't be done. "Too many notes, Mozart!" "I'm re-editing your film, Orson!"

As a result we are all saddled with this yoke of narrative in games; even though it need not exist. We have stuck our heads into it almost without complaint. "They're only games, after all." Yet we have progressed, as we'll see in this look at the story structures we have to choose from today.

Figure 14.2 Emperor Joseph II (Jeffrey Jones) counts the notes in Amadeus.

Traditional Story Forms in Games

In the earliest text adventures, we saw the beginnings of an exciting possibility: gameplay and storytelling emerging into a single entertainment experience. It was non-linear, much like the web form in Figure 14.4. with the boxes being the rooms, and the arrows interconnecting tunnels. The player could explore many different rooms of *Colossal Cave* in whatever order she chose. Other areas of the cave were opened upon solving a particular puzzle.

Colossal Cave (aka *Adventure* and *Adventure in the Colossal Caves*) was first written and programmed (in FORTRAN) by Will Crowther circa 1975, then expanded and distributed by Don Woods in 1976. Crowther was a caver, and his game was always intended to simulate the exploration of a cave. In fact, Colossal Cave does exist. It's a section of Mammoth Cave in Kentucky, reimagined in a fantasy setting. And at that it succeeded well. The game is loaded with references to actual features of the cave system; and caver jargon is used throughout.

True, the puzzles were only that, and not dramatic obstacles; and they weren't always consistent with the loose fantasy fiction of the world. Other characters, like the troll and the thieving pirate, were nothing more than puzzle elements; and the "story" was more an environment or arena built on some backstory. Yet it was the start of a promising trend.

Then graphics arrived and we got distracted by the pretty pictures. The graphics improved year by year, but the stories stayed sketchy. When we attempted to develop the stories, they seemed to get more and more linear. However many areas there were for the player to explore, the stories started to fall into a familiar, comfortable line.

Video forced us into a truly linear path from which we have never recovered. The best video seemed to offer was branching storylines, covered in a moment. *The Riddle of Master Lu* and *Dark Side of the Moon*, I'm proud to say, avoided both linear and branching. Too bad that fact went largely unnoticed.

So even though our first attempts at computer games with at least story "elements" like *Colossal Cave* and the *Zork* Trilogy hinted at non-linear storytelling, their influence faded, and the torch was kept lit but flickering by other text adventure games until graphics snuffed it out. Gameplay and stories headed down two very different paths.

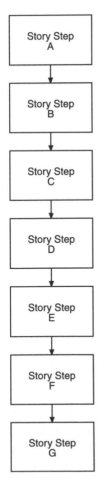

In the diagrams that follow, the boxes indicate any number of moments in the progression of a story. They may be scenes, levels, locations, character encounters, puzzles, any of the various storytelling devices we talk about in this book. They are all points where story is advanced. The arrows indicate how players can move from story point to story point.

Traditional (Linear)

Storytelling, even with its variations, is still to a large extent linear in other media. There's no reason for it not to be. Other than standard techniques like flashbacks, which rarely fail to advance the story in a single direction, books, movies, and television tell their stories in lines, straight or otherwise. In many games it's no different.

In Figure 14.3 the story starts at A, proceeds from obstacle to obstacle until B is reached, then in the same manner to C, all the way to the end. The arrows point inexorably in one direction from the introduction to the endgame. It looks a lot like a stack of children's blocks, doesn't it?

Figure 14.3 Linearity: storytelling at its simplest.

This is how writers of games thought other media wrote stories, and the first attempts slavishly copied the structure. Why not? The traditional linear story structure has a lot going for it.

- It is time-tested.
- It is successful in a variety of media.
- It is familiar to the writer and comfortable to the player.
- It guarantees authorial control over the progress of the story.
- Traditional stories enjoy the added benefit that lots of people have had experience writing them. The difficulties are limited to the same craft issues found in other media.

Figure 14.3 also looks a bit like our python from Chapter 7 standing on its tail. If we increase the size of the lettered boxes, that's exactly what it is: balloons of non-linear gameplay connected by narrow one-way funnels like those found on crab traps to ensure there is no turning back.

The most obvious limitation to this structure is that it ends up forcing gameplay into a linear structure. This construction could be obvious, as in level-based games, or disguised as in the python structure.

It's a fair question to ask why linear gameplay is such a nasty thing. Designers can track and control the player's advancement in the game, advancing her skills at a rate balanced with the increasing difficulty of gameplay, making sure she doesn't get too powerful too quickly. Even though the two may feel quite different when they're implemented, they are structurally similar. It would therefore seem to foster the illusion that the story and gameplay are part of a single entertainment experience.

But there are too many factors working against that illusion. The storytelling is predominantly passive, and the gameplay active. They are often segregated from one another by the use of cut scenes, long game engine scenes, pages of text, and so on. Why add one more immersion-breaking element?

Linear structures are completely at odds with what players want to do in games. Linear structures force them on to rails, or limit them to small areas in obviously larger worlds. In a linear adventure game, a single puzzle can stop a player's progress dead. We know we need to limit them, but why choose a tactic that makes it so obvious?

Players want freedom. The more freedom, the more real the game world feels to them. When we start holding up signs saying "You can't go here" or "You can't do that," and they know in the real world they could go there, or do that, we're rubbing their faces in the fact that the game world is actually a very limited subset of the real world. James Bond isn't going to visit every exotic locale on the planet in every film. The audience knows that. They accept the illusion that he is able to. We have to exert ourselves to create that illusion.

I worked on an interactive storytelling project with a lot of money and technology behind it. There was no gameplay as such, only narrative, so the player controlling the avatar was called a "user." I want to support any efforts in interactive storytelling. The fact that more than one person could move independently through the narrative interested me. It was doomed from the start for several reasons, only two of which are pertinent to our discussion. The team in place when I arrived had made two assumptions that were absolutely wrong.

First, their way of maintaining the illusion of a world beyond the areas of the game was to herd and punish the avatar. We often feel as if our player-character is being dragged from point to point through linear stories, but in this case the dragging was literal. The avatar was first asked by NPCs to go someplace or remain someplace or do something. If the player tried something the narrative didn't support, the NPCs would grow more insistent. If the player remained recalcitrant, the NPCs would manhandle the avatar, physically moving him, or the engine would remove the avatar's ability to move.

At the very beginning of the narrative, the avatar was somewhat at the mercy of outside forces. But very soon the player would move on to sections where taking him prisoner, or holding him in place wouldn't work at all.

Snatching control from the user whenever it was expedient, and at moments when it would be obvious to the user what was happening and why, would be calamitous. Users would get angry at being forced to march from moment to moment in the story. They were being treated like incarcerated felons.

Their second assumption was that users would "understand" that this straight-jacketing of the avatar was necessary, and go along with it. All I could think of were the thousands of game message boards out there pelted with posts from gamers when designers make a mistake. How forgiving they are! I tried to show them other ways of limiting the game world that weren't so invasive, that worked within the context of the story and the world, but the creative lead remained adamant.

Players want freedom of choice and action. Linear storytelling clearly limits their choices and actions. They want the world affected by their actions. It's a technical hurdle to add bullet holes in walls and make most objects destructible. It's a writing/design craft hurdle to create moments of story and character based on their decisions.

Luckily a number of writers and designers realized the corner linear storytelling was pointing them towards and looked for alternatives. The first alternative was branching storylines.

Branching (Linear-Thinking)

The branching story is a great idea, poorly implemented. The game frequently loses track of exactly what information you have learned. This means you're presented with conversation options like "Tell me all about X" when you've never heard of X at all! Similarly, the non-linearity of the plot means it's possible to advance along one storyline past a point of no return before you've collected essential items from another area.

—PC Gameworld review of Post Mortem (2003)

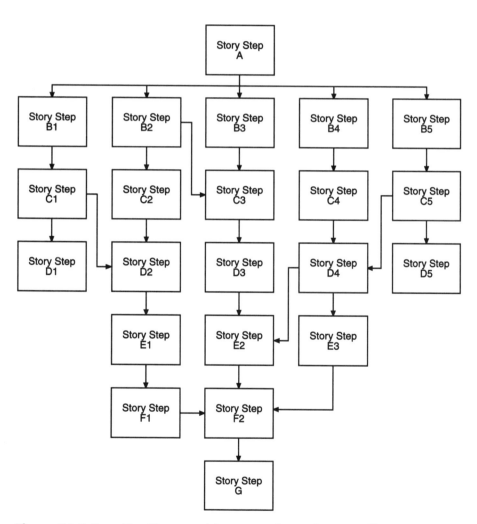

Figure 14.4 Branching: The perennial answer to interactive storytelling.

I entered the games industry as the result of my frustration with two games. The first I mentioned in Chapter 6, "Character Encounters"; it was *Return to Zork* in 1993. The other was *Sherlock Holmes: Consulting Detective* released in 1992, one of the first computer games on CD-ROM. In *SH:CD*, players moved through the story by interviewing various characters in full-motion video clips (FMV). You found these characters by selecting locations from a menu. The story was linear. The presentation was not. To use our analogy of the children's blocks, players could select a character on Block D before Block C even if the questions they were given to ask that character were dependent on the conversation on Block C. Look at the date on the review quoted above. Over a decade later, game designers are still making the same mistakes.

A far more fundamental mistake also occurs on a regular basis. Branching stories have been with us since text adventures, yet every few years another company arrives on the scene, announcing they've solved interactive storytelling. Their solution is always branching storylines. Often it includes FMV too. The theory goes that branching is not only "interactive," but it encourages repeat play.

Branching breaks down into two main types: single point branches and games structured with many branches. The first is most often seen in the endgame where the storyline will happily proceed on its linear way until the conclusion where players will be faced with a choice that sends them into one of several alternate endings. These endings may be of equal value, or one may take precedence over the others, completing the golden path.

My favorite example of this is *Titanic: Adventure out of Time*, Andrew Nelson's adventure game from 1996 that got a big boost from the release of a certain movie one year later. It was a beautiful-looking adventure game with a fanatical attention to historical detail. What made the alternate endings work so well was that Andrew had real history to play with. In one ending, players could even prevent World War II. Each ending was equally interesting. There was no golden path ending. There was no entirely happy outcome. Given the nature of the material, this isn't surprising. *Blade Runner* is another example of a game with interesting alternative endings.

A rarer type of single point branching is when the branch point is located at the beginning of the game as in Hal Barwood's *Indiana Jones and the Fate of Atlantis*. Another of my sidebar contributors, Noah Falstein, was a co-designer on the game. He suggested custom-tailoring gameplay to a player's preferences by giving him a choice of how he wanted to play the game: as a lone adventurer; with an NPC companion; or as an action game hero. The choices were carefully integrated into the fiction of the game world. Quite a bit of additional work was needed to support all three paths, although some assets were re-used.

However, most games use branching storylines simply for additional interactivity or to encourage playing the game more than once. There is, in fact, anecdotal evidence to suggest that the majority don't replay the games to try out different paths or endings. This is probably because many branches are there just to be branches. The story may shift slightly, but the differences are not meaningful. I'm not saying the choices may not result in significantly different gameplay but that they do not expose the core themes or emotional stakes of the story very often.

In the Xbox game *Tom Clancy's Splinter Cell: Pandora Tomorrow* (actually written by J.T. Petty) there are multiple branches in story progression as well as multiple endings to the story. These can involve ethical decisions on the part of the player to the point of questioning and even defying orders. NPCs react to players' decisions, and the game difficulty adjusts as their attitudes to the player-character, Sam Fisher, change. The branches are meaningful therefore both to the story and game mechanics.

Meaningless branches make branching meaningless. Story branches that require the player, not only to think, but to feel as well, are the best use of the form. The verdict is still out on whether they encourage repeat play.

I would much rather see games that are so dramatically compelling and fun to play that they are played multiple times for those reasons. We don't watch *Casablanca* over and over again to see if Rick and Ilsa will finally wind up together. We watch because the characters touch us; the ethical choices are meaningful; the story is engaging; and the theme of self-sacrifice for a greater good is a powerful one. Also the film's sense of humor is timeless!

Games that rely on branching for their entire structure reached their first peak of popularity in Hollywood's second major assault on computer games. Or was it the third? Just as branching refuses to die, Hollywood's invasions are remounted every few years.

As recently as March 25, 2004 an article in *The New York Times* by Michel Marriott was entitled "Movie or Game? The Joystick Is a Tipoff." Joystick? Well maybe. Bruno Bonnell, CEO of Atari is quoted in the article as saying, "We are starting to see, effectively, the best of both worlds. I am convinced that we are, right now, inventing the format of video games."

In that same article Bruce Feirstein, writer on *Everything or Nothing*, adds, "We are decades away from Pong. Now we can put you in the movies." *Broken Sword: The Sleeping Dragon* sports the slogan "It's the game that plays like a movie. Really!"

George Santayana's quote "Those who cannot remember the past are condemned to repeat it," is not from a recent article on branching storylines or Hollywood discovering games.

Games entirely made up of FMV have vanished, yet branching endures. Why does branching remain so popular? A number of reasons:

- It is time-tested. Maybe not as long as linear storytelling, but it's been around for over two decades.
- It has been somewhat successful despite being tied so closely to FMV. Remember *Night Trap* (1995)? *Silent Steel* (1995)? *Black Dahlia* (1998)? *The X-Files Game*

(1999)? As we see, it's continuing to be used. (Note: *The Riddle of Master Lu* and *Dark Side of the Moon* both contain FMV. There is branching only in the dialogue trees of Lu, and none in DSOM.)

- It's still locked into paths. There can be a golden path, and less satisfactory paths.
- It's familiar to the developers of games. There are still many who think it is the only way to tell interactive stories.
- It's familiar to the players of games and the reviewers of games. They recognize that even the limited choices branching gives us are more interactive than linear traditional storytelling provides.
- There is still authorial control over the progression of the story because branching is really just a form of linear storytelling. Each branch is still a stack of blocks piled from A to B to C and so on. Over the course of a game with the most branches imaginable, the story progression is still headed in the same direction from beginning to end.

People who are locked into linear story structures in games and are fearful of branching don't understand a fundamental principle involved. They fear the branches will keep spreading like some huge genealogical family tree.

When I took over the job as head writer of *Edge of Night*, I was told that a huge chunk of stations carrying the show were going to be dropping it in a few months no matter how successful we were. It was the last soap of the afternoon because of its title. And that time slot bumped up against the period when network programming gave way to local programming. Our half hour was coveted by local stations for cheaper programs, reruns, programming more geared to school kids, and for many more reasons. And sure enough that September our station coverage took a major hit. *Survivors* would not have survived.

I had been flirting with interactive storytelling since 1981 when I wrote a pilot for a television series that Atari was involved in. The story involved a family who could use their large-screen TV as a gate to other worlds. The plan was to release episodes based on games, and to base episodes on Atari games. I'd been a part of a panel at the first interactive storytelling conference in New York.

When *Edge of Night*'s ratings dropped solely from the loss of the stations in 1983, we tried to figure out what we could do to attract new viewers. The 900 number was a brand new phenomenon at the time. I suggested allowing the audience to vote, then taking stories in the direction they preferred. The reaction was similar to what we still find in games over two decades later. They pictured multiple story branches headed in all directions; scenes being shot that would never be aired (remember we only had a couple of weeks lead time); and they saw this all happening in real time: phone calls tallied, scripts hastily rewritten, and stories that were out of control, at the mercy of the viewer. No more authorial control!

I pointed out that our lack of lead time, and the nature of soaps, actually made the idea workable. I'd learned my lesson. I understood about coffee-table scenes. I knew there were times to slow one story for a couple of weeks or more and allow an overlapping story to pick up its pace. Given our short lead time, it would not have changed the pace of the show at all to create a suspenseful branch point; slow the pace of that storyline while we focused on another story (this also increased suspense); tally data on what the viewers wanted to see; write the new scenes, shoot them, and have them on the air a couple weeks later. My writing time for an entire episode averaged less than three hours. The writing time of a few transition scenes would be insignificant.

When they asked about out of control story branches and horrors! abdicating authorial control and allowing the audience to dictate story, I drew a diagram for them. It didn't look like Figure 14.4. It looked like this:

Instead of letting all those housewives, law enforcement officers, and convicted felons write our stories, I would present them with choices that I could fit back into the overall story arc. Any experienced writer knows that even if you're moving from A to B to C, there are many alternatives you can choose to get there. If we offered the audience a choice once a week in different stories (there were many in play at any given time), we'd still only be giving them two or three choices in stories that ran for several months.

Well, it didn't happen. We opted to refocus on some core characters, and up the stakes in their lives. It would have been an interesting experiment, particcularly in light of some of today's reality TV shows where viewers can vote whether participants can stay or must go.

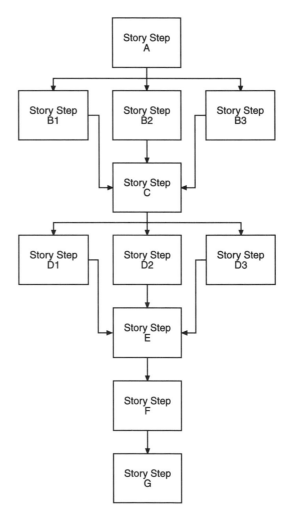

Figure 14.5 Retaining authorial control in branching stories.

Branching is all about illusion. No authorial control is given up. In solo boxed games, writers don't have to adjust to players. We may have to write more, but not as much as one might think. Entire scenes and swatches of dialogue, if they are never seen by the player, can be positioned in any number of places.

Virtual worlds have bits and pieces of branches, such as a quest that may change a player's alignment from one faction to another depending upon a choice she makes. But it is unsuited as an overall storytelling structure. Virtual worlds are (or should be!) as non-linear as you can get, and even the disguised linearity of branching is contradictory to that.

What if players want to revert to a saved game and try other options? In earlier video disk games like *Dragon's Lair* and *Space Ace*, players had no choice but to replay scenes. This problematic design concept (learning by dying) was adapted unquestioningly in interactive movies. Yet if written and designed correctly with no golden path there is no need for players to rewind and try again.

This allows us to still use branching in dialogue trees where its use is not as outdated as it is in overall game and game story structures. But even here there are more sophisticated structures we can use. My use of dialogue branching in my earlier games led me in parallel with other designers (I'm not the only one tackling this stuff after all!) to the next level of sophistication in story structures: the web.

Web (Simple Non-Linear)

Kenneth Millar was a mystery writer who lived in Santa Barbara, California. He was the direct stylistic descendant of Raymond Chandler. Under his pen name of Ross MacDonald he wrote intricate hard-edged detective stories featuring his detective Lew Archer. Paul Newman appeared in the film adaptation of the first Lew Archer novel, *The Moving Target* with the character name changed to Harper to fit in with Newman's other hit "H" films like *Hud, Hombre,* and *The Hustler.* The screenplay was by William Goldman.

Millar constructed intricate murder mystery plots around one of his favorite themes: the decay and corruption that lay beneath the surface of seemingly ordinary American families. He would walk along the beach every morning, a spider weaving his stories like webs, spinning out long strands, then connecting them again and again in the most unexpected places. He didn't know until the last minute which of his many characters was the culprit. So cunningly were the characters trapped in the web any one of them could have done it. This image of his stories as webs has remained with me till this day.

When I played those first text adventure games I mapped every room on graph paper. I still have some of those maps filed away. I remember one particularly difficult game built with ASCII "graphics" on my green phosphorescent monitor. It was called *Asylum.* You started out trapped in a padded cell. It took me forever just to figure out how to escape from that cell! I would never have been able to complete it without drawing a map.

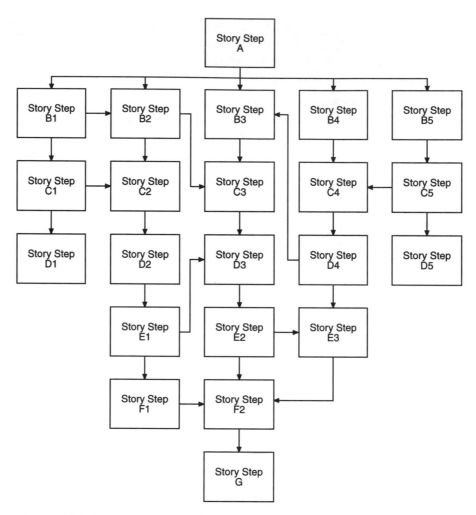

Figure 14.6 The Web: Less linear but still with strings attached.

Any of you who have mapped games, whether early adventures and RPGS or some text MUDS still with us today, will recognize Figure 14.6. In our maps the squares were not story points, character encounters, levels or scenes, they were called rooms. These rooms could be indoors or outdoors. They might be only part of a bigger room within the game world like a ballroom divided into sub-rooms such as the entry, dance floor, banquet tables, stage, and so forth. The arrows indicate the exits from and entries into these rooms.

These maps not only kept me from getting lost in the game (particularly in mazes!), they were also a map of the game's structure. When I became interested in the design of games, I realized that, thanks to mapping, I had a good first leg up on how games could be structured. It wasn't until I'd actually had a couple games released that I realized that they could also be maps of story structure.

Here are the main items of interest about the web story structure:

- It is the first truly non-linear storytelling form, even though it is not a very complex one to imagine. For the first time, the progression from A to B to C is no longer clear. You can actually go from A to C to B. By allowing progression in more than one direction, it breaks the linear pattern. It is definitely the beginning of a new paradigm.

- Webs are still fairly new. It's hard to find examples of them at all in many types of games. We do find webs in console action games that don't depend on explicit levels but open up new areas after players complete certain tasks. When these areas can be opened up in different orders, as in *Jak & Daxter*, the web structure is present.

- It still feels familiar to gamers and reviewers because they mistake it for branching. This indicates that it's working because they don't recognize it.

- For the first time we loosen the author's grip on the story, which is why you don't see writers unfamiliar with web structure embracing it. The more perceptive light fires to push back the darkness it suggests. Others don't even notice it.

- It is definitely more difficult to write than its two predecessors. An entirely new element has entered the mix.

- It moves us one step closer to a structure that resembles true non-linear gameplay.

- It provides a useful transition from linear thinking to true non-linear modular storytelling, story designed in the same way gameplay is designed.

Riddle of Master Lu was built with a few huge modules. Within those modules it was business as usual. The dialogue was structured as branching dialogue trees. It wasn't until *Dark Side of the Moon* that I was able to put the web structure to use in the dialogue trees. Parts of that game's structures are not modular, but web. This was necessary when I had to limit the paths players took to reach certain goals. I don't necessarily see this as a flaw in the game's design, although sometimes it revealed flaws we were unable to correct.

In *Dark Side of the Moon*, there are several unfortunate choke points that must be completed in order for the player to progress. What is worse, a couple of them are not obviously connected to the player being able to advance. As far as I'm concerned, this is as bad as forcing players to hunt for pixels and search for the story. I apologize to the players. I screwed up.

Hopefully, an example of the corner I painted us into will illuminate one of the challenges non-linear storytelling presents. At the beginning of the game, the lower levels of the mining colony are inaccessible to the player-character Jake. The reason for this was technical, not story-related. Because of all the FMV involved, the game first shipped on six CDs (later it was released on a single DVD as well). At the time (1997), that was a lot to load onto a player's hard drive, although they had that option. Assuming that most players would be swapping disks, I needed to find a way to minimize that as much as possible.

I divided the disks according to mine level, so that players knew that if they needed to take an elevator ride, a new disk would probably be required. So for a technical reason there were sections of the game that were modular, but they were stuffed into a python-like structure (sort of the reverse of *The Riddle of Master Lu*). In order to work within the belly of the python I backed up a step to the web structure of the following puzzle.

It is necessary to receive a Proof of Claim, Jake's right to his uncle's mine, before he can proceed to lower levels of the mine. But the mining clerk is never in his office. Furthermore, players have to find out where the clerk spends most of his time: a gravity dice table. Like lotto players, the clerk plays a certain "lucky" number every time, and that number is the very one needed to enter into the security keypad to gain access to his office. The problem it creates is the fact that there is no indication that it has any connection whatsoever with the player's inability to access the lower levels. That's sloppy puzzle design. Knowing that I had to create a choke point, I should've reworked the puzzle so players could early on connect it to its reward.

This type of puzzle structure is not uncommon in adventure games. And you can get to the important information by several routes, but it remains a web, not true modularity. True modular storytelling (and puzzle design as we've seen is storytelling) would have removed that chokepoint. It took another six months for hardware to catch up with the design. If we'd been able to release on DVD to begin with, such artificial choke points (there weren't many!) would have been unnecessary.

It's not a real python structure, of course, because the choke points are not one-way. As each obstacle is removed, the player has access to a greater part of the game world, until eventually all locations in the world are "open," at least in the sense that the player knows how to access them. So the web structure falls away to reveal modules underneath.

One benefit of such choke points was that, even though they were a nuisance to the purity of my concept of modular storytelling, they were helpful as flags. As soon as the game engine was notified the player had accessed a new area, any situations, puzzles, character encounters, and so on connected to that new step in the story could be flipped to a new state. Characters who could once reliably be found only on an upper level could now appear in new spots. Jake's status changed within the story. He moved from busybody to fugitive from a murder charge, and colony announcements changed to warnings to be on the lookout for him. And the nature of puzzles left unresolved changed.

I'm giving you clues here to which method of storytelling I overwhelmingly prefer. Let's move on now to a new storytelling.

Relinquishing Control

Modular (Non-Linear)

The thrust of these last few chapters has been towards an integration of story and game-play. It makes sense that the closer the way we construct our stories comes to the way we build our games, the better chance we have for that integration. Even though I've tried to prepare the way for a modular concept of storytelling, there are several scary issues we need to address.

First of all, let's look at Figure 14.7. What's missing? All of those comforting little arrows. It might seem more accurate if we drew the diagram with two-way arrows from every box connecting to every other box. I didn't do that for two reasons.

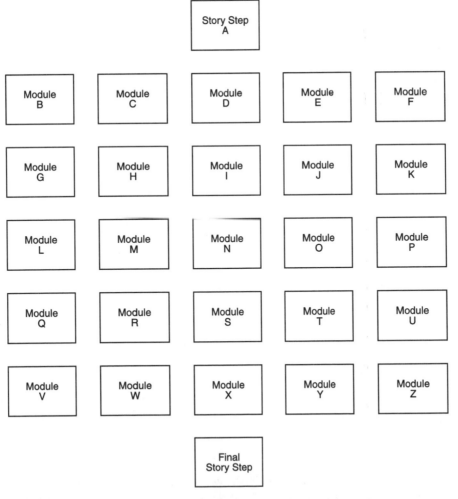

Figure 14.7 Modular: Storytelling that matches the way gamers play.

The first is that it would look like a hairball. I didn't want readers to take it as a personal challenge to trace every one of the connections. The point should be clear without them: The story can progress from any single box (module) to any other single box with two exceptions: the first box and the last. A game has to begin somewhere (point of attack!) and end somewhere (final resolution!), or at least a single-player game does. Virtual worlds don't need that last box any more than soap operas do.

The second reason is that I want to wean us from the idea of paths. This concept, firmly established by the first three storytelling forms we've looked at, fails to acknowledge how the gameplay in many games is already designed. In many treasure hunt games like *Jak & Daxter*, the gameplay is already laid out in modules. You start the game in a large area with a number of locations to explore. There are boundaries at the edges of the area, but there are no rails. While the entire structure of the game may not be modular (there are choke points) players can move over a lot of territory in any direction they choose. And like *Dark Side of the Moon*, the choke points are not one-way only. The world doesn't continue in a linear way, it expands.

Virtual worlds are even farther from a path structure. There are no true choke points. This is why linear quests and storytelling seem so odd when we encounter them in virtual worlds. How did they get there? Why do designers think they're good ideas? It's due to the parallel development path they took to solo player games. Their pedigree stems from tabletop role-playing and small MUDs, not text adventure games. Text MUDs and text adventures look very much alike if you examine obvious things like the text format, player input, maps, and so on. They are really quite different. In Chapters 18, "Bringing Virtual Worlds to Life," and 19, "Enabling Story in Virtual Worlds," we'll look at the challenges their independent history has created for them.

If we can get beyond the idea of paths being the way a player moves through a game, we'll be able to progress to new paradigms. Paths promote linear thinking. Do all games need to be non-linear? No. I don't believe that anymore than I think all games should tell stories. What I'm saying is that if you choose to make your game linear, don't do it because you think it's the only way to tell your story. Don't copy the paradigms of the past before you understand them. Once you do understand them, you hopefully will be able to see how they can be repurposed. Remember Picasso's mother and daughter!

Okay, what distinguishes modular storytelling from the first three forms?

- It is unfamiliar to designers, particularly those who routinely segregate story and gameplay.
- Its structure is not immediately apparent. Without all those comfortable arrows in the diagram to hang on to, it can look frighteningly vague.
- There is apparently no authorial control. It looks as if the direction the story takes is totally at the whim of the player. Players may love this, but writers don't.

- It can be difficult to grasp. It requires a new way of looking at story, especially for someone who is not already experienced in constructing linear stories. You didn't read that wrong. I'm not suggesting it should be easier for someone not tied down to the old "outdated" ways. Look around. It's one of the core themes of the book.

- Modular storytelling requires much more effort. Once the mind clicks over to how it is done, there are other factors that we begin to look at in the web form, the first non-linear structure. However, we are used to those issues from gameplay design. They are not as foreign as you might think. It is the application of them to storytelling that is not obvious.

No other structure is better at integrating story and gameplay than modular. Those boxes in Figure 14.7 can be of any size. They can be entire scenes if you must have it that way, or brief moments captured in the rush of gameplay. All that is required of them is the same thing required of any step in a story, that it move the story forward.

But what is forward? No matter what order the story steps are experienced by the player, the momentum is always from the story's beginning to the story's end. The player may jump around on the diagram from box to box, but eventually she will find herself where the author has always wanted her to go.

J.T. Petty, in an interview with Amazon.com said, "At the stage of interactive narrative we're working with now, I feel like we still need to control the narrative pretty strictly. I've never been a fan of multiple endings; they make me feel as if none of the endings are actually valid." But he then appears to contradict himself: "With current technology and innovations, I think the best we can do is create the illusion of narrative control, and create the most manipulative/sympathetic situations possible."

He is expressing the anxiety a lot of writers have when faced with interactivity. He's obviously intrigued by its additional challenges enough to try branching, but seems to think multiple paths are his best storytelling tool. Anything beyond that is unexplored territory.

While there is apparently no authorial control in modular storytelling, there really is. Now that we know the story still starts at A and will eventually end at Z, we should be able to relax a little. What's next? Adjusting the modules.

Not only are they different sizes, the modules are also dynamic. Just as we break down the elements of a scene or level to see what we need to save if we're dropping it, we do the same in modules to see what components are tied to that particular story step, and which are more flexible. Most are flexible.

Setting remains tied to a specific module. We don't change a module's location from a corporate office in Manhattan to a Libyan desert oasis. Physical action is tied to the module, just as it is often tied to the setting. Most puzzles remain constant for the same reason, although we can see where the game engine might lock or unlock a door and place a key in a scene, depending on previous player actions.

Characters may or may not be tied to the module. If an NPC is mobile, he's free to sit in our digital green room like an actor until he is called upon to make his entrance. We'll maintain the illusion for the audience that he has a real life offstage just as we do in plays. "Where has that no account brother of mine gone off to?" "Probably gambling at the casino again!" No, the closest he'll come to that is playing cards with the actor playing the character he murdered in the first act.

Most importantly, as we saw in our discussion of cutting levels and areas almost all story steps can be fluid. As we discover when we edit and must move story elements around, exposition works in a surprising number of places in any given story. Remember that to the player the story is always moving forward along a single linear path. Modular structure is entirely invisible to the player.

Now that we've freed the necessary steps of our story from being tied to any individual scene, we need to track the player's progress. We do that in the same way we track player progress in any other parts of our game like skills or quests or acquired items. We pass tokens. We set flags. Even though the player has been successfully derailed and is now wandering freely through our world, every action she takes, every choice she makes, is dutifully tracked.

The backpack is a classic game device for inventory. We know it holds far more in a game than it would in real life. It is a game convention we accept. Think of the player-character hiking through our story carrying a backpack containing the various objects, story steps, and NPC character developments possible in the story. It's a database just as it is in the inventory analogy. The game can pick through it at any moment and find out where the player has been; what the player has done; what the player has learned; what NPCs think of the player; and so on.

Having that information, the game can automatically salt the next module the player visits with the next step along all those "paths." If the player fails to experience all the possible elements now available to him because of his progression through the story so far, they go along with him in his backpack to the next module to become available again.

None of these variables in the backpack need to be tied to any of the others. Some may, but it's not necessary. We may need a specific story step to reveal growth in an NPC, but even that is fluid.

This might sound like we could be tracking unwieldy numbers of variables. This isn't true. The number of story steps and character revelations in any scene are very few even in the most complex stories, or audiences could never follow them. In our stories that are simple even when they're disguised as complex the number is very manageable. The tricky part comes in testing all the possible variations, and making sure they track appropriately.

It may take a certain kind of personality to handle as much of this as possible during the writing. As J.T. Petty says (and remember he's only talking about branching!):

> I've got my sock drawer organized according to the Dewey Decimal system. Low-level compulsion comes to me pretty naturally, and keeping track of the narrative threads is usually pretty satisfying. The script format we came up with for the first SC [*Splinter Cell*], the documents we call "Mission Bibles," are also helpful, (especially since the level designers have to know the various threads as well as or better than I do.)

I have that same compulsive nature and feel the same satisfaction when the pieces of a story or conversation match up like dominoes.

Time for an example. In Figure 14.8 we see a portion of Figure 14.7 magnified so we can better see the building blocks that make up the module. This is one possible story progression based on choices made by a player named Jane. The letter P stands for permanent features. The letter D stands for dynamic features that are present dependent on player actions.

In Figure 14.9, we see the same story as it is experienced by another player named Dick, who made different choices. (Their dog Spot doesn't play computer games.)

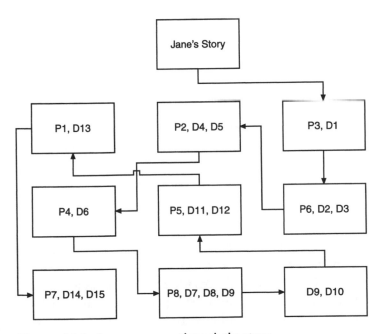

Figure 14.8 Jane progresses through the story.

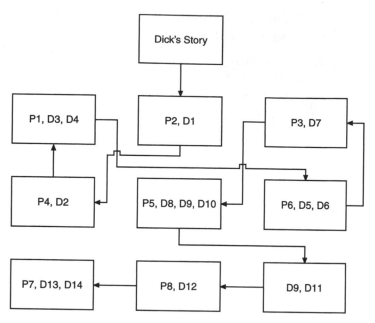

Figure 14.9 Dick progresses through the same story.

Even though Dick and Jane have made very different choices in where to go and what to do, both find themselves at exactly the same point in our story. We are maintaining authorial control. In a virtual world, of course, Dick and Jane may be simultaneously involved in the same quest, following it from step to step at an identical pace, and still never meet. The divergent experiences prompt a lot of discussion at the ingame pub.

Another question may have occurred to the reader. Maybe we can tell stories in this fashion in our games. But isn't modular structure too loose to give us compelling stories? The answer to that question lies in Chapter 13, "The Roots of a New Storytelling," and scattered throughout this book. It was that question that prompted me to rediscover *Don Quixote de la Mancha*. That story would remain great literature no matter in what order we followed its picaresque adventures.

We don't want to throw out all that we've learned on how to write stories, but we do need to look at them with different eyes. Divorcing story steps and character development from setting happens every day when writers rewrite. If it's raining, shooting at a practical location may need to be rescheduled to an existing indoor set. If an actress in a TV series becomes pregnant, that may need to be written into the storyline (or disguised—I've done both), and her physical action scenes altered or shifted to another character. Actors' contracts sometimes dictate story moves. Mike Muscular is asking for too much money? Involve the character in an auto accident, keep him a helpless paraplegic for a couple of heart-wrenching weeks, then write him out. Writing for a television series is already being aware about how dynamic and flexible story (and careers!) must be.

But if you were paying attention in the earlier chapters, you know there are some other issues to be dealt with. What about rising action, and tightening the emotional screws? What about the crisis, climax, resolution trio? What about reversals?

These are dealt with in several ways. I realized how flexible we could really be with story and character while working on *Dark Side of the Moon*. It took me awhile to realize what word I was looking for to describe the effect I saw, and for quite awhile thought it was symbiosis. That's dead wrong. It's *synergy*.

note

> SYNERGY: occurs when two or more substances, organisms, or elements combine to produce an effect greater than the sum of their individual effects.

To explain this effect, I developed the following example that I give at my tutorials and lectures. I call it "A Bad Day at the Office". Please remember this is only one example of a way to escalate tension or suspense in a modular story structure. It is by no means the only one!

Suppose in the course of any workday, six bad things can happen. These are not earth-shaking, such as getting fired. Nor are they so minor as to pass beneath our emotional radar. All are of a similar intensity, somewhere in the middle ground between minor irritation and total calamity. A misunderstanding with a coworker, a meeting that went nowhere . . . whatever.

Okay, one of these happens to you. You go home, and your significant other asks how your day was. Balanced against that one bad thing is an entire day of good, or at least neutral incidents. So you reply, "Pretty good!"

Suppose three bad things happen. Depending on your outlook on life, you might reply, "So so." "Not bad." "Not so good." Etc. The cup is either half full or half empty.

Suppose all six happen. You would say you had "a bad day at the office."

Now, these six things could happen in any order. And none is of a higher intensity than any other. One of the reasons *Don Quixote* is such a good example is because, as I said when I described it in Chapter 13, the incidents in the main part of the book have a similar emotional level. Yet, simply by juxtaposing them in a single day or story or game, then adding them up, something interesting happens.

The resulting emotion is stronger than any one of the individual pieces. Synergy. This phenomenon is the real world's gift to us, the writer of games. It is a gift our linear media colleagues would never appreciate. They have no need for it. We can manipulate that synergy in a modular story. At the end of a game session in which we rescued a child from bullies; helped a baker deliver his pies; defeated a bandit in combat; solved an intriguing puzzle; and completed a mission that required stealth and ingenuity, we can say we had a great time no matter what order we experienced those modules in.

Here's another way to tackle some of the storytelling challenges we face. And it's the solution to the question I posed at the end of the section on web story structures. Which form do I overwhelmingly prefer? Modular storytelling, right? No. I prefer none of them; and all of them.

In the sentence length of your dialogue; the types of characters you use to populate your world; the quests you create; and in so much more, variation is everything. It keeps the player interested. And it's no different in story structures.

While I may prefer modular for overall game structure because of its flexibility and how closely it mirrors the way gamers like to play, it is not the only possibility. The web structure got me out of a corner in *Dark Side of the Moon*. I also use it in most of my dialogue trees.

Branching is still a viable alternative for dialogue trees, especially for exchanges with minor characters or "conventional" dialogue (bartering with merchants, talking to town criers) where the exchange follows fairly strict rules. Branching also can be useful as we've seen to present players with meaningful choices that can pose ethical and moral questions or alter the player-characters relationships with NPCs.

Linear story structures are perfectly fine for cut scenes, if we must have them. They are more effective when used sparingly in the non-linear structures web and modular. Want to guarantee an immediate climax and resolution to a crisis? Tie all three together and move them as a single piece. We can also use choke points (either one-way or two-way) to guide players to an important story goal.

Reversals aren't the problem they may first appear anymore than interim rewards are. They can be attached to specific modules or allowed to float freely, ready to be plucked from the backpack at emotionally satisfying moments. We always control the removal of items from the player's backpack. It's an illusion that the player is in control of the story. She is only in control of her own actions, how she experiences our story. Just like the magician who forces a card on an audience member, we can force moments on the player at will.

In *The Gryphon Tapestry*, we, of course, had random encounters with adversaries, mobs like bandits, wild animals, and magical creatures we could choose to fight, negotiate with, or run from. Sometimes, however, for story purposes, we wanted to force an outcome of a battle. To the player, the battle seemed as random as any other. The messages describing the action were the same. Yet we knew whether the player was going to win or lose. Writers are magicians. We manipulate and misdirect, and the audience loves us for it.

We've been discussing modular storytelling in only two dimensions. Like our characters and our game worlds, modules can be three-dimensional. I've mentioned the third dimension once before. Let's enter it now.

Nesting Modules

Just as modules contain static components like setting, and dynamic variables like story steps, they can also contain other modules, as illustrated in Figure 14.10. The largest module can be the entire game world. Within that game world can be as many stories, characters, quests, encounters, puzzles, and so forth that our time, budget, energy, and brain capacity can support. And each of those can be made up of even smaller modules.

Figure 14.10 Nested modules.

A small module, such as an encounter with a minor character may contain a module consisting of exposition, faction, advancement, reward, any number of things.

Nesting modules is also a way to retain a familiar level structure but with a more flexible appearance. Console treasure hunt games can present us with several areas that may be entered from the very beginning of the game. Maybe we can't progress very far at first, but as soon as we acquire the necessary item or skill or knowledge, we can proceed a bit further. These areas can be nested modules with components also broken down into modules, which are variable depending upon what the player has accomplished and experienced.

It would be an interesting experiment to see how far we can drill down in this third dimension. I've never made a purely modular game myself. I'm part of a commercial enterprise, after all, with milestones and budget restrictions. The amount of effort necessary may not provide enough value. And I do believe variety is the spice of games as well as life.

How far you want to take the nesting of modular structure remains dependent upon many factors. Take it only as far as it adds value to your game.

Structuring Chaos

Those writers with faint hearts may want to skip over this section. It strays outside the scope of the book, and I only include a couple of brief ideas to tickle your brains. But if moving beyond linear or even branching feels too much like diving into the ocean from a cruise ship at sea, you aren't going to want to dive in with the following lead weights attached to your boat shoes. I'm not going to go into much detail, but with apologies to Stephen Hawking I wanted to share with you my forays into some theory that reminds me of attempting to connect up quantum mechanics with the theory of relativity (being tested for the first time as I write this, by the way). Still with me? Okay, don't say you weren't warned.

A few years ago I began messing around with chaos theory. The theory was popularized by Dr. Ian Malcolm, Jeff Goldblum's character in *Jurassic Park*. I'm going to give you a couple of definitions:

note

CHAOS THEORY: describes the complex and unpredictable motion or dynamics of systems that are sensitive to their initial conditions. Chaotic systems follow precise laws even though they appear to be random.

We are seeing it applied to studies of the weather and attempts to predict stock prices. It seems like it could be put to good use in politics too. My first brush with chaos theory was many years ago when I had a screen saver that drew terrain using fractals.

The term fractal was coined in 1975 by Benoit B. Mandlebrot, a mathematics professor at Yale. It refers to objects built using recursion (each iteration is a reduced version of a previous iteration—sorry, I warned you) where part of the object is defined and part is variable. Despite the apparent randomness of each individual screen of that screen saver, I could set several variables such as mountain height and the ratio of land mass to water.

It seems to me very likely that instead of concentrating on what we traditionally consider A.I. storytelling or what we traditionally think of as structured writing, chaos theory offers us the best of both worlds. A modular structure built as a fractal would have a top level consisting of a row of seed modules chosen by the author. They can contain all of the ingredients of story and characterization we use when we write our stories: characters with traits that will set them in opposition to other characters; settings that support story; values assigned to conflict that when added up will create climax.

These are not just tossed at random into the mix however. They are very deliberately chosen to steer the story into a recognizable genre toward a satisfying, if undetermined conclusion. Furthermore the structure is tweaked with specific authorial story moments triggered when a critical mass of ingredients is reached. Turn the heat up on a pot of water, eventually it boils.

I've never tried this. I haven't had a lot of spare time. And nobody has been loony enough to fund a project based on the theory. But I have gut instincts about writing and storytelling. They almost always pay off. And I have a gut instinct that there is something very useful here for the storyteller in a medium that embraces freer story structures other media only flirt with. I'm done now. I said it was just a tickle.

Adventures in a Non-Linear World

That modular storytelling can help us integrate story and gameplay, and create a game environment the player is free to explore is not just theory. It's proven. Every day we're seeing examples of it in games. Most examples are small. I use it all the time. You may have sensed a greater freedom of action, but have not pinned down exactly how it was achieved. Or like some of the reviewers who played *The Riddle of Master Lu* you may never have noticed.

That sophisticated story can survive the demolition and separation necessary to the process is also proven. It is being done daily in other media every time we rewrite.

We can maintain authorial control over the story and its steps, even as we unbind those steps, and let players encounter them as they choose. The order is irrelevant.

Tracking the progression of the player and mapping our story moves to that progression is something we do routinely in gameplay.

Modular storytelling allows us to throw off the yoke of narrative we've been harnessed with for decades. It gives us a chance to tell our stories as part of a single experience that is both narrative and game. It's time to stop bussing our players back and forth between story and gameplay. It's time for true integration.

PART IV

GAMES PEOPLE PLAY

Interlude in a Twisty Maze of Passageways

> go east

The tunnel narrows here to a low east-west crawl.

> go east

This is a large cave. Stalactites hang from the ceiling, glistening in the light from your brass lantern. A solitary figure sits on a nearby boulder, shoulders slumped, head in hands. The figure's T-shirt and jeans look remarkably like your own.

> look

There is a lost adventurer in the cave.

> talk to adventurer

The adventurer stirs and looks up, blinking at the light. "Hello!" he exclaims. "Another one, eh? Lost as I am, I expect."

> talk

"I've been wandering these passages for who knows how long, existing on little more than spring water and blind fish. I took a wrong turn back in 1976 I think it was. What year is this?"

> talk

The lost adventurer looks stunned. "That long? I was a young man when I went astray, and now...well I'm not so young now..."

> talk

"All I can tell you about is our immediate surroundings. At least I think I can." He points behind you to the west. "Back the way you came is the real world...somewhere.... Further to the east you'll find action, if it's action you crave. South of here more adventure awaits. To the north you'll find children playing, and in the room beyond them are adults dressing up and pretending to be people they are not. Climb up through that hole and you'll find simulated countryside and sky; but don't be fooled. It isn't real. You may find it a worthwhile strategy to lower yourself into that crack in the floor over there, although I've heard what sounds like clashing armies down there."

> talk

The lost adventurer scowls. "Parsers haven't improved much in all these years, have they?"

> talk

"That's easy for you to say. But I see no point in beating about the bush, if there were a bush nearby. Here there are only games. It's best if you pick one direction and see if it suits you. If you get bored you can always try a new one. Just remember you're now lost like I am in a twisty maze of passageways. There's no returning to the real world. Would you like me to show you how to catch blind fish?"

CHAPTER 15

GAME TYPES

A s I mentioned in the introduction, the word *genre* gets misused a lot in our industry. In this book I've tried to make the distinction between genres of games that
break down the same as they do in other media, and types of games that are
uniquely our own. We'll get to genres in Chapter 16, "Game Genres," but first let's take a
look at the types of games that lend themselves to storytelling.

Throughout the book, I've discussed issues that are common to character creation and
storytelling across various game types. Each type of game presents unique challenges and
opportunities. I'm going to look at them in alphabetical order.

Action

Action gamers, particularly those who play
shooters, demand a greater adherence to real
world physics than any other type of game
outside of simulations. The first few generations of shooters would acknowledge when a
hostile target or the player was hit, but that
was about all. The amount of blood varied,
but it wasn't a lasting condition. Both it and
the bodies of dead targets would disappear
from the game world much like the title aliens
in the 1967 Quinn Martin TV series *The
Invaders*. In that case, the bodies vanished so
David Vincent, the lead character played by
Roy Thinnes, would have no evidence to support his claim of an alien invasion.

ABC

Figure 15.1 Roy Thinnes had a hard time
convincing people *The Invaders* walked
among us.

In games we often take our cues from Hollywood even if we aren't experiencing the latest full-scale Hollywood invasion. The mayhem in our action games wasn't as realistic as that of movies or television. We needed to change that.

The next stage was to allow the destruction of objects within the world that were obstacles. Crates stacked in front of a doorway could be blown up. Gates could be smashed through by cars. Their states changed from undamaged to blown to smithereens. In most cases, the obstacle was removed from the game world just like the bodies of fallen enemies. Yet that was still not "realistic" enough so we began to break down the objects into several states: undamaged, partially damaged, seriously hurting, scattered bits of debris. As computers and consoles acquired more memory, we could store more objects. For those of you who are writers but not designers, it's important to know that every one of those states of destruction is an object that must be stored by the game separately. The last state, bits of debris, if it were to remain in the game world, usually occupied the same amount of memory as the undamaged object. It doesn't become a whole mess of individual objects.

When memory is an issue, dead bodies will still wink out of existence after a short while, or as soon as the player has had sufficient chance to loot them, but in some cases, they remain. One way to get around the increased memory needed to hold the new object called "dead body" is to stamp it into the background and treat it as just another hot-spotted feature in the room.

As we moved from straight shoot-em-ups, we found different ways to affect the game world. In games ranging from *Thief* (the first true *stealther*, not really a shooter) to *Tom Clancy's Splinter Cell*, we added the ability to manipulate the environment in a number of ways much as adventure games had been doing for years.

Figure 15.2 *Tom Clancy's Splinter Cell: Pandora Tomorrow* allows players to affect almost anything.

The lines between the two types of games began to blur. The first few attempts at this melding of game types resulted in what we used to call hybrids, like action-adventure games. *Wild Wild West: The Steel Assassin* was a hybrid. James West solved puzzles as in a regular adventure game, or he gunned down bad guys as in an action game, although even in the action sequences there were optimum ways to approach each shootout. Today almost all action games allow for at least simple adventure game obstacles. The word hybrid doesn't really apply any longer.

Not only can bodies now remain, but gamers are demanding more and more realism. No longer are the only objects that can be affected by the player those that are obstacles or otherwise related directly to the plot. Now bullet holes pockmark walls. Anything in a room that can be damaged in the real world by automatic weapons fire can now be damaged in some games. Innocent civilians can get caught in the crossfire.

Memory issues aside, this is important to writers for several reasons. First, it makes it easier for us to hide which objects are puzzle-related, a temptation we should resist because it puts us right back in the realm of hide-the-pixel puzzles. We need to believe enough in our obstacles, and the challenges necessary to surmount them, that we don't conceal them from players. This requires two different classes of objects: those that are just collateral damage, and those that are meaningful.

A balance must be struck between immersion and ease of gameplay. If we're using a cursor to target, unless it's the dot from a laser sight, we're already moving from the real world to game convention. If it glows a bit brighter when it moves over an important object, it's not intrusive, and the player accepts it. I think of it as a visual representation of instinct or experience in the game world, depending on who the player-character is. If the PC is the member of a SWAT team, experience would tell him which objects in a room are more important than the others. If the PC is one of Hitchcock's innocents on the run, then it is the survival instinct, or senses heightened by fear, whatever we need.

All of this additional detail means that something has to give. In the case of action games, we limit the world. The player does not have free access to the entire city of New York in an action game set there. Not every floor of every high-rise will be accessible and loaded with gameplay. We pare back scope just as we do in television and movies. The only medium that allows us the entire universe and all its inhabitants is prose. But even there, novelists are constantly making choices of where to cut back. At least for them the reason is not budgetary, but focusing and heightening the drama.

Another thing worth considering is the moral and ethical issues that are raised. I'm not talking now about the explicitness of the violence in the game, or sexual content. I'm talking about the choices we are giving the player. In the section on adaptations from other media (Chapter 7, "Once Upon a Time"), we talked about making sure to stay true to the morality—or lack of it—of the adapted characters. In Chapter 13, "The Roots of a New Storytelling," we discussed using branching as a way to introduce ethical choices. These are specific issues we address as we write and design. But in a game world where almost anything can be destroyed, we're opting out of making the decisions, and leaving them entirely in the hands of the players.

Should players be able to gun down or run down innocents in the street? This creates a serious dilemma for storytellers. One solution might be the smart cursor approach. Just as we alter the targeting crosshairs to point out important objects, we might disable them entirely when passing over an innocent NPC. This keeps a character "good" but at the expense of the very shooting range challenge designers were trying to emulate.

We may not care if players think we're condoning such activity. I hope we do. And if we do care, then there must be consequences for players who recklessly take or endanger life in the game world.

Some shooters try to emulate the difficulty of real gun ranges that train SWAT team members and anti-terrorist squads. The trainees in real life get points deducted from a session when they kill hostages instead of terrorists. But in actual fact, games that simply punish players by taking away points or even making them restart a level are presenting supposedly real life situations to which they attempt to apply game rules.

Maybe restarting a level is not punishment enough. Maybe the player-character must sit through a debriefing with a senior NPC investigating the shooting incident the way Internal Affairs (IA) officers would investigate a shooting in real life. But what would that do to the fun factor of the game?

A better way out would be to include consequences in the game, like capture and execution by opposing forces for war crimes; or the appearance of an overwhelming force that wipes the PC out because he was distracted by his bloodlust. Outside the game world, a screen announcing the immediate termination of the mission might appear. But if there is an ingame consequence, then ingame mission termination by the PC's boss or superior officer is also possible, just as it is if we're killed or discovered by the enemy.

The best answer is consequences for the player's decision within the fiction of the game, either by itself or as a transition out of the situation. It is a thematic solution. It doesn't break the fourth wall. It gives us another opportunity for storytelling and character revelation.

There's another moral issue: the killing of other human beings. For decades, the Star Trek franchise has been accused of xenophobia. The good guys are all human or at least humanoid with recognizable human values. The bad guys are often heartless humanoid aliens like the Romulans, or outright nasty non-humanoids like the pool of tar that ate Tasha Yar. Gene Roddenberry vigorously fought this sentiment. Over the course of the series more benign aliens were discovered, and more humans turned murderous for balance.

Movies and television can easily accommodate the slaughter of human beings by other human beings for one major reason. The audience isn't doing the slaughtering. In games the player pulls the trigger. To avoid dealing with the moral issues this raises, we have a number of fallback positions.

- There's the *Star Trek* solution. Nobody cares if you're blowing away slimy creatures with five eyes.

- There's the historical solution. Nobody cares if you're defending democracy from World War II Nazis or neo-Nazis. You have to be careful of race, of course. In World War II combat games, you can kill Japanese soldiers. Today they are our allies. I can't imagine any mainstream developer creating a game that pitted real world races against one another in violent conflict.

- There's the foreign nationals solution. Nobody cares if you're taking down armed hostiles from a nation bent on the destruction of your own country.

- There's the generalized terrorist solution. Nobody cares if you're terminating with extreme prejudice terrorists who owe no national allegiances, as long as you avoid too many references to religion.

- There's the generalized criminal solution. Criminals are bad guys. They deserve punishment as long as the punishment fits the crime. Slaughtering shoplifters in a department store might raise some eyebrows. *Grand Theft Auto: Vice City* is dealing with criminal gangs modeled on reality. Despite the protests, there's no evidence the developers are trying to say all Haitians are criminals any more than a theme of *The Sopranos* is that all Italians are in the Mafia.

- There's the mindless evil solution. It doesn't matter who the antagonist is if he is hell-bent on destroying all the good things in life like children playing; butterflies flitting; lovers walking hand-in-hand on a sunny day in the park. I feel like I'm going to break into song . . . it's okay. Luckily the urge passed. Of course, the mindless evil solution also pertains to all of the antagonist's minions if they remain indistinguishable from one another, spawning as needed like ants from an anthill you've poked a stick into. If they *are* distinguishable, all the better. Yet another opportunity for us to write zealots, traitors, weaklings, snitches; adversaries who are honorable, greedy, clever, stupid, sentimental, humorous, long-winded. . . .

- There's the fantasy solution. *Toontown* allows you to cause the bad guys, humorless robotic cogs, to break down, by using gags (jokes) for weapons. In virtual worlds, races become things like elves or Wookies. If there is PvP combat, players can play different races that are at odds with each other, and kill each other. It's an interesting dynamic we'll look at in Chapter 17, "Console Games."

Figure 15.3 Comedy gags are weapons in *Toontown*.

A casual glance at these solutions will give us a preview into why most games remain mired in only a few genres. We'll tackle that one in the next chapter.

Action games require pace, more so than any other type. As in action movies, we must keep our dialogue and stories lean. Robert Ludlum had 900 pages in which to tell his stories. With a couple of exceptions, the plots were so convoluted they do not translate well to movies, let alone games.

We don't have 900 pages. We don't want them. Every time we brake for exposition, we interrupt the race to the climax. That doesn't mean we have no twists. Surprise is an important part of storytelling. But we make it easy on ourselves as writers by creating twists that explain themselves even as they occur, rather than requiring elaborate explanations. Here is an example:

Mission briefing for Tara Boom, crack NSC agent: the player-character is told by her superior that there's a traitor in the NSC. There are three suspects. She'll have to storm an enemy safehouse to get the truth. Her superior gives her the escape plan to use once her mission is complete.

- Twist #1: a guard looks at her ID and lets her pass an early checkpoint (exposition in action).

- Twist #2: a higher level spy shakes her hand, believing she is the enemy's inside contact (twist #1 explained in action).

- Twist #3: Tara is assigned to hunt down the spy that has infiltrated the safehouse. (We already know Tara has been asked to hunt down herself.)

- Twist #4: Tara is contacted by her superior and told the three suspects are all dead. She must abort her mission before the enemy realizes their mistake (brief exposition).

- Twist #5: Her cover is immediately blown. Everybody's gunning for her (exposition in action).

- Twist #6: Tara overhears the safehouse boss getting instructions. The real traitor is still alive! (exposition in action).

- Twist #7: Tara finds bad guys waiting along her secret escape route, kills the safehouse boss, and automatically loots a significant clue from his body (exposition in action).

- Twist #8: Tara escapes only to find herself under arrest by her fellow agents. She's accused of being the traitor (exposition in action).

- Twist #9: Tara confronts her superior with the clue. He was the spy after all. (Brief exposition ties clue to superior.)

- Twist #10: Tara's superior escapes and swears revenge (exposition in action and beginning of transition to next mission).

That's ten twists in the simple linear storyline of a single mission. None of the twists require more than a sentence or two of exposition at the worst, and some are instantaneous. All should heighten the player's interest, yet none are so complex as to baffle the player. There is a very clear through line.

Weapons, ammo, health packs, and so on are not unique to action games, but they lean far more heavily on game convention than they need to. We don't want to pause the game to scoop up items, so we have the convention in action games of simply moving over them. Weapons are automagically loaded. We accept these conventions. In story terms, training a top operative would require them to grab anything they can use, and slam new clips into weapons without much thought. A less experienced character might be too concerned with dying to notice when the survival instinct kicks in and accomplishes the same tasks.

Health is a bit trickier. One of the conventions used in balancing an action game is that health is often automagically restored. If the player can find enough health packs or bandages or healing plants or whatever the game world's fiction accepts, their effect is nothing short of miraculous. The bad guys can spawn as many of their number as necessary to create the necessary challenge in a given level. The player is stuck with the PC and counters like health points and lives. We discussed the death of the player-character in Chapter 4, "Character Roles." This instantaneous health thing though is also a bother. It is a game solution to game balance that steps on story and character.

Like alternatives to player death, one solution doesn't appear to fit all unless it is stated as simply as: make it true to the game fiction. In a science-fiction or fantasy setting such miracles may find justification. In a game set in the present day focusing on stopping Columbian drug runners both in the U.S. and on their own turf, if we want to preserve as much of the fourth wall as possible, it's much better to place things like health in context.

A more realistic metaphor would be number and severity of wounds. Bandages staunch the bleeding, but a counter is activated, increasing the suspense. If the player doesn't complete the mission in a certain amount of time, the wounds become debilitating and the mission fails. Miraculous recovery can then occur *outside* of the game world.

Again it's all about balance. If the player heedlessly rounds a corner and comes face to face with the muzzle of a Kalishnikov, whatever happens next to the PC is deserved. If we go for suspense instead of shock, we can warn the player that there is a hostile around the next corner. We can give the PC the ability to peek or provide a security mirror or sound effects.

Usually there is no explanation whatsoever as to why hallways are littered with such items. Yet it is a simple matter to place them in context when the scene is set for a mission. The level is the scene of an earlier failed firefight. Bodies and weapons are still strewn about. The level is a warehouse where military supplies are stored. An earlier operative has planted the necessary tools here and there. These might be stashed in specially marked containers among similar containers that belong in the location. Scooping them up on the move is still permitted.

Half-Life was ground-breaking in its painstaking efforts to keep such conventions grounded in reality. The use of the biohazard suit gave the player-character a shell that had to be recharged, the equivalent of regaining health and armor. Weapons and ammo are found in supply cabinets. This attention to the reality of the experience is why *Half-Life* is more immersive than any ten other shooters on the market. Everybody knows we have to shorthand the game mechanics, but when the effort is taken to place such activities in the context of the narrative's fiction, we all win. The game mechanics no longer fight against the storytelling; they are part of it.

Shooter and stealther action games can take a couple of different forms: solo games for a single player-character and squad-level games where the player either controls several characters, or the computer controls them. Most of what we've been focusing on so far are solo games. Squad-level games where the computer is in control of team members allow greater chances for storytelling and character because of the additional interaction.

The player has his own Greek chorus tagging along to comment on the action; create relationships with the PC for the purposes of generating emotion; offering updates to mission briefs, opinions, and jokes. We can create an emotional attachment between any PC and NPC. If we're told we must free hostages, we can give them context which is emotionally charged like recognizable human plights: they've been tortured or are victims of genocide; they are women and children. There are lots of buttons to press, but the relationship remains static. When the NPCs are squad members, the relationships are continuing and can ebb and flow.

Once we've rescued hostages, we may still need to get them to safety, creating an interesting *Ico*-like dynamic. The NPCs *become* team members, and possibly can now be directed. And of course, they are all available for exposition, complaints, heroics, and humor.

Action games aren't all shooters or stealthers. Traditional sports games rely on the game itself for their storytelling. This isn't a rule carved on a stone tablet. It is a convention. A story involving a sports team is very viable, if players indicate interest. The same holds true for racing games.

Extreme sports are even more flexible. Traditions aren't solid yet. Anything goes. The games *Jet Set Radio Future* and *Dark Summit* take the action of an extreme sport (rollerblading and snowboarding, respectively) and translate it into a story in the way the movie *XXX* did.

Figure 15.4 Vin Diesel gets extreme in *XXX*.

There are as many solutions as our imaginations allow. Too often, if it fixes our gameplay problem, we stop there. The key is to think about a story context as well as a game context for our game design issues. Once a solution fits into the game world and is consistent with the fiction of the world, the problem is truly solved for both parts of the entertainment equation.

Adventure

Even if you couldn't already tell, it should come as no surprise that my first games were adventure games. When I entered the industry in 1994, adventure games were where you wanted to be if you were interested in story and character. Role-playing games caught up with them first, then action games, and finally, strategy games. But by their very nature adventure games ruled the roost.

There are a lot of theories as to why adventure games plummeted in popularity, and have never regained the imminence they once had. To a certain extent, all of them are true.

- Developers of adventure games grew complacent and our games stagnated. Puzzles were the chief obstacle, and their nature rarely changed. Monotony is not a primary goal of entertainment.
- Failed experiments in FMV limited the flexibility of our gameplay. The quality of the FMV was far below the standards of Hollywood production, even when Hollywood got involved.

- Improved graphics gave *Myst* and adventure games in general a new lease on life. People wanted something to show off their new video cards. But as CPUs became faster and able to drive more pixels, adventure games did not look so good when placed alongside action games.

- The demographics of the marketplace and our gaming culture changed. The first kids' games were adventures or interactive picture books. Soon the early kids' games were also action games. As they grew, they weren't interested in slowing down their entertainment.

- The fortunes of adventure games are tied to the personal computer, and for gamers, the computer is not the machine of choice at the moment. Consoles reign.

- The industry is cyclical. This is the second market peak for consoles, remember. RPGs were once dead, buried beneath thick manuals, and far more options than the average player could ever hope to learn or care to use. Then *Diablo* revived them with its RPG-lite style of play. Strategy games were on the outs until real-time strategy games like *Warcraft* and *Command and Conquer* appeared. Again simplicity was in. Adventure games were never sold as simple games. Theirs was the challenge of the crossword and the chess board.

Adventure games are still being made, of course. They also have been simplified, and there is a loyal following served by publishers and development houses like Dreamcatchers and Microids, and publishers with international connections (where adventure games fare better than the U.S.) like Ubisoft and Vivendi. Big budgets are allotted to other types of games. Still, there have been worthy examples in recent years: *Syberia*, the *CSI* games, and of course *Uru: Ages Beyond Myst*. Others are games for younger players built around franchises like Harry Potter and Nancy Drew.

Unfortunately, with sales of less than 20,000 for even a premier title like *Uru*, adventure games are currently a small niche. I'd love to revive *Sideshow*, or design a massively multiplayer adventure/RPG, but nobody has been beating down the door. In fact at this writing it looks like my next design *will* be an adventure game. I'd love to do it. Maybe, thanks to Harry Potter, a new generation of kids raised on adventure games will want to play them as adults!

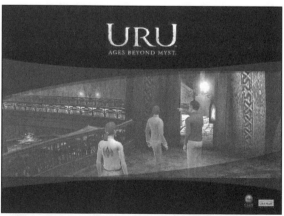

Figure 15.5 *Uru: Ages Beyond Myst* continues the best known adventure franchise.

Still, let's take a moment to look at challenges unique to adventure games. We find puzzles in all types of games these days, but they remain at the core of adventure games, and for that reason need more care taken in: 1) treating them like dramatic obstacles, and therefore opportunities for story advancement and character revelation; 2) making them logical within the fiction of the game world; 3) keeping them thematically consistent throughout a game.

In *The Siberian Cipher*, I had a complex puzzle suite centered on the player breaking into a Swiss bank vault. (You can find this section of the design on my Web site, if you'd like to see the entire puzzle suite.) One puzzle was based on O'Henry's short story *The Gift of the Magi*. It involved Ripley as a go-between, attempting to prevent two young lovers from making the mistake the characters in O'Henry's story made: giving up their most prized possessions to purchase gifts for one another that could only be used if they retained those prized possessions. The puzzle was not simply a mechanical puzzle, but a dramatic obstacle. It was logical within the fiction of the game world, and true to the characters. And it related to one of the major themes in the game: the nature of sacrifice.

Adventure games allow us the chance to construct more interesting puzzles than simple "find the key" exercises. The players have the time to appreciate them. Let's look at time for a moment. We have four kinds of timers at our disposal in game design.

- First there is *real* Real Time. The player is sitting at his computer and the clock on the wall is ticking. Few games use this timer. Virtual worlds occasionally do. In *Horizons*, players accumulate debilitating death points whenever they die and are resurrected. The counter on these continues to fall even if the player has logged out.

- Next is Game Time. The player-character is within the game world, and a clock in the game engine is ticking. If a shooter or strategy game measures the passing of time, this is the timer they use.

- Third there is Event Time. The player-character is within the game world, and there is the *illusion* that a real clock is ticking. Events are actually in control of the passage of time. The player may be given a limited amount of time to finish a mission but, in fact, may have as much time as he needs. Or the clock may only advance as the player does. To create suspense in *The Siberian Cipher* during the completion of a puzzle where Ripley finds himself locked in a trunk and dumped into the middle of Lake Geneva, I used Event Time. Every time the player completes one step of several in the necessary escape sequence, the level of water in the trunk rises, increasing the tension. The last step in the escape can only occur once the trunk is completely filled with water and Ripley is holding his breath. Yet Ripley will never drown. Event Time can be one solution to player-character death. In the game I'm currently working on, I'm using Event Time to create the illusion that the NPCs are going on with their lives even if the player-character is not present. It will appear as if it is just a lucky break that the PC seems to arrive at the most dramatic moments.

■ Last is turn-based. The game *explicitly* doesn't advance until the player completes her move. All strategy games used to be built as turn-based. *Civilization* is a good example. Now few are. Most are "real-time." Adventure games are almost always turn-based to give the player time to think.

Turn-based and Event Time give adventure game writers an added opportunity to tell story and reveal character. The game convention allows the player to sit there as long as she wants mulling over an obstacle. Designers occasionally add Game Time puzzles, but they remain unpopular with players. There are times when adventure gamers do not want to be rushed.

Another challenge is the same as action games, but different. That's pace. In action games we don't want to interrupt the pace. In adventure games the pace must lag to give us time to think, and solve puzzles. So the trick is how to get the pace revved back up again. Like other games, adventures fall back on cut scenes and the inherent problems of segregation of story and gameplay. They allow for far more flexibility in game engine storytelling because of the changes in pace built into their design. It would seem the blend of story and gameplay should be much farther advanced, but it seems to be at exactly the same point as other types of games.

How can we create pace? By varying the difficulty of puzzles. Start out with simple puzzles to settle the player into the game, then increase the challenge. Then when the game is approaching the climax again, simplify once more. Not only does this increase pace, but the player will think the game has made her smarter. This is not a bad thing. It will look good on the box—"Our game will increase your I.Q.!" It's certainly every bit as true as announcing that the game will put you in the middle of a movie, or that MMORPGs have somehow reached their second and third generations without actually leaving the first.

Another way is by narrowing the world. Adventure game worlds are like action game worlds: subsets of the real world. There are even tighter budget and time restrictions. But because adventure gamers don't require that every bottle on a bar be destroyable, attention can be paid to those elements of areas that are directly connected to plot and gameplay. This focus is of great benefit to the storytelling and presenting the theme. And this allows us to expand the world a bit more. Adventure games adapt easily to the modular structure. Then as story threads are tied off, the size of the world can shrink, to compel a faster race to the finish.

In *Dark Side of the Moon*, we had a perfect context for narrowing the world: the moon was becoming unstable and was going to explode. Earthquakes shook the mining colony. Shafts caved in. Passages players once explored were blocked. In the final rush to escape the moon, there was really only one route open to the PC, Jake. This kind of situation is like all those action movies and multiple-jeopardy movies that are structured the same way. Movies don't like to give their characters multiple ways to escape from danger. That leads to discussing options, not action. Give them one option, make it seem impossible, then force them into it. That's how movies increase suspense and pace. Adventure games can do the same thing. (So can action games of course; the need simply isn't as great. The pace of the game is already there.)

Narrowing the world need not necessarily mean only its geography. Another related way to increase pace is to reduce the number of tasks to be performed; number of characters to interact with; or the player-character's inventory.

A villain emptied Ripley's inventory near the end of *The Riddle of Master Lu* as a third act reversal. I broke my own rules by allowing the actions of an NPC in the world of the game to break the fourth wall when the villain bent over a fallen Ripley, and as he rifled his pockets, the player saw the inventory display on the interface drain item by item. My reasoning went like this: it was a third act reversal scene we've watched over and over again in movies and television and I wanted to spoof that. Also the game convention of inventory is directly related to possessions, so theoretically anyway, a villain in the game world should have access to the PC's possessions. And finally, by the end of an adventure game, the player has a huge puzzle-solving arsenal at her disposal in inventory. I wanted the player to start from scratch for the endgame.

Adventure games have more opportunities to tell story built into them than any other type of game. With all those chances, you'd think adventures would be miles ahead of other types of games in thought-provoking themes and rich characters. They aren't.

Two popular recent adventure games, *Syberia* and *Syberia II*, are beautiful-looking dream-like fairy tales, but at their core they are as insubstantial as a snowflake. I know *URU* well because I worked on it in one of its incarnations. You aren't going to find any of the cultural satire of *Grand Theft Auto: Vice City* or the ethical geo-political situations from *Splinter Cell: Pandora Tomorrow* in any of the recent adventure games I've seen.

This is disappointing and surprising to me. It doesn't cost any more to create games that push the envelope of ideas. If you want to break out of a niche, you have to make waves. I see no more than ripples. The paradigm remains stagnant.

Figure 15.6 *Syberia II:* dreams are sometimes not enough.

Role-Playing

Just as weapons and ammo litter hallways in shooters, treasure boxes have been left lying around in most dungeons. It's one of those conventions copied, but not thought about very much. As in shooters simply finding a reason for the litter is sometimes all that is necessary. The game mechanic may remain the same: click on the box and it opens. Either the contents go directly into inventory, or the player can choose which items to take. But answering the design question without addressing the fiction of the game world is to needlessly treat the storytelling as a second class citizen.

Character exposition in computer RPGs started as simply the stats and abilities the player-character or other party members had. The advantage of strength a warrior had over a wizard, or the ability the wizard had to cast spells that the warrior lacked, were the only differences in character. This is a direct result of the development of RPGs from tabletop games where the players gave their characters personality and dialogue.

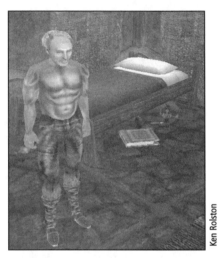

Over time however RPGs began adding more typical character traits. In contrast to RPG-lite games like *Diablo*, two series of RPGs embody for me the current state of affairs in RPG character development beyond stats and abilities: *Baldur's Gate* and *Morrowind*. In the sidebar *Morrowind* designer Ken Rolston describes revealing character through environment.

Figure 15.7 Caius Cosades from *Morrowind*.

Ken Rolston, Writer/Designer

To have weight, a primary character requires exposition.

Obvious methods of exposition, like dialogue, are perceived and resented by the player as awkward and manipulative. Dialogue, in particular, appears awkward and manipulative because it is, in a game, so far inferior in flavor and freedom to its real world counterpart.

Visual cues to character are discovered by the player through the player's free and unconstrained exploration and observation, and, as such, are more subtle, less awkward and obtrusive, and more unconsciously acceptable in shaping the player's response to the character.

Caius Cosades is the player's first and most important informant and patron in Morrowind. He is a spymaster, an agent of the Empire and Emperor, and your primary quest giver.

Three visual details define Caius Cosades: his bare chest, the skooma pipe beneath his bed, and the book he is reading.

Caius Cosades is the only character in *Morrowind* with a bare chest. He is an old man, which makes his bare chest seem more peculiar. And it is a strongly muscled chest, which is even more peculiar. He will be your boss. He is an old, creepy guy who lives in one room—but he looks like an old creepy guy who could kick your ass.

The skooma pipe openly visible beneath his bed reveals that Caius Cosades is a drug addict. A spymaster who is a drug addict? That does not inspire our confidence in his judgment as our spymaster.

The book, "The War of the First Council," a historical summary of the political and religious conflicts of *Morrowind*'s major factions, presented in the voice of a serious and reflective Imperial scholar, introduces the major characters in the backstory of the ancient events inciting the major action of *Morrowind*'s plot. The old man is a creepy crack addict, but his bedtime reading is serious history.

Thus, by looking at Caius and exploring the items by his bed, we get the impression that Caius Cosades is an eccentric, creepy old man, with a disordered but fundamentally earnest and serious mind.

Figure 15.8 Ken Rolston, as he appears in the person of Socucius Ergalla, your guide through character generation in *Morrowind*.

At first, we have a strong emotional reaction to what we see. The bare chest is odd, vaguely sexual, and repellent in an old man. The skooma pipe is worrying—I'm taking orders from a drug addict?

But the book tempers our uneasy response with a reflection of Caius's mind—a serious mind studying the exotic culture of the foreign country of his posting.

Thus we begin our relationship with a strong, at best ambivalent, emotional response to Caius Cosades, tempered by an intriguing hint of his mind's inner workings.

These are the features I'm proud of in his exposition.

On the other hand, I'm sorry we didn't take the same care with the other 3,000 characters in *Morrowind*. If we had, we would have rewarded the inquisitive and observant player every time he encountered a new character, and would have taught him to explore and savor their intriguing personalities—before he killed them and went through their pockets.

RPGs were the second type of game after adventures to embrace storytelling. As in the case of RPG characters, RPG storylines matured to fill the gap left by the lack of a human Game Master. In tabletop role-playing, just as players bring their characters to life, it is the job of the Game Master to bring the world and the story to life.

Computer RPGs are perfect for storytelling. In them the story is authored just as it was when it was written by the GM. The difference is that the GM could react to the gameplay on the fly, and adjust the story like the parent telling a story to a child who bombards her with questions. In single-player RPGs, players don't demand such flexibility (although they do in virtual worlds, as we shall see). This gives writers of solo RPGs the freedom to create elaborate worlds full of interesting characters and thrilling adventures.

There is a trade-off however. RPGs today are less limited by geography than action or adventure games. There are entire worlds to explore. Some, like *Dungeon Siege*, try to emulate earlier, simpler story structures by limiting player exploration even more than most action and adventure games.

Other games are far more open. The *Baldur's Gate* series uses a modified python structure controlled by the ingame mapping system. Some areas of the world that players would normally be able to visit do not show up on the map until certain conditions are met. This allows the writers to advance the story in a linear fashion while the gameplay permits players to roam within revealed areas.

Other games open their worlds, but restrict player access by making the challenges in certain regions far too dangerous for low-level player-characters. As players gain in skills and abilities, they can survive these more advanced areas. This recognition of level is used in character encounters as well where NPCs carrying high level functions in the world can refuse to deal with player-characters until they are stronger.

Such methods are gameplay solutions only thinly disguised as belonging to the world fiction. It is because they are capable of allowing open-ended exploration that RPGs have attracted me in recent years as a perfect opportunity for modular storytelling. In fact the *Might and Magic* RPG series used a simple modular structure for many of the quests. To fill out the world quests were added that did not advance the story, only the player-character by providing xp and items. These quests may have been consistent with the world fiction, but because they were not tied to the narrative there were no variables that needed to be tracked. So while the basic structure was there, the designers did not take advantage of all those quests to advance narrative as true modular storytelling would have allowed.

Because RPGs track so many stats, the stats themselves can be used in storytelling. We've talked about how relationships with NPCs can be affected by player actions. They can also be affected by player stats. The first time a player-character enters a village she may be low-level, unskilled, and dressed in cast-off leather. Villagers can treat her with disdain. Perhaps a kindly cleric has sympathy for her and sends her off to do some errands. Later the same player-character, now battle-hardened and wearing shining mail may return. Now she is respected.

Hopefully the villagers she interacted with at the lower level remember her, and are quick to apologize for their behavior. The cleric may react with pride, and now humbly ask if the PC can undertake a much more important mission. The relationships can be further affected by how the player decides to respond to this new state of affairs. She might bully merchants into reducing their prices, or shrug off the cleric's entreaty. Or she could find forgiveness for their past behavior and be offered lower prices. Doing the good deed for the cleric could result in no monetary reward, but a blessing that increases her chances of survival. Even though stats are a game mechanic they can support storytelling, given a chance.

Simulations

We are going to look at two types of simulations. Combat simulations focus on military equipment such as planes, helicopters, and tanks. Social simulations focus on social systems such as families, cities, and industries.

Whereas action games run the risk of alienating players if they cast them as crack pilots then allow them to crash over and over again, players of combat simulations accept the challenge. Where action games simplify controls as much as possible yet still try to maintain verisimilitude, simulations take pride in accurately modeling controls, maneuverability and physics. If a simulation features an Abrams tank, the tank had better look and act like one, or the simulation player will be up in arms.

Combat simulations have become another niche market like adventure games. As the games industry has grown, more players are attracted to the razzle-dazzle than the finely detailed environments of simulations. Racing games in particular take great pains to keep controls simple whether the player is at the wheel of a Ferrari, straddling a Harley, or balancing on a skateboard. These more free-wheeling action games recognize their younger demographic wants to be able to do cool things they can't in real life. Simulations appeal to an older demographic who takes pride in the mastery of the simulation.

In recent years, simulations have added story, but they face a couple of challenges unique to their game type.

- First, they are only borderline games anyway. They must be far more aware of real world details, even at the expense of action.

- Secondly, they have difficulty inserting story into the simulation because it can distract from operating controls. If there are plot moves, they are brief and to the point: a comrade is in trouble; mission parameters abruptly change due to increased numbers of hostiles; new information, not available at the mission briefing, is suddenly communicated to the player.

As a result if there is any storytelling to be done, it is confined to mission briefings. Some may not even attempt to tell a story from mission to mission in any other terms than a campaign such as the Battle of the Bulge or rescue missions during a natural disaster.

In no other game type do story and "gameplay" feel more at odds than these kinds of simulations. It isn't impossible, but writers need to recognize the rigid limitations of the form. As soon as a simulation begins to concentrate on story it almost invariably becomes an action game.

The second type of simulation holds more promise for storytelling, yet ironically its most successful example leaves all the storytelling up to the interaction between game and player. These are social simulations like *Rollercoaster Tycoon* and the standard-bearer of this type: the *Sims* franchise. *Sims* adventures would seem a natural next step.

Other variations of social simulations center on interesting and visually exciting industries such as theme parks and transportation. All such arenas are as ripe for storytelling as they are in other media. Here story can be tied to the fortunes of the player the way they are in RPGs. As the player advances by mastering the simulation, story twists like natural disasters and computer-controlled rivals are obvious. Even *Sim City* added tornadoes and fires to spice up play.

Taking such incidents to the next stage and building an entire story on player advancement makes perfect sense. It is, in fact, the area I've looked at most when my mind turns to chaos theory and fractals. You didn't read that section? Shame on you! Seeding story in social situations is as obvious to me as it is in psychology when researchers confront participants with variables. "What if?" they ask. There are sociologists who deliberately break *Star Trek*'s Prime Directive when modeling cultures to see how they will respond. They are seeding stories the way we seed fractals. Okay, enough about fractals. Let's move on to the next section.

Strategy

Strategy games, like all types of games we've discussed here except adventures, did not start out telling stories. They began by presenting players with a broad canvas in contrast to simulation's detailed models. Over time, as action games and simulations began to place their missions in context, strategy games did the same.

Civilization, arguably one of the very few games that will stand the test of time and be seen as a classic, presented a diversity of turn-based gameplay that took players from a single wandering tribe to the establishment of a colony on

Figure 15.9 *Civilization*: one of the best computer games yet.

a planet circling Alpha Centauri generations later. It needed no more story than that. Characters were either units or opposing rulers controlled by the computer.

A few years ago, strategy games had reached a plateau shared by RPGs and simulations and adventures. The number of players was not growing. Action games were attracting most of the players. RPGs were finally reinvented as RPG-lite. Combat simulations were simplified and became action games centered on a specific piece of equipment. Strategy games moved to the action of "real-time." Interest in all three benefited as a result with strategy games and RPGs becoming very popular.

What all three types of games gave up was depth. Heavy manuals shrunk to almost nothing. Choices were reduced. They had to be. Players needed to make decisions as the game clock continued to tick. The computer opponents weren't sitting around, leafing through manuals. They could react to player moves instantly. It became necessary to artificially slow them down. And it became necessary to simplify the gameplay so us mere mortals could compete.

Just as in RPGs and action games, strategy games substituted action for depth. Some stopped there. Others like *Age of Empires* added specific campaigns. Games like *Command and Conquer* wrapped their campaigns in story told in cut scenes.

The difficulty in integrating story into gameplay in strategy games is the omniscient POV they require. Strategy players need to see as much of the geography as possible. *Starcraft* balanced its "unit view" somewhat with large-sized character profiles that talked. As we zoom back, we don't have characters anymore. If a game has only units, they lose their individuality.

It's not impossible to create individual characters players can care about or tell their stories, but it's more difficult. It may help to remember that stories are not tied to the medium. They can be shaped by a particular medium, but they require little more than the ability of the storyteller to touch the imaginations of the audience. That hunter spinning yarns by the fire, or a grandparent telling a story to a sleepy child, are not relying on pictures to advance the story. We have our picture book metaphor from children's games, but that is due to the demographics of the player. They aren't necessary. The tribe's artist may have painted the story of a hunt on the wall of the cave, but words came first, not graphics. (The most famous cave paintings in the world were found in France, also home to some of our most celebrated artists. I wonder if there's a connection.)

If the story is compelling enough, the characters involved in it can be the size of ants. They can come alive as characters if we allow them to. Must every unit in a strategy game be treated so well? Of course not. Not every one of the thousands of slaves in *Spartacus* gets dialogue, only the stars like Kirk Douglas and Tony Curtis. But any slave could have a three-dimensional character and a story to tell in the strategy game version of *Spartacus*. We, the writers, get to decide which ones.

God games, a sub-type of strategy game, usually share the challenges of other strategy games. Only one in recent memory, Peter Molyneaux's *Black & White*, attempted to chart a new course. A kind of kitchen-sink game design in that game overshadowed the story and often players as well resulting in an interesting, if bewildering and ultimately frustrating, experiment.

Strategy games may not lend themselves as readily to narrative as action, adventure, and role-playing games, but there are still avenues to be explored, just as there are in social simulations. All it takes is a designer willing to try and a receptive audience.

Multiplayer

Many action games, strategy games, and RPGs feature Player versus Player gameplay. Player versus Player is outside the scope of this book. The only multiplayer type of game that really interests us as writers is cooperative multiplayer where two to four players share a console; or two and up play over a network or online. The difference is that in cooperative multiplayer the players work together. Computer-controlled team members are routinely replaced with human beings, although this doesn't need to be the case. There's no rule that says you can't have both.

Cooperative players can experience any encounters or plot twists together. An interesting variation allows players to separate. On consoles the screen must be split, and therefore both players can experience first hand what one is doing. Over a network connection or the internet players can retain full screen. This is much more "realistic" because players must communicate their adventures to one another.

Once cooperative players are able to split up, the storytelling becomes a greater challenge, but the rewards are commensurate. Players can immerse themselves more easily, relaying information, or calling for help. The story can be made up of areas and incidents that can be played separately or together with differing results. Players may encounter the same NPCs at different times, and form dissimilar relationships with them.

Whether the stories are linear, branching, web, or modular doesn't matter. Diverging gameplay allows us to explore alternatives; come at obstacles from different sides; and experience many more variations on single-player play. It promotes more socializing—and remains fertile ground for different storytelling structures in the future.

Virtual worlds belong on this list as well, but their differences are significant enough to warrant a couple of chapters on their own.

CHAPTER 16

GAME GENRES

In this chapter we're going to examine various genres and how well they map to games; to which types of games they are best suited; and which challenges each one presents to the writer. There are hybrids, of course, that contain elements from more than one genre. The *Resident Evil* games take horror conventions and mix them with science fiction and, eventually, post-apocalyptic science fiction.

This is not meant to be an all-inclusive list. Comedy has been with us since the beginning of this book, and hopefully it hasn't all been unintentional. In particular, we looked at various styles of comedy in games in Chapter 11, "Story Chiropractics." The genres that remain are heavily weighted towards *melodrama*.

Melodrama is a term I've deliberately avoided up till now, mainly because it suggests a low grade type of entertainment and I didn't want to confuse the issue by defending it. If I were to admit up front that most of what we do is melodrama, it might have seemed as if I was saying it's okay to go for the lowest common denominator. Saying "It's just melodrama," is as bad as saying, "It's only a game." We do not deserve to be let off the hook so easily.

But now that you understand the importance of three-dimensional characters, and the care with which stories should be constructed, you're ready to handle the monkey wrench melodrama tosses into the works. Let's bring melodrama out on stage and have a look at it.

The word melodrama began life as a description for musical theatre. In the 19th century, it attached itself to florid dramas where characters were starkly contrasted and broadly written as either virtuous and good or dastardly evil. The plots were simple, and the acting style over-the-top. The critics twirled their moustaches and sneered at melodrama. Society matrons turned up their noses at it. Common folk lapped it up.

www.dazeofourlives.com

Figure 16.1 Melodrama took center stage in the 19th century.

In fact, most of entertainment in any medium is melodrama. The pit at the Globe The-atre was home to common folk, and Shakespeare wrote to them as much as he did to the aristocracy in their balconies. Almost all film and television is melodrama. Drama is still found on the stage, one of the reasons certain plays perform wonderfully in London's West End or on Broadway, then fail when they go on tour. With a rare exception, the *New York Times* fiction bestseller list is a list of melodramatic novels.

Today the pit is the mass market, not the aristocracy. If you want to sell big, sell to the pit. Let's look at a couple of definitions of melodrama.

note

MELODRAMA: a dramatic form that depends on sensation, simplistic plotting, stereotypical char-acters, coincidence, implausibility, and artificially happy endings.

Ick. Here's another.

note

MELODRAMA: a dramatic form that focuses on action, clear plotlines, characters who personify good and evil, plot twists, and morally unambiguous resolutions.

Hmm. Not so bad. Which is the true definition? Both are, of course. Or the answer lies somewhere in between. A discussion pitting melodrama and drama against one another—Drama good! Melodrama bad!—is as pointless to me as one pitting story and gameplay against one another.

The difference to me is in the quality of the execution. Two more definitions illustrate this.

note

PATHOS: a dramatic quality that evokes sympathy, pity, or sorrow.

note

BATHOS: a dramatic quality that attempts to evoke sympathy, pity, or sorrow, but fails, often arousing laughter instead of tears.

We recognize 19th century melodrama today as being packed with bathos. And it certainly shows up in popular media where a failure to establish an audience's empathy in characters leads to irritation, not compassion. However, if we are able to craft characters the audience identifies with and cares about; if we write such scenes with some restraint and sensibility, we can achieve pathos in either drama or melodrama.

The lines are blurred, and it is to our benefit to blur them. It may help critics and college professors to draw rigid distinctions, but it doesn't serve writers well. Just as it is counterproductive to analyze to the point where we lose sight of the whole experience; or dangerous to rely on lists without history and context, trying to find the lines of demarcation between drama and melodrama only serves to cut off useful aspects that are applicable to both.

Remember William Archer unapologetically defending drama in Chapter 9, "Bringing the Story to Life"?

> "It may be thought a point of inferiority in dramatic art that it should deal so largely in shocks to the nerves, and should appeal by preference, wherever it is reasonably possible, to the cheap emotions of curiosity and surprise. But this is a criticism, not of dramatic art, but of human nature."

Is he yelling at the common folk down in the pit? He wouldn't be that silly. No actor ever won an argument with the pit. Don Rickles, the famous comedian of insults known as "Mr. Warmth" and "The Merchant of Venom," has been attacked more than once by audience members over his nearly 50-year career. The pen may be mightier than the sword, but the fist can often end the joke. What is it called? Ah yes: the punch line.

Archer, writing in 1912, is able to defend drama even as he derides melodrama elsewhere in *Playmaking*, because he sees what the two share in common, yet appreciates the difference in execution. It's *all* in the execution.

Bathos, one-dimensional characters, implausibility, and artificial story construction don't belong in today's melodrama anymore than they do in drama. That they crop up all the time is a testament to bad writing, directing, acting, or any combination of those. No one denies that melodrama goes for the throat, yet it can do so with some grace and style, and when it does, the audience welcomes it with willing suspension of disbelief.

Are the recent movies *Mystic River*, *The House of Sand and Fog*, and *The Human Stain* drama, melodrama, or tragedy? They are all three. A third definition of melodrama would incorporate its heightened drama, but at the same time allow for its human drama as well. I write melodrama. We all do. To do it well is the key.

Figure 16.2 *Mystic River.* Currents of melodrama and tragedy flow as one.

As I said, almost all of the genres that follow are home to melodrama as much as drama. Comedy is the only exception, although it has its own versions of melodrama in farce, slapstick, and burlesque. A classic moment in both a murder mystery and a farce is the flinging open of a closet door. In a mystery, a dead body falls out. In a farce the body is alive and wearing only underwear.

What are the most popular genres in games? Fantasy and science fiction. Why? The reasons aren't hard to find.

- The roots of many of the first games came from these genres: tabletop games like *Dungeons & Dragons* and films like *Star Wars* were popular at the beginning of the personal computer revolution.

- The primary crossover audience from other media is still a fantasy and sci-fi audience. The audience remains predominantly young and male. Cross media fertilization is now a big marketing focus.

- They are overwhelmingly the genres of preference for many game developers attracted by technology, interactivity, and the possibility of creating anything our imaginations can conjure.

- Fantasy and sci-fi allow us a wider range of solutions to fiction-breaking game problems like player-character death, tissue regeneration, and so on.

- Locales are more flexible. They may resemble real-world models, but the genres allow for all sorts of bending of the rules. It's easier to create an alien world than to duplicate our real one. In games set here and now on planet Earth, we're more likely to spot details that aren't correct or shortcuts taken to reduce the game world to a manageable size.

Let's take a look at each of these two popular genres in turn.

Fantasy

When we speak of fantasy in computer games, we mainly mean high fantasy, the realm of elves and dwarves and magic handed down to us from various mythologies, such as Celtic and Norse, codified by J.R.R. Tolkien, borrowed by tabletop role-playing, and digitized in role-playing games from *Wizardry* and *Ultima* and *Might & Magic* to *Morrowind, Baldur's Gate, Diablo,* and their massively multiplayed cousins like *Ultima Online, Everquest,* and *Dark Age of Camelot.*

Curiously enough, when one attempts to define high fantasy, it starts to sound familiar. High fantasy is concerned with epic battles between good and evil; stereotypical *types* of characters; simple plotlines with clear goals; and morally unambiguous resolutions. Do I have to state again that there are exceptions? No? Good. High fantasy sounds a lot like melodrama, doesn't it? It should, and God bless both their houses.

Fantasy is a comfortable genre. We grew up with it via fairy tales; then watched it take over the bestseller lists, thanks to the acolytes of Tolkien, such as Raymond Feist with his Riftwar Saga, Robert Jordan and his *Wheel of Time* series, Terry Goodkind and his *Sword of Truth* series, David Eddings' *Belgariad,* and on and on. Interestingly enough, high fantasy has not done as well as you might expect in other media, not at least until Peter Jackson's triumphant return to the source in the *Lord of the Rings* trilogy of films.

Figure 16.3 J.R.R. Tolkien, father of Middle Earth.

So the crossover here is from books to games, an unusual occurrence, but potent enough to drive the sales of many games. The type of game most known for fantasy is, of course, role-playing, although we see the console action version in games like *Baldur's Gate: Dark Alliance;* strategy in games such as *Age of Mythology;* and action games like Glen Dahlgren's *The Wheel of Time,* based on the Robert Jordan series.

The first challenge the writer of high fantasy has is facing the conventions of the genre. Fat axe-wielding elves and tall wise dwarves just won't play outside of comedy. No matter whose world we base our game on, or even if we invent a "new" one, we must be respectful of high fantasy's conventions the same way we would be respectful of a license. If we make an exception, we do it because we know the rule, and have a very definite reason to break it.

Being respectful of the source material creates all sorts of challenges. Earlier, I said we expect certain stereotypical types of characters. We need to recognize this as not being a license to write stereotypes. Instead, the skillful author should bring them to better than one-dimensional life.

Plots should not blindly follow the same "small band of adventurers on an impossible quest" cliché. We need our quests in our games, but should find other dramatic situations as well. Some authors focus on the politics of their worlds; others on the romantic lives of their characters.

Raymond Feist and David Eddings slavishly follow Campbell's hero's journey in their first books, but are then faced with a similar predicament. Their heroes reach the end of their journeys, but there are still more books to write. Pug in the Riftwar Saga becomes the most powerful wizard in most of the known universes. How does the author put such a character in danger? How do we empathize with him?

We usually avoid answering these questions because our game stories end at the moment of ascension to power or riches, Campbell's *The Return*. But sequels challenge us again. As our player-characters and other party members rise in levels, we must boost the power of their antagonists. This is not simply a question of game balance, but of story balance as well. If we just keep leveling our characters up, we risk losing the empathy even if we continue to provide danger.

Many game writers and designers seem to view a genre only from the outside. They copy the conventions without knowing why they are there, or where they came from. Then they find themselves wallowing in cliché. Me-too games are the equivalent of direct-to-video movies. The moves are all there, but something essential is missing. It is the creative commitment of a writer or designer who doesn't do his job.

Too often, the answer is to cop an attitude and distance themselves, as if to say "This material is really beneath me, so I'll just have some fun with it instead." The genre isn't beneath them; they are beneath it. Learning the conventions of the genre and respecting them is a sure sign of an experienced professional writer. She then knows when it's time to add her own vision into the mix and bring that genre truly alive once again.

Other forms of fantasy crop up of course. If high fantasy takes us to hopefully fully realized worlds, low fantasy concerns the intrusion of fantasy into our more rational world—like horror in Bob Bates' *Blackstone Chronicles*, based on a story by John Saul, and Jane Jensen's Gabriel Knight adventures.

It's easy to follow the silver bullet, stake through the heart, conventions of most forms of fantasy. As Curt Siodmak wrote for *The Wolfman*: "Even a man who is pure at heart and says his prayers by night, may become a wolf when the wolfbane blooms and the autumn moon is bright . . ." It's much harder when you start from an entirely blank page.

Many console games create wacky worlds all their own like *Rayman*, the *Mario* series, and *Spyro the Dragon*. These worlds are unique unto themselves and offer the greatest opportunity for the writer's imagination to run riot because they are not based on accepted traditions of the genre. The writer/designer must be particularly careful to be consistent in whatever laws govern their worlds.

The fact that these games are also comedic and whimsical gives the authors some leeway, but it is also a danger. However crazy the logic, it must still make sense in context. A schizophrenic's logic is never crazy to the schizophrenic.

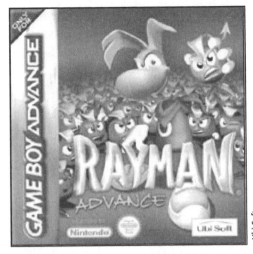

Figure 16.4 *Rayman:* a world all his own.

Ubi Soft

Writing fantasy characters is its own challenge. All of a sudden we are faced with a huge variety of creatures at various stages of sentient evolution that we can interact with. Here too, it's important not to get carried away when given all that freedom. To keep the characters grounded in emotion and behavior that is recognizable to an audience, and that can therefore create empathy, we *anthropomorphize* them.

note

ANTHROPOMORPHIC: describes assigning human characteristics to non-human creatures and inanimate objects.

How far we want to take this depends on the character and the world fiction of course. But the combination of human qualities with the non-human substance of the character can create delightful characters like Yoda, Ents, or Dorothy II from *The Little Shop of Horrors*.

Fantasy will remain popular. No genre connects more directly to our imagination than fantasy. All worlds are possible. It's our challenge to make sure they're believable too.

Science Fiction

Science fiction games share with fantasy an exhilarating unrestraint in their ability to portray alien worlds that stretch our imaginations both as writers and as players. The difference in science fiction, as the term implies, starts with some basis in recognizable science. Flying horses who take wing through magic are replaced by flying saucers that soar thanks to anti-matter drives.

There are many sub-genres of science fiction. Just a few are space operas like *Wing Commander*; alternate realities and parallel universes as in *Half-Life*; post-apocalyptic games like *Fallout*; cyber-punk like William Gibson's *Necromancer*; time travel as in *The Journeyman Project* series; and like fantasy, the creation of entirely new worlds and cultures like Frank Herbert's *Dune* or Anne MaCaffrey's *Pern* series of books.

Many of these sub-genres have been strip mined enough. How many stories have we seen in so many media where someone from the future journeys into the past to correct something, or someone stumbles into the future from the past? Do we really want another post-apocalyptic or cyber-punk vision of the future any time soon? I need one about as much as I need another player-character with amnesia. Please . . . just say no.

If RPGs are the most likely home to fantasy, shooters seem to be most attracted to science fiction these days. It makes sense. Shooter players enjoy the potent weaponry science fiction can provide. As we've seen, blowing away aliens is less ethically problematic than human beings. And difficulties with health and player-character death have more possible solutions.

Science fiction also shows up in strategy games like *Starcraft* and *Command and Conquer*, both notable among this type of game for their interest in storytelling. Whereas *Command & Conquer* is wholly reliant on cut scenes, *Starcraft* deserves an additional mention for the attempt to combine gameplay and story.

Adventure games too are comfortable with science fiction. In addition to the confined settings of space ships and remote outposts on distant planets, the relatively sterile environments can

Figure 16.5 Story and strategy coexist in *Starcraft*.

help with puzzles. One way to avoid pixel hunts is to limit the number of interactive objects in an area. This works against immersion when, in an environment meant to simulate the world we live in, only one book on a shelf or only a few items scattered on furniture are interactive. In space, we seem to accept the fact that desks are cleaner; corridors are devoid of plants; all reading material is confined to files on a computer; and so on. We don't need to clutter our sets with non-interactive objects in the name of verisimilitude.

The percentage of interactive objects goes up as the overall number of objects decreases. It becomes that much easier to find the important ones. I used this "less is more" philosophy in *Dark Side of the Moon*. The player needed to be able to purchase items from the company store. One way to do that was to find ore and sell it to Hunter, the owner of the mining colony's casino. I could scatter bits of low grade ore here and there for players, and because of the lack of clutter, they weren't that hard to find. (Later on, I gave them access to another character's credit card, giving them the ability to buy out the store if they wanted. This was another way of increasing the pace of the game. The necessity of gathering ore was bypassed.)

Whereas high fantasy can be limited by convention, science fiction is limited by its roots. Since science fiction must be at least an extrapolation of some facet of real science, we must be cautious in writing it to make it at least plausible. It is that tie to science that demands more care be taken to ensure a willing suspension of disbelief.

A major reason *Half-Life* works as well as it does is because of the hard science feel of the Black Mesa Research Facility where something has gone horribly wrong. We've already talked about how gameplay necessities, like guns and ammo and health and armor, are in sync with the reality of such a research facility.

One of the *System Shock* games, RPG-shooter hybrids, takes place on a space station taken over by a computer gone mad named SHODAN. Its sequel is set on a research vessel, the *Von Braun*, bound for Tau Ceti to investigate a mysterious transmission. Here again the game world is based on hard science. Story delivery in the *System Shock* games is surprisingly one-note: messages, data disks, and even psychic transmissions in the sequel. What sets them apart is the oppressive, menacing atmosphere created by their confined settings, and most importantly, sound that can alert the player to danger ahead. Again, the verisimilitude of the locations helps us to accept the fiction.

Another challenge for writers of science fiction games is similar to the concern in fantasy about the level of power of the player-character and her antagonists. In fantasy anything can happen if it's set up properly. The same is true of science fiction. Because science fiction looks at the unknown and asks "What if?," just about anything can descend from the night sky with evil intent.

We ran into this challenge all the time on *Star Trek: Next Generation*. Too many times, we were faced with alien beings that were unlike anything the crew of the *Enterprise* had seen before. And every time an unbeatable alien was beaten by the *Enterprise*, the ship and its crew gained in levels, at least in the audience's mind. So the most unstoppable, unbeatable enemy imaginable, the Borg, was introduced.

Every story structured like this has what we call a *penny drop* scene; that moment when a character suddenly gets very excited and yells, "Of course! They live on an arid planet!

What if we sprayed them with a garden hose???" The term comes from that satisfying clink you hear when a coin drops into the telescope on an observation deck, a vending machine, or pay telephone. You've done the one thing that will gain you the result you want.

The Borg's weakness was realized in the first penny drop scene. They were all linked as one mind, apparently wired in series. Like a string of Christmas lights, you can take out all by breaking one. Then sometime later the Borg reappeared in the *Star Trek* universe. Only now they were able to adapt to the weapons that had previously defeated them. Another penny drop scene was needed.

This scenario illustrates another term, *formulaic*.

note

FORMULA: a string of clichés, plot moves so predictable the audience can recite them as the action unfolds.

Science fiction games fall into formula even more than fantasy: *System Shock II's* mysterious signal is a perfect example, and its predecessors range from Arthur C. Clarke's Rama books to *Alien*.

We can't make the mistake of confusing formula with convention. This is the same as mistaking a paint-by-the-numbers picture for a school of art. Recognizing formula is not easy. You attend that writing seminar, rush home to your keyboard, and start pounding out a three-act structure with arcs and reversals in place. The story flows! It may not be until you're 50 pages in that you suddenly realize you've seen it all before. You're not following the conventions of the genre, you're marching to a formulaic tune. I wonder if Dolph Lungren's available?

One of the most problematic characters we dealt with on *ST:NG* was Q, and again it was because of the power the character wielded. How do you combat something that can do anything? You can't. So Q had to remain, not evil or good, but beyond those: irritatingly arrogant and cavalier, operating on a god-like plane we couldn't hope to understand. Given a choice, I'd much rather write a peasant than a god any day.

Speaking of characters, science fiction adds to the range of fantasy characters. Not only can we create non-human creatures, but manufactured entities as well, like robots and androids. Isaac Asimov recognized that not only was there a need to keep the power of robots manageable for the story, but it was an opportunity for exploring what it might mean to be a robot. For books like *I, Robot* and *The Naked Sun*, he created his often-borrowed Three Laws of Robotics:

- A robot may not injure a human being or, through inaction, allow a human being to come to harm.

- A robot must obey orders given it by human beings except where such orders would conflict with the First Law.

- A robot must protect its own existence as long as such protection does not conflict with the First or Second Law.

One of my favorite episodes of *Star Trek: Next Generation* is "The Measure of a Man" from the second season, written by Melinda M. Snodgrass. The story concerns an attempt to disassemble Data to see what makes him tick, so that other such androids can be made to serve Starfleet. Data at first agrees until he learns that all Starfleet's horses and men may not be able to put him back together again. Wonderful philosophical wrangling surrounds the legal hearing when Data tries to resign from Starfleet to avoid disassembly.

Robots from Steve Meretzky's Floyd to *System Shock*'s SHODAN, a female version of *2001: A Space Odyssey*'s Hal, are great chances for characters not found in the real world, and can be used, as in the case of "The Measure of a Man" to explore very human issues like civil rights as well.

Fantasy and science fiction share a great attraction for audiences and writers alike because of their seemingly unlimited possibilities, and that's their greatest danger as well. If we don't appreciate that paradox, our games run the risk of inviting players to take a thrilling space walk, then snapping off their umbilical.

Figure 16.6 Life where no life should be: SHODAN, a chilling artificial character in *System Shock*.

War

"War! Huh! Yeah! What is it good for? Absolutely nothin'! Say it again, y'all!"

—*Norman Whitfield & Barrett Strong*

Edwin Starr (1942–2003) sang that back in 1970. But you couldn't prove the sentiment by looking at video games.

War games were once the number one sub-genre of simulation and strategy games. Simulations of conflicts, campaigns, even single battles like Gettysburg were everywhere. There wasn't just one simulation of Gettysburg on store shelves at the same time either; there were many.

Then, in a trend we've already witnessed in several types of games, this genre slimmed down, sped up, and reinvented itself for the gamepad generation. Those detailed combat simulations with their thick manuals have been replaced by action games: simpler and far more visceral.

Not only do war games come in just about any type imaginable, each type is defined by how it approaches combat. Let's start with the real-time strategy game style that we still find. These are omniscient-view games either in isometric 2-D or true 3-D giving a view of entire battlegrounds. The strategic war game can be found as a primary component in more general empire-building strategy games like *Age of Empires* and more focused games like *Close Combat*. (Despite the title you were a long ways away.) *Close Combat* was interesting in that it attempted to model troop morale, one of the few RTS games to acknowledge these were not just units, but might be human beings worthy of characterization.

Conflict in the original *Civilization* was indicated by an icon representing an entire army landing on top of another icon and blinking for a second or two. Combat in today's strategy games is full of sound and fury: individual units moving independently with swords clashing, guns firing, and nicely animated mini-explosions.

These war games can be divided into two camps. The first is based on actual conflicts as were most of the original war games. The second group is more fanciful. Two of its biggest hit series are *Warcraft* and *Command & Conquer*.

Story in the first camp is handled mainly as historical background to provide context for the upcoming battle. The second camp often needs to create its own backstory to explain what's going on. Such is the case with the *Command & Conquer* games and their video cut-scene interludes. *Warcraft*, relying on high fantasy, needed much less explanation. Everybody knows what an orc is.

For writers, strategy war games don't provide much challenge. If you go the route of *Command & Conquer*, the story is reassuringly linear and segregated from the gameplay. If your scenario is historical, this type of game doesn't give you much chance to get down and dirty with the foot soldiers, so character revelation is at a minimum.

This isn't to say that strategy war games can't be created with more sophisticated stories and characters. But the need for storytelling beyond context hasn't been proven, and the audience doesn't appear to be clamoring for it the way they are in the other incarnations of war games. Developers of these games spend their resources on the addition of player vs. player more than on storytelling.

If we zoom in to the next level of war games, however, things change . . . er . . . dramatically. Whether first or third person, these are squad-level war games such as those produced by Tom Clancy's company Red Storm and many others. The player is now down in the trenches, firing weapons and hunting for ammo just as in other shooters. The squad is of two different types. Either the player controls all members, moving from player-character to player-character, or they are AI controlled.

We find both in PC games. Plus a necessary hybrid where the player can choose when to drive other characters. This is used in an attempt to retain the strategic element that was otherwise lost when squad-level war games moved from turn-based like *X-Com* to real-time. As stated before, human players can't keep up with computer-controlled enemies. Computer-controlled enemies don't need to take breaks from the almost constant action, so some relief, in the form of AI was needed for human players.

In any of these three cases though, there are many more story and character opportunities. Now we have buddies with distinct personalities to interact with. Now we build friendships with those buddies, so if one is killed, the player can be touched by the loss. This is not true only for foot soldiers. Squadrons of fighter planes or tanks or ships are treated in the exact same way. In *Star Wars*, I never really cared about Wedge, another pilot along for the ride with Luke Skywalker, but his death was necessary in the final battle because of what he meant to Luke, even though most of his dialogue comes over the radio. This use of characters heard but not seen is a staple of war movies in general and can be used to good effect in squad-level games. As long as we give them voice, we have a chance to give them something interesting to say.

Historical scenarios are popular, covering just about all of our modern wars from World War II to Iraq. Depth of simulation has given way to a cinematic feel of being in the action.

We find this cinematic immersion as well as we zoom down to the last level of war game: single-player. Here is where we find most of the console war games. We'll examine some of the unique challenges of console games in the next chapter.

One PC game deserves mention for music as immersion tool. The use of period music adds immeasurably to immersion in *Battlefield: Vietnam*. This game is one of several that allow players to experience the war in several different roles: from dog soldier to sniper to helicopter pilot. Despite single-player scenarios, the major focus of this game, like its predecessor *Battlefield 1942*, is on multiplayer, so storytelling is reduced to the bare minimum.

Figure 16.7 Blast away to the top tunes of the late 60s and early 70s in *Battlefield Vietnam*.

With this technology, we have the tools to make a story-based single-player war game every bit as compelling as a war movie that explores the human side of war beyond the morale calculations of *Close Combat*. Out of all the genres, war games can explore themes that are difficult and not easily resolved. There is no fantasy or science fiction patina to soften the life and death issues. Right now, we're stuck in the safe John Wayne world of *The Green Berets*. Would anyone want to play a grittier game? If it's written with the conviction of the HBO mini-series *Band of Brothers*, I'd say yes.

Espionage

"Stealth and secrecy are our only weapons now. You gentlemen are, I trust, stealthy and secretive."

—Alistair Maclean, *Where Eagles Dare*

Like fantasy and science fiction, there is a lot of crossover between this genre and the next, crime. Because games in this genre are almost invariably action games, there is a lot of similarity with war game first-person shooters although espionage games are more likely to resemble the play style of *Thief* than *Doom*, where being stealthy and secretive can gain you almost as much as firepower and reflexes.

Yes, *Where Eagles Dare* may look like a war movie, but it's not. Long before Indiana Jones was a gleam in Steven Spielberg's eye, Richard Burton and Clint Eastwood starred in this 1969 super-charged action film about a commando raid on an impregnable German castle perched on a mountaintop, which defined the modern cliffhanger. And it is also a workable model for the structure of our espionage games.

What games fall under this genre these days? There is a wide range that includes *Everything or Nothing* and *Splinter Cell: Pandora Tomorrow*. Developers of espionage games have become increasingly interested in storytelling as a way to stand out from the crowd (although major licenses don't hurt!).

Being stealthy and secretive gives writers the potential for other obstacles than simply enemies to be gunned down. These obstacles then can be overcome in a variety of ways: cracking a safe's combination lock; accessing computer files by deducing a password; borrowing credentials that get the player-character past a suspicious guard; using special stealth moves like the player-character being able to pull himself over a fence or wedge himself between two beams in the ceiling, and many more.

In *Everything or Nothing*, Bond finally escapes from the first-person shooter mode he's been imprisoned in since *Goldeneye*. The new Bond game allows players to drive an array of typically high-tech Bond vehicles as well as utilizing Bond's arsenal of gadgets and exotic weapons.

Electronic Arts

Figure 16.8 *Everything or Nothing.* Bond never was all that stealthy and secretive really.

By varying the gameplay, we not only keep the experience fresh for the player, but we provide ourselves with a variety of different approaches to the storytelling. Let's look at the opportunities presented in the previous paragraph's examples of gameplay.

- Cracking a safe's combination lock. Does the character use a digital tumbler detector or a stethoscope? Where did the character pick up safecracking? What exposition does the safe contain?

- Accessing computer files by deducing a password. Instead of just finding the password taped to the bottom of the keyboard, provide clues to the password. It'll require a search of the office the player might not otherwise bother to make, revealing the character of the computer's owner: is he married? Any kids? Pets? Birthday/how old is he? What are his hobbies? Hmmm . . . he's colorblind and has a black belt in karate . . . might be useful knowledge later on . . .

- Borrowing credentials to get past a suspicious guard. This gains you knowledge about the true owner of the credentials; provides the opportunity for revealing dialogue with an NPC who trusts the player-character; maybe ensures his friendly recognition of the player-character later on after the credentials have been destroyed.

- Wedging himself between the beams of a ceiling not only may save the PC from detection but give her a chance to overhear NPC conversation in the corridor below her that may include character insights or exposition crucial to the mission.

Because espionage games are set in a world that more closely resembles our own than fantasy or science fiction, we are constrained somewhat by real world natural laws and physics (at least as much as James Bond is). It also means that we don't have to police our imaginations as closely. We should automatically recognize when credibility is being stretched to the breaking point.

Espionage games can take the player to new locales, like Paris and Indonesia in *Splinter Cell: Pandora Tomorrow*, and Moscow, Cairo, and elsewhere in *Everything or Nothing*. Real locations mean we don't have to make everything up. We can do research. The famous *jet d'eau* is a major puzzle element in the Geneva section for *The Siberian Cipher*. The fact that the city is home to so many well-guarded and secretive banks suggested the main puzzle: breaking into one. The design also took players to New York, Africa, Australia, China, and yes, Siberia.

Few genres immediately suggest such an interesting variety of skills the way espionage does. Fantasy and science fiction are wide open. You start from scratch. War is . . . war. You start with an M16. Espionage makes you as close to Super-Renaissance Man as a human is likely to get.

The major issue for the writer is how realistic the game is going to be. In 1965 *Thunderball*, the fourth James Bond film, was released. That same year saw the release of *The Ipcress File* starring Michael Caine, a far grittier look at the world of espionage. Both films were produced by Albert "Cubby" Broccoli and Harry Saltzman and featured much of the same behind-the-camera talent. *The Ipcress File* wasn't any more realistic, featuring as it did a psychedelic brain-washing room I paid homage to (stole) for *Edge of Night* almost 20 years later. It was simply done in a realistic style of British cinema popular at the time that also produced such non-espionage films as *Room at the Top* and *The Loneliness of the Long-Distance Runner*. The style meant the characters felt more like real people than James Bond. They weren't all glamorous and neither was their work of stake-outs and prisoner exchanges. Harry Palmer, Caine's

Figure 16.9 Michael Caine's Harry Palmer, the ordinary bloke in *The Ipcress File*.

character, didn't much fancy being a spy at all. He wore glasses, spoke with a working-class accent, made mistakes, and in the end almost kills the wrong man.

The reason I chose *Splinter Cell: Pandora Tomorrow* for this section along with *Everything or Nothing* is because its grittier style and ethical considerations exist in a very different world from the other game. Both provide a depth of storytelling missing from most console games. Both stories turn on dangers that threaten the entire globe. Their treatments are miles apart.

Crime

Crime might look like it belongs linked up with the next genre, mystery. But crime games are actually much closer in structure and gameplay to espionage and non-strategy war games. This genre includes both sides of the law: *S.W.A.T* and *Grand Theft Auto*. Cops and robbers. Like many war games, players can play both sides.

We don't see crime-based strategy games much, but both squad-level and single player-character are well represented. We let players play bad guys because it appeals to the naughty side most of us have within us. *Grand Theft Auto: Vice City* is unapologetically not politically correct. You can hear the developers giggling maniacally even now. If *all* games *only* gave us the option to be criminals, we might risk encouraging a generation of social misfits. But for the rest of us, playing villains is a fun diversion, and release.

Playing honest officers of truth and justice appeals to the hero within us, and is a reaction to the chaotic world we live in. Mysteries try to deny that world exists. Crime confronts it; knows we're frustrated that we can't do much about it; and hands us the weapons to change that.

This section is shorter than most of those in this chapter because gameplay and opportunities for character and story have been discussed in the sections on earlier genres, particularly war and espionage. Deciding whether hostages are taken by bank robbers or terrorists doesn't affect the mechanics of the gameplay, only the details. The major difference is in the storytelling.

Sierra

Rockstar Games

Figure 16.10 Cops (*SWAT 3*) . . .

Figure 16.11 . . . and robbers (*Grand Theft Auto: Vice City*).

Deciding whether the game casts the player-character as a S.W.A.T. member or a single detective on a homicide case determines the style of gameplay in a shooter, whether the genre is science fiction, war, espionage or crime. But there are two primary considerations when designing a crime game I want to bring up.

The first is that, of all the genres, this one is most real and most known to us. With a couple of exceptions, usually dealing with 30s gangsters, crime games are modern day, or near future. We need to get the world right, and we need to get the facts right. If we screw up on police procedure, or on how to handle terrorists, players will know and rightfully be annoyed. Remember our characters and stories don't have to be real, but they have to *feel* real.

The second is thematic. Playing cops and robbers is fine, but because crime games are based in a recognizable world, the consequences for actions must be carefully weighed. Even in *Grand Theft Auto: Vice City* there are degrees of villainy and lines certain characters won't cross. This is not only for dramatic variety, but because the game's creators have committed themselves to a point of view. We make choices every time we write. Being aware of that, and making meaningful choices, are the most important and often the hardest part.

Mystery

Ah, my favorite genre. I was a mystery writer long before I was a game designer, and a mystery lover long before that. The next game I design (I begin as soon as this book is completed) will be a mystery. Mystery is the chameleon of genres, showing up in all the others, adapting itself to its new surroundings without missing a beat. There is mystery in every game I've ever designed, and most of the TV shows I wrote. Even when I worked in a non-mystery genre like *Eight Is Enough* (family comedy) or *Father Murphy* (family western) I usually wrote a mystery.

I love traditional mysteries because they are windows on an orderly universe far removed from uncertainty and injustice that are a part of everyday life. In a well-constructed mystery story, clues are followed to a logical conclusion. There are no loose ends. Good triumphs, and evil is punished. This wasn't true of life in the golden age of mysteries any more than it's true today. There is no guarantee of such tidy resolutions in this world. But that's okay because mysteries deal with illusion, not reality.

Figure 16.12 My title for the *Eight Is Enough* episode suggests the genre.

Classic mystery stories fall into two major camps. *Cozies* evoke cozy English villages with their elderly tea-sipping spinsters and deacons and bicycle-riding constables. Most of Agatha Christie's mysteries are cozies, but even at their coziest her amateur sleuth, Miss Marple, had a keen edge to her that belied her lace and granny glasses. *Hard-boiled* mysteries originated in the United States. Among the more famous hard-boiled writers were Dashiel Hammett and Raymond Chandler.

Mystery writers are often compared to magicians, and with good reason. We use some of the same techniques, like misdirection and sleight-of-hand. We'll look at some of these in a moment.

Being a mystery writer has helped me in *all* my writing. Traditional mystery structure is unforgiving. You need to know where you're going. The clues must pay off and the motives tie up. At the end of the story if your reader tosses the book aside or walks out of the theatre and goes, "Huh?" you failed.

It's because I'm a mystery writer that I stress such elements of writing as consistency and clarity. You need to play fair with your audience. And this is the primary difference between mystery stories and crime stories. Crime fiction is more firmly based in the real world. It may contain one mystery or more, just as any other genre, but it's sloppier, and in the end, justice is not always certain. Misunderstanding this distinction leads a lot of unaware writers to confuse the two, just as *noir* and mysteries are often confused by the undiscriminating. For the record, Raymond Chandler wrote hard-boiled mysteries with noir elements. Cornell Woolrich caused the French to first use the word *noir* to describe his work because he used *black* in many of his titles. He did not write mysteries. He wrote psychological thrillers that sometimes contained elements of mysteries. *Rear Window* is based on a Cornell Woolrich story.

When the mystery has loose ends, or the solution makes jumps in logic, or depends on wild speculation or coincidence, it is doomed. The result can be dissatisfaction in the audience much like when the director crosses the axis for two matching shots. They may not know what's wrong, but they know something didn't work. It can also be worse.

It's like the feeling we get matching up our socks after doing the laundry, when we are left with a stray. We can usually track down its mate in the washer, or retrieve it from that linty space between the dryer and the wall. If a mystery reader flips back through the pages to check on a stray clue, the result can be catastrophic if the clue isn't there. The plot is exposed in all its unfair artifice. If a magician's illusion fails onstage, the audience sees the smoke and mirrors used to construct it. "Don't look at the little man behind the curtain!" cries the all powerful Wizard of Oz. But it's too late. We've seen him.

As I said, mysteries are a component of many games. But as a genre they are fairly rare. They've been with us from very early on. The first was probably Infocom's text adventure *Deadline*. They are with us today in games like *Post Mortem*. Why haven't they enjoyed the popularity of fantasy and science fiction? I think there are three reasons. All have to do more with we who create games than those who play them.

The first is that mysteries can seem very complex, and simple stories work best for games as in any other action medium. We need to separate story structure from mystery problem and solution here. The underlying solution to most mysteries is as simple as Mrs. White in the library with the candlestick. The rest is all as much smoke and as many mirrors as we want to use to disguise that fact. The plot moves must be clear even if we don't reveal their true meaning.

The second is that even if you've created a new world for your science fiction game, as long as you're consistent, you can make up all sorts of natural laws. Spells can be whipped up in a fantasy game on demand. Mysteries force us to plant both feet firmly on the ground. We must play fair.

The third is the reverse of the number one hackneyed metaphor that shows up in so many mysteries. You know the one I mean: the pieces of the jigsaw puzzle line. Please! Swear an oath. Swear now that you will never refer to the clues in a mystery story as "pieces of a jigsaw puzzle" or observe that "we don't have all the pieces" or "the pieces don't fit" or "there's only one piece to the puzzle missing." Swear it.

Thank you. Now that I got that out of my system, back to the reverse. When we write a mystery, we start from the end when the jigsaw puzzle is complete. We then take it apart and plant the clues like Easter eggs throughout the story. We may change a clue, or add more or alter details in the solution as we write, but we must start with that damned completed jigsaw puzzle. Too many attempt to wing it with just the culprit's identity and motive and a vague clue or two. The pieces don't fit. The player notices. Just as stories are unfairly looked down upon in games, mysteries are looked down upon because they often are not done well. I swear I will never mention jigsaw puzzles again in this book.

Being a fan, I'd like to see more mysteries in games. If you accept the three reasons I've given for our lack of mysteries, and are willing to try and make the effort to write one, I have a few helpful hints.

Use *misdirection* in all sorts of ways, refine it, and layer it. Different types of people will play your mystery. Start with a coarse layer of obvious red herrings that the helpful sidekick or other looker on will point at. These are innocent suspects, false clues, motives that could lead to murder but didn't, and so on. The canny mystery writer will often double bluff and point at someone, exonerate her beyond a shadow of a doubt, then reveal she committed the murder after all.

note

MISDIRECTION: the art of focusing a watcher's attention on one place so he doesn't see something happen in another.

Create a second layer that waits to trap the clever player who sees through the major red herrings. Then a third, and a fourth if you like. The term *red herring*, of course, stems from British fox hunting (Oscar Wilde called it "the unspeakable in pursuit of the uneatable.") where early pro-fox activists would stuff burlap bags with smoked (red) herrings, and drag them across the trail between the fox and the pursuing dogs, hoping to throw them off the scent.

Want to know who the killer is in far too many books and movies? Wait until the detective's sidekick, or the dumb police officer lists the suspects. They have to, of course, to remind the audience. One of two things will happen. He'll make the mistake of saying, "So, it must be Professor Plum, Colonel Mustard, Miss Scarlet, or Mr. Green. We know it can't be Mrs. White." Who's the killer? Quick! No looking at your neighbor's paper! Or he'll say, "So, it must be Professor Plum, Colonel Mustard, Miss Scarlet, Mrs. White, or Mr. Green." The killer is the same in both cases.

Somewhere sometime in the dim past (long before R.D. Laing) somebody must have done a study on human perception and concluded we pay a lot of notice to the first item in a list, but then our attention begins to drift. We pay almost as much attention to the second item, even less to the third and so on until the end when we snap back to consciousness and zero in on the last item to prove we were actively involved the entire time. Mystery writers routinely place the killer's name in the bottom third of the suspect list. It takes a confident writer to double-bluff and pick the first or last name.

As for the first case, even if a master of the puzzle mystery like Agatha Christie allows a character to be ruled out because they couldn't possibly have done it, be suspicious, and watch them like a hawk. Once suspicion falls, clues can leap into view.

Withhold explanations. In Chapter 9 I talked about the crisis, climax, resolution triplets. We saw that by stretching the time between any of these we could heighten suspense. The same thing is true with exposition. Every time a detective collects a clue, it's the A side to a joke. The punch line is the moment the meaning of the clue becomes clear. You can't have one without the other.

It's like the classic situation that gives rise to the phrase, "waiting for the other shoe to drop." Where did it originate? Nobody knows. It was called an "old chestnut" in a copy of *The New York Times* published in 1921. It probably originated with some poor soul in a downstairs lodging house room trying to go to sleep who hears his upstairs neighbor getting ready for bed. The neighbor takes off a shoe and tosses it aside. It lands with a thump. The longer that neighbor takes to toss the second shoe the more excruciating the suspense becomes. The man downstairs will not be able to sleep until the second shoe drops. Human beings, even the less anal ones, need closure. Keeping it from them only makes them desire it more.

A variation on this is don't try to hide clues. The best clues are those where you can jump up and down in front of the player and point at them. "Look! A clue!" The player sagely guesses what the clue means, and is totally wrong.

The close-up magician who works his illusions right under our noses uses physical dexterity called sleight-of-hand. By carefully choosing words designed to mislead, we work our sleigh-of-hand with those. Frederic Dannay and Manfred B. Lee, writing under the pen name Ellery Queen (also their detective's name) were particularly adept at presenting the "dying" words of a victim that appeared to mean one thing when actually they meant something entirely different.

Mysteries flourish in other media. Many of our most popular films, from *Chinatown*, (at its core a simple story about different kinds of parental love), to *Pulp Fiction*, *Memento*, and *The Usual Suspects*, are mysteries. Action and mystery go well together when they are in balance. Understanding the craft of mystery writing is a necessary step to writing games whose mysteries satisfy as much as their action.

Horror

We find horror intermixed with other genres just like mystery. *Alien* is a horror tale set in a science fiction universe. The *Resident Evil* games as I mentioned are similar. The genre is inhabited by monsters. There's a wide range of monsters to choose from, human monsters like *Hannibal*, or the prehistoric reptiles from *Jurassic Park*. The scariest seem to not be the mindless killers of dead teenager movies like *Friday the 13th* that must rely solely on effects like shock and gore, even if they play on our standard fears of isolation and vulnerability.

Rather, the most effective monsters are human, or at least anthropomorphic. The biggest monster in *Jurassic Park* is the T-Rex. But it is the raptors with that unsettling glint of intelligence in their eyes that are saved for the spine-tingling climax. Universal Studios owes its success in the 30s and 40s to its monsters, and the most popular were *Dracula*, *Frankenstein*'s creation, *The Wolfman*, and *The Mummy*. Hammer Studios replicated their success in the 50s and 60s. Zombies have been with us just as long (*White Zombie* in 1932, 1943's *I Walked with a Zombie* and others), but came into their own in the 60s first with Hammer's *Plague of the Zombies* in 1966 and more spectacularly with George Romero's *Night of the Living Dead* in 1968.

Figure 16.13 *Resident Evil*'s science fictional zombies still lurch with their arms stretched out.

It is the fact that there is a horrible caricature of humanity in all of these creatures that makes them resonate longer with us than non-human monsters, and keeps them coming back to scare us time and again.

We're not going to linger on gore, but it is one of the elements of horror we address as writers. Again it hits the player harder when humans become rotting corpses or begin to mutate than when unrecognizable tentacled blobs attack. The stories of horror writer H. P. Lovecraft have been a favorite source of material for movies and games. Very few low budget horror film writers can resist the temptation to drop a reference to Arkham, Massachusetts, or place a Miskatonic University sweatshirt on a character.

The most effective of Lovecraft's writing comes when he describes the alterations in humans after their brushes with his mythical beings called The Old Ones. Whenever the Old Ones themselves make guest appearances, he relies on suggestion and warnings that the descriptions are too horrible to imagine. Not something that translates well into literal mediums like computer games and movies.

Three other elements worth mentioning here show up in other genres. But horror is particularly dependent on them. We've discussed them: suspense, surprise, and shock. The key to their use is a word I've used many times: balance. Shocks and surprises are only effective if they are not over-used, and if we take care to vary their rhythms. An endless string of shock after shock after shock deadens the player. We want to vary when the shock occurs in our game; and where the box is that Jack is going to jump out at us from.

We want to vary their intensity, all the while trying to avoid escalating things too far too soon. It's the same problem as player-characters becoming too powerful. If we rely solely on shock and surprise, each instance must cap the previous one.

Far easier, and in the long run far more effective, is to string the shocks together with suspense. Lengthen the time between the setup (a first dead body?) and the appearance of the thing that did the deed. Create a red herring surprise. Cause some laughter in the player, then choke it off with a blood-soaked claw.

In shooters, we send armies of drooling, bloodthirsty mobs after the player to keep the action intense. But just like the James Bond games added gameplay as they evolved from *Goldeneye* to *Everything or Nothing*, we need to do the same. The arsenal of gameplay stealth and secrecy give us can be far more rewarding than simply bigger guns to splatter bigger monsters.

Romance

These last two genres are included for completeness. But I think it's safe to say neither romance nor the western have found a home in games. Infocom's *Plundered Hearts* was an attempt at a text adventure version of "bodice-ripper" romance novels. It was not a commercial success. And it's not because the player-character was female. This fact didn't stop Roberta Williams' *King's Quest* series from being successful, or *Lara Croft:Tomb Raider*. It's the idea of romance that causes difficulty.

Now that more women are playing games, maybe this will change. I hope so. I don't mean that the female audience is more interested in romance. But they do seem to have less trouble than we males with emotions. And romance is about emotion. There is no denying that.

Over the past few years I've been approached several times about a multiplayer world of romance. On the surface, these sound like a great idea. There are certainly a lot more women online than those we see blowing things up in shooters, even though women can enjoy the action just as much as men.

The problem isn't that the women who play shooters are less comfortable with computers and consoles as men. Their generation has been raised on them. The majority of the women online are playing social games like hearts where friends and chatting are as important as who wins. Most game types are off their radar.

Romance is already online in a big way in chat rooms and dating services. And it's real. These are the romance equivalent of PvP. And they bring all the nuances human opponents bring to those games that AI can't provide. There are two sticky points the developer of a romance multiplayer game must get past. That's the first one. Romance arrived without our help. We may have missed our chance.

The second is that other very interesting element to romance: sex. Again, the Internet is already there, and we've seen the results both good and bad. The sensational stories make the headlines: online relationships that break up marriages, serial killers and pedophiles on the prowl for new prey. For every one of those, I expect there are quite a few healthy relationships that develop, as they can among singles anyplace.

But this is a book on writing, not sociology. And my writing answer to this dilemma is one word: *Titanic.* I was in Beijing when it was first released there. It was the number one movie by a wide margin for weeks.

Figure 16.14 Romance on the high seas: *Titanic.*

Romance in movies does not only occur in romance movies. Even romance novels are comprised of other genres. *Edge of Night* was the mystery soap. In *Titanic*, there is an almost perfect balance of elements that appeal to a huge proportion of the mass market: the mystique of the subject matter; the suspense; spectacle; action; and yes, romance. It didn't even matter that the screenplay was nothing to write home about. It was the elements chosen and how they were balanced that made *Titanic* a phenomenal hit that appealed to just about every demographic in every country on the planet.

We will eventually see games that are romances at their heart. A way to get to that point is to add legitimate romance, not just Bond girls, to the games we have now.

Western

Westerns have long been considered a wonderful genre for storytelling. What was the first narrative film? *The Great Train Robbery*. After falling out of favor in the 70s due to saturation and the changing sensibilities of a post-Vietnam country, we have seen a quiet resurgence in them over the past few years in other media.

What about games? Remember LucasArts' *Outlaws*? That was quite awhile ago. I see a single western title being advertised during the period I write this. Its awkward title is *Red Dead Revolver*, and it's from Rockstar, the developers behind *Grant Theft Auto*. I also read that it is yet again the same old revenge premise, ". . . a young man's innocence was lost when he witnessed the brutal murder of his family . . ." Sigh. Families of player-characters just don't survive long in games like this. Red, meet *Max Payne*. Max, meet Red. Boys, meet *The Bravados*, *The Godfather*, *Once Upon a Time in the West*, *Gangs of New York*, and 300 other movies, all of whom I bet did it better than you. Cliché meet cliché. It's okay. It's only a game.

In fairness I'll point out that my own *Dark Side of the Moon* does begin with the death of the player-character's uncle. Although his sister is never even threatened! And the plot has nothing to do with revenge. None of my other games feature the opening death of the player-character's loved one or ones, and revenge is a theme I've left in cold storage.

Rockstar Games

Figure 16.15 It doesn't look like Red's taking in this varmint alive.

Red becomes a bounty hunter, I see. Hopefully, he won't gun down all those he goes after; there will be a variety of crimes; and once Red confronts the bandits who killed his family in the obvious endgame there may be some irony during the inevitable shootout. Do they have families too? Do we introduce the young hothead Billy Clanton from the O.K. Corral who really doesn't want to fight? Do we let the women and children go? Does the chief villain turn out to be kindly old Sheriff Potter we've been getting missions from? We'll see.

Making Red a bounty hunter does avoid one tricky aspect of westerns: the cowboys and Indians thing. Native Americans are no longer portrayed only as soulless monsters who booze and rape and torture the innocent settlers and ranchers who only wanted their share of the American dream. Thanks to global terrorism the gunsights of that brand of casual racism have swiveled over to Arabs now. The *ghoutra* and the *agal* have replaced the feathered war bonnet.

The best thing about the classic western films is that they explored large themes like courage (*Shane*); family relationships (*Red River*); friendship (*Gunfight at the O.K. Corral*); the nature of violence (*The Gunfighter*); responsibility (*High Noon*); and yes, even revenge (*The Searchers*). They were often morality plays firmly grounded in melodrama, and happy to be there thanks.

They are a fallow field that is largely unplanted by writers and designers of games. Maybe *Red Dead Revolver* will do well and waken interest in other developers. Who knows? Rock-Star got the spaghetti western music right.

CHAPTER 17

CONSOLE GAMES

Most of the character and storytelling topics in this book apply equally to all game hardware. There are some challenges that become more acute on consoles. We'll take a look at some of these in this chapter, then briefly look at the even smaller platforms: handhelds, PDAs, and cell phones.

Console games are the biggest part of the current gaming market. As I write this, there are three major competitors for a gamer's hardware dollars: the Microsoft Xbox, the Nintendo GameCube, and the Sony PlayStation 2. I'm not going to get into the specifications of the three current video game systems beyond a few general comments on those hardware characteristics that affect our ability to tell stories, and that set the consoles apart from personal computers.

The first is memory. Not one of the three contains anywhere near as much memory as a personal computer. Due to this smaller storage capacity, they must sacrifice certain features useful to us as storytellers. The major one is game variety. Console games worlds are narrower than personal computer worlds and in one respect at least, quieter. The gameplay offered has less variety, and is often not as deep as that found on personal computers. NPCs can speak, but the moments when they do can be few and far between. Although things are changing rapidly, spoken dialogue is often supplemented by text. Text is a step back from the way dialogue is treated in plays, movies, and television.

Action games, of course, emphasize action. These sequences are far more extended than comparable scenes in films. They take up far more of the gameplay time than dialogue. Yet a game like *Everything or Nothing*, which features the voices of the actors like Pierce Brosnan, Dame Judy Dench, and John Cleese voicing characters they play in the recent

Bond films, will obviously benefit from more dialogue. The *New York Times* quoted John Cleese as saying about voice acting in *Everything or Nothing*, "I didn't have to shave, I drank a decent cup of coffee, sat in a comfortable chair, and it was kind of fun."

The developers are adding player-controlled action to the movie-going experience. So something has to give someplace else to make room for the sound files. The result is the world narrows even more. We have to find ways to justify that within the context of the fiction.

While game consoles may skimp on general RAM and ROM memory, they are far more generous when it comes to graphics memory. This is hardly surprising.

Figure 17.1 John Cleese, first "R," now "Q" in film and game.

They are game machines first, not generalized computing devices. This means that they can handle the spectacular action gamers demand with a lot more agility than personal computers, and they don't have to worry about such niceties as video card compatibility. All games run just fine on their intended Nintendo. This gives us the opportunity and the challenge to create all sorts of wild action with less effort than on a PC.

But what we gain in video memory we lose in display resolution. Console games are meant to use the television as their display device. While many games now support HDTV, most are still played on sets whose resolution is far below what a computer monitor can deliver, and a monitor is already reduced in resolution from the printed page. So even as we're often obligated to use text, reading that soft text for any length of time on a television is even worse. The text is larger, so less can be displayed on the screen at any one time. This forces us to reduce dialogue, and to deliver it in irritatingly small bits. This is one of several factors that can lead to simplistic storytelling on consoles.

The last piece of hardware game consoles use that is different from computers is the control device called a game controller or gamepad. Here the limitations are not in what the game can deliver, but what the player can deliver to the game. Moving from keyboard and mouse to a single input device with only a few buttons and a couple of miniature joysticks makes player text input far more tedious, as even the standard personal computer input paradigms of pointing, clicking, and dragging become trickier.

Figure 17.2 Microsoft Xbox controller.

Figure 17.3 Nintendo GameCube controller.   **Figure 17.4** Sony PlayStation 2 controller.

Gamepad controls are simpler to learn, of course. And more versatile methods of input are always being explored, voice being an obvious choice for consoles. The recent PlayStation 2 game *Lifeline* (a rare console adventure/action hybrid) attempts to allow players to not only control the female player-character, but converse with her as well. The results are mixed, combining as they do both voice recognition and an optimistic parser.

For now gamepads remain the control device of choice for consoles. Gamepads are built for action, not story. That may not appear to matter much. Let's take a look at the demographics.

Figure 17.5 *Lifeline*: "She'll do anything you tell her to!" the ads coyly promised.

Demographics

Much as we may not like to admit it, personal computers are meant to perform a variety of tasks, not just to play games. Consoles are dedicated game machines. They have traditionally targeted a younger playbase. The balance between gameplay and story is heavily weighted toward gameplay, action gameplay. Nintendo's audience is the youngest. The 18–24-year-olds are heaviest on the Xbox. The PS2 has the broadest market. None are actively targeting older games. You don't expand your market by turning your back on the core group of players.

For the youngest players, very simple stories are fine. Simple does not equal sloppy. They should still be as well crafted as the gameplay. Here is one of the rare cases where prose seems to be more analogous to writing games than drama, film, or television. Major children's plays are heavily dependent on spectacle. Movies and TV shows directed at kids try to reach a wider age group. Books, though, can still be focused on much tighter age ranges. As a result, more care is taken to appeal to the child in that age group alone.

Younger players are even less interested in stopping the action to move the story forward than adults. Recent reports verify what many of us have long suspected: attention spans are getting shorter. I'm going to save the social implications of this until Chapter 20, "The Responsible Writer." For now, what this means is we have less memory, less input options, and less time within which to tell our stories on consoles.

Yet console game developers are now finally catching up with personal computers in their desire to tell stories. And lo and behold, the challenge of how to do that is causing video games to leap past computer games in a key area: integration. Out of necessity comes innovation.

Push the Button, Get the Story

With few exceptions, all games have been designed within some rigid parameters and console are no exception. Many of these can be summed up by saying that the gameplay waits for the player to interact with it. Obstacles sit there, animated or not, until the player attempts to overcome them. All mobs are like murderous cows contentedly chewing their cud inside a fenced field until the player-character wanders inside their *aggro range*. The fence may be invisible, but it's there.

note

AGGRO RANGE: the area surrounding a mob or NPC that, when breached, triggers the mob to action. The word comes to us from British slang meaning aggravation or aggression.

The game world is like a car waiting for its owner to show up and drive it. Even patrolling guards in shooters have limited paths they travel. Once aggroed, however, new code kicks in. The mob goes into attack mode and can pursue the player-character outside its territory, for example.

The same paradigm applies to the storytelling. The player-character arrives at a source of exposition, whether it's an object or an NPC. The player presses a button on the gamepad, and the story bite is delivered in a spoonful or a few spoonfuls separated by more increasingly impatient button punches.

If we need to provide the player with choices, a menu appears (see the "Dialogue Systems" section in Chapter 6, "Character Encounters"). Confining selections to those chosen by pointing and clicking with a joystick or an arrow pad limits interaction as well.

The knee jerk reactions to this are familiar: remove choices from players; keep NPC encounters few and far between; remove all non-mob NPCs entirely from the gameplay, and maroon them in cut scenes. If an NPC appears in both cut scenes and gameplay, he is treated differently. In gameplay, he becomes a mob or a vending machine. He still acts in ways consistent with his character, but his action queue becomes combat or commerce oriented.

In *Baldur's Gate: Dark Alliance* when player-characters confront the boss mobs of each level there is a short game engine cut scene to set up the confrontation, then gameplay resumes. The only choice players have is to fight or die. This is not an attempt at integration. It simply places the cut scene side-by-side with the gameplay.

In the next section, Nate Fox describes using level design choices to truly integrate story and gameplay.

Integration Versus Cut Scenes

Nate Fox is the writer and lead designer at Sucker Punch, responsible for *Sly Cooper & the Thievius Raccoonus* and *Sly 2: Band of Thieves*. In an interview with GameSpy, he said, "My Role on *Sly 2* is to write the story and the dialogue and create the spaces which the gameplay takes place in." I like that word *spaces*.

Nate Fox, Writer/Designer

As a designer who sort of fell into story and dialogue, I've got a different take on how narrative should show up in games. I believe that it's a game designer's responsibility to support narrative through *level design*. Make the story an integral part of the play experience and the synergy between the two will draw people's interest ... both to the game play challenges and why they should care about overcoming those challenges.

Ok, so here's a working example of what I'm talking about. The first level of *Sly 2: Band of Thieves* features a scene in which Sly (our hero) runs through a Cairo museum to avoid getting captured by his nemesis/love interest Inspector Carmelita Fox. Sly runs down screen (facing the camera) while he dodges blasts from Carmelita, who all the while shouts clever phrases like "Stop thief!" The three design elements at work here are: setting, character use and camera set up.

Nate Fox

Figure 17.6 Nate Fox.

First things first: why is Sly breaking into a museum? How come he's not breaking into a military base or sorority house? Well, we weren't trying to portray Sly as a commando or frat boy . . . no, we were going for "high brow thief," hence the museum. And it's not just any museum, it's a museum in *Cairo*; we're talking world class here. Where you take your hero says a lot about what sorts of things they're interested in. Levels should not be a random collection of locales based primarily on artistic variety, but rather meaningful environments that help advance the theme (and story) of your game.

All right, let's cut to the chase—why have Carmelita pursue Sly? In fact, why have Carmelita in the game at all? Well, she's there to label Sly as a thief. Without her, he's just an everyday do-gooder. But with a policewoman hot on his tail, he's a wanted criminal. Making playable sections of the game, like this museum chase, that reflect the characters' association to each other, provides the players with first-hand experience in their relationship. Is Carmelita talking to the player or Sly Cooper when she yells "Stop, thief"? If the player fails in making an escape she's caught by the cops; if she succeeds, it's a clean getaway. Consider this: how many games have you played that feature an unmotivated obstacle course, with no real goal other than to unlock another unmotivated obstacle course? By making gameplay sequences that are also motivated challenges, the player is living out the story . . . not just being informed of it in a cut scene.

Finally, we come to the camera setup, Sly faces downscreen while running from Carmelita. Anyone familiar with character action games has seen this "run from the boulder" style gameplay. Why use it here? Why not have a rappelling sequence or safe cracking mini-game or something else that helps support Sly's character? The answer . . . face time! By having him run downscreen, the player gets to know Sly and Carmelita through their facial expressions. Imagine if you watched a movie in which the main character always had his back to the camera. That's exactly the experience you'll get 95 percent of the time with the standard game perspective. From a playability standpoint, running down screen is not that interesting . . . but, the personal connection it creates between Sly, the player and Carmelita is worth the tradeoff.

As a designer, I'm well aware that the average player is not going to sit there and ponder all the steps being taken to advance the characters and theme during the 40-second scene described above. However, I believe that the player will feel a greater connection to Sly than to the average game character because of these nuances. As you put together the story for your game, really think about how that story fits into gameplay. And while you design your levels, think hard about how you can make challenges which support the story.

If you get both right, you'll have a narrative you can play . . . instead of just watch.

Camera angles are carefully chosen in cut scenes and often ignored in gameplay. Too many angle changes can easily disorient a player. Yet in Nate's example, a single angle change for a complete gameplay sequence accomplishes the same thing. The key to finding this approach to level design is to not blindly accept the idea that story and gameplay must be segregated simply because they are so much of the time.

Realizing that integrating the two is not only possible, but desirable and not all that difficult is the first step. Once that first satori hits, the next step may be simply tossing a few lines of NPC dialogue into the action. Even in a game with minimal storytelling and little variety of gameplay like *Diablo* there is a groveling character who begs you not to kill him and gives you a quest instead. And then you get to kill him later!

Step three is specifically making gameplay decisions that not only produce great gameplay, but great story as well. I really believe the reason video games have begun to be more successful at this new paradigm than computer games is because of the inherent limitations in their hardware. It forces designers to think outside of the box.

Whatever it takes, it's okay with me. I said very early on in this book that technological limitations are no excuse not to tell wonderful stories. Story has never depended on technology. Ready for interactive TV? Look at your TiVo controller. We can tell interactive stories just as easily with that as we do with gamepads. It's all in how we approach the design.

How Story Enhances Gameplay

Once you accept that gameplay can be used to tell stories, the next obvious step is seeing that story can help your gameplay. Without constant nurturing, gameplay can become as monotonous as bad storytelling. One way to avoid this is through setting.

When I first started writing for *Charlie's Angels*, my producers Ron Austin and Jim Buchanan allowed me to accompany our location manager when he scouted locations. It was not common practice for freelance writers to tag along on scouts. But ours was very much a teaching relationship. I wasn't just a writer they'd hired. They were investing in me. I was also allowed on the set for every day of shooting of several episodes, a rare privilege for a freelance writer. All of it made me better at my job.

Columbia Tri-Star

Figure 17.7 Charlie's Angels' second season was my first.

My first script, *Magic Fire*, featured characters that were professional magicians. We went to Hollywood's famous Magic Castle to shoot, and I incorporated what I saw there into the teleplay. Not just the physical rooms, but the playful atmosphere, the camaraderie and rivalry of working magicians, and more all contributed to the episode. Scouting locations for my second episode, *The Jade Trap*, allowed me to use the physical features of a hotel in Marina Del Rey to bring a couple of action sequences to life. We shot in famous silent film star Marion Davies' mansion for *Rosemary for Remembrance*, directed by Ron. It was seeing the ballroom in the house that gave me the idea for an impromptu Charleston by Cheryl Ladd's character Kris Munroe, and for the final shot in the episode. That last shot is unique. It is the only one in the entire series that ended without the traditional Angels' tinkly "sting" music.

We've talked about setting as a tool for storytelling. The more vividly drawn the setting, the more opportunities for gameplay present themselves. The mining colony in *Dark Side of the Moon* suggested the ore cart ride action sequence. The museum exhibits in *Temüjin* helped me in my frantic last minute search to find puzzles in an already nearly completed game.

Another obvious way story can help is by forcing more variety of gameplay into the game. Altering the camera angle in *Sly 2: Band of Thieves* not only gave us character reactions to the action, it allowed for a new perspective. This is most applicable to third person games. First person games show you the faces of both NPCs and mobs. They hide yours. How could such a sequence be adapted to a first person game?

Figure 17.8 Guns and mirrors in *The Lady from Shanghai.*

I can think of several ways, but I'm only going to give a single example. The climax to Orson Welles' *The Lady from Shanghai* is so effective it has been borrowed over and over again. The identical sequences in the Bruce Lee film *Enter the Dragon* and *The Man with the Golden Gun* are probably better known than the original source. Two characters stalk one another and battle to the death in a mirror maze, either in an actual funhouse, or in a mirrored room that becomes a maze.

Figure 17.9 Fists of fury and mirrors in *Enter the Dragon.*

Imagine a first person shooter where the player-character is not the player, but playing a character (see Chapter 3, "Respecting Characters"), maybe one adapted from another medium, maybe not. Consider the implications. We might even prepare the player for our house of mirrors by revealing the player-character's face in passing earlier in the game much like Robert Montgomery did in *Lady in the Lake*. Eventually, the player-character arrives in our mirror maze. And everywhere she turns, she sees her own reflection.

We can ratchet up the suspense even more by the fact that the camera can now reveal the enemy or enemies creeping up behind the player-character. Sound effects can become instrumental in targeting. If there are several reflections of an enemy, his true position might be determined by sound. Then comes the need to break mirrors in order to escape or gain the upper hand. So just as the way out becomes more apparent, the information gained by the mirrors is removed. The player now knows things can creep up on the player-character from behind, but the player can no longer see them.

Variety isn't the only way story can enhance gameplay. It can raise the stakes. Higher stakes in the outcome of the action grabs the emotions. The gameplay fits more solidly into game fiction. There is more depth to the gameplay.

What do I mean by that? It's another console game, *Splinter Cell: Pandora Tomorrow*, which we've seen is one of the few currently in release to confront ethical issues. They don't overwhelm the entertainment. The designers didn't stop the spectacular action as Sam Fisher races along the top of the train pursued by rival helicopters and try to hammer home the theme. But by carefully finding moments where player choices have resonance, the entire game gains depth.

Are all of these examples only true in console games? No, but right now console games are leading the innovation. That's why this section belongs in this chapter.

So story can get us thinking about gameplay design. Once we are thinking about it, so many opportunities present themselves. And with both gameplay supporting story and story supporting gameplay the entertainment factor increases exponentially. Nate used the same word I did earlier: synergy. It's a beautiful thing.

Cooperative Games (Minimally Multiplayer)

Video game hardware supports up to four players. Many of these games are competitive racing or sports games or player versus player shooters. Others allow for cooperation between players instead of competition. This is usually a mode choice the player makes at the beginning of the game just as players choose between single player and multiplayer competitive games.

Very few personal computer games feature cooperative gameplay. This has made the paradigm somewhat difficult to accept in team games like *Tribes* or virtual worlds like *Dark Age of Camelot*. Players are far more accustomed to competition than cooperation. When cooperation is required, it can take some getting used to, and some players never seem able to make the adjustment.

Far more console games support cooperative gameplay. I could never have played several of the games I examine in this book without the help of my son Graham. I'd still be stuck trying to jump across those sinking platforms in *Dark Alliance* without his help (although in that case he just got his player-character across, then guided mine). Not too long ago, I worked on a cooperative product for the console market that emphasized storytelling over gameplay. A first for me. Again it was a console product, not one for a personal computer.

Consoles are finally adding online play, but most cooperative play is designed in third person on a single screen. Player-characters cannot wander far from one another. Split screen is mostly reserved for PvP first person shooters. It would not be much of a reach to combine the two. If the two PCs get far enough apart, the screen splits, maybe either horizontally or vertically depending upon the initial direction the two player-characters were from one another. You wouldn't want to alter it every time that relationship altered, but it could orient players to help them get back together again.

Splitting cooperative players is much the same as what we did in *The Gryphon Tapestry*, the difference being there is no need to incorporate flashbacks. All participants learn at the same time when a new item is found or exposition is delivered. This omniscient view doesn't do as much damage to immersion as you might think. We're used to gaining information in other media as well as games from scenes the protagonist doesn't participate in. Allowing the audience/player knowledge of such events is a convention.

Even if we constrain cooperative players on a single screen, we have chances for gameplay unique from solo-player mode. If we track factions in our game, NPCs may respond differently. If my character is a police officer and my partner's character is a streetwise convicted felon in my custody as in the film *48 Hrs.*, a suspect may be more willing to talk to my partner than me. I can stay seated at the bar while my partner crosses the room to sit at a table with the suspect.

We call these "buddy pictures." Two very different characters are thrown together because of circumstances and must learn to cooperate to be successful. It's a perfect structure for a savvy cooperative video game. Players will find themselves role-playing if you're not careful!

We have yet to explore a lot of the aspects of cooperative mode already built into the hardware of consoles. Personal computer games rarely support multiple players at a single machine. Network and online games might approach cooperative play from a similar

Figure 17.10 *48 Hrs.*: a buddy picture model for a cooperative video game.

perspective. Gameplay on multiple machines allows split screen action to be designed as part of the experience. James Cameron used the video displays of the squad of soldiers in *Aliens* to suspenseful effect.

The Incredible Shrinking Game

There is one family of game platforms that I've only flirted with and never designed for. That is the handhelds, PDAs, and cell phones. The challenge for handheld-dedicated gaming systems like the Game Boy Advance are similar to those faced by consoles only more so. Or less so. Less memory, pixels, colors, and controls.

PDAs face the same dilemma as personal computers. They are not dedicated game machines, so memory restrictions can be more severe. Interestingly, their keyboards are not laid out for games, but they are for text input. Despite the size of the keys, frequent users of PDAs input text at a faster rate than moving the cursor over a grid of letters and clicking, the method on consoles. This is one of the reasons text adventures and interactive fiction have found a new home here.

I'm going to let John Szeder, Director of Development at Digital Chocolate, Inc., take over. John has been doing it for awhile. Then I'll finish up with a few final comments.

John Szeder, Designer/Programmer

The best way to describe the mobile platform is "constrained." It has a slow processor, limited memory, a small screen, poor input mechanisms, and is not always connected to the network. Many of these constraints are a function of trying to extend the device's limited battery life, be able to fit it in your pocket, and also keep the cost of the device low.

The screens come in roughly three sizes: the "cheap phone" with a 96x56 pixel display, the "feature phone" with a 120x120 pixel display, and the "smart phone" with a 176x202 pixel display. Input on the cheaper phones is limited to one key press at a time, which inhibits multi-press behaviors like diagonal movement, and simultaneous move and fire options. There are usable memory limitations, often around 200k, and on many of the popular phones, there is a total application download limit of 64k to 100k.

Figure 17.11 John Szeder

Operating within these technical constraints is a challenge, but these challenges have existed on all of the early platforms at the dawn of the video game industry. There are some unique constraints to the mobile phone that are more based on social and usability expectations. The phone is a very casual device and is rated among the three most important things that most people take with them when they leave the house; keys and wallet being the other two. When people use their phone, they tend to make frequent light social connections with people for short durations of time. This is also how people expect to use mobile applications.

When designing an experience that tells a story to the mobile consumer, the best way to make it meaningful for the medium is to design the episodes to be one to five minutes in length. Having the ability to share the results of this drama through messaging features in the phone is a great way to tap into the power of the medium, and is also a great viral way for people to share their stories.

There are two additional emerging technologies that can provide better immersion for mobile users, and real world context to their experiences. The first is having access to location data in the phone (using GPS or assisted GPS). The second is the presence of a digital camera on the phone. The game designs that can incorporate these technologies effectively into their storytelling will have a chance at dominating the marketplace of tomorrow.

John's game *Portals of Arnak* (Figure 17.12) looks a lot like those graphical RPGs we played not all that long ago. If we could tell story then, we can tell story now.

Many years ago a classmate of mine at CalArts, Michael Pressman (*Frankie and Johnny Are Married*, *The Brotherhood of Poland, New Hampshire*), and I pitched a TV series to ABC called *Danger Games, Inc.* about a company that hired actors to portray characters in a real life adventure tailored to a customer's requirements. A year later, *Fantasy Island* debuted on ABC, and our idea became redundant. Years later of course, the film *The Game* with Michael Douglas and Sean Penn mined the same dramatic territory.

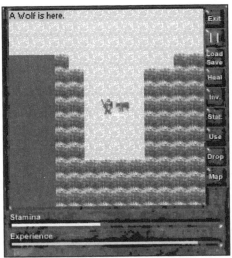

Figure 17.12 Story does not care how many pixels you have.

Thanks to Global Positioning Systems, fiction and reality are converging. GPS is taking us a fascinating next step beyond multiplayer gaming. The game board becomes the streets of Tokyo in *Mogi, Item Hunt,* where players invest real shoe leather tracking down items in collections of virtual treasure they can then trade with one another ala *Magic the Gathering* or *Pokemon*. Travel to Hong Kong and you can play the first massively multiplayer *persistent* (we'll define this in the next chapter) game, *Smart Mobs*. Other titles include the PvP title *Gunslingers* in Singapore. In Europe *Can You See Me Now?*, *Botfighters* (complete with role-playing elements), and *BattleMachine* all use GPS.

You don't need to literally take to the streets. Convergence is the current buzzword in mobile devices. Nokia's N-Gage is the most aggressive attempt to date to combine high quality mobile gaming, online connectivity, standard wireless phone features, personal information management, and even MP3 playback. *Pathway to Glory* is an impressive squad-level multiplayer game set during World War II. Even with its constraints, mobile computing has come a long way from the cute little time wasters shipped with my cell phone.

All of the same rules apply to storytelling on these devices, storytelling not being dependent on hardware as I've been drumming into you over and over again. However, glitz and glamour go a long way to convincing publishers to develop ever more interesting games.

A design for a massively multiplayer game I worked on a couple of years ago allowed players to access certain functions of a personal computer-based world from other hardware such as telephones, cell or not. There are still technical considerations when we start to mix and match all these platforms, but allowing players to make simple game decisions like beginning to craft, buying and selling items, and arranging expeditions with other players all from their phones is just around the corner. As games like *Pathway to Glory* indicate, even more will be possible in the not too distant future.

I was approached at GDC a couple of years ago concerning a proposed reality TV show that would challenge players to capture another player trying to make it across the United States without being caught. Take the current craze for reality TV, add the convergence of fiction and the real world possible with a variety of GPS-compatible game devices and the possibilities for storytelling become fascinating to contemplate. *Danger Games, Inc.* may become a reality yet!

CHAPTER 18

BRINGING VIRTUAL
WORLDS TO LIFE

Throughout this book when I have mentioned *virtual worlds* I have concentrated on massively multiplayer games because they are the mainstream entertainment progeny of MUDs (Multi-User Dungeons), and because they are the ones I know best. It's now time to examine this type of game. I've devoted two chapters to virtual worlds because, while on the surface they remind us very much of their single-player cousins and especially the multiplayer variations on those games, they are very different. Even in two chapters, I feel like I'm only scratching the surface, which is why I've tried to thread discussions of their unique qualities throughout the entire book. Someday there will be a book as long as this one just about story in virtual worlds.

In this first chapter, I'll set out some of the challenges writers and designers of virtual worlds face, and how they evolved. I'll suggest some approaches to tackling them here, then continue with more ideas in the second chapter.

When single-player games offer multiplayer versions, they are not virtual worlds. Popular multiplayer versions of games like *Diablo*, *Half-Life*, *Tribes*, *Age of Empires*, and many more are single sessions created for players when they are ready to play. There is no *persistence*.

note
___
PERSISTENCE: A virtual world or multiplayer game is said to be persistent because it remains even when individual players do not. Time passes, events occur exclusive of whether players are present.
___

Any storytelling of the original single-player game is stripped away. Players are left with the world for context, its weapons, skills, and mobs. Most of these are solely player versus player (PvP) games. Some games, like the newest incarnation of *Neverwinter Nights*, incorporate storytelling in their single-player versions, and player versus environment (PvE). *NWN* allows players to design their own worlds with their own stories that a limited number of players can experience together. Game states and player statistics can be saved to be resumed at a later play session in these games, but the planets stop spinning; all the NPCs head home to dinner; and the mobs go into hibernation.

Figure 18.1 Aribeth, the tragic figure from *Neverwinter Nights*.

Virtual worlds have many other unique qualities as well as persistence. It will be helpful to know a little about their development over the years to understand how this happened—and why storytelling is a far greater challenge than in single-player games.

Once upon a time, the majority opinion was that storytelling and gameplay would never mix. We still hear it today, although more often it's the variation that demands the two be segregated. Yet we have been steadily filling our magician's trunk with tricks and gadgets that enable us to tell stories every bit as compelling as those found in any other medium. If you run across someone who says it can't be done these days, translate that into him saying that *he* can't do it, and move on. If you meet someone who claims to have very recently figured out how to do it all on her own, you've met someone who is ignorant of the history of our medium. If you are confronted with someone who claims to be bringing emotion to games for the first time, you're in the presence of either a fool or a charlatan or both. Move along. There's nothing to see.

There are now a growing number of people who grew to storytelling from within our industry like Bob Bates, Nate Fox, Glen Dahlgren, and James Ohlen. There are those, like Hal Barwood and Mark Barrett and me, who have successfully made the leap to games from other media. And we're seeing new blood arrive such as J.T. Petty from the same direction. An annual workshop that I attend composed of writers and designers in our industry interested in storytelling, and from which many of the contributors to this book have been drawn, had nine participants in 2000. Now a list of well over 100 people supports the workshop.

We've seen how storytelling in single-player games flourished very early on, then stagnated to a certain extent. Yet over the past decade as more and more publishers and developers have become interested in stories as a means to distinguish their games from other products and reach new players, we've solved many of the problems that have made single-player stories so challenging.

Virtual worlds entered mainstream entertainment late in the game. Those in our workshop interested in virtual worlds has grown from me in 2000 to at least half our number today. Much of the resistance to story and misinformation about how to tell stories that we're finally overcoming in single-player games is still firmly entrenched in multiplayer. Let's see why.

Though computer games are by no means as mature an industry as film, that has been with us for over a century, or television, which has been around for over 60 years, we are approaching our 30-year anniversary. We'll deserve some fireworks, cake, and champagne. Out of that 30 years, many lessons have been learned.

The vast majority of players may think the first virtual worlds were *Ultima Online* (1996) and *Everquest* (1999) and, maybe if they're really up on their history, *Meridian 59* (1995). In fact, virtual worlds in one form or another have been around almost as long as *Colossal Cave* that developed in 1976 into the adventure that we all remember.

Richard Bartle ably chronicles the true history of virtual worlds in his book, *Designing Virtual Worlds*, so I'm not going to repeat the details here. I com-

Near Death Studios

Figure 18.2 *Meridian 59*: the first of the massively multiplayer games as we think of them today.

mend this book to you for insights from the man who helped create the first MUD or Multi-User Dungeon in 1978. It was called simply *MUD*. Mr. Bartle is quite rightly one of the most respected figures in the field of virtual world design. It's an excellent overview of the subject. My chapters will confine themselves to character and story.

I'll mention only one early virtual world that was significant for me, and that was the first manifestation of *Neverwinter Nights*. This game was the reason I became one of the original 50,000 subscribers to a new online service called America Online, or AOL, that was born in 1991 out of an earlier service called QuantumLink. The experience of playing in a game with unseen strangers from who knows where scared the hell out of me. In the 13 years since then, I've managed to get past that fear. A little. The best thing about a virtual world is all those other people you're playing with. The worst thing about a virtual world is all those other people you're playing with.

It's important to note that there are very few crossovers between the development of single-player RPG games and virtual worlds. The first *Neverwinter Nights* sprang from a series of single-player "gold box" games based on the *Advanced Dungeons and Dragons* license. *Ultima Online* was based on the highly successful single-player *Ultima* series. For the most part, however, the two types of entertainment developed along parallel tracks. Each school took its settings, themes, and archetypes from the same sources, like *Lord of the Rings* high fantasy, but approached them in very different ways.

While not the first multiplayer worlds, *Meridian 59*, *Ultima Online*, and *Everquest* were the first *massively* multiplayer games. Their designs made it clear that while some elements of tabletop and MUDs scale quite well, others do not. Today, less than a decade later, we are handcuffed by a patchwork design style that borrows, often indiscriminately, from many, not always compatible, sources. One of the themes in this book that I bring up as often as I can is summed up by Richard Bartle: "Time and time again, designers have made the same mistakes their predecessors made, either because they were simply not aware of the earlier work or they were too arrogant to believe it could possibly be relevant to their greatly superior products." This truth does not just apply to virtual worlds.

Writers and designers of our current virtual worlds fall into two factions, sometimes warring, sometimes allying. The first is comprised of people who have moved from tabletop role-playing games like *Advanced Dungeons & Dragons* and/or MUDs into massively multiplayer. For that reason, most writers and designers of that first crop of massively multiplayer games to hit mainstream computer gamer radars were culled from this tight-knit fraternity, and most of the paradigms for the games that followed are drawn from these.

The officers and many of the staff of the company that developed *The Gryphon Tapestry* (1999), the first virtual world I worked on, were all Live Action Role-Players (LARP), and the world and backstory of the game had been built as a LARP over several years before adapting it to a massively multiplayer game. It gave us a deep well of rich lore to draw upon. Figure 18.3 shows one of the first crude maps we worked from while translating the LARP world of Averndale to a massively multiplayer game.

There's another obvious benefit to this type of background. Tabletop roleplayers, MUD-ers, and LARPers share a common history of humans interacting with one another to create their storytelling that prepared them well for massively multiplayer. This has shaped how story has been approached until now. We'll examine this evolution of massively multiplayer storytelling in the next section.

The second faction is made up of writers and designers from single-player games who have been attracted by the new challenges virtual worlds filled with many players present us. Until recently we were rare. While I played some tabletop RPGs; dabbled in text MUDs; and slunk around in AOL's *Neverwinter Nights* in near catatonia, I belong to this hardy band. Ever since my first experiences with *Ultima Online* and *Everquest*, I've been fascinated by the storytelling possibilities of virtual worlds.

I don't even come entirely from the second group since my origins as a writer were theatre, film, and television. I guess you noticed that a long time ago! If you've made it this far through my book, it should come as no shock to hear that I disagree with Richard Bartle's

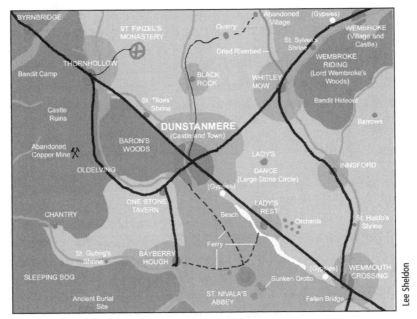

Figure 18.3 The area surrounding the market town of Dunstanmere in *The Gryphon Tapestry*.

assertion that "Books and movies, well known and respected art forms that they are, nevertheless rarely contain practical information that virtual world designers can actually use."

I don't blame him. His is a majority opinion of those who developed their design philosophies along the tabletop/MUD track. As such, we approach this type of game from two very different backgrounds. One of the major themes in this book is that storytelling in games is not as divorced from other media as many believe. Virtual worlds are no exception. While I continue to write and design solo-player games, I have been working on virtual world projects for the past five years now. I would guess Mr. Bartle has not worked on many plays, movies, or television. Looking at a field of endeavor from the outside is liable to lead one to draw some odd conclusions very much like the blind man attempting to describe an elephant. Hopefully, I can change his mind some day.

I mentioned earlier a story structure called "multiple jeopardy" or more accurately, "multiple character." Multiple character films have been popular for years, and have their roots in Victorian novelists like Dickens who had to fill so many weeks with new content he wove the stories of many characters throughout his longer books. *Grand Hotel* (1932) is a famous example of this type of storytelling.

The term "multiple jeopardy" was coined for disaster films that became so popular in the 1970s like *The Poseidon Adventure*, *The Towering Inferno*, and *Earthquake*. Here, while there

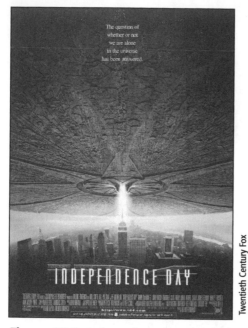

Twentieth Century Fox

Figure 18.4 *Independence Day:* massively multiplayer movie.

may be a hierarchy of stars, many characters and stories are given equal screen time. *Independence Day* is a more recent example of this. *Pulp Fiction* and *Eight is Enough* both fit in the broader multiple character category too. Soap operas, of course, fit into the multiple character category and for the same reason Dickens needed all those characters. It helps fill the hours just as it helped fill the pages.

Because I enjoyed this style of storytelling, and had used it in other media, I saw the implications for virtual worlds, and how stories might be structured for those worlds. There were some hurdles to get over first—the same hurdles people had been struggling with all the way back when we sat around the kitchen table and rolled the combat die. A big stumbling block for many people is "Why bother?"

The Roots of Role-Playing

Face-to-face role-playing goes back to the dawn of man when children pretended to be those brave hunters I wrote about in my prelude (back at the dawn of this book). Such play is every bit as structured and ritualized today as it was in the Paleolithic. As I mentioned earlier, it teaches as well as entertains, and the behavior is easily spotted in other species. Lion cubs learn to be the king of beasts through role-play.

When I was a boy, my friends and I used to play games based on a popular show of the day called *Combat* that starred Rick Jason and Vic Morrow. We role-played the various characters. My friend Joel always wanted to play the French character played by Pierre Jalbert. He would introduce himself in appropriate accent as "My nem is Caje. I spik Frranch." I liked to play Vic Morrow's character: chisel-jawed Sgt. Saunders. Nobody wanted to be strong but kind of slow Littlejohn.

ABC

Figure 18.5 The cast of characters from *Combat* that we role-played.

Dave Arneson and Gary Gygax created the original *Dungeons & Dragons* in 1972. Instead of moving units around on a board as in previous games, this time players were cast as individual heroes who could gain experience as they adventured in a high fantasy world. That world existed in the set of rules governing play and in players' imaginations. Both rules and gameplay were very flexible. In 1978 *Advanced Dungeons & Dragons* was released. This version was far more structured, and it is the game most mean when they say *Dungeons & Dragons*.

The casual role-playing of childhood, filtered through the sensibilities of two guys who had played many board and war games, became codified. Soon worlds from many genres were developed. And of course, the timing is significant. 1978 also saw the birth of MUD.

Many of the features that distinguished tabletop role-playing also shaped how the stories were told. The rule sets were the game engine. Character attributes gave role-players the foundation to build characters upon. The backstories and world details provided the context for their adventures. The individual stories that players experienced came from the same bardic tradition we've talked about before, the give and take of oral storytelling.

DMs or *GMs* construct outlines for a play session's adventures; create characters for players to interact with, monsters to slay, and loot to be discovered. They base their games literally or loosely on the structure and rules of the role-playing franchise their adventure is a part of. But that is only half the job.

note

DM: stands for the Dungeon Master, overseer and manipulator of a live role-playing adventure often involving exploration of a dungeon.

GM: Game Master, a more general title that covers all role-playing games, including those not involving dungeon crawls.

Some GMs use campaigns and scenarios provided by professionals to play. Others use these only as springboards for original stories. It may seem as if new GMs form the biggest part of the first style, then when they become more comfortable they also become more original. But while the source of the story may indicate more or less writing talent, it is no indicator of a good or bad GM. It's how they direct the story once it's written.

GMs must keep on their toes to adjust to player input. They are good GMs because they are good bards. More than one tabletop session has dissolved into arguments and even the occasional fight between inflexible GMs and frustrated players. Flexible GMs who can adjust without missing a beat to the unexpected choices role-players make are what change the experience from a scripted by-the-numbers, role-the-die experience to a dynamic and volatile entertainment.

On the other hand, good GMs also find many of their talents make them good designers of MUDs and MMORPGs. Moving to MUD design allows the GM/designer to hand over to the computer a lot of the busy work. Die roles to determine outcomes of encounters and battles are programmed into the game. Stats and levels are calculated automatically. And the GM no longer has to be present for her game to be played by others. This last fact is both a blessing and a curse.

It is a blessing because MUDs tend to run 24/7 unless there's a glitch. Once the MUD is launched, while the world still needs to be administered, maintained, and updated, the designer can actually get some sleep occasionally. It's a curse because the biggest thing lost is the GM's direct involvement with the players experiencing the quests and story in the game. MUDs are at their best with combat, levels, and loot. They are at their worst in responsiveness to players. The human element is still there. Most designers are human. But they are now one step removed from the player experience. What takes their place? What now reacts to the unexpected choices players make? The computer. And the computer is not as good at being human as it is at arithmetic.

The first solution, one that still occasionally shows up in MMOPRGs, was to allow GMs to stage special events within the world where they actually assume the roles of NPCs or mobs. They might take over NPCs and mobs already in the game as computer-controlled characters, or they might play all new ones.

Everquest's events were not especially successful, consisting as they did of GMs taking over powerful mobs, then proceeding to slaughter every low-ranking PC in sight. Eventually, a large enough crowd of high-level players, usually an uber guild, would roll up, defeat the GM-controlled mob, and reap the rewards. I remember that when players complained, the senior customer service representative replied that he didn't see the problem. In fact, he enjoyed playing a victim sometimes. This was certainly an interesting insight into his character, but most would agree players would rather be heroes than victims. The *Everquest* events were isolated occurrences in a static world, short bursts of activity casually connected to the world fiction.

Ultima Online continued to feature live events. Some were successful; some not. Their variety was impressive however, from the appearance of GM-controlled NPCs to major invasions. But again, the world was effectively static. Once the invasion was repelled, PCs who had participated returned to their every day lives of hunting, crafting, and battling each other.

Another solution was to take the ongoing story of a tabletop or LARP world away and replace it with an essentially static world (like *Everquest*, with backstory and characters) but one that didn't change substantially unless it was added to by incorporating new areas to explore, quests, monsters, and NPCs. This approach, even more popular now than the first in MMORPGs, should not be mistaken for ongoing story even when writers and designers introduce seasons or try to glue words like arc on to it.

The distinction is important. Additions to the virtual world do not significantly impinge on the state of the world that was in place before they are introduced. The world expands. The story does not progress.

As we saw in our discussion of quests, the world of *Dark Age of Camelot* is no more dynamic than one of those paddle toys with the ball attached to it by a rubber band. No matter how hard you hit the ball, it always zips back. Over time, ball and paddle remain the same. Unless of course the rubber band breaks. But we don't want our games breaking.

Finally, we come to attempts to actually duplicate the ongoing bardic story of tabletop. *Asheron's Call* combined live events with scripted events as part of their monthly updates. *Asheron's Call 2* and *Earth & Beyond* settled on scripted events for their story progression. In all cases, these events were package deals including new quests, new items, physical changes to the landscape, and so on. These events are delivered as monthly episodes. *Horizons* delivers its scripted events on a weekly basis, although they are often on a much smaller scale. We'll be talking more about this episodic structure for the delivery of content at the end of this chapter.

Figure 18.6 *Asheron's Call:* The first MMORPG to feature regular ongoing story.

What this short history of role-playing reveals is that however MMORPGs attack the problem of replacing the GM, we cannot approach the level of engagement enjoyed by tabletop, at least if we look to developers to provide it. Developers of these games rightly missed this interaction between GM and players. They recognized that the storytelling was a collaboration between bard and audience. If the bard was difficult to replicate, is it any wonder then that they backed away and looked in another direction?

The most common solution has been to decide that the players can take over the jobs of both bard and audience. If they were able to role-play their way to exciting stories in tabletop, the thinking goes, why not let them do it in massively multiplayer? We would give them context through the world design and backstory, then set them free. This is the sandbox approach to virtual world design. We build the world, players provide the stories.

If there is another name that comes to mind when we talk about the most influential people working in virtual worlds today it is Raph Koster. Raph came into the commercial industry directly from the well-respected *LegendMUD* that his wife, Kristen, still runs today. From there, he went on to be lead designer on *Ultima Online*, *Star Wars Galaxies* and is now Chief Creative Officer at Sony Online Entertainment, makers of *Everquest*, *Star Wars Galaxies*, and *Planetside*.

In response to a question asked of a panel on next-generation persistent worlds at the March 2002 Game Designer's Conference Raph said:

> I hate to say this to all the film directors, writers, poets, [and] painters: Get over yourselves; the rest of the world is coming. Okay? The thing is that people want to express themselves and they don't really care that 99 percent of everything is crap, because they are positive that the 1 percent they made isn't. Okay? And fundamentally, they get ecstatic as soon as five people see it, right? It's all them, guys, and, fundamentally, "authorship" is about *us*. And it's the wrong medium for it. It's not what the medium is for.

I condensed that a bit, but I think the message is intact. In *Designing Virtual Worlds*, an over 700-page book (I don't want to scare you. If you're interested in virtual worlds, buy it anyway.), Richard Bartle devotes 12 pages to storytelling. This quote may explain why:

> Virtual world designers can't add story, they only can add content. Content provides experiences that can be made by those who come through or observe them into story. If the content itself is story, players' own stories become worthless incidentals.

Mr. Bartle goes on to say:

> Narrative is linear. Virtual worlds are not linear. You can't control the order in which players do things without railroading them, removing significant freedoms. There is only one path into the past, and thence comes story; there are infinite paths into the future. Virtual world designers build a bagatelle board and release the ball but have no way of knowing where it is going to land. If they did, where would the fun be?

There's more, but I think you get the idea. Mr. Bartle and I obviously disagree. One of the reasons for that disagreement is how we look at narrative. If you think narrative is only linear, it's not surprising you believe it has no place in non-linear worlds. If you can imagine non-linear ways of telling story, then those stories and the world may not seem quite so at odds with one another.

To me the loss of true GMs in our massively multiplayer words is significant. The GM didn't just create the setting for her players then go out to order pizza. She helped shape the experience by providing her players with an ongoing story they could play.

I suspect you can see why storytelling has faced a rough (and linear?) road in virtual worlds. If two of the most influential names in this field feel this way (and they are by no means alone), what hope do author-developers have? Please note that they are both from that first faction I mentioned, both on the track that runs parallel to my development. Their conclusions rise naturally from the bardic approach their experiences took to story. I just think they've thrown the bard out with the bathwater.

This is where my question in the previous section rises from. Why bother? If you believe that players can entertain themselves sufficiently, it certainly takes some pressure off. You can concentrate on providing enough sand and plastic shovels without worrying too much about narrative. Kids make up their own stories after all in real sandboxes.

This is the uphill battle faced by storytelling in virtual worlds. I think we need to bother, and happily some developers like Turbine (*Asheron's Call*) and Artifact Entertainment (*Horizons*) do bother. These aren't the most successful of MMORPGs, however, and a case could be made that's a reason why their approach is wrong. But I find fault not in their aspirations, but in their execution. We'll revisit both games in these two chapters.

Single-player games were in a very similar state for many years. Developers overwhelmingly chose gameplay over story. Eventually enough designers began to realize a balance between the two might create a synergy out of which a richer entertainment experience might grow. Things began to change.

In the Academy Award winning romantic comedy from 1934 *It Happened One Night* Ellie Andrews (Claudette Colbert) and Peter Warne (Clark Gable) are two healthy, attractive, but unmarried adults forced to spend a night together in an "auto court," the forerunner of today's motels. In a scene affectionately dubbed "The Walls of Jericho," Gable was perfectly willing to explore the possibilities, but not Claudette. So he gallantly hangs a sheet on a clothesline between their beds to protect Claudette's virtue while they disrobe slightly for bed. Gable's removal of his shirt reportedly caused female members of the audience to swoon (and started a shirtless fashion craze). I

suspect the ladies fainted for different reasons than the gun fired at them in *The Great Train Robbery*. At the resolution of the film, a married Ellie and Peter return to the auto camp, and ask the bewildered managers for a blanket, a clothesline and . . . a trumpet . . .

Just as Ellie came around, solo games are coming around. It is inevitable virtual worlds will follow. We just need to find a loud enough trumpet. Getting away from ideas like "narrative must be linear" will help. Realizing that just as gameplay and story can support one another, so can authorial storytelling, and player created story (see the next chapter) will

Figure 18.7 Story on one side, virtual virtue on the other.

help too. It's one thing to observe that players can find themselves entertaining just as the clichéd drunk at the Prohibition party wearing a lampshade is delighted in his wit. It's another to throw out centuries of proven story-based entertainment, and hope the players will make up the difference. That's sort of like discovering a shortfall at the bank and hoping the customers will cover it no matter how rich they think they are. Okay, enough Depression-era analogies. Back to the present.

Why couldn't human GMs continue to effectively oversee events? Why did we have to look for other toys to fill our sandboxes? The answer lies in our next topic.

Scope and Scale

One of the primary issues in the development of virtual worlds and the way they traditionally view story is scope and scale. We'll look at growth in several areas as we scale up from the intimacy of the tabletop to those melting pots of humanity called massively multiplayer persistent worlds: the size of the worlds; the number of designers needed; and especially, the number of players. Scope and scale have been a challenge in every massive game to date, just as they were when MUDs attempted to duplicate the tabletop experience.

The size of the world in a tabletop game is usually much larger than that of a massively multiplayer game. It's easy to do. It exists in the imaginations of the players. It doesn't have to be rendered in breathtaking 3-D graphics. Also the GM only needs to recreate a small portion of that world for any given play session. Text MUD worlds can be huge as well. All that is required is the time and the descriptive talent to bring to life whatever locations are required. Massive worlds, despite their name, are the smallest. *Everquest,* even with all its expansion packs, is only a fraction of the size of the *Advanced Dungeons and Dragons* universe.

What does this mean to us? Our worlds are more easily explored. The sense of mystery can fade. The most exciting journey I've ever taken in an MMORPG was in the first weeks of *Everquest* when my friend, Adar, and I were guided across the continent of Antonica from Qeynos to Freeport. The most powerful players in the game still ran from the beasts that roamed in our path. In one particular canyon we had to inch along a crack halfway up a sheer cliff to avoid minotaurs wandering below.

Soon every location on that continent and the others in the initial game had been explored and mapped. The Kunark expansion pack gave players new lands to explore. But nothing had really changed in the story or the fundamental gameplay. That initial fear of the unknown and awe at the wonders it held was never recaptured. Even in the first version of the game, teleports allowed players to bypass vast distances. The world shrank. *Everquest* did one thing right that I think *Asheron's Call* missed. The teleports in *Everquest* could only be activated by certain classes. The rest of us had to hitchhike a ride.

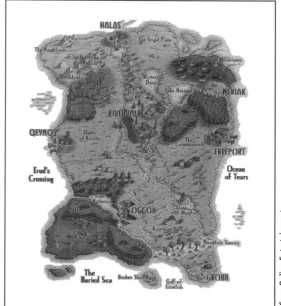

Sony Online Entertainment

Figure 18.8 At first, the geography of *Everquest* seemed vast and unknown.

Even more important, their use was based on level. Players in those first weeks had no one yet to hitch a ride with. We were forced to experience the vast world on foot. *Asheron's Call* allowed all players to teleport immediately. The mystery of the land diminished, and it was far more difficult to orient myself. I had a clear picture in my head of where the cities and other features of the lands of Norrath were in *Everquest* because I explored for a long time on foot. The Dereth of *Asheron's Call* and its successor remained much harder to orient myself within.

Not only are our worlds smaller, but the populations are larger. So the worlds become even smaller. It's hard to lose yourself in adventure when you're competing against dozens of other players for the chance to slay some poor mob. If hell is repetition, as some philosophers say, then a mob's life in these games is hell. They respawn over and over only to be killed over and over again. No wonder they're cranky. We'll look at some ways around this issue in the next chapter.

Because the worlds are smaller and the population is larger, content is easier to find, which means more must be added and faster. Unfortunately, this caused designers to try and hide content. We'll revisit the conundrum of revealing story in the next chapter.

The next challenge of scale is that whereas one designer alone can design a single-player game even today, one person cannot design a massive world, at least given the production schedules necessary to get them from conception to profit as quickly as possible. Design teams have mushroomed. Various designers tackle different game components. Mimicking Hollywood with its long lists of story editors and producers, developers seem intent on calling everybody who works on a game some kind of designer or other. There may even be several lead designers. Given the rock band mentality we've already discussed, its obvious communication becomes an enormous challenge.

Several writers or quest designers, for example, working without a strong lead, will churn out stories and quests that only marginally resemble one another in style and their interpretation of the world. As I began to play through the quests in *Dark Age of Camelot*, I could recognize which quests were written by the same person. Someone should have been smoothing over the inconsistencies in language and style of the quests. Writing on a staff demands the writer be a forger who can duplicate style and character or her fellow writers as closely as possible. This issue is discussed in detail in the appendix on building writing teams.

Even worse, lead designers can lose touch with what individual level designers, being overseen by other designers, are up to. I was embarrassed for a lead designer on a game I played recently who confessed he didn't know why a particular design glitch had made it into his game. How does a design vision survive, or a theme for that matter, if its implementation is sabotaged by poor communication?

Now let's look at players. In a tabletop game you have a handful of players, usually grouped together, overseen by a GM. Even though party members could split off from the main group, the GM only needed to create a single adventure for a play session. In a MUD, there can be dozens, even hundreds, online at any given time. The code is usually there for a GM to intervene in gameplay at any time and theoretically on any scale he desires. Events can be limited to a quest for a single group, much like tabletop, or a world-wide announcement as if called down by the gods of Olympus. But if the MUD is small, chances are the staff is as well; and it may be all volunteer. There may not be enough GMs to participate in the world on a regular basis and in such a way as the most players benefit.

This results in GMs offering selected groups special interaction, and the rest of the population feeling left out. Now move to MMOs where there can be thousands playing simultaneously on each of many servers. GMs must coordinate their efforts or, as in *Asheron's Call*, move from server to server like a traveling minstrel show. The value of live events begins to diminish rapidly when you consider live humans may need to be paid, the events are only one-shots, and the percentage of the playerbase able to experience them is relatively small.

Ultima Online used to be able to draw on an enthusiastic crowd of unpaid volunteers to stage their events both large and small. This kept costs low. Then in 2000 a group of former and current volunteers were told that their free *Ultima Online* service, plus other perks they'd enjoyed, were being withdrawn. A recent judgment against AOL had already recognized that such volunteer work might fall under the jurisdiction of federal legislation establishing minimum compensation.

A class action lawsuit was filed asking for past wages. Very recently, rumors have surfaced that the suit has finally been settled and checks issued. If true, that may sound like a long time between crisis and resolution until we remember England's Chancery court. The result everyone agrees upon is that it spelled the end of the volunteer programs as we knew them at all three of the then major MMORPGs: *Ultima Online*, *Asheron's Call*, and *Everquest*. Most live events these days are player-led, not developer.

Another issue of scope and scale is how quests are handled. The most important gameplay mechanism in tabletop is the quest. Quests in tabletop are designed for small groups of players to experience together. Just as the players are playing one story, they are involved in one major quest. It is during that quest that their ongoing personal stories and character advancement occurs, much as we've seen television shows like *Sex and the City* use individual episodes to advance their characters' stories.

Quests in MMORPGs, when they do appear, are most often written and designed exactly the same way as single-player quests (see Chapter 10, "Charting New Territory"). This is one of the patches in the design quilt of virtual worlds that simply does not match the others. Quests that worked fine for small groups or in single-player games make no sense in the world fiction of massive worlds with thousands of players. It results in players lining up to slay fearsome beasts that respawn moments later; cure plagues that immediately re-infect the populace; and find fabulously rare lost treasures that a thousand other players also have exact duplicates of.

The attempt is to make heroes of the players, yet their transitory fame rarely extends beyond their immediate circle. This is true of most people's real lives. Why do we impose the restrictions on their chances of fame and glory in a fantasy world where they want to be larger than life? We'll look at true multiplayer quests in the next chapter, but the fact is quests are no longer the primary gameplay mechanism in most MMORPGs. It's *camping*.

note

CAMPING: refers to the repetitive behavior of killing the same mobs over and over again as the most efficient way to gain levels and loot.

A variation of this, called *farming*, emphasizes loot over level.

note

FARMING: a term used to describe the repetitive behavior of players killing much lower level mobs for their loot.

Both are primary game mechanisms in massive worlds. Another is player vs. player combat. Quests are so tied to storytelling, they are harder to do than the calculations of hits and misses and rewards accompanying combat. Here we have another example of the circular logic that limits the growth of story in virtual worlds. Because the numbers are easier to do than the stories, fewer stories are told. Because fewer stories are told, it appears obvious they don't work as well in virtual worlds. The computer is being used not simply as a tool, but as a critic as well. It is being allowed to decide what it wants to include based on what it does best, never mind the human at the keyboard.

www.rainforestventures.com

Without live GMs, generation of new content becomes a primary challenge. Players are army ants relentlessly devouring everything in their path like the short story "Leiningen vs. the Ants" made into a movie called *The Naked Jungle* in 1954. The bigger the world, the more minds are pitted against the designers, attempting to solve their puzzles, complete their quests, kill their mobs, and obtain phat l00t. Adding new mobs is easier on the computer, and on designers mired in believing story doesn't belong.

Figure 18.9 Actual photograph of players consuming content.

Many writers will argue it's impossible to keep up with a player's appetite for new quests. All of them should spend a month or two writing for soaps. We looked at some ways of streamlining the creation of new quests such as Chinese menus, but we can't rely totally on such repetitive errands. We need to write quests. We can. Stop whining.

Writers must take into account the rate of character progression, just as designers do. It is always faster than we plan for. Watching the baby boomer spikes that ripple through our player base we can track what percentage of players are at which levels and adjust our content generation accordingly. Obviously, as more story and quests are added over time, newer players won't notice the frantic addition of new material we generate to keep the leading edge of power gamers entertained.

Single-player games have endgames and then we put the box on the shelf, but our worlds go on and on. Just as characters grown too powerful can harm sequels in other media, the same challenge presents itself to us in virtual worlds. A world with all of the players squashed together at the very top end of the power scale needs something more, at least assuming its progression is the typical one of levels and loot. Most current games are based on MUD engines that emphasize this progression. This is when what Raph Koster refers to elegantly as the "elder game" kicks in.

Elder games can be extensions of the gameplay already in place. *Everquest* churns out new zones and expansions. They are still running ahead of the ants. Other elder games are almost like a new game. *Dark Age of Camelot* has its realm versus realm warfare. Players are teased with this new *Tribes*-style capture-the-flag gameplay early on, but cannot really take part in the full-fledged version until they are extremely high level, and can play it as an elder game. *Shadowbane* even accelerates the normal tedious level and loot treadmill to help players get powerful enough to survive its no-holds-barred PvP elder game as quickly as possible.

This is a reasonable game solution, but it is not a happy story solution. For those games like *Dark Age of Camelot* and *Shadowbane* it doesn't really matter. They proudly hold tickets for the "players will make their own stories" bandwagon. But in our search for more things for players to do, massive persistent worlds have borrowed from another type of online experiences: MUSHes.

note

MUSH: stands for Multi-User Social Habitat. These online communities emphasize the social aspects of virtual worlds.

Our current massively multiplayer worlds are not only about combat. For example they include closed economies for the buying and selling of loot as well as player-crafted items. The importance of crafting varies among the current games. *Star Wars Galaxies* and *Horizons* have robust crafting systems. In *Horizons* the crafting system is far more satisfying to crafters than the adventure system is to the level and loot crowd.

MUSHes also often allow players to assist in the actual world-building. This is an area most massive games pay only lip service to. It's become common for games to provide the ability for players to build housing. *Star Wars Galaxies* allows players to litter the countryside with mining and harvesting machines like pumps in a west Texas oil field. But like realm versus realm gameplay, this is not truly dynamic, and the world is only changed in its aesthetic appeal. There are more social elements introduced into virtual worlds that we'll discuss shortly.

This is just an overview of some of the challenges scope and scale hand designers of virtual worlds. There are many more outside the range of this book like numerous balance issues, policing of players, communication between server and client computers, and more. We will mention story solutions to a couple of these in a moment. They don't completely solve all of the problems, but intelligent methods for delivering story can help some.

In the next chapter, I'm going to refer back to the challenges brought up here, and explore some more far ranging solutions to them.

Death of a Player-Character Revisited

Virtual worlds add a new wrinkle to the issues of player-character death we discussed in Chapter 4, "Character Roles." Not just one player-character is dying again and again, but thousands might be. I don't consider permadeath a reasonable solution for most virtual worlds. Unlike single-player games, the investment of time and effort makes it an extreme penalty. If a virtual world isn't going to kill the player-character ever as in *Toontown*, it's not an issue at all. But most do.

To make certain players don't heedlessly ignore their safety; to create some tension and a sense of consequences and loss, massive persistent worlds do impose death penalties. One of the most interesting challenges for me as a player in *Everquest* was corpse retrieval. While a player's body lay rotting where it had fallen, the player was reborn some distance away at a magical location called a bind point. She then had a generous amount of time to return to her corpse before it was gone forever. This was important because all of the player's weapons, armor, loot, and so forth remained with the body. It was challenging because the player often died in very nasty places, and strategy had to be worked out to get to the body.

There were more death penalties. Players lost experience needed to gain levels and power. Lose too much experience, you could lose an entire level and the abilities you enjoyed there. Other games cause you to lose some items you had in your possession.

At the other end of the spectrum, consequences in *Horizons* are slight. A player is whisked back to a bind point inventory intacta. But there is another key difference between the two games. *Everquest* makes little attempt to explain why the player is reincarnated or how her corpse can coexist in the same world with her healthy body. The storytelling opportunity is squandered.

In *Horizons*, all players are called The Gifted, and a backstory explains how they can be resurrected. This is not just explained in a manual. There is the quest suite in the game called the Trials of the Gifted that players can undertake very early on. It teaches players about the world and their place in it. One of the quests retells the story of The Gifted and allows players to experience this resurrection firsthand. Here the designers did not simply repeat the convention without explanation; they took the trouble to place it within the context of their fictional world.

Figure 18.10 In *Horizons*, The Gifted die a thousand deaths, but it's okay.

Other quests reinforce the special nature of this "gift." Certain NPCs express opinions about it. A gameplay problem—what to do when a player-character dies—has not only been solved, it's a solution that addresses the storytelling as well.

The Social World

The best thing about a virtual world is all those other people you're playing with. The worst thing about a virtual world is all those other people you're playing with. It bears repeating. I've mentioned crafting. It's part of the social world of the game because it requires interaction between players: sellers, and buyers. Another important issue is interfaces. The ease with which players can communicate with each other, NPCs, and the game world in general is incredibly important.

There is also the matter of choosing how we can dress up player-characters before they go out into the world to interact. We talked about professions, classes, races, and sexes in Chapter 5 "Character Traits," and relationships in Chapter 6, "Character Encounters." First I want to briefly revisit the concept of factions brought up then.

Factions

As we saw, factions are a relatively simple way to create relationships and rivalries between players and NPCs or other players. The choices we make about these factions can affect the way our entire virtual world is perceived. Setting players in opposition with NPCs is obviously a good thing. If our worlds contain PvP, it's necessary to place players in opposition with one another. *Dark Age of Camelot* and *Shadowbane* go the basic imperialist route: grab land, become more powerful. Is there any real reason in DAoC for Hibernians, Albions, and Midgardians to hate one another? No. Is anything more at stake than power and bragging rights? No.

This is not a particular problem in worlds where storytelling takes a back seat to gameplay. It helps if those factions are more historically opposed such as in *World War II Online*. That game is all gameplay, no story. It attempts the almost impossible feat of taking a war that ebbed and flowed then only a few years later ended, and reducing it to a timeless static situation that may shift like realm warfare in DAoC, but then never shifts too far. The challenge would be greatly increased if the developers attempted some kind of ongoing story in addition to the warfare.

What happens when we adapt opposing forces from another medium that our audience has already become familiar with? Let's look at *Star Wars Galaxies*. It makes perfect sense in gameplay terms to allow players to play either rebels or Imperials. If you're going to have PvP in a *Star Wars* game, that is the obvious choice. But what happens to both story and the game world itself?

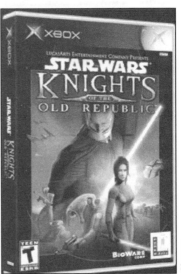

We already know from the franchise that the Imperials are the villains. No problem so far: some players love to play villains. There's a naughty thrill involved in doing what thou wilt. Bioware's single-player game *Knights of the Old Republic* is a good example of the fun that can be had going over to the dark side. In a massively multi-player game, another factor intrudes. While some players want to be villains, more want to be heroes. In *Star Wars Galaxies*, there are far more rebels than Imperial soldiers.

The entire nature of the universe is shifted away from the one players are familiar with. All of a sudden the rebels are no longer in hiding, small brave bands fighting against insurmountable odds as heroes are wont to do. They are kicking serious Imperial butt all the time. One of the complaints in the first three months of the game when I was playing, was that the universe of the game didn't feel much like the Star Wars universe. There's not much writers can do about the fact that there was no true space travel in the game. Virtual worlds always have to cut corners, knowing that eventually, if they are hits, they can add features. But what might writers do with the entire shift in the balance of power towards the underdogs?

Figure 18.11 Play either side of the force in *Knights of the Old Republic*.

As attractive and balanced as it must have appeared to allow players to play both rebels and Imperial soldiers, it might have been better in story terms, and for the good of the game universe, not to allow it. If the Imperials were solely NPCs, their iron fist would remain intact. They could swarm rebel uprisings whenever they grew too out of hand. Players could still have played one of the factions allied to the Imperials, or other factions like pirates opposed to the rebels to be villains and for PvP. The overall balance of power in the game would have remained as it is in the other products in the franchise. The climate of danger would be intact. The Imperials would continue to be a force to be feared, and the rebels would have a chance to be the kinds of plucky, under-gunned heroes players loved in the movies.

Factions in virtual worlds are far trickier than in single-player games. Their ramifications are great. They can be a great boon to providing conflict and variety of gameplay, as we saw earlier in the book. They can also be a subtle trap, even if they're true to the desired gameplay, if they fail to take into consideration the storytelling needs of the world.

Guilds

Guilds are one of the primary social systems we can construct for our players in virtual worlds. They can go by many names: clubs, factions, unions, and so on, but we use guild the most because they are inspired by the medieval guild system that began around the 11th century with merchants who gathered together for mutual aid and protection. Craft guilds soon followed, and today we still have them. I've been a member of the Writers Guild of America for 30 years.

Role-playing is easy in tabletop. Whatever their role-play abilities, all participants are there with role-playing in mind. Role-playing in MUDs is a bit more problematic, but most MUDs can successfully police it. The numbers of players are still manageable. And it's relatively easy when you're not dependent on revenue to toss players who refuse to go along. Role-playing in a world populated by thousands, even hundreds, is an uphill battle. These games want to appeal to the greatest number of players possible. As a result, strict role-players often find themselves in conflict with gamers mainly interested in the game of level and loot. These are often referred to by role-players in derogatory terms such as l33t d00ds.

Some games launch role-playing servers, but the problems remain due to lack of policing on the part of developers naturally concerned about alienating the larger non-role-playing base. Guilds give players the chance to join together for exactly the same reasons they did in the middle ages: mutual aid and protection. Pure role-playing guilds who deliberately attempt to isolate themselves from non role-players are common.

Another reason guilds are popular is that when the population of a game world grows too large players gravitate to smaller groups where the interactions of the world will not overwhelm them. Raph Koster has estimated that after a server reaches a population of about 250, sub-populations will begin to be needed. All worlds provide tools for the creation and management of guilds. Guilds provide a comfortable venue for exchanging player stories and disseminating CNN-like reports from the front lines of battle. But to the best of my knowledge, no massively persistent world to date has used guild systems as authorial story devices.

One of the systems I worked on for *URU: Ages Beyond Myst* was a guild system, based on preliminary work we'd done in *The Gryphon Tapestry*. It was near the end of my tenure at

Cyan, and I'm not sure how widely distributed that document was, or if any of it made it into the multiplayer version of the game, another one that died in beta. On *TGT*, we were already toying with the idea when a well-meaning member of the team revealed to fans that, yes, we would indeed have guilds. Even before alpha and players could enter the game world, guilds sprang up on our message boards. Unfortunately not all of these guilds fit the fiction of our world very well. What to do? Necessity became the mother of intervention.

Always on the lookout for story opportunities and ways to engage more players in the world fiction, I approached guilds the same way I did NPCs and quests. We may be able to build a sandbox and expect people to play in it, but we cannot guarantee that they'll play the game we expect them to. More than one designer has complained bitterly that players are ignoring the design and doing what they'd rather do. I think they're actually playing the game *as designed*, and the designers simply have failed to design the game they were hoping for.

In addition to tighter designs—a difficult thing to imagine when you're building acres of sand surrounded by four boards—another way around this problem is to pay more attention to seeding the world with tutorials of gameplay. My thought was to create "state-run" guilds (Hey, it works for totalitarian regimes!) that players can join, with solid structures, paths for advancement, and special skills or products non-guild members would need. The guilds can be based on adventure aspects of the game, crafting, or any other major factors.

In the beginning, man the guilds with NPCs. Then over time allow players to succeed to those positions through elections, even the highest. Such guilds can be a source for quests and stories. When a particular NPC has been voted out of office in a guild, we can give him a story. He moves to another guild, or becomes an embittered opponent. The story progresses as the world moves on.

We also allow players to form their own entrepreneurial guilds in competition with the NPC-run guilds, and give them all the tools necessary to match the gameplay of the others, including the ability to create quest objects and rewards. It never got to this point, but eventually we expected players would control all the guilds, but those guilds would be solidly anchored within the world fiction, and would still be resources for authorial storytelling.

Politics

Guilds are a form of political system, even if they are not developer-run, to seed player behavior. Politics is one of our most prominent social systems in real life, always in the news and always affecting our lives. However, politics in most MUDs and MMORPGs mainly seems to be just another form of player versus player or guild versus guild combat and diplomacy. Ignoring structured politics in virtual worlds removes yet another support for storytelling. One designer who believes politics should have far more importance is Matt Mihaly, the creative director of *Achaea: Dreams of Divine Lands*, continually one of the most successful commercial text MUDs in existence. In his sidebar Matt discusses what he calls "constructive" politics.

Matt Mihaly, Designer/Entrepreneur

What do we mean when we speak of "constructive politics?" For our purposes, we'll define politics as struggles for power over fellow man via some sort of organization and involving a major non-violent component. In other words, standard PK-oriented PvP isn't what we're talking about here.

Constructive politics are those politics which are interesting to some decent portion of your players. In a MUD (text or graphical), this might take the form of anything from an election for Guildmaster to negotiations between city-states over the status of an accused war criminal to formation of a trade consortium in order to drive up prices for a particular product. We'll briefly look at two major reasons why a political system that allows for large-scale player organizations can be of significant benefit to story creation in a virtual world.

Figure 18.12 Matt Mihaly.

The first is immersion. In order for players to become immersed in a story, they need to buy into the world first. It's no use crafting an epic story for your players to participate in if they don't take the milieu somewhat seriously to begin with. By creating political systems that can rule organizations with some level of control over a part of the world (such as a city-state), the power of players to influence the world around them in a structured fashion is increased, which facilitates immersion in the world. Ask yourself what's more likely to grab a player's interest: Going to the local Baron's castle to "talk" to an NPC that is nothing more than a quest dispenser, or to go down to the local Baron's castle to demand that your Baron do something about those darn Druids and their restrictive policies on harvesting herbs in the nearby forest? The keys here are that the organizations have to be able to exercise meaningful control over the world around them, as otherwise there's little reason for the organization to be important to anyone but the members themselves, and the organization members must feel some ownership over the organization (often accomplished via democracies and republics).

The second is broader participation. One of the major difficulties in MUDs of any size (even the larger text MUDs) is creating a design that will allow for valuable-feeling participation by more than just a handful of players. Using the political structures in the game as actors lets story flow down from the leadership to the organizational membership. If one allows only individual action, or action by very small groups, the stories of most individual players will be fairly chaotic and lacking in cohesion. On the other hand, by treating these political structures as actors, the players within those structures are similarly empowered to a greater extent than otherwise possible. Instead of 10,000 people purely doing their own things, which is little more than noise, you might have 50 political structures that players focus some of their effort through. Providing the organizations have an ability to impact the world in real ways, this allows story to emerge from the web of relationships and inevitable conflicts between these entities. It's the difference between interesting complexity and indistinguishable chaos.

Matt's essay shows that politics can allow players to have a considerable effect on a virtual world. It is essential to seduce players into the life of the world. Then the fiction of the world becomes more important than backstory or context. In the next section we'll look at other ways of allowing players to help shape our worlds.

Footprints in the Sand

"In the future everyone will be famous for 15 minutes."

—*Andy Warhol*

Well, that's not long enough in virtual worlds. Players want to leave their tracks on our worlds, visible to all. Allowing players to have a real and lasting effect on our worlds may sound like we're ceding too much control. But it isn't really, no more than allowing players to choose how they will experience modular stories removes authorial control. Yet it is one of the hardest challenges we wrestle with in virtual worlds. Many developers would rather just avoid it.

When we looked at quests in Chapter 10, one aspect of the various levels of quests was how much they affected the world. We're now going to revisit quests for a short time; look at other ways players can affect the world; and see how this essential attribute of virtual world gameplay in turn affects storytelling.

In our hierarchy of quests, we found that even fairly intimate quests can affect the world. If there is a robust news gathering and dissemination system in place, other players can learn ingame of the achievements of their peers. *Earth & Beyond* had such a system for major events, but even minor incidents can also be covered. Local happenings can be picked up by town criers or displayed on notice boards in town halls or pubs. These moments of glory can be as fleeting as an appearance or two on the nightly news; or become permanent additions to the world as souvenirs that can be discovered or citations and rewards that can be issued to individual players for display in their homes.

Again, as we seed guilds and other political systems, then allow players to gradually take them over, we can do the same with information systems. Players who run pubs would be able to control their messages boards. In *TGT*, we announced local events like a limerick contest with prizes on such a board, then listed the best poets there. Explorers who discover new and interesting features like beautiful waterfalls or uncharted caves can be honored by naming those things on ingame maps. In *Anarchy Online*, players and guilds can get powerful items named after them.

As in MUSHes, almost any system that allows change in a massively persistent world can be adapted for the use of players with the proper seeding and policing. There are obvious opportunities for abuse if you allow players the ability to type in public notices. "The developers suck!" is not the worst of these. But the potential for involving players and allowing them to affect their worlds make the attempt a worthy one.

Rewards may be even more tangible, like the personalized bricks I proposed for *Disney's Virtual Kingdom*, that could be accumulated and used to build bridges to new islands. As I discussed in Chapter 10, *Horizons* allows both crafters and adventurers to participate in the opening of new zones and adding new playable races. The steps necessary to free the satyrs for example were very immersive, involving crafters rebuilding several mines and tunnels while protected from marauding bands of undead that increased in size and ferociousness as the construction projects got closer to completion.

The execution of other such endeavors has been less successful. Rebuilding a destroyed elven city was stalled because the developers were apparently unready for the consequences. The freeing of a second race, the dryads, moved along by fits and starts while players finished quests to gather clues to a logic puzzle that had nothing at all to do with the ritual it was supposed to reveal, and necessitated the creation of a grid outside of the game to keep track of the possible permutations.

If instead an ingame context for the puzzle had been found, it would have been fine. A nearby druid tower tied to the story of the dryads could have been used to keep the puzzle elements rooted in the game world. Also, the story potential for the various quests was largely squandered. They were only loosely interrelated by their connection to the clues they rewarded players with. For example, an NPC mentioned in the first quest sent players in search of him, but he didn't exist. He was just local color in one quest backstory. It's all in the execution. Still, *Horizons* continues to take evolutionary steps in the quest to allow players to affect the world.

Players can be allowed to affect our worlds in small ways like winning a local beauty contest. But we must have mechanisms in place to publicize their achievements, or at least be able to reward them in a way they can share with their peers. In time, as more heroes emerge and more achievements have been recorded, chronicles of the world can be written for players to read. This may be authored by the world's team of writers. Part of these chronicles may also be fan fiction, which we'll look at in the next chapter. The more story that is produced from either source, the more the world has a sense of history, a true passage of time, and the more players feel a part of it. This gives players a huge stake in the world, yet another reason to keep playing, and to play the world as designed.

The Trap of Episodic Structure

Asheron's Call was the first MMORPG to institute regular updates to content. They based their delivery mechanism on television episodes. Every month, the servers were brought down and new quests, NPCs, and items were added. Geography was changed. Towns could be permanently wiped from the map. Unlike *Horizons*, which came four years later, these changes occurred, then players reacted to them. *Earth & Beyond* followed this release pattern of monthly updates. *Star Wars Galaxies* was attempting to do the same in those first few months when I played it, but without much success. *Horizons* is tackling the daunting task of releasing new content on a *weekly* basis.

This seems like a perfectly logical application of episodic structure to virtual world storytelling. How is it a trap?

In the hot summer months when air conditioners are draining the power grid, utility companies will institute what they call "rolling brownouts" to prevent a total blackout. As we saw in 1966 and again in 2003, blackouts still happen. But by lessening the load, they can prevent more from occurring. They spread the load out over time and geography.

Figure 18.13 *Horizons* launches a weekly installment.

We face a similar situation in virtual worlds that rely on episodic structure, and several potential problems quickly become clear. When a new event occurred in *Asheron's Call*, everybody on a server would flood the location where it occurred. To prevent them crashing the server, a unique form of involuntary teleportation was awkwardly worked into the game fiction to explain why players found themselves booted out of the area.

Here the dilemma is we want as many players as possible to participate in a major event like the release of new content, but our servers can't handle the load. One solution is to spread the effects of the content over more than one location. This fits in with the concept of providing things to do for players of all levels in each content release.

In order to release the satyrs in *Horizons*, players needed to destroy certain machines in the new zones. Only high level players had any chance of surviving attacks by the monsters that guarded them, and of doing reasonable damage to the machines. But low level players wanted to be a part of the story. This created friction between them and higher level players who were already fighting serious lag, and didn't see the value in constantly *rezzing* (slang for resurrecting) PCs who could contribute little. It would have been much better to provide other activities for lower level players to do so they could contribute to this part of a story that took several weeks to complete.

Over the course of freeing the satyrs and dryads, there were some roles lower level players could play, others that crafters could play, high level adventurers, and so on. But these were rarely ongoing simultaneously. Often one or two groups watched from the sidelines while others participated.

Every major story event we add to the world should have components that can be experienced by any player in the world simultaneously. Delivering that spread of activity will create only the occasional brownout of lag, and not force a server reboot.

When story is provided in episodes, there is also the legitimate concern that players will complete one story episode, then stop playing. In episodic television, every act between commercials is not the same length. The first act is often the longest to hook viewers. The other acts vary in length so that commercials don't all happen at the same time.

Networks try to steal audience share from one another. If a viewer switches channels between programs or during a commercial, other channels want to avoid him hitting another commercial and surfing right past them. They also hope that if the viewer tries to switch in the middle of the show, he'll be penalized by running into a commercial on another channel. With staggered breaks and overlapping content, the channels hope to grab and retain their audience.

Most TV shows are stuck in regular schedules that begin and end on the hour or half hour. Our content release is only formalized because we copied television exactly, even if the analogy between the two mediums wasn't as explicit as it seemed on the surface. We need to re-evaluate whether it really makes sense for us. I don't think it does.

Episodic content dumps at regularly scheduled times give players the chance to exit cleanly. Overlapping content increases the chances they'll stay put because the story doesn't end. *Horizons*, trying to keep ahead of their army ants, often leaves players with no new story for far too long. If they forgot about regular weekly updates that players now expect, and surprised them with staggered updates, impatient players wouldn't be given time to think about giving up and going elsewhere.

Another problem with episodic structure is players only logging on when new content is released. Players saw this in *Asheron's Call 2*, a game with a limited player base. A world often as empty of players as it was of NPCs would suddenly have a population spike like a resort town on the weekend the day new content was released. This is a given of episodic television, and not a problem. Every week, regular as clockwork viewers tune in. It doesn't translate to virtual worlds at all well.

Designers of virtual worlds work hard to encourage players to play with each other. One solution I hate is to provide higher levels of content (always involving the defeat of powerful mobs) that one player cannot enjoy by herself. The idea is that once a player has played enough to advance that far they will have made enough friends to team up with to defeat the bigger mobs. In actual practice, however, friends come and go, guilds dissolve, people live in different time zones. Players may be ready for such an experience yet unable to have it for reasons that have nothing to do with their sociability. This enforced grouping remains an aspect even of the upcoming *Everquest II*, it seems, whose designers look as if they're convinced it is a perfectly legitimate mechanism to encourage social interaction.

When new content only attracts the critical mass of players necessary to enjoy it in a short period of time once a month, you can bet it will be even worse the next month. Players who can't participate during that small window of opportunity can find themselves left out in the cold. There will be fewer and fewer online in the troughs between the swells. A rigid episodic schedule works against the very social interaction designers want to encourage.

Yet another problem is our old friend immersion. All TV shows take place in universes that can be revealed as needed. It doesn't matter if that universe is a small town in Ohio or the neutral zone between Federation and Romulan space. Want to set a couple of scenes someplace we've never been, like a Romulan bowling alley? Do it. Want to introduce that wacky Klingon next-door neighbor? No problem.

In a virtual world, players explore every square inch. Every NPC is found and interacted with. Players know there's no bowling alley yet, and if new NPCs are needed, their arrival will be noticed. Bundling up all of our new content in one neat episodic package tells the players they are playing a game. The world isn't real. "Here's new stuff you didn't have before!" Every time we deliver new content, we just push the fourth wall aside and stuff the content into the world.

Figure 18.14 A character makes a big entrance on *Edge of Night.*

In soap operas with their multiplayer storylines, when we introduce new characters, we have two choices: the big splash and the slow build. The big splash is nonsubtle. The character no one has ever seen before marches into the nearest crossover set and confronts the most saintly regular on the show with their love child. The slow build introduces the character in an almost offhand way and gradually either works him into an ongoing story, or begins to reveal his own story. This builds suspense. Why is this character here, the audience wonders?

Instead of plunking down a new set of static characters at the moment you need them, all primed with exposition or a quest, introduce them over time *before* the story's point of attack is reached. One week a new merchant replaces a familiar

Figure 18.15 And a big splash.

face behind the counter, and says she's new to town. A few days later, a strange forester, taciturn and preoccupied, is spotted in the woodlands intent upon some unknown search. The forester may actually be a part of the next story step. The merchant may not become involved in story for quite awhile. We don't have to create new characters. Move an NPC players know from one town to another. Give him a reason for the change of scenery. Whether it's true or not remains to be seen.

This type of movement brings the world to life in any case, and helps ease story into that life. And we can do the same thing with events, like dropping a meteor on a thriving city at the end of *Asheron's Call*'s beta. The big splash. Or gradually introducing dangerous mobs into a formerly safe part of the countryside. The slow build. One week there are three. Two weeks later there are twelve. The reason they've appeared is discovered to relate directly to the new merchant who showed up in town last month . . .

If we stagger our delivery of new story and other content; if players don't know when to expect it; and provided it's compelling enough to generate interest, we have a win-win situation. Population spikes will smooth out over the course of a week or a month. More players will be online more of the time for other players to interact with. And we create anticipation. Players won't know when the next big thing is going to happen, but they'll sense that something wicked this way comes.

We need to plan far enough ahead that we don't have to slow down the release of relevant content when the population is ready for it, but that's a rule we *can* take from episodic television. If the new content is tied to ongoing story where they can't wait to find out what is going to happen next to themselves and their world, we can create pleasurable suspense like in a good horror film. The shark in *Jaws* did not attack every afternoon at three o'clock.

CHAPTER 19

Enabling Story in Virtual Worlds

Story in all games is not just written; it must be designed as well. The design dictates whether it is linear or modular, something in between, or a mixture of structures—and how it will be revealed. The design explains story's relationship to the other parts of the game. In virtual worlds, it is also important that mechanisms be in place to allow story to reach the greatest number of players. It shouldn't be forced on them. A lot of different types of players play massive persistent worlds, and not all will be interested no matter how much we may want them to be. But it should be offered to all.

This goes back to the concept of value we discussed in the previous chapter. If the story is to help replace the GM, it must be worth the effort. Little stories can justify their telling because even if only a few players at a time experience them, hopefully many players can experience them over the weeks and months and years that follow. Epic stories better invite participation by many gamers all at once.

Backstory is no trouble. Even static worlds have backstory. It is easy to segregate it or ignore it to make sure it doesn't get in the way. It's even easy to balance gameplay with story by revealing it in quests or through the characters of NPCs. The challenge comes when both world and story move into the future together.

Thousands of Heroes

All those players running around in our virtual worlds and all of them want to be heroes. We can't write individual stories tailored for each one the way we could in tabletop. If the only stories we have in the game are repetitive errands so players can be legends in their own minds, but no one else will notice, they'll feel cheated. Real heroes get noticed! How can we possibly tell stories that they can drive, and make them think their deeds matter? The challenge then becomes this: if all those protagonists don't get to launch major stories, who does?

In Chapter 4, "Character Roles," we examined some of the important roles NPCs can play in our game stories. They are particularly useful in virtual worlds because the few elements supporting authorial story are so often shoved aside. One of those roles is as pivotal characters. Chris L'Etoile, one of the original writers on *Asheron's Call*, knows several of these pivotal characters intimately, and in his sidebar introduces us to some "surrogate heroes" who helped drive story.

Chris L'Etoile, Writer/Designer

In the traditional single-player RPG, the player is the hero. The human participant should be the prime mover of plot in both consideration and action. They decide how to advance the story and then accomplish it. Friendly NPCs may have their own compelling story arcs and play a pivotal role in the story, but they do not set the course of the game.

MMORPGs potentially have millions of "heroes" with differing opinions on how to solve plot points. To tell the monthly serial story content in *Asheron's Call*, the original live team developed certain NPCs as "surrogate heroes." Rather than allow multiple solutions to a plot point, we imposed a single solution in the sugar coating of a trustworthy NPC with a Brilliant Plan that he or she could not accomplish alone. NPC heroes "decided" how to resolve a problem, and players saved the

Figure 19.1 Chris L'Etoile.

world by enacting their plans. NPC-imposed solutions allowed us to complete the following month's content as the current month's was playing out. Though it is arguably better to allow the playerbase to "vote" between several solutions and go with the majority, carrying the story forward in a timely fashion often requires plot points to be resolved predictably.

For example, the conclusion of *AC*'s first story arc saw the release of the nemesis NPC Bael'Zharon. Using quests and NPC dialogue, we emphasized his godlike power, beyond the ability of players to resist, and established that certain powerful monster races opposed him. In the climactic month, our titular NPC, Asheron, informed players of the means by which Bael'Zharon could be defeated. Objects held by the monster races opposed to Bael'Zharon had to be recovered and combined, then given to Asheron. Offscreen, he used these to "cast a spell" making Bael'Zharon vulnerable to attack. Players could then enter Bael'Zharon's lair and kill him.

An advantage to using "hero" NPCs to drive the plot is that they can suffer. Players are unhappy when their game avatar suffers. Even in *Warcraft III*—an RTS rather than an RPG—many players react negatively when the paladin hero Arthas "falls" and joins the undead. In an MMORPG, killing or abusing player avatars with months of play invested in them alienates subscribers. Yet a story needs the threat of loss to sustain dramatic tension. Beloved hero NPCs can be freely broken, abused, nobly sacrificed, horrifically murdered, or descend into madness and evil due to their own weaknesses. As in single-player RPGs, the potential or realized suffering of a well-written NPC can supply the necessary tension.

The second story arc of *AC* introduced the memorable NPC Candeth Martine. Players followed a trail of notes left by Martine as a monster race abducted him for vivisection and brainwashing. Martine, driven mad, overcame his captors and ran amok, his blind thirst for vengeance creating obstacles for players to overcome. As his sanity frayed, he mistook another NPC, Elysa Strathelar, for his lost wife. Trying to reach her, he nearly killed Asheron. With Asheron and Elysa's help, Martine regained his sanity, and helped players defeat the nemesis NPC Gaerlan. His act of contrition, however, apparently killed him.

In any MMORPG, it is vital that the players feel *they* are the heroes. However, strong NPCs are important for the same reasons as in single-player RPGs. They illuminate the plot and evoke sympathy by absorbing the burden of tragedy that players would be unhappy assuming themselves. An MMORPG that hopes to tell serial stories cannot limit NPCs to being bland, static quest distributors.

Chris's examples are great ways to use NPCs as pivotal characters in virtual worlds. Being a hero can't mean always taking center stage in a virtual world, but being a part of the events set in motion by these major figures gives all players who participate a chance to share in the excitement. Chris also reiterates one of my concerns from Chapter 2, "The Story Remains the Same," about the lack of tragic figures in most games. Players may not want to play such characters, but interacting with them can be very powerful.

Ongoing Story

In this section, I'll suggest a possible template to use for the release of ongoing story and new content. Don't mistake these for hard and fast rules that guarantee success. Adapt them to your own needs.

The current fashion is to continue an ongoing narrative in episodic chunks. We want to go beyond that. As we saw in the last chapter if we stagger the content delivery we support the feeling that the virtual world is real and continuing. Characters come and go, their entrances and exits overlapped. Stories may begin subtly or with a bang, and they too are overlapped just like in soap operas.

In *The Gryphon Tapestry*, there were wolves in the forests to the southwest of the small village of Thornhollow. Most were mobs that players could kill. Occasionally, a local NPC farmer may have placed a bounty on them if his livestock was being attacked, increasing the benefit of hunting them. There was also an old gray wolf who had been in the forest no one knew how long. He did not kill livestock, was only occasionally glimpsed, and he didn't act at all like the other wolves. There was an aura of mystery about him. He was there from the first moment players entered the world, even figuring in a quest or two. Months later, he would be revealed to be a shape shifter, a local beggar already established as a separate character, and much, much later as a powerful mage.

Another character was a kindly, but somewhat befuddled cleric at a local church, much loved in his community, and of great help and comfort to players. We were going to kill him off about three months into the game.

The first thing to do is prepare the way. Establish the foundations of upcoming story. The next step is to mix the scale and length of narrative pieces in a single story, or of stories themselves. Hang stories of all sizes and shapes on the overall arc. Connect them to each other by interesting and surprising means. Make some simple Chinese menu quests, some one-offs, still others that change the world in ways that support the narrative.

Before I get into detail, there's a very important concept from episodic television we need to be familiar with: *lead time.*

note

LEAD TIME: the time between the scripting, pre-production, and production of an episodic television show and its air date.

If a TV show's premiere is scheduled for September 1, preparations for that and subsequent episodes begins in April or May. By the time September rolls around, shows want to have several episodes to choose from "in the can" (shot and ready to air), and scripts for as many more as possible in shootable form. Even then by the end of the season, the lead time will have been chewed up and production companies will often be scrambling to stay two or three weeks ahead. Sound familiar? Virtual worlds aren't the only medium plagued by army ants.

And because our assets can take longer to create than television, we need even more lead time. In the suggestions that follow you may be surprised by how far apart the writing and introduction of content must be to stay ahead. I'm not even being conservative. The thing to keep in mind is that because the material is written in stages there are several chances to be flexible even with such extended lead times.

Think of these stories in several layers. Start with the ongoing story arc of the world that hopefully will never end. Next lay out content that will last a significant length of time, say three years. Now triple the amount of that content since the army ants always chew faster than you expect. Next, outline a handful of major storylines of three to six months' duration. And finally, toss in a varied selection of smaller stories that can be completed before the next new content is released. Make sure to overlap them all.

Write your quests to support the stories. Plan to stagger and vary the introductions of NPCs who will launch the stories or figure prominently in them. Create new items thematically consistent with the stories that introduce them. How do we keep track of all of this?

It doesn't matter if you use Word, HTML, Excel, or any of the other popular programs for creating design documents, but I would suggest first writing everything as if it were a continuing narrative. Want to build your stories modularly? Bravo! The first pass at this can be as simple as describing each module in a separate paragraph. Just remember that if you don't use some kind of hypertext-style environment like HTML or Excel or a database program, make sure that your paragraphs do not directly reference one another. The references lie in floating variables that will attach themselves to the appropriate modules depending upon any individual player's choices of where to go and what to do next.

Write four types of story document so the task doesn't seem so overwhelming. Start with the over-arcing, never-ending story for the game. This is as much a vision statement as it is a story, and is probably only a few pages at most. Have a pretty good idea where you want to be a few years down the road, but know that this will almost certainly change based on the actions of your players. The key to all of this is having the flexibility to respond to players' needs without compromising your overall vision.

Next write a macro story document that describes your three-year story arc. This could be about 60 pages long and includes the major storylines that take several weeks to several months to complete, and as many shorter stories as possible. You just hit the major events and connecting tissue. The storyline should be dynamic. The players should be able to affect it. But you don't want your players in such control you have no idea what your world will look like in three years.

The major characters of all of these should be represented. And the story start and completion dates should, of course, overlap. Production management software can be used to track the dates you plan to release and complete stories. Know that here too the players will have a major effect on your plans, and prepare to improvise if necessary.

When I was writing *Edge of Night* I planned out the beginnings and endings of stories down to the day. Yet real life constantly intruded. Actresses became pregnant; cast members became ill or fidgety about their contracts; sets were not quite ready in time. Anything could happen.

The audience could even affect us. One story I was very proud of was based on a news item I'd read about a Native American burial ground that real estate developers wanted to move to make way for a subdivision. I used that as the basis of a story of the clash of cultures, tradition, greed, even mysticism. I planned to run it for three months. The audience didn't like it. One woman from Iowa wrote in that the Indians were always trying to take our land. ABC asked us to shorten the story. I had to finish it up in six weeks. And then come up with something entirely new to take its place. I moved up the beginning of another story even as I prematurely wrapped up the first story.

Figure 19.2 The writer rewriting on the set. Not as much fun as it looks!

If I had not been ready with the next story, I still had a fallback position. Most of us squirrel away a couple gallons of water, a few cans of food, and extra flashlight batteries in case of a natural disaster. I keep files of stories, ideas, characters from my imagination, news clippings, moments from other stories that struck me. More than once emergencies arose and these scattered bits and pieces, separate or combined, became stories I could use.

The next step is to write separate long term story documents for each of your major storylines. The length will vary with the lengths of your major stories, but not every detail needs to be in place as yet. Then write story breakdowns (outlines) that indicate most of the beats of any story and exactly how they are going to be revealed to the players. Is an NPC going to tell players a crucial piece of exposition if a quest is completed for them? Is a beat going to be announced on the news? Found on a scrap of parchment? Blurted out by a cocky NPC right before he's unexpectedly killed? These will probably run about 15 to 20 pages.

Finally, write "scripts" that include *all* of the detail needed for the content, including NPC dialogue, step-by-step quests, new items, mobs, and so forth.

The first two macro documents (vision and three-year story arc) should be written early in pre-production. To give the team enough lead time, the long term story documents for the first year or so should be completed well before alpha. Six months of story breakdowns and scripts should be ready when the first testers arrive to begin playing. These detailed content scripts should be written with approximately two to three months lead time. This time frame gives you a chance to adjust to players' actions, but still stay ahead of them. I could be only two weeks ahead on *Edge* because the physical production only took a day.

Remember, these stories will be staggered and overlapped so the three months of material will not begin or end cleanly. Some stories will end before the three months are up. Others will extend long past that time.

Three months is a reasonable compromise between staying ahead of the army ants and remaining flexible to their changing appetites. Any longer than that and your ability to respond to short term player trends drops. Any shorter than that and you risk ant bites on your ankles.

In Appendix B, I describe how to build a writing team to implement this schedule. It may feel relentless and unforgiving, but it is no more so than weekly episodic television, or soap opera where content is added on a daily basis. If you don't take the time to properly prepare, and do it as early in the production process as possible, the authorial storytelling in your virtual world will suffer. And nay-sayers will have one more "proof" it can't work at all.

Revealing Story

It remains a mystery to me why the company that made *Asheron's Call*, the first massively multiplayer game to boldly incorporate ongoing story and that had devised several ground-breaking techniques for doing it, would then turn around and build *Asheron's Call 2*, where the story is almost totally divorced from gameplay.

In our efforts to attract new blood to our virtual worlds, we use Web sites. Here potential players can hopefully get a feel for a game before they decide to try it. Developers often use these sites to inform players of new content. Games like *Everquest* and *Dark Age of Camelot* use their game engines to directly launch their worlds, bypassing internet screens. Separated from their official Web sites, they have a proprietary way to make announcements if they wish to do so. Games that actually launch from Web sites like *Asheron's Call* and *Horizons* can connect directly to material on the developers' other Web sites.

Using Web sites and extra-game announcements are fine to attract new players, and to bring players up to date without forcing them to load the game. But if we are going to use Web sites outside of our worlds to tell story, they

Artifact Entertainment

Figure 19.3 *Horizons* is launched from a Web site.

should not be our only mechanism for doing so. It is lazy and non-immersive to require that players read such text, and/or watch cut scene introductions if they want to participate in ongoing story. In movie theatres or television when we do trailers or teasers about upcoming episodes we are at least doing them in an identical fashion to how the stories will be told. Film is film. But these are the tools of non-interactive media.

In any type of game we have far more immersive ways of revealing story, and I've spent a good portion of this book suggesting how to do just that. The scale of a single-player game is not broad, and the delivery mechanisms at the writer/designer's disposal can be restricted by choices made as the game is designed. It could be something as obvious as non-speaking NPCs or a setting that doesn't contain books or videos.

Virtual worlds, because they have the potential of allowing us the entire range of methods to reveal story, are far more flexible. Unless we overlook or ignore their storytelling potential. Let's keep Web sites where they belong as teasers and supplements to our storytelling and remind ourselves of some of the ways stories can be revealed in game.

- The vaults in *Asheron's Call 2* are actually grouped as sets of modules. Players can choose among several to visit. In order to provide an overall linear progression to the backstory as it is revealed, level restrictions are used as a sort of combination lock. The items necessary to access the vault drop from a certain level of mob, and the vaults are infested with mobs appropriate to the level of players the developers wanted visiting them. A new set of higher level vaults would then contain the next pieces in the story.

- We can use town criers, bartenders, journalists, and other similar NPCs to dispense exposition, or to direct players to where it can be found. This includes backstory and current events. In a sense, such NPCs are the virtual world equivalent of the "coffee table" scenes in soap operas, reminding players of what is happening in the world around them, and keeping them up-to-date on events they may have missed. We can't create events that all players can participate in, even though we should spread the love as much as possible. Providing ways to share the story draws interested players in and keeps them involved even if they arrived late to the game or missed some major story event.

- NPCs that are not the usual information sources can be mined for gossip and rumors. (See Chapter 4 for more detail.) Other NPCs may have windows on the future: magic spells, scientific devices, or simple intuition and deduction to foreshadow upcoming events.

- Some NPCs may be fixated on certain plot points. Others, like town criers can be regularly updated with new exposition. Quest givers can change the quests they assign based on current events. Nowhere is it written that they must be static. Their interests can change as the story progresses.

- Inanimate objects like books, journals, message boards, signposts, video screens, and so on can be used in obvious ways. Keep the text succinct by supplementing it in other ways. Ruins may have plaques like historical buildings do: "On this site eleven months ago stood a flourishing city . . ." We could provide an overview on the plaque (the official version), then salt the surroundings with NPCs who are witnesses; or who are present to study and rebuild. They can provide details in bits and pieces.

- In all of the above, story points do not have to be accurate or correspond to points from other sources. We can establish reliable story sources and less reliable story sources, as we discussed in Chapter 4. These are not only NPCs. Books can lie. Everything you see on TV is not necessarily true.

Players don't need to start at the beginning of a story to become actively involved, if we provide entry points like the flashbacks in *The Gryphon Tapestry*'s multiplayer quests. "The story up till now" is a part of the world's history, and should be readily available to newcomers in a variety of ways like chatty NPCs, quests like *Horizons'* Trials of the Gifted, news archives, and more.

World-changing, ongoing story is easy to write. It retains its mysteries just like the ongoing story in other media. Players do not know what is coming until it is revealed at the designer's pleasure. Smaller stories and repeatable stories found in NPC encounters or quests are not so straightforward. For these smaller storylines, there is a trap in writing them the way you would a mystery. As we know, there are no secrets in MMORPGs. It's much better to embrace that fact, and encourage players to spread the lore. There are other ways to provide surprise, the cheapest of which, of course, are random story elements, a gameplay solution.

A subtle variation is to keep those random elements within the context of the story. Use the reliability of witnesses, gossips, and commentators as random story elements. A pathological liar is about as random as you can get. Keep her in character and you have a story solution as well.

I've talked about quests and missions, and how they are excellent mechanisms for the delivery of story; but also how in virtual worlds they are too many times constructed the same way they are in tabletop and single-player games, one of those patches in our design quilt that doesn't match. Let's take a look at how to build quests that better fit our massive worlds.

True Multiplayer Quests

What do I mean by this? A single-player quest in a multiplayer game is one that resets its conditions for every player who undertakes it. If one player kills a creature named Randy the Rancorous Raccoon and is rewarded by the grateful Quest Giver, the next player in line will receive the exact same assignment, and Randy becomes Randy the Resurrected Rancorous Raccoon, ready to die again.

Why bother with true multiplayer quests? Everybody accepts the convention of solo quests, don't they? We accept conventions if there is no alternative, but when there is a plain alternative that supports story and immersion, there is no reason at all not to pursue it. If we don't the verisimilitude of the world is broken, and the player's success is diminished because a thousand other players managed to do exactly the same thing. The quest story details are trivial compared to the gameplay mechanisms it serves. It is there simply as another way for players to receive experience or loot as rewards.

We already have respawning mobs and magically replenished resources in virtual worlds as a game convention, so that players will never be able to kill everything; and lumberjacks don't have to wait for new growth in forests to mature. Alternatives have not fared well. But if one were to come along that made sense, these fiction-breaking conventions could be done away with as well.

Just as developers want content that renews itself automatically to lessen the amount of new content we have to create, it would seem to follow that respawning quests can work the same way. Replayability in single-player games is a feature. In virtual worlds it is a necessity. We welcome it wherever and whenever we find it.

Replayability is not a concern when designing epic quests that advance story, but in all other cases it must be, or it chops away at the fourth wall, immersion, and players' willing suspension of disbelief. Even epic one-off quests to advance individual characters must feel like true multiplayer quests. This may sound like a paradox, but it isn't. There are actually two types of replayability:

- One player can do some quests over and over again. The Chinese menu Fed Ex quests fall into this category. When written simply, as in *Dark Age of Camelot*: "Creature X is a nuisance, kill as many as you can," they are repeatable, and truly multiplayer.

- One player can only do a quest a single time, but the quest remains available for all other players, or at least those who match whatever requirements might be imposed. Most of this kind of repeatable one-off quest in current MMORPGs fall into the category of single-player quests masquerading unsuccessfully as multiplayer.

Let's take at look at some single-player quests disguised as multiplayer quests, and see how we can tweak them in the writing to become multiplayer. We'll start with the Journeyman Boots quest from *Everquest* I've mentioned before in the book. This quest is admittedly old and very simple, but almost all quests in *Everquest* proceed along familiar single-player lines. It was added to *Everquest* to address players camping in a dungeon called Najena for the reward: boots that made player-characters run faster.

The quest begins with a little guy speeding around the Rathe Mountains. His name is Hasten Bootstrutter.

The player waits for Hasten to spawn. This can take quite awhile. Then she must catch up to him and chat. She'll learn that Hasten has need of three items: a ring from an Ancient Cyclops, a scimitar from a shadow man, and a bunch of gold. Why does he need these items? Nobody knows. But if you give them to him, he'll give you his prized boots that will make you run faster. Players can actually skip the reason for the quest entirely and just return to him with the items he needs. No secrets in MMORPGs, remember?

Next the player kills the Ancient Cyclops, and loots the ring. Why did it have the ring? Nobody knows.

Next she kills a shadow man, and loots a scimitar. It vanishes if you leave the world, so forget about taking a break.

The player stops at the bank to withdraw the necessary gold from her account. Now it's time to go find Hasten again and wait for him to reappear.

Finally, she is able to deliver the items Hasten requires, and is given the speedy boots. End of quest.

Figure 19.4 Hasten pauses long enough for a photo op.

The player has killed respawning mobs that inexplicably carry items they need to trade for this unique pair of magic boots. But look! That player over there is already wearing them! Which are the true Hasten Bootstrutters, and which are the knockoffs? Well, at least the player can run faster now.

Now look at the same quest rewritten as a true multiplayer quest:

The player learns from Hasten that even though he appears to be moving at a good clip thanks to his ability to make the Journeyman Boots he's wearing, he actually could be much faster. However, due to an ongoing feud with Ancient Cyclopses, some of whom occasionally can be seen in the desert of South Ro, he can barely trot along. These Cyclopses carry rings they use to cast spells on him, slowing him down. These spells can only be lifted by killing an Ancient Cyclops, and bringing Hasten its ring. Ancient Cyclopses are so powerful they can't be killed by ordinary means, but an orc in South Ro supposedly has seen one downed. If you kill a Cyclops and bring Hasten a ring to lift the spell, he will sell you a pair of Journeyman Boots at cost.

The player finds the orc Hasten mentioned in the northwest corner of South Ro. This orc saw an Ancient Cyclops killed by a group of adventurers wielding scimitars that vanished when the thing died. The orc's cousins in West Commons have told him of such weapons wielded by shadow men. Those weapons vanish after awhile. Maybe they used those.

The player kills a shadow man and loots his scimitar.

The player uses the scimitar to kill an Ancient Cyclops, and loots its magic ring.

She stops at the bank for gold on the way back to Hasten.

Hasten accepts the ring, removes the spell, fashions the player a pair of boots Ferragamo would envy, and sells them to her at cost. He then speeds off to taunt the Cyclopses with his restored powers, setting up an obvious sequel for the next player to run him down.

The moves are very similar on purpose. Tokens are passed in the same way. I deliberately limited myself to the same items already in the quest. The same creatures must be slain. But the entire quest is approached from the direction of multiplayer story not a single-player Fed Ex structure. Another player can repeat the quest without breaking the world fiction. Hasten, thanks to an obvious character flaw, is off to get into trouble once again. At this rate, he'll never make a profit from his boots!

I've alluded to the next quest before in the book as well. It is from *Dark Age of Camelot* and is called Connla's Fever.

The player's trainer in Connla will tell him to talk to Keaghan, a healer, about curing the fever in town.

Keagan says, "Have you come to help collect ingredients so that I may [cure the town] of this horrid fever going around?"

No other NPCs in the town show signs of fever. (The player clicks on the bracketed words to continue Keagan's monologue— see the topic of dialogue systems in Chapter 6, "Character Encounters.")

Figure 19.5 Connla won't look very feverish when the player arrives.

Keagan next says, "It's truly a miracle you've not been affected. I think I can make a poultice or a brew that will break the fever, but I'm too weak with it myself to go and get the ingredients. It's nothing difficult really. Do you know [what is needed]?"

A final click brings up the last of Keagan's monologue:

Kaegan says, "First, I need two bits of mud. You can collect them from the mudmen wandering just outside the village. Then, I'll need, oh, the fever has taken my mind, I can't remember if I need a dried sand cake from a sandman or the shinbones from a skeletal pawn. Oh, and I need to rest. I can't think of which one it is. It's one or the other. When you get the ingredients, bring them to me. I'm going to lie down and rest while you collect the ingredients."

Keaghan doesn't move.

After the player collects two bits of mud from mudmen, and a dried sand cake from a sandman, or a shin bone from a skeletal pawn, he brings the ingredients back to where Keagan is still standing.

Keagan, feeling the effects of the fever, says, "Rhodry, you're back. Oh wait, you're not Rhodry . . . this fever is making me lose my memory. I hope you have the ingredients. Here, give me a bit of mud first."

The player transfers the various ingredients as Keagan asks for them, then he says, "Well, let me put this together for the townspeople. This should surely cure the fever."

The player is rewarded, but Keagan doesn't even cure himself. When the next player clicks on him, the quest begins again by rote.

The multiplayer version is even simpler than in the first example.

The player's trainer in Connla will tell him to talk to Keagan, a healer, about curing the fever in town. Some other local NPCs exhibit symptoms of the fever as they conduct their business with players.

Keagan says, "Don't get too close! I too am infected! Have you come to collect the ingredients so that I may try and [cure the townsfolk] of this horrid fever?"

Keagan next says, "It's truly a miracle you've not been affected. I think I can make a brew that will break the fever, but most hereabouts are too weak with it to go and get the ingredients. It's nothing difficult really. Do you know [what is needed]?"

A final click brings up the last of Keagan's monologue:

Kaegan says, "First, I need two bits of mud. You can collect them from the mudmen wandering just outside the village. Then, I'll need, oh, the fever has taken my mind, I can't remember if I need a dried sand cake from a sandman or the shinbones from a skeletal pawn. Oh, I can't think of which one it is. It's one or the other. When you get the ingredients, bring them to me. They should be enough to create a small amount of the healing brew. If only I had time to rest, but I must be ready to speak to others who will hopefully come to our aid."

After the player collects two bits of mud from mudmen, and a dried sand cake from a sandman, or a shin bone from a skeletal pawn, he brings the ingredients back to where Keagan is still standing.

Keagan, feeling the effects of the fever, says, "Rhodry, you're back. Oh wait, you're not Rhodry . . . this fever is making me lose my memory. I hope you have the ingredients. Here, give me a bit of mud first."

The player transfers the various ingredients as Keagan asks for them, then he says, "Well, let me put this together. This should surely be enough to cure one or two of the townspeople. I'd ask you to get more ingredients, but you've had too much contact with me already. Others are helping. We'll soon break the back of this fever."

If the player clicks on Keagan again, Keagan will reply, "For mercy's sake, stay back! After all you've done, I'd hate for you to become infected!"

Writing true multiplayer quests is about perspective as much as anything else. Chinese menu quest structure can make it easy. Even one-offs like these two examples can be reshaped once we stop blindly following the old paradigm of shoving single-player quests into our worlds and calling them multiplayer simply because more than one player-character can experience them. Almost any quest can be written as single-player or true multiplayer. The choice is ours. All that is required is the will to do it.

Crowd Control

A new buzzword in MORPGs these days is *instancing*. It's an important concept that allows us more control over the environments we place our content in.

note

> INSTANCING: Creating a private but identical section of a virtual world such as a dungeon to limit the number of players who experience it at any one time.

This is usually done to remove the necessity for rival groups to compete for the same mob camps or loot. A private dungeon (Dungeon 1A) is created at the moment players choose to enter it (Dungeon 1). If a second group of adventurers want to enter the same dungeon they find themselves in Dungeon 1B. When we used a form of this in *The Gryphon Tapestry* in 1999, we did it to support the storytelling since the camping of mobs was not a major part of the gameplay. It evolved like this:

One of my favorite settings in *Everquest*, which I was heavily involved in at the time, was Mistmoore, a sinister castle where high-level undead walked. The spooky atmosphere was painstakingly created. But then something happened. Players wanted to play there. The atmosphere was destroyed by rooms and graveyards crowded with groups of players camping mobs. The graveyard was alternately funny and annoying, as players lined the walls ready to be the first to pounce on poor skeletons and zombies as soon as they appeared.

Sony Online Entertainment

Figure 19.6 Castle Mistmoore was not a healthy place to be for the undead.

I wanted to avoid this so we could maintain control over the atmosphere in some of the crucial sequences in our stories. In *TGT*, we created what we called story locations. One was a graveyard. When a player or a single group of players chose a story that took place partly in the graveyard, a version of the graveyard was created especially for them. When they found themselves there at night, they would be alone. Or rather there would at least be no other players with them. Any company they had belonged there. The spooky atmosphere was preserved, and a ghost story could be told without disruption from other players. If another group reached the same point in the story, they would find themselves alone in their own graveyard.

In a design of my own I'm currently working on, I extend this story location metaphor. Not only are there story locations that are instanced the way dungeons are beginning to be instanced, I instance *hiring scenes* and even certain forms of transportation, and of course, housing.

note

HIRING SCENE: initial contact with a quest giver where a player is offered the quest.

In a hiring scene players can choose to accept or refuse the quest. (Some virtual worlds force players to accept quests before they've heard all the details. This is quest giver as used car salesman and should be avoided.) There are a number of very famous characters in my design that players would be familiar with. In none of the stories featuring these characters are their homes or places of business crammed from floor to ceiling with players begging for work.

Most developers approach the problem from the point of view of gameplay only. If 15 people are all asking for quests simultaneously, and all that text, including NPC dialogue, is streaming past, too much can be lost in the process. So we suppress the text display. A player only sees the text of her encounter. But still there may be dozens of other players standing nearby when the super secret mission is granted to a player. This crowd ruins the illusion. The player is no longer special, with her own relationship to the quest giver; she is just one of many faceless adventurers lined up in a homeless shelter waiting for her soup bowl to be filled.

So in my design, just as graveyards are instanced, these meetings with quest givers, where appropriate, are instanced too. Just because we are creating games is no reason to subject our players to each other 24 hours out of every day. Just as in real life, and certainly as in real drama, sometimes private moments are important.

In this same game, I want to emphasize a rigid class structure. I therefore allow those of wealth and position to travel by private means, while only public transportation is available to the lower classes. While they are traveling they cannot be disturbed by other players, only scripted story events. Rest assured that there are attractions in all classes in this system. There are a lot of reasons players might want to forego private transportation for some other benefit.

Finally housing is instanced. The geography of the game is urban, and therefore, its boundaries are limited to a certain extent. You can't add housing to an urban environment the way you can the vast expanses of countryside in *Star Wars Galaxies*. So private homes are instanced in two ways: there can be many wealthy addresses on certain streets, reached by private transportation, and many rooms in less affluent "apartment buildings." *Dark Age of Camelot* added housing fairly late in its development. It uses a form of the same technique by creating zones specifically for player housing so as not to clutter up the countryside with new subdivisions.

When we moved from text to graphics, we entered a literal world where walking from one side of the room to the other was a thrill. It didn't take long for the thrill of this literal geography to wear off. My idea is to get away from the literal interpretation of virtual world space that has been copied from game to game simply because it can be done, and the games that came first did it that way. I'm not suggesting such an approach will work for all virtual worlds. Obviously, it won't. But this particular world is designed to accommodate it.

Instancing right now is being used to solve a gameplay problem, but there is no reason at all it can't be yet another tool in our storytelling arsenal.

Variety

We've discussed varying story lengths to keep them from falling into ruts. We've talked about varying the length of lines in speeches to prevent their rhythms from falling into predictable, boring patterns, We can vary types of stories too. Just because your world is high fantasy doesn't mean you can't tell stories drawn from life back here in the mundane world. Just because your themes are about greed and destruction doesn't mean you can't leaven them with laughter. Some stories can be funny, some sad; some thoughtful, some bawdy. Look at Chaucer's *The Canterbury Tales*. There is a rich spectrum of life on display, and the tales are better for it.

Trying to keep stories thematically consistent is good, but you don't have to illuminate the theme with the same color lights. Make people cry over it, make jokes about it. In *Seabiscuit*, the narrator, biographer, and historian David McCullough is heard in voice over putting in perspective photographs from the Great Depression: "They called them forgotten men, but it was really a misnomer. They were wanderers. Men who left a shattered life in search of something new. . . . Men who left something new, desperately in search of something old. . . ." As Charles Howard, Jeff Bridges' character in *Seabiscuit* proclaims: "Our horse is too small . . . our jockey's too big . . . our trainer's too old . . . and I'm too stupid to know the difference!"

Both lines nail the theme. There is worth in everyone if you dig down deep enough, and give them a chance. The first is solemn and sad, the second boisterous and optimistic. Our themes deserve all the ways we can possibly find to illuminate them.

Figure 19.7 Laughter and sorrow both drive home *Seabiscuit*'s theme.

We can take recognizable characters from our own world and place them in any setting. As long as we're true to them in that new setting, they can provide a recognizable anchor for our audience. As long as we avoid anachronisms or parody, they keep us grounded in the humanity of our stories. They are recognizable because their human traits are universal.

Variety can and should be pursued when writing any game, but it is especially important in virtual worlds. We know we're going to find every opportunity to be repetitive to win the content race with players. We need to hide that repetition in any way possible. If two quests are basically Fed Ex of about the same length, difficulty and with the same rewards, but one is heart-wrenching and the other hilarious, the player won't notice.

One of our smaller stories may concern a former hero's lost honor, another might be about farmer's rights, and still another the forbidden love between teenagers from rival clans. It is the diversity of our stories that adds to the breadth of our worlds as much as their acres of geography.

Hiding the Numbers

Some massive persistent worlds can remain happily ensconced in level and loot paradigms. But the market isn't there to support more than a handful of them. If they bring nothing distinctly new to the table to grow the market, their long development cycles and huge budgets doom them to a small piece of a niche in video games that won't support their business models. After only eight years of massively multiplayer worlds this paradigm is already showing its age. Players complain constantly about the level and loot *treadmill.*

note

TREADMILL: A term that describes the repetitious nature of killing or crafting to achieve the advancement of characters in massively multiplayer games.

Other paradigms are needed for persistent worlds to reach a broader audience. Other metaphors for the progress players make through these worlds must be found that appeal to an audience not all that interested in racking up kills, obtaining phat l00t and number-crunching. The fact is there is a huge untapped market of people who have computers attached to the Internet who would be perfectly happy to play in a virtual world that offered a viable alternate metaphor for entertainment. Other types of sandbox experiences like *There*, a world that drops most gameplay and offers only commerce in its place, are not the answer. Storytelling is a far more workable alternative once designers decide that yes, maybe it can be done successfully after all. We have a history centuries long to prove human beings are attracted to storytelling.

The odd thing is that MUDs, particularly text MUDs, are a far more diverse lot than MMORPGs. The practice these days is to suggest that MUD stands for multi-user domain or multi-user dimension for those who want to distance themselves from the clichés of *Dungeon & Dragons* clones. There's quite a bit of authorial storytelling going on it MUDs, and a lot of thought is given to seeding player-created content.

But somewhere in the transition between MUDs and MMORPGs something was lost. Partly, because of such challenges as the increased complexities of more graphics and more players, developers dumbed down their content, and went for the easiest model: kill things, gain experience, gain power.

The two areas that most help define the potential differences between virtual worlds are happily familiar to us: character development and storytelling. Some writers and designers can sit around trying to think up new names for their high fantasy or science fiction game worlds and fill them with new races, but in the end, if that's all they do, their games will play like all the others.

Character development in virtual worlds normally follows patterns long established by tabletop and RPGs. Characters are mostly defined by their skills, attributes, race, and profession. Simply through utensil selection, we dictate to players how to play our games. If the only choices are either weapons or tools, then it is obvious to players they are meant to either kill or build. The names of professions like warrior or blacksmith also guide players. It is left up to the players to add distinct personalities.

This is not a bad thing. We can assign numerical values to all those things. That allows us to use the power of the computer to track a player's progress through the world. And tracking such advancement is important. Progress suggests forward momentum. It allows us to simulate progression in even the most static of virtual worlds. The world may not change, but the player can change within it.

The problem arises when these numbers are shared with players. If stats like hit points and health points, damage inflicted and taken, and so on are explicitly served up to players with numbers floating off the tops of characters' heads, it shouldn't be a surprise if players seize on those numbers as important. Certainly in *Advanced Dungeons & Dragons* the numbers are right there on the die that determines the outcome of battle and in the value of weapons that have their power indicated by a number. A short sword +2 hits harder that a short sword +1. Levels are tracked from 1 to 20, and are important for the additional power and skills a new level can add to a player-character.

But because a GM is in charge, the story of the game can move forward. There is no time for repetitive behavior like camping, or making the same weapon over and over again for experience. In a massively multiplayer game, however, if a player notices that a certain kind of mob is easier for his profession to kill than others, and that it provides reasonable amounts of experience every time one is killed, she is more likely to camp it. There is no GM to nudge her and say, "While you are hunting the Minor Clerks, you come upon a group of Middle Managers by the water cooler." Oops, no more camping. It's clear a larger battle is about to take place.

So again, we have a convention, share the numbers with the players, copied only because that's the way it's been done in the past. Some players will tell you they like the numbers. They will keep track of every experience point total needed for every level; which weapons hit for the most damage; and which armor protects best. These players are already here, making up a large portion of our market. They may be fickle and move from game to game as the next "generation" of MMORPGs is giddily announced, but they've bought into the metaphor currently offered.

Even a game like *Horizons* that tries to concentrate more on ongoing story, and throws most of its content generation at that goal, still follows the level and loot paradigm, hit points, explicit values for items, and numbers floating off from a mob's head when it is wounded. Variations on a theme don't change the theme. We're still on the first generation of massively multiplayer worlds, folks, sorry.

A new model that I've been exploring is one that concentrates on living in the virtual world and experiencing its ongoing story. The numbers are still there tracking player progress, but they are not shoved into players' faces. Since players can enjoy their lives in the virtual world without trying to become immensely powerful there is no pressure to level or acquire loot. There are definite markers of progress players see, but the hierarchy is more flexible. Instead of advancing up a ladder like career-obsessed corporate executives, players are allowed to find their own niches in the world and expand. Take a look at Figures 19.8 and 19.9.

The first figure is a typical linear advancement for a character wanting to improve himself while remaining within the ranks of the Church of England. It illustrates the progression of characters in current MMOs. Gain a level, gain more power, new skills, and so forth.

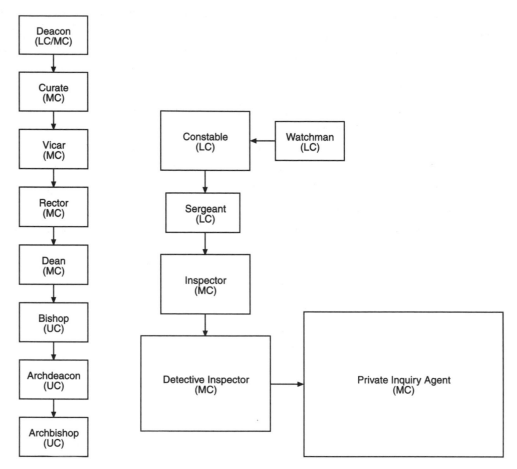

Figure 19.8 The typical massively multiplayer world leveling ladder.

Figure 19.9 Players might want to expand instead of climbing via the typical leveling treadmill.

Figure 19.9 is an illustration of how a player-character might progress as a crime fighter without needing to climb the ladder. Here the player has experienced two linear progressions from professions within a police force and in private law enforcement. The resident started life as a private Watchman, moved to the police force where he chose to stay a bit longer as a Constable, breezed through Sergeant, spent a bit more time as an Inspector, solved a good number of cases as a Detective Inspector, then headed back to the private sector and settled on life as a Private Inquiry Agent where his reputation continues to grow and grow.

Imagine within each box there is a list of cases (quests) this resident has solved. As a Watchman he may have solved only a handful before he decided to join the police force. As an Inspector he needed to solve more to be promoted. He enjoyed life as a Detective Inspector quite a bit, so he has far more cases to his credit. And that reputation made it easy for him to gain clients once he decided to leave the force and take up detection on his own.

There is also no need to limit players to a single profession. *Asheron's Call 2* and *Horizons* offer particularly wide open potential for career choices. Our detective friend in Figure 19.9 may, of course, change his mind and decide to become a surgeon. A noble calling, but a reputation for dissecting crimes will not serve in a hospital. He will have to begin again on the ground floor.

The bottom line is this: the player-character should be able to choose not to advance or at least not in the traditional sense of MMORPGs; yet always be assured of being a viable and productive part of the virtual community, offered new challenges, stories, recognition, and opportunities to affect the world. Once other paradigms for achievement are explored, the need for numbers diminishes.

I'm not the only writer/designer talking about hiding the numbers from the players, but so far, no massively multiplayer world has attempted it. My reasons are simple, focused entirely on increasing immersion, protecting the fourth wall, and of foremost importance, supporting story. I'm advocating removing all those numerical equivalents of tabletop die rolls. Not just for combat or leveling, but everything.

Any die roll result or check for balance the game makes can be expressed in a standardized way that players will recognize. Even provide a chart in the documentation, if you wish, just don't have those numbers flashing past in the middle of a fight. You don't see them when Jackie Chan goes after 20 bad guys with a ladder. Sure, a martial arts movie isn't interactive, but it would also destroy the fourth wall, and therefore harm your willing suspension of disbelief.

What makes us think the same isn't true in our worlds? They are commonly referred to as games, and they contain gameplay, but they are not games. They are far more.

We've seen how we can escalate suspense and track the player-character's progress in the world by attaching a database to the character. In this way, the game engine can know which modules the PC has visited, and in what order, and can adjust the experiences in the remaining modules before the PC reaches them. We can create the illusion of a dynamic world that is altered by the actions of the player within it, a world where events pile on top of one another with purpose. Since the PC may alter the world in any number of non-story ways as well, it provides a consistency of experience. We don't stop world-affecting gameplay for an insular story. The story affects the world, too. Maybe not in the same exact way. But it *will feel* the same, and that is what we are striving for.

So we use NPCs who are not simply props or functions; we set up *a standardized* description of action so the player can quickly spot trends, success or failure, and specific text messages (again *standardized,* but not necessarily entirely repetitive) to report the outcome of encounters. If you're dying to use numbers, feel free to allow the merchants to count out change.

We can replace explicit numbers with real world-style accomplishments for players to truly feel as if their characters live in the world of the game. If the player-character's career path is military, her progress can be tracked through ranks. Corporate? Promotions. Different job titles, increases in salaries and perks.

We already maintain databases to track things in our games: items owned, skills learned, abilities acquired. We can use the same databases to track stories completed; scenes of stories completed; knowledge acquired; general reputation; NPC relationships. And by tracking all these story, or at least character-based conditions, we as designers can ensure that the experience, even in a dynamic, open-ended world are as consistent, believable, and as logical a progression as in any linear story. We can allow the world to react to the PC's ever-changing knowledge of the world.

It is our duty as writers and designers of story-based genre games to do everything we can to guarantee the player a rewarding, fun experience. Therefore, we cannot totally abdicate authorship. We only need to keep it as integrated as possible through vivid characters who have lives of their own; gameplay that is consistent with world fiction and that supports ongoing story; and social systems that encourage emergent storytelling.

If you want your players to immerse themselves in your game world, and the stories and characters you populate it with, use every trick you can think of that you've seen in the best movies, TV, drama, and literature as story-related substitutes for the usual simplistic tracking of statistics. Use any techniques you have to *hide* the mechanics of the storytelling and the gameplay. You want as little as possible to get in the way of entertainment. And meaning.

Even if we hide the numbers, we can still present players the same satisfaction that comes with successfully playing the game. At the same time, there is nothing to get in the way of our storytelling, or theirs. We'll conclude our discussion of virtual worlds with a look at non-authorial storytelling.

Empowering Emergent Storytelling

We have concentrated on authorial storytelling in these two chapters for two reasons. The first is that this book is about authorial storytelling. The second is that there are so many people developing virtual worlds today who believe the players should be telling the story they don't need any additional support from me. In this last section they're going to get it whether they like it or not. Despite the fact that many don't see room for authorial narrative when they promote players telling story, I see a perfectly valid reason for encouraging player stories, even as we tell our own. We call this phenomenon emergent storytelling because it emerges from the world; we don't place it there.

We *want* players to be storytellers, but we cannot leave them to flounder. We must help them be *good* storytellers. I disagree that it doesn't matter if they're terrible, as Raph suggests. We cannot create worlds and expect the players themselves to do all the work. The worlds must be focused and covertly manipulated to help non-storytellers create their stories.

Where did this idea of community storytelling come from? I see its origins in a couple of places. The first is the same as role-playing: children's games. The second is the phenomenon of the fan. I've had my share of fan letters over the years, as well as some a lot less friendly. When I was head writer of *Edge of Night*, I wrote a particularly intricate mystery centered around a murder in a hotel. As the story unfolded over several months, suspicion fell at least once on every single cast member, regular or supporting. When the story was at its peak, fan mail poured in. I remember one letter in particular.

To set this up I need to explain something about fans. Most are regular people who keep their fondness for a show or star or sports figure or team in perspective. At the far end of the spectrum are people who tangle up the object of their interest in their own lives. This can lead to stalking. The letter I'm going to tell you about falls somewhere in between. These are letters from fans who *seem* to know the distinction between fact and fiction, but can confuse the two.

When I was writing for *Quincy*, there were two prominent celebrity deaths within a short period of time in Hollywood: Natalie Wood and William Holden. Jack Klugman, the actor who played Quincy, a forensic pathologist, got more than one letter from fans asking him to investigate these "suspicious" deaths. An actress on *Edge of Night*, Sandy Faison, played a psychologist named Beth Correll. She showed me a fan letter whose author complimented her on her acting performance, then proceeded to go into great detail about the fan's marital problems, asking for Sandy's advice. Get the idea?

Mine was a several-page letter, frantically written in long hand. Since I was the head writer of the show, the letter writer had concluded that I was the best person to communicate with police chief Derek Mallory and detective Chris Egan (characters on the show played by Dennis Parker and Jennifer Taylor), and inform them that the letter writer had discovered the identity of the killer. The letter went on to explain in detail the author's solution to the crime. He was 100 percent wrong.

I've responded to a few fan letters over the years. That was not one of them, nor was the invitation to join a coven in San Diego I received (complete with provocative Polaroids) when I was writing for *Tucker's Witch*. For the record, even though I wrote an episode of *Charlie's Angels* about the supernatural and was on staff on *Tucker's Witch* and *Blacke's Magic* I am not now, nor have I ever been, actively involved in promoting the "old religion" in my work. Please don't reach for the wax and the pins. I'm not judging, only clarifying!

Fan fiction, something I believe the writers of those letters were engaged in even if they didn't know it at the time, occurs when non-professional writers become so enamored with the world created by the original authors they want to add their own stories to it. It can be a very positive thing. *The Sims* phenomenon is fueled by player-created content. The important thing to realize is that that content is not created in a vacuum.

Fan fiction attached to our worlds lies outside the game worlds on Internet Web sites for the most part due to copyright and liability issues. In game we can guide players, but we need ways to enforce rules.

How do we go about empowering emergent storytelling? We stimulate the players' desire to tell stories. We can do this in several ways:

- Construct a game world players will want to inhabit, and that sparks their imaginations. Basically, take everything suggested in these two chapters, then add a hundred more things of your own that make your world immersive, exciting, and fun.

- Set the stage for emergent storytelling with a detailed backstory, or lore, as it is sometimes called in virtual worlds. Unlike a single-player game that can get bogged down by backstory, the stronger the backstory in a virtual world, the more liable players are to seize on it, rather than having to create their own that may conflict with it now or in the future.

- Compose with a single voice—not necessarily a single composer, but rather design and write with thematic and stylistic continuity no matter how many developer-side authors are involved. (See Appendix B for more on this.) Consistency in style and vision can help new storytellers find their voices. If you feel a crying need to have your dwarves speak like Scots, make sure they all do.

- Provide platforms and tools for storytelling that are epic like theatres for large performances and those that are more intimate. *Asheron's Call* featured writeable books. Areas can be set aside in pubs for individual or small group performances. Overturned boxes placed on the corners of public gardens might encourage popular oratory and fiery debate like those in Hyde Park. Create a journalist class or profession that can submit material to newspapers or broadcasts. Allow for "amateur" submissions from non-journalists, too. One way to police this material is to retain editorial control. Players can't publish, they submit to NPCs, and then developers make the decisions. The more avenues for expression the better, both formal and informal.

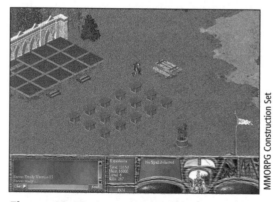

MMORPG Construction Set

Figure 19.10 A stage on a village green ready for player-characters to perform.

- Create a filter so that the best stories can emerge. Acknowledge their authors in rankings, or grant them awards.

Figure 19.10 is from a version of *The Gryphon Tapestry* I built years after the real game closed up shop. I used a buggy program called the MMORPG Toolkit that had great potential, but not enough resources to realize that potential, much like *TGT* before it.

All of these empower emergent storytelling that in no way interferes with the ongoing authorial storytelling writers and designers add. One kind of storytelling supports the other. Just like narrative and gameplay, they are not at odds with each other. To limit either is to limit a huge opportunity for the widest range of players to enjoy our worlds.

PART V

REFLECTIONS

Postlude: Endgame

* * *

SELECT doors.

The vast doors, wood, black with age and studded with rusting iron, swing open. The Player can choose to return to the cliff above the now impassible chasm, or move into the lair.

INT. WIZARD'S LAIR

A vast space filled with unfathomably complex devices and magical implements. The Wand of Yearning floats on end, slightly angled above a pedestal to one side. It isn't glowing. Incongruously, there is what looks like a playpen on the other side of the room, but as the PC and however many of the group have survived enter it's impossible to see what may be inside it. The Wizard stands waiting. He is huge, no frail magician, but a well-muscled giant standing at least 15 feet tall. In his headband, the Tormentor's Jewel blazes with a potent green light.

> WIZARD

You've come at last, I see, but not with heads respectfully bowed. Very well. May your valor prove worthy of your choice.

The Wizard begins hurtling Flame Bolts at the party.

1. IF the Player chooses to ATTACK the Wizard, the weapons and spells of the party will do one tenth of the usual damage. The Wizard has over one million hit points.

> WIZARD

Where are all your dreams now, mortal? I will eat them as you die.

Eventually the Wizard will kill the entire group.

2. IF the Player tries to TAKE the Wand of Yearning, it can be picked up and equipped, but it remains cold and lifeless. ATTACK the WIZARD with wand:

WIZARD

The wand is useless against my strength!

Eventually the Wizard will kill the entire group.

3. IF the PC moves to the playpen, the player-character
   can see inside where a baby squirms about, gurgling
   softly, a greenish glow encasing it. Its eyes are
   fixed on a small green jewel that floats in the air
   above it. The jewel is exactly like the one the
   Wizard wears. It's the PC's baby, alive after all,
   but in some way a part of all the disasters that have
   torn the PC's homeland apart.

4. If the Player tries to ATTACK the baby with weapons
   or spells, it is unharmed.

WIZARD

You would kill your own child? Your lack of parental
affection surprises me. But no matter. It is
invulnerable while under my protection!

Eventually the Wizard will kill the entire group.

5. IF the Player tries to ATTACK the floating jewel with
   weapons or spells, it is unharmed.

Eventually the Wizard will kill the entire group.

6. IF the Player tries to ATTACK the floating jewel with
   the wand, the wand begins to glow brighter and
   brighter. The Wizard screams.

WIZARD

Noooooooo!!!

Jagged bands of green energy are discharged from the
jewel to the one in the Wizard's headband. Green energy
encases his body as he shakes uncontrollably. The jewel
in the crib shatters, and a moment later, the Wizard
disintegrates in an earthshaking explosion of green
light.

Pieces of the jewels and the Wizard vanish. The baby is
unharmed. The protecting green glow is gone. The baby is
looking directly at the PC, waiting.

The Player has two choices:

1. Comfort the baby.

2. Kill the baby.

* * *

CHAPTER 20

THE RESPONSIBLE WRITER

> Our revels are now ended. These our actors
> As I foretold you, were all spirits and
> Are melted into air, into thin air;
> And, like the baseless fabric of this vision,
> The cloud-capped tow'rs, the gorgeous palaces,
> The solemn temples, the great globe itself,
> Yea, all of which it inherit, shall dissolve,
> And, like this insubstantial pageant faded,
> Is rounded with a sleep.
>
> —William Shakespeare, *The Tempest*

We've come to the end of the quest. I hope you've found a reward or two along the way. Don't take a word I've said, or anyone else quoted in this book living or dead, as law. Feel free to disagree, and go your own way. At least you will be choosing and not making it up as you go along. Ah, one of my themes! Listen to the echoes of the past. Surprise, surprise. My favorite theme is memory, after all. Learn the work others have already accomplished before you begin. Learn from other media. Build on those games that have gone before, don't just copy them. Know a rule before you break it.

Have respect for your characters. Give them lives and purpose. Avoid stereotypes. Respect your stories. Give them a weight equal to your gameplay. Avoid clichés. Balance is important in all things from gameplay to characters in opposition to real life. Construct gameplay and story together, allowing them to support one another. Synergy. Be consistent in the worlds you construct.

Have respect for your players. If they have been kind enough to buy your game, and the word "story" is on the box, give it to them with all the craft and professionalism you use to deliver stunning 3D graphics and exciting gameplay. Design the story as part of the entire experience, don't segregate it.

I'm sure I've forgotten some, but before we're through Mr. Laing would like me to take a moment to put all of this into some perspective. There are three topics worth addressing I think. Remember Art with the capital "A"? That's one. Next, I think we should remind ourselves of some of those questions from the first chapter: questions like "Why make games?" "What kind of games do we want to make?" "Should they have meaning?"

I'm going to start with a third (why be linear?). There is one other thing that is worthy of respect: writing. I remember . . .

A long time ago I was invited by a friend of mine, Christine Foster, to speak to an extension class she was giving at USC. Christine was an executive at Columbia Pictures then, and her class covered a lot of aspects of script development for movie and TV production. One of the students asked me a question about breaking into TV and the movies as a writer I will never forget: "How little do I have to write?"

I admit I just stared at him for a moment in disbelief. I don't remember what my answer was. I'm sure I talked about the length of treatments or how detailed story pitches should be or something. But that question shocked and offended me, and I know what I wanted to say: "Get up. Walk out the door. Go away. You will never be a writer. Stop wasting your time and ours."

Writing is not just a craft you can learn. For most writers, it is a vocation. I know I would write whether or not anybody was willing to pay me. I have no choice. Writing defines who I am. I don't know what age I was when I began making up stories and poems and songs. I know I started writing them down as soon as I could write. I have been very lucky. Except for a few months as a clerk in the Samuel French office (the play publishers) in Hollywood (when I would often come home and write all night), I've made my living as a writer my entire adult life. I intend to write until the day I die.

While I hope you have found some suggestions in this book that may help you, I haven't attempted to dictate surefire techniques to writing successful games. I cannot magically turn you from a tyro to a professional. That happens inside. Rather, I've tried to share with you a lot of thinking, much of it by writers far wiser than I, about what it takes to create characters and write stories—thinking that spans centuries and media.

We do not need to reinvent the wheel. To try is hubris. One book can do little more than scratch the surface of all that's out there that can assist us to grow as writers. The bibliography that follows this chapter has some more suggestions. And beyond that is an entire

And that leads me to our next question: What kind of games do we want to make? Should we decide just to make games that are cool, and let meaningful stories remain the province of other media? We can fall back on all sorts of excuses like "Stories and games are different." But that's all they are: excuses.

Should games have meaning?

Not all of them. But some should. For every hundred clones of last year's bestselling action game, a few games that strive for more will be welcomed. We need balance, not saturation.

Here are a few more questions to ask ourselves as we create our games. Some are simple to answer, some not so simple.

"Is the game fun?"

One of our primary concerns, as it should be. We are part of an entertainment medium, not professors or theologians. If our games aren't fun, it won't matter if we had any other lofty aspirations for them.

"Does the game move me?"

I wrote an episode of *Quincy*—a show that occasionally stepped over the line from entertainment into the lecture hall—based on a true case about a father accused of electrocuting his severely handicapped son. The boy had a particularly gruesome degenerative condition that was calcifying his brain, literally turning it to stone. As I wrote some of the scenes, tears rolled down my cheeks. I knew what had to be said, as difficult as it was to say it. We are masochists at times, I guess. But it was my responsibility to convey that emotion to my audience. I hope I succeeded.

We can't write true emotion into our games if we shy away from it, just as an actor will never move an audience unless she can find the necessary emotions within her. We need a balance between craft, talent, and our own sensibilities. Otherwise, the performance will stay mechanical and uninvolving; the words will remain ink on a page.

"Does the game make the world a better place for its having existed?"

If all we create is a shadow, glimpsed briefly then gone, what purpose have we served? If we squander this power—this gift—granted to us, we are diminished.

Not all of us would like to make, or are capable of making, a game that will endure or touch those hearts and minds. But some of us must try. Imagery without meaning is empty and artless. We owe it to ourselves and the future to strive for more.

There are no universal answers to these questions. But a failure to address them is a lost opportunity to communicate with the player, our audience. It is a failure to communicate with ourselves.

PART VI

APPENDICES

APPENDIX A

APPENDIX B

APPENDIX A

OPINIONATED BIBLIOGRAPHY

This bibliography is a collection of books, movies, and television shows that will aid you in writing for games. Some are background. Others are attempts in other media to do narrative in interesting and unexpected ways. Some of these works are referred to in the text; others are not. There are a lot of worthy titles in the book that are worth looking up. I'm only hitting some of the most significant, or the ones you may be less familiar with here. I'll try to give a brief reason why I feel each is important.

James Agee. *Night of the Hunter*
Based on a novel by Davis Grubb, but it's the film you should see. Listen to Agee's language, and watch Laughton's remarkable expressionist compositions. My favorite movie.

William Archer. *Play-making*
I've quoted from this book quite a bit, especially in the opening chapters. Out of all the books I've read about the craft of writing, this one, written in 1912, is one of only a handful I've found to be truely useful.

Aristophanes. *Lysistrata*
Send a copy of this comedy to your congressman. Better yet send it to his wife.

Aristotle. *Poetics*
This Greek, even writing way back then about drama that was limited by the fashion and culture of the time, still lays out some of the basic principles that remain with us today. If you ignore them, you won't die, but your drama might.

Alan Ayckbourn. *The Norman Conquests*
Ayckbourne's comedy is actually three full-length plays: *Table Manners, Living Together*, and *Round and Round the Garden*, usually performed over successive nights or, upon rare occasion, as a marathon. Each play concerns events that occur during the same period of time in three different areas of a house: the dining room, kitchen, and garden. The reasons for the characters' behavior in many scenes is not apparent until you've seen all three. The three plays fit together like the pieces of a . . . I mean like a glove . . . no, I mean like . . . oh, never mind. An assured experiment worth seeing and dissecting.

Joseph Campbell. *The Hero with a Thousand Faces*

As I said in the second chapter, this is the best book on writing that isn't really about writing. I may not have quoted as often from Campbell as I did Archer and Egri, but it is required reading. Every page.

Miguel de Cervantes Saavedra. *Don Quixote de la Mancha*

If it isn't clear why this book is on this list by now, it will never be. Read it even if you're confused.

Geoffrey Chaucer. *The Canterbury Tales*

Read it in a good *inter-linear* translation. Watch how our language evolved.

Cirque de Soleil

Talk about playing with narrative! If you've never seen them live, you've never seen them at all. Go. Plug directly into that childlike sense of wonder you tap when you write. Don't try to deny it. I know you do. *Cirque de Soleil* is more than worth the arm and leg you'll have to pay.

Ronald Davidson & Joseph Poland. *The Adventures of Captain Marvel*

Actually any of the serials from the 30s and 40s will do. Pick one, watch it all the way through. See the picaresque construction still alive.

Charles Dickens. *Bleak House*

My favorite book by my favorite author. *A Christmas Carol* may show more modular potential, but if you can create a modular structure from *Bleak House*, you can create one from anything.

Lajos Egri. *The Art of Dramatic Writing*

I'm pretty sure I've quoted this book more than any other. Between Aristotle, Archer, and Egri, you have the three best books on drama ever written.

William Faulkner. *The Sound and the Fury*

I talked more about *Intruder in the Dust*. Read that one too, but this book's title is taken from *Macbeth*'s last soliloquy:

> "Tomorrow and tomorrow and tomorrow
> Creeps in this petty pace from day to day
> To the last syllable of recorded time.
> And all our yesterdays have lighted fools
> The way to dusty death.
> Out! Out brief candle!
> For life is but a walking shadow,
> A poor player who struts and frets
> His hour upon the stage
> And then is heard no more.
> It is a tale told by an idiot
> Full of sound and fury
> Signifying nothing."

I quoted that from memory, but I think it's pretty close. The story of the novel *is* told by an idiot, giving a context for Faulkner's stream of consciousness tale of the Sartorius family you can also read about in my favorite Faulkner novel, *Absaolm! Absalom!*. Incidentally, Alastair MacLean borrowed *The Way to Dusty Death* for a novel of his own. Shakespeare's a great source of titles.

Michael Frayn. *Noises Off*

The movie version doesn't do justice to this fall-out-of-your seat funny play that chronicles all the things that go wrong in a touring production of a typical British sex farce called *Nothing On*. And in keeping with the two titles, we get to see what happens both onstage and off. The blurring of reality and illusion played for high comic effect are delicious.

William Goldman. *Adventures in the Screen Trade*

Required reading for anyone who wants to write for Hollywood, or who is already working there.

D.W. Griffith. *Birth of a Nation*
Riveting and hard to watch all at the same time, this film is still the one that single-handedly turned movies from curiosities into a new art form.

Lillian Hellman. *The Autumn Garden*
Besides being married to Dashiell Hammet, hard-boiled detective author of *The Maltese Falcon*, *The Thin Man*, and *Red Dust*, Lillian Hellman is one of the masters (mistresses?) of structure in the theatre. Want to read (or hopefully see) a well-made play? Start here.

Homer. *The Odyssey*
Okay, so maybe the guy didn't write it! Give him a break! He wrote it down! I wonder if he could see the modular structure more clearly because he was blind?

Peter Howitt. *Sliding Doors*
Cute movie about alternate realities spinning off from a single moment in time. Remarkable only as an example of movies messing with narrative structure.

Henrik Ibsen. *A Doll's House*
This is one of the most quoted plays in all books on drama. See it or read it and learn why.

James Joyce. *Ulysses*
The book wasn't banned for its use of stream of consciousness. If you want to read the naughty bits, they're in Molly Bloom's last soliloquy. Otherwise, listen to the English language burst in your brain like a ripe peach.

Carl Jung. *Man and His Symbols*
Read the guy who got Campbell all revved about myth and symbolism. Learn what déjà vu means, and the collective unconsious we all share, not just politicians.

Charlie Kaufman. *Adaptation*
This movie is worth a look by writers for three reasons: the twisting of reality and illusion, the structural complexity that makes the last 20 minutes far less baffling if you realize what the story is really all about, and it's gleeful portrayal of writing guru Robert McKee.

Akira Kurosawa & Shinobu Hashimoto. *Rashomon*
A movie that not only experiments with non-linear narrative, but profoundly succeeds. Try to overlook Toshiro Mifune's way over the top performance. Jack Nicholson obviously went to school on this film to prepare for his role in *The Shining*.

R.D. Laing (with H. Phillipson and A.R. Lee). *Interpersonal Perception*
A perceptive book, undeservedly overlooked.

David Mamet. *Glengarry Glen Ross*
The film is every bit as riveting and harrowing as the play. Listen to the staccato rhythms, words used as blades: rapiers, pocket knives, and machetes. Want to hear less raw Mametspeak? Try *The Untouchables* or *Ronin*.

John Mortimer. *Rumpole of the Bailey*
All episodes are available on VHS, some on DVD. Series television writing of a high order. His autobiography, *Clinging to the Wreckage*, is worthy too.

Gaspar Noe. *Irreversible*
Extremely controversial film, and rightly so, but still worthy of a look (if you can stomach it) for the non-traditional narrative structure. Remember, we can learn from *Birth of a Nation*, even as we may abhor its socio-political sensibilities. No, this film's no *Birth of a Nation*.

Christopher Nolan. *Memento*

Nolan wasn't the first to tell his screen story backwards, but it's intriguing to watch as we try to piece together the . . . never mind.

Irma Phillips. *The Guiding Light*

Just like any serial will do, so will any soap. Try to find one you can stick with for awhile. Of course writing ongoing story in a virtual world is a fool's game. But if it could be done, you will learn much watching soaps.

Harold Pinter. *Betrayal*

Before *Memento* Harold Pinter wrote this scintillant screenplay that marches back in time from the end of a relationship to its beginning. Well worth seeking out.

Edwin S. Porter. *The Great Train Robbery*

The robbery isn't all that great, and neither is the movie, but it is only one reel, and then you can say you've seen it. Recently released on DVD too!

Alain Robbe-Grillet. *L'Année dernière à Marienbad*

If we're going to talk about film directors playing with narrative (or lack thereof), we must include Robbe-Grillet. I've never been a fan, but he's certainly playing with narrative all right.

Gary Ross. *Seabiscuit*

One of the best-constructed screenplays in a long time. It had the good fortune to be nominated for every major writing award. Unfortunately, it was released in the same year as *Return of the King*. Don't get me wrong, *The Lord of the Rings* was a brilliant adaptation (*Seabiscuit* is an adaptation too), but as rambling as its source material. *Seabiscuit* tells its story like a thoroughbred owns a quarter mile.

Geoff Ryman. *253*

The modular Internet novel also in book form. It's not terribly gripping, but it isn't a long read either.

William Shakespeare. *The Tempest*

My favorite of the Bard's plays. The Bard? That's what he was called. Noteworthy, don't you think?

Lee Sheldon. *Impossible Bliss*

Because no self-respecting author should pass up an opportunity to sell his books.

Sophocles. *Electra*

Or *Oedipus Rex* or *Antigone*. Skip Aeschylus and come straight here. These are the same stories more compactly told, and for some reason, his translations are more readable.

Quentin Tarentino. *Pulp Fiction*

More messing with narrative structure. Tarentino didn't invent it, but he's sure in love with it. Compare it to *The Norman Conquests* if you dare.

Tom Tywker. *Run Lola Run*

A far more interesting film than *Sliding Doors* with which it has been compared. Get the DVD. Watch it a couple of times, then listen to the commentary from Twyker and his star. You'll be amazed at the connections you missed. I'll give you a hint. The three episodes are not simply variations on a theme, they comment on each other. Highly recommended.

Billy Wilder and I.A.L. Diamond. *Some Like It Hot*

Izzy Diamond added those extra initials because he thought they looked cool. More great dialogue, and a classic last line. Also check out *Double Indemnity* for some true *noir*.

APPENDIX B

DEVELOPER PRIMER ON BUILDING WRITING TEAMS

Writing teams are everywhere in television, and movie studios routinely hire several writers for a single film. Yet writing teams are rare in single-player games. We find them occasionally as staff writers or writer/designer *hyphenates* at companies like Bioware where they are assigned a succession of titles.

note

HYPHENATE: a TV and film industry term to designate someone who fulfills more than one role on a project such as a Writer-Director or Writer-Producer.

More often than not, if professional writers are used at all, they are contractors, hired for a single project and let go. There is no opportunity for a pension, profit sharing, or health plan. Yes, programmers and artists and designers may be hired as contractors as well, but many, especially the leads, are full-time with all the benefits and perks. It's a sad commentary on how much our industry values a writer's contributions.

We are reluctant to go beyond our own ranks for talent, and it's true we've been burned in the past, especially by the last few Hollywood invasions. How many world-class writers have been hired from outside the industry? We're seeing a few Hollywood writers being hired for exactly the same reason we hired them in the past, the *wrong* reason: because we want our game to be like a movie.

If these new writers succeed, it will be because of their talent and skill and ability to adapt to our peculiar needs, not because they have mapped their keyboards to churn out games just like Hollywood movies. It's still a rare enough occasion to attract comment when an outside writer is hired. Why?

The reason we give for not hiring writers from other media is "They don't know games." How easy it is for us to say they don't know games so they shouldn't write them, but even though we game developers may not know how to write, it's okay for us to write them.

Since there is one type of game where writing staffs are not just used, they are a necessity; we're going to discuss how to put such a team together. Its members can come from inside the industry or out, inside the development studio or out. It does not matter. What matters is whether they have the correct skills for the job. These games are, of course, MMORPGs where the amount of content required demands more than one writer.

After having worked on a few of these and observed a few more, it's become clear to me that developers, not having had much experience in these things, don't seem to know anything about forming writing teams. Some of the basics that every television show producer understands are completely ignored when developers put out the Help Wanted sign. Well, you can relax now. Developers, producers, this one's for you. A survivor from one of those earlier Hollywood invasions is here to help ease your pain.

Introduction

Writing massively multiplayer games is not simply a massive challenge; it is a conglomeration of massive challenges.

First, there is the sheer amount of material that must be in place when the game launches. Second, there is all the additional writing that will be needed as new content is added. Third, there are all kinds of writing required: quests and stories; NPC dialogue; informational text; help systems; on and on. Fourth, each kind of writing requires a different style, talent, and craft knowledge.

Anyone who has written professionally knows that just because a writer can write trenchant dialogue does not mean he can tell a story to save his soul. And a brilliant novelist may be unable to tame her literary style to the needs of clarity and brevity journalistic prose demands.

Given time, a single writer might supply all the material for a year of television sit-coms or a single issue of a daily newspaper or even a massively multiplayer game, provided we ignore irritants like budgets and deadlines. But that isn't feasible, so we look to teams of writers to do these jobs.

When I was the head writer of a daytime soap opera, I turned out more material each week than most writers are required to complete in two or three months. I wrote the long-term story documents (projecting story from three months to a year into the future), all daily breakdowns (outlines for each episode), and two or three scripts (the actual action and dialogue for each episode). My output averaged 500 pages per month, not including the sometimes extensive editing I had to do to scripts written by my writing team. That's

6,000 pages per year, the equivalent of 20 novels or 60 screenplays. What I wrote in week one was produced in week two and on the air in week three. And that pace needed to be maintained day in and day out 52 weeks a year.

I mention this for two reasons. Massively multiplayer games aren't the first medium to require massive amounts of writing. It can be done, but it can't be done alone. Like an MMO, a soap opera is a merciless, forever-hungry monster voraciously devouring everything in its path. The monster that is daytime television demands 260 programs per year. Even at the comparatively sedate pace of nighttime television, where production companies are only required to turn out 22 shows per season, the monster is almost impossible to keep ahead of without a writing team.

At the height of the Hollywood studio system, which stretched from the mid 1930s to the early 50s, movies were routinely written by teams. One writer or more would construct a storyline, another would flesh it out with dialogue, another would embellish action sequences, another would supply the expertise needed for a particular genre, and still another would "punch up" the script with jokes. This practice continues today. The number of writers who worked on the feature film version of *The Flintstones* has entered popular Hollywood mythology, and seems to increase with each new telling. Were there really more than 20? I suspect only the bookkeeping department knows for sure.

Team Configurations

There are two major configurations of writing teams in virtual worlds just as there are in television. The first type was initially confined to hour-long drama, but has now been almost completely abandoned. Usually there is a writer-producer and/or a story editor on staff, and the first drafts of scripts are written by freelancers—what we call contractors in the game industry. Here the burden is on the in-house writer or writers to shape the freelance material into a style consistent with their show. And while the producer or editor may come up with the original story ideas, freelancers often bring in their own, broadening the selection of ideas to choose from.

The second type of writing team—the full-time staff—has always been the province of TV sit-coms and variety shows, and is now used by most hour-long dramas as well. In comedy in particular, the writers all sit in a room for hours on end shouting out ideas while the one with the best penmanship copies the outlines of the story on a wallboard. Here the chief writing burden is sorting through the ideas and fashioning them into a coherent—and hopefully entertaining!—structure. (This also explains why many successful TV comedy writers have difficulty transitioning to movies. Their dialogue may still be funny, but often their structure is weak.)

Either configuration is possible for virtual worlds. Most single-player game developers hire writers on contract to save costs, while most massively multiplayer games want writers on site as part of the development team. In fact, these writers often have other roles such as art or programming, which saves even more money, but usually diminishes the quality of the work.

Still, given the tools for telecommuting at our disposal, it is perfectly feasible for most writing team members to be off-site contractors. I've had two jobs as lead writer where I was off-site: one worked fine, one did not. For such an arrangement to succeed it needs copious amounts of trust, open lines of communication, and a willingness to spend a lot of time on airplanes.

The Lead Writer

The most important member of the writing team is the lead writer. In television, this is usually a writer-producer. In games, many titles are used, but I'll keep it simple here and call her the lead writer. This position requires several more skills in addition to simply good writing, and should be the first position filled on the team. This seems obvious, yet often writing staffs are hired simultaneously or in no particular order. Having a qualified lead writer in place before the rest of the team is assembled means that designers and producers don't have to be expert writers themselves any more than they need to be expert artists or programmers to make those hires. An experienced lead writer knows what is needed, probably has her own contacts to draw from, and will be far more likely to hit the ground running with a team she has helped put together because of the added familiarity.

Stories may differ in length, tone, theme, and many other things. Characters must speak in their own voices. Disparate elements should all appear to exist naturally in the same world. For these reasons the lead writer must be a master forger, able to take the work of several often very different writers and mold it into a single consistent style. When done well, it should be impossible for players to discern different authorial voices.

The lead writer must be the voice for the entire writing team, representing them in meetings with producers, designers, and other department heads. Communication is critical to the development team, and good communication occurs when lines of communication are clear. If a writing team member takes a question directly to a designer tasked with implementing the quest system, they may end up with a brilliant solution that enables a greater differentiation between NPCs, but that also kicks out a supporting leg from the faction system. And if this new solution is not communicated to the people whose own areas are affected, the damage may not be discovered until a disastrously late date.

Note that I am not suggesting the lead writer should be communicating directly with a designer or programmer or artist either, but with their leads. This addition of middlemen in the process may seem unnecessarily convoluted or time-wasting, but it keeps everyone on the same page, and does not preclude times when the leads themselves will put two team members together.

All of which means a lead writer must be a diplomat both to those above, and to those in his charge. Ways of selling a new story idea, or asking for an engine design change, must be found that are positive and non-threatening. The lead writer must also convince every member of the team that their ideas have worth, but yet make it clear that it is the lead writer's job to sort through them like tomatoes, only choosing the plumpest and juiciest. In a team setting, knowing when to drop a pitch to the designers for a new feature, or close a blue sky discussion with the team and move on, can be as important as knowing how to write.

(Here are a couple of tips for everyone who needs to pitch an idea: listen to the *pronouns* your audience uses when they respond to your pitch. Listen for the moment when *you* segues to *we* as they discuss your idea with you. The moment that happens, you know they are on your side. By the same token, try to get a sense for how much you should push an idea if you aren't hearing that pronoun switch. The first moment you think you've hit an idea hard enough, move on. Continuing to press the issue will only distract your listeners, forcing their attention on their perception of you (stubborn? arrogant?), and will make the next idea all that much harder to sell.)

The lead writer must also be part producer, aware of budget constraints, milestones, staff priorities, art asset and engine limitations, and able to veto even good ideas that are simply not possible given the constraints of production. To this end, a lead writer must gauge value constantly every day, and balance ideas with their effect on production. Hundreds of ideas generated by a truly creative environment that, out of context, sounded good or even great will be lost during the production cycle. Rejecting them will sometimes feel like the "death of a thousand cuts." But it must be done.

The luxury of the "We'll release it when it's ready" philosophy is granted to only a few mega-successful designers, and even then I'm of the opinion it should not be indulged. It comes across to me as amateurishness instead of professionalism. If Shakespeare managed to write on budget and on time; if Hitchcock managed to direct on budget and on time; who are we to conclude that quality cannot be achieved by adhering to a schedule?

The lead writer must be able to lead both by example and direction. She must be able to write what she preaches. She need not be the best writer on the team, but she must hold her own, teach her staff writers to be the best possible writers they can be, and be willing to learn from them as well. I always try to hire writers who will challenge me by their talent and enthusiasm. It saddens me every time I see an insecure lead writer or designer deliberately hire staff members he feels will not threaten his position.

The Staff

So where does the lead writer go to find his team? It is a mistake to narrow the search to the genre of the virtual world and think that's all you'll need. Being the creator of a *Dungeons & Dragons* module is absolutely no guarantee that a writer can be a potent member of a team in a massively multiplayer game set in the *Dungeons & Dragons* universe. Being the author of *Star Trek* spin-off novels is no guarantee that a writer can keep up with the never-ending demand for new material a *Star Trek* virtual world would generate. Being a writer of single-player games where linear story structures remain a viable (if limited) option is no guarantee that a writer can adapt to the open-ended narrative of a virtual world. (Is it any wonder that single-player quests are so often carelessly stuffed into multiplayer environments?)

Familiarity with the story world or the genre is important, but more selection criteria are needed. A staff writer needs to have experience writing to deadlines. A staff writer must understand the nature of value, and be willing to sacrifice even good ideas if they prove too unwieldy to produce, or might overbalance some other aspect of the world. A staff writer must be able to apply as much professionalism to descriptive text as to epic adventures.

All writers on the team must have, to some greater or lesser degree, the talent of forgery. Staff writers need to be able to recognize, copy, and maintain a consistent style, so that regardless of who wrote what, *all* of the writing appears to come from a single source. It is not a staff writer's job to bring a unique and idiosyncratic style to the table. Rather they have to do their best to write in a style that mimics the vision of the material, and each other.

This is not to say that one writer must be adept at all the different jobs required in a virtual world. Only that what he writes must mimic as closely as possible the overall style of the writing, whether it be scene descriptions, NPC behavior, or dialogue.

The final consideration in the construction of the writing team is its size. This is somewhat dependent on the abilities of the team members, and how jobs will be divided. Will everyone write quests or will one person write all the descriptive text for items and mobs? Each team will be different, and the lead writer must be flexible enough to adapt the structure of the staff to the strengths and weaknesses of its members. (Since writing quests and stories is one of the "fun" jobs—and writing item descriptions isn't!—I usually allow everyone the opportunity to participate, assigning additional quests or more sophisticated stories to those who are more accomplished.)

In my experience, a team of three to five staff members under the direction of a strong lead are more than capable of meeting the demands of writing content during pre-production. Often, one of the staff members becomes a second-in-command, assisting where possible with various lead writer duties, and making sure the pipeline of material keeps flowing.

Each staff writer may have a particular area of responsibility, but all contribute wherever needed. To supplement the team, freelance contractors may also be hired to script planned-for events or stories far in advance of their production, in essence creating lead time even when live production is underway.

It is customary for the development team to be replaced with a live team once the virtual world launches, yet my experience has been that there is much to be gained by maintaining the continuity of a writing team familiar with the demands of a particular world after it goes live. This is the standard in television, and it makes just as much sense here.

Additional Considerations

Once the team is in place, the pipeline for material must be constructed. Who delivers what to whom? When? What is the green light procedure? In what format should ideas and stories be written? Who is in charge of seeing that the writing gets into the game world? Must the text be translated into code? Is there a scripting language the writers need to learn?

How much new material can a team be expected to turn out in a set amount of time? Far more than most developers believe. Far more than many writers want them to believe! Go back and look at the amount of material a soap opera requires, then look at the amount of material in any of the large commercial massively multiplayer games released so far. Listen to the cries of designers and developers who say they can't keep up with the new-content monster, let alone stay ahead of the beast.

There was an interesting presentation at GDC a couple years ago on *Majestic*, Electronic Arts' ill-fated and ill-conceived Internet-based push-technology storytelling experiment. An EA executive in charge of the project listed some of the lessons learned after the experiment had failed. I was dumbfounded by the list. Most items on it were things the development team should have known going in, particularly since several members supposedly came to the project from television. One of the most blatant mistakes was the huge underestimation of the lead time needed to satiate the hungry monster's appetite. They ran out of new material in a few weeks!

Lead time, as we've learned, is a television industry term meaning the time allotted to put as many shows as possible in the can (ready to be viewed) before the first episode airs. Nighttime shows need this lead time because it can take two to three weeks to produce an episode, yet there must be a new episode every week. (It takes one day to produce a daytime soap opera episode which is the only reason soap writers have any chance at all of keeping up with their monsters.)

In game development, the pre-production period is the lead time. Yet, over and over, we see months of pre-production spent on design, art, and programming before the first writer shows up. If game writing is ever to have any chance of overcoming the myth that "New content takes too long to create. That's why there's so little of it!" or "The writing doesn't have to be as good as other media. It's just a game!" or "Players want player-generated content, not developer-generated content!" we'd better at least give writing a development cycle and budget so it can compete with the quality and quantity of the art and programming.

It's one of those vicious circles. Writing in games isn't very good because developers don't think it can be; therefore, they won't do what is necessary to make it good. Which brings up two other very important reasons to have the writing team in place from the very beginning. First, it gives them time to get to learn the game engine and to adjust their writing styles and expectations. Second, it also gives them an opportunity to suggest features of the game engine that can be designed specifically to facilitate storytelling.

Conclusion

The keys to building a successful writing team for a virtual world can be summed up as follows:

- Hire a talented lead writer who possesses the skills to be leader, diplomat, salesman, producer, and master forger.
- Hire staff writers used to deadlines and balancing quality and value issues.
- Build the team at the very beginning of pre-production to create lead time, and so the team can learn the game engine and aid in its construction.
- Create open yet formal lines of communication to minimize misunderstandings and time-consuming glitches in the development process.
- Empower team members to present their ideas, yet keep the hierarchy clear so all understand how decisions will be made.

There is no reason players must endure empty worlds and unfulfilled promises of story in massively multiplayer games. With the right team in place, virtual worlds can enjoy the same level of story quality as the *best* episodic television shows, with the added benefits of far more story, and the excitement of living the stories instead of simply watching them.

INDEX

Index